OF LABOUR AND LIBERTY

OF LABOUR AND LIBERTY

DISTRIBUTISM IN VICTORIA, 1891–1966

RACE MATHEWS

UNIVERSITY OF NOTRE DAME PRESS
NOTRE DAME, INDIANA

Published in the United States in 2018 by the University of Notre Dame Press
Notre Dame, Indiana 46556
www.unpress.nd.edu

First edition published by Monash University Publishing
Monash University
Clayton, Victoria 3800, Australia

Published by arrangement with Monash University Publishing

Library of Congress Cataloging-in-Publication Data

Names: Mathews, Race, author.
Title: Of labour and liberty : distributism in Victoria, 1891–1966 / Race Mathews.
Description: Notre Dame : University of Notre Dame Press, 2018. | Includes bibliographical references and index. |
Identifiers: LCCN 2017057357 (print) | LCCN 2018000914 (ebook) | ISBN 9780268103439 (pdf) | ISBN 9780268103446 (epub) | ISBN 9780268103415 (hardcover : alk. paper) | ISBN 0268103410 (hardcover : alk. paper)
Subjects: LCSH: Distributive justice—Religious aspects—Catholic Church. | Distributive justice—Australia—Victoria—History—20th century.
Classification: LCC BX1795.D59 (ebook) | LCC BX1795.D59 M38 2018 (print) | DDC 261.809945—dc23
LC record available at https://lccn.loc.gov/2017057357

∞ *This paper meets the requirements of ANSI/NISO Z39.48-1992 (Permanence of Paper).*

CONTENTS

To Don José María Arizmendiarrieta (1915–1976)

Light in darkness. Hope in the face of despair.

ACKNOWLEDGEMENTS

I am deeply grateful to the many colleagues and friends whose support made this book possible. Thanks are due in particular to Melbourne's Catholic Theological College and University of Divinity where it was researched and written as a DTheol thesis; to my supervisors Fr Austin Cooper and Fr Bruce Duncan for the excellence of their guidance and support; and to my examiners Jay Corrin and Michael Hogan for their empathetic and insightful reports.

I thank also Tony and Stella Kitchener for their encouragement and assistance; Mark Brolly for the input with which he has so comprehensively deepened and enriched my understanding of the origins and experience of the Catholic Church in Australia; David Kehoe for access to his unpublished history of the Young Christian Workers (Y.C.W.); Jean Ker Walsh, Leon Magree, Des Ryan and the late Fr Cyril Hally for further Y.C.W. insights and information; Helen Praetz for her 'The Church in Springtime: Remembering Catholic Action 1940–1965' interview transcripts as deposited in the University of Divinity Repository; Ben Arnfield and Michelle Goodman at the Australian Credit Union Archives for transcripts of interviews conducted on behalf of the former Credit Union Historical Society by the late Richard Raxworthy and related records; Rachael Naughton at the Melbourne Diocesan Historical Commission for her guidance and assistance in accessing and evaluating records held in the diocesan archives; Lucy Shedden at the State Library of Victoria for her facilitation of my access to its collections;

the consistently helpful staffs of the Catholic Theological College Library, the Victorian Parliamentary Library and the National Library; Philip Ayres and the late Jim Griffin for advance access to their then forthcoming biographies respectively of Cardinal Moran and Archbishop Mannix; John Best for his input to the selection and presentation of the illustrations; and my Mondragón friends Mikel Lezamiz and Fred Freundlich for again enabling me to observe at first hand the operations and aspirations of the co-operatives group.

I am grateful finally for the recollections, records, images and other memorabilia which so freely and in many instances spontaneously have been made available to me; to Kathryn Hatch for her assistance in securing permissions for the use of copyright material; to Jeannette Harlock for meticulous secretarial support; and to Nathan Hollier and his Monash University Publishing staff for their unfailing helpfulness and the pleasure of working with them. And to my wife Iola for the love that lightens my life and her support and forbearance in the face of my long pre-occupation.

ABBREVIATIONS

ACCCS	Association of Catholic Co-operative Credit Societies
ACTU	Australian Council of Trade Unions
ALP	Australian Labor Party
ANSCA	Australian National Secretariat for Catholic Action
CBL	Catholic Boys Legion
CSM	Catholic Social Movement
CSSM	Catholic Social Studies Movement
C.Y.M.S.	Catholic Young Men's Society
CDC	Co-operative Development Society
CEC	Co-operatives Education Committee
CMC	Co-operatives Management Committee
CPA	Communist Party of Australia
CUHC	Credit Union Historical Co-operative
DLP	Democratic Labor Party
ECCA	Episcopal Committee on Catholic Action
ECCSSM	Episcopal Committee of the Catholic Social Studies Movement
JOC	*La Jeunesse Ouvrière Chrétienne*
NCC	National Civic Council
NCGM	National Catholic Girls Movement
NCRM	National Catholic Rural Movement
NSW	New South Wales
THC	Trades Hall Council
VCCA	Victorian Credit Co-operative Association
WFTU	World Federation of Trade Unions
Y.C.W.	Young Christian Workers
Y.C.W.CCCS	Y.C.W. Central Co-operative Credit Society

Chapter 1

INTRODUCTION

The philosopher George Santayana wrote famously that 'Those who cannot remember the past are condemned to repeat it'. Those who can may hope to improve upon it. This book highlights the potential of the social teachings of the Catholic Church and the now all but wholly forgotten Distributist political philosophy and program that originated from them as a means of bringing about a more equal, just and genuinely democratic social order.

It is a response in part to evidence of a precipitous decline in active citizenship consequent on a loss of confidence in politics, politicians, parties and parliamentary democracy; the rise of 'lying for hire' lobbyism; the inexorable upwards creep and concentration of capital in the hands of a wealthy 'one per cent' minority; endemic tax evasion by the rich; and widespread corporate wrong-doing. It points to Distributism as a possible antidote for the passivity and 'bread and circuses' mind-set into which Australians have allowed ourselves to be seduced, and our consequent inability to acknowledge much less confront the several convergent catastrophes including climate change that threaten to engulf us. It questions whether political democracy can survive indefinitely in the absence of economic democracy.

The challenge is seen to lie in restoring to their proper pride of place citizenship and the public interest, as opposed to the narrowly economic categories of 'customer', 'client' and 'consumer' in which we have been misled to think of ourselves – in short, in empowering ourselves to become truly 'masters of our own destinies', and like Dante 'emerge and once more see the stars'. The approach is through serial biography - to capture through the prism of emblematic reformers the attendant clash of ideas, circumstances, aspirations and ambitions. Quotation has been preferred to paraphrase, and protagonists and researchers to the greatest possible extent speak for themselves.

A previous book, my 1999 *Jobs of Our Own: Building a Stakeholder Society*, stemmed from research in the course of a series of visits dating back to the middle 1980s to the great complex of manufacturing, financial, retail, civil engineering and agricultural co-operatives as first brought to fruition in Mondragón in the Basque region of Spain in 1956 by the philosopher-priest Don José María Arizmendiarrieta (1915–1976), whose cause for canonisation the Vatican is currently examining. It identified a way ahead through ownership and control by workers of their workplaces – through labour hiring capital rather than capital hiring labour.[1]

It tracked back on an international canvas the evolution of Mondragón's 'Evolved Distributism' from its origins as a gleam in the eyes of great late 19th century princes of the Church through its shaping at the hands predominantly of their lay adherents including the British writers Hilaire Belloc and G.K. Chesterton into the coherent political philosophy that became known shortly as Distributism; the heroic but ultimately unsuccessful attempt by the

1 Race Mathews, *Jobs of Our Own: Building a Stakeholder Society* (Sydney: Pluto Press, 1999) and 'Cause for Canonisation of Fr José María Arizmendiarrieta the Apostle of Cooperation', as accessed 14/1/14 at http://www.canonizacionarizmendiarrieta.com/en/.

Distributist priests Moses Coady and 'Jimmy' Tompkins to give hands-on effect to it through the Antigonish Movement that thrived briefly and attracted worldwide attention and acclaim in Nova Scotia in the 1930s; and its ultimate Mondragón apotheosis. It documented in detail how Mondragón has evolved and its principles, objectives, structure, governance and achievements.

It is to the Australian canvas that the current account necessarily now turns. The accession of Pope Francis (1936–) invites a re-assessment of responses by Australian Catholics, predominantly in Victoria, to the social teachings of their Church, beginning with the 1891 social justice encyclical *Rerum Novarum* on the rights and duties of capital and labour and culminating with the creation by the Australian bishops in 1938 of the Australian National Secretariat for Catholic Action (ANSCA), and their subsequent adoption and promotion of Distributism. A window of opportunity for this re-assessment is evident in Pope Francis's advocacy of transformative mutualist and co-operativist principles and practices, as exemplified in particular by his 2013 apostolic exhortation *Evangelii Gaudium*[2] and the 2015 encyclical letter *Laudato Si'*.[3]

The preparation and promulgation of *Rerum Novarum* in the English-speaking world was instigated and facilitated by the Archbishop of Westminster, Cardinal Henry Edward Manning (1808–1892), who had long worked for the betterment of the working poor. In Australia, the Archbishop of Sydney, Cardinal Patrick Moran (1830–1911), was the first ecclesiastic to spread the *Rerum Novarum* message. Later, the Archbishop of Melbourne from 1917 until 1963, Daniel Mannix (1864–1963), was the most high-profile supporter

2 Francis, *Evangelii Gaudium*, Apostolic Exhortation (2013).

3 Francis, *Laudato Si'*, Encyclical Letter (2015).

and promoter of Distributist, mutualist and co-operativist thought among Catholic Australians, notably through Melbourne-based bodies including the Campion Society, ANSCA and the Young Christian Workers (Y.C.W.). A key role was played by formation of the Catholic conscience in the mould pioneered by the founder of the Y.C.W., the Belgian priest Josef Cardijn (1882–1967), and enhanced and expanded later by Arizmendiarrieta and his local Y.C.W. associates in their development of the Evolved Distributism that Mondragón so triumphantly now exemplifies.

The example and advocacy of Cardinals Manning and Moran and the support of Archbishop Mannix encouraged laymen such as the influential Melbourne Campion Society members Frank Maher, Kevin Kelly and Murray McInerney and the 'Y.C.W. Co-operator' activists Ted Long, Bob Maybury, Frank McCann and Leon Magree to spread the Distributist message. Inspired by their faith to seek through credit unions and other co-operatives an alternative social order reflective of its papal encyclicals, the example of these young Catholics is a challenge to the 21st century Australian Church to again endorse and advocate Distributism, this time in the evolved form to whose feasibility Mondragón so comprehensively now attests.

Interwoven throughout the narrative is the role of the 'controversial layman' B.A. Santamaria, whose failed bid for control of the Australian Labor Party (ALP) and the consequent party split paved the way for the election in a new century of conservative governments led by upwardly mobile Catholics who had no interest in the social justice policies of their Church or their Labor predecessors and pursued the most reactionary policies in living memory.[4]

---

4 T.R. Luscombe, *Builders and Crusaders: Prominent Catholics in Australian History* (Melbourne, Vic: Lansdowne Press, 1967) 175.

About Distributism

Akin to the hedgehog of Isaiah Berlin's essay on Tolstoy, Distributism 'knows one big thing'.[5] Its basis is the passionate conviction that a just social order can be achieved only through a much more widespread distribution of property. Distributism favours a 'society of owners' where property belongs to the many rather than the few, and correspondingly opposes its concentration in the hands either of the rich, as under Capitalism, or the state as advocated by some Socialists. In particular, ownership of the means of production, distribution and exchange must be widespread. Other than in the case of sole proprietors or hands-on partnerships, labour hiring capital should be the rule rather than the exception.

'Distributism', in the view of the US Social Catholicism studies scholar Jay P. Corrin, 'represented the single most important synthesis of Catholic social and political thinking to emerge in the English-speaking community in the early twentieth century, and its values had a telling impact on Catholic intellectuals in Britain and America'.[6] As noted by the prominent lay Catholic writer, Maisie Ward, in her 1944 biography of her fellow author, Gilbert Keith (G.K.) Chesterton:

> In Australia, Distributism has given a fresh slant to both Labour and Catholic leadership. ... Most important, however, of all the Australian developments has been the approval by the Australian Hierarchy of the main Distributist ideal as the aim of Catholic Action.[7]

---

5 Isaiah Berlin, *The Hedgehog and the Fox: An Essay on Tolstoy's View of History* (London: Weidenfeld & Nicolson, 1953).

6 Jay P. Corrin, *Catholic Intellectuals and the Challenge of Democracy* (Notre Dame, Ind: University of Notre Dame Press, 2002) 3.

7 Maisie Ward, *Gilbert Keith Chesterton* (London: Sheed and Ward, 1944) 446–447.

Distributism, in its distinctively Australian form as refined and elaborated in the deliberations of Catholic bodies including the Campion Society, ANSCA, the *Catholic Worker* magazine's Council and Central Committee, and the Y.C.W., was spelled out to definitive and succinct effect by the scholar Fr James Murtagh in his 1955 study, *Australia: The Catholic Chapter*. Murtagh identified as its fundamental principle 'the restoration of property to the average citizen' and as its slogan 'Property for the People':

> This was to be achieved gradually by a reform of the wage system and the reorganisation of economic society on vocational lines. The wage contract, it urged, should be modified by a contract of partnership by which wage earners could become sharers in ownership, management and profits. Where the business admitted of individual ownership, as in the small shop, farm or factory, individual ownership should be encouraged and extended. Where the enterprise called for the division of labour and numerous workers, as in large engineering plants, chain stores, or sheep stations, all the workers engaged should co-operatively own it. The reorganisation of society in vocational groups or guilds representing all interests concerned with the industry would enable worker-owners to plan economic activity, ensure and promote widespread ownership and build an economic democracy within the framework of the existing political democracy.[8]

A key question to be addressed is how a cause and convictions in good standing in the eyes of many Australians as recently as the early and mid-20th century could have been erased from the nation's political agendas and public consciousness so totally as if they had never existed. Was there a point at which they might have put down enduring roots and secured a niche or beach-head for themselves

8 James G. Murtagh, *Australia: The Catholic Chapter* (Melbourne, Vic: Angus & Robertson, 1959) 175–176.

within the wider social order, and, if so, how is it that defeat was snatched so comprehensively from the jaws of victory? Is there now evidence that the Distributist vision for a better future was more practical than many have supposed, and, if so, what lessons can be learned from it? Might we not, like the Old Testament prophet Ezekiel, ask 'Can these bones live?[9]

Catholics in the 20th century drew inspiration and example from co-operatives and other mutualist bodies, as models for self-help independent of the state, exemplars of the key Catholic value of solidarity and a broad social movement with which they could identify in their pursuit of a fairer distribution of wealth and opportunity and alternatives to Capitalism.

Distributism comprised in all these respects a largely but by no means exclusively Catholic subset of the wider 20th century struggle for social justice. Had a unity of purpose among disparate elements within the wider movement been fully achieved, an alternative social order worthy in every respect of the Church's finest teachings and noblest aspirations might well have been brought within its grasp. A mighty confluence of interests might have carried forward the Distributist cause to glory.

The theological context was the papal encyclicals *Rerum Novarum* (1891) and *Quadragesimo Anno* (1931), and the assigning by the Church of a central significance to personhood and personalism, as reflective of longstanding Judeo-Christian tradition, and defined in particular by the French philosophers Jacques Maritain and Emmanuel Mounier through the journal *Esprit* which Mounier founded in 1932.

---

9 Ezekiel 37.

Personalist strategies included the co-operativism that had been applied with conspicuous success in Belgium. Mounier wrote in his influential *A Personalist Manifesto* in 1938:

> A personalist civilisation is one whose structure and spirit are directed towards the development as persons of all the individuals constituting it. They have as their ultimate end to enable every individual to live as a person. That is, to exercise a maximum of initiative, responsibility and spiritual life. ... The central move of any personalist revolution is not, then, to unite incoherent forces for an attack upon the coherent and powerful front of bourgeois and capitalist society. It is rather to implant in the vital organs, at present diseased, of our decadent civilisation the seeds and the ferment of a new civilisation.[10]

Nor were the core tenets of Distributism necessarily incompatible with the wider conventional wisdom. Significant affinities were apparent with the Democratic Socialist, Social-Democratic and Labourist thought of the ALP and the trade union movement, to which Australia's predominantly working-class Catholics had looked traditionally for sympathy and support. Common ground between the respective traditions was exemplified by the welcome extended by the then prominent Fabian Society and ALP activist and future Australian National University Economics Professor, Heinz Arndt, to a 1948 Social Justice Statement in the series issued by ANSCA on behalf of the bishops.

Noting that the statement read 'The Church recognises that, under present conditions, there are certain forms of enterprise and industry which are of quite extraordinary importance to the community and which may legitimately come under public control in one form or

10 Emmanuel Mounier, *A Personalist Manifesto* (London: Longmans, Green & Co, 1938) 167, 281.

another, though not necessarily by means of nationalisation', Arndt wrote:

> One could hardly find a more succinct statement of the point of view of intelligent, modern Democratic Socialists. It precisely represents, for example, the attitude of Fabian Socialists today and of the present British Government. The appearance of a remarkable coincidence is strengthened still further by this forthright condemnation of the two ideologies to the right and left of social democracy: 'The Church condemns in equal measure both Communism and the social system of monopoly capitalism which had denied property to the masses and thus created the division of classes on which all class warfare is based'.[11]

A relevant reflection by the long-serving New South Wales (NSW) secretary of the Australian Railways Union and leading ALP historian and theoretician, Lloyd Ross, reads:

> It is only because modern Labourites and Socialists have neglected their own history, and no longer read their theoretical classics, that these strains of liberty, industrial democracy and workers' self-government, have been forgotten and their lessons for today neglected. And it is essentially in these features that the possibility of an understanding between the Socialist and the Distributionist can be reached and the problem of industrial unrest be tackled.[12]

Support for reform stemmed in the first instance from Manning's precept and example in promoting *Rerum Novarum*, as embraced locally by his Australian counterpart Patrick Francis, Cardinal Moran. Daniel Mannix's appointment as coadjutor to Melbourne's

---

11 Heinz W. Arndt, 'The Church on Socialism', in *Australian Observer*, October 1948, as appended to Arndt to Santamaria, 6 August 1956. B.A. Santamaria Papers Series 5 Box 3. MS13492.

12 Lloyd Ross, 'Socialism and Distributivism', *Twentieth Century*, Vol 1, No 4, June 1947, 41.

Archbishop Carr in 1913 and subsequent succession to the See on Carr's death four years later gave rise to a short-lived golden age or 'one brief shining moment' of inspired lay idealism and social activism between extended episodes marred by failed strategies and disappointed hopes.[13]

Radicalisation

Impoverishment in 19th century Europe and the United Kingdom engendered a widespread revulsion and agony of conscience. 'In a massive surge of social consciousness', writes the American poverty studies scholar Gertrude Himmelfarb, 'respectable middle-class people pronounced themselves Socialists, and Socialist organisations vied for membership with each other and with a multitude of other causes and societies – land reform leagues, charitable associations, settlement houses, model building projects, children's homes, "missions" to the poor'.[14]

Catholics were no exception. Their concern for the predicament of the poor was reflected in a social Catholicism that, like Socialism, initially assumed forms that differed radically from one another. Disparate responses to poverty were forthcoming from reformers such as in France Félicité de Lamennais (1782–1854), Henri Dominique Lacordaire (1802–1861), Charles Montalembert (1810–1870), Frederic Ozanam (1813–1853), Léon Harmel (1829–1915), René de La Tour du Pin (1834–1925) and Albert de Mun (1841–1914); in Germany Wilhelm von Ketteler (1811–1877) and Karl von Vogelsang (1818–1890); and in Italy Guiseppe Toniolo (1845–1918).

13 A.J. Lerner and F. Loewe, *Camelot* musical, 1960.

14 Gertrude Himmelfarb, *Poverty and Compassion: The Moral Imagination of the Late Victorians* (New York, NY: Alfred A. Knopf, 1991) 71.

The times were ripe for radicalisation. De Mun and La Tour du Pin fought in the 1870 Franco-Prussian War, were interned as prisoners of war at Aachen and subsequently were appointed by the military governor of Paris to inquire into the causes of the 1871 Paris Commune revolt. The social conditions that their inquiry uncovered and their first-hand observation of the brutality of the suppression of the Communards convinced them that it was to the excesses and arrogance of the wealthy and powerful that the insurrection primarily had been due. De Mun, released from his captivity and stationed back at Versailles where the Communards were being imprisoned and executed, 'never forgot how one of them dying, cursed the defenders of order – "Les insurgés, c'est vous" ("You are the rebels")'.[15]

De Lamennais, Lacordaire and Montalembert advocated that, far from the Church standing aside from politics, its advocacy should be on behalf of the poor and in defence of democracy. Their journal *L'Avenir* adopted as its masthead 'God and Liberty'. The projects and propositions of later reformers ranged from reconciliation of the poor to their station in life subject only to such alleviation as charity and alms-giving might provide, through the paternalistic and even authoritarian vision of von Vogelsang's 'social kingdom' and de Mun and La Tour du Pin's Working Men's Clubs to the authentically co-determinist (management and workers co-operating) industrial advisory councils, worker-directed mutualist welfare bodies and unions made up exclusively of worker members as favoured by the industrialist Harmel. Consistent with Harmel's advocacy, his factory

---

15 John McManners, *Church and State in France 1870–1914* (New York, NY: Harper and Row, 1972) 81, as quoted in Bruce Duncan, *The Church's Social Teaching: From Rerum Novarum to 1931* (North Blackburn, Vic: Collins Dove, 1972) 28. In all, some 28,000 Communards were executed, after having themselves shot seventy-four hostages including the Archbishop of Paris and twenty-three priests.

at Val-des-Bois – seen by some as 'a model of Catholic industrial co-operation'[16] – featured, in addition to its industrial advisory council, wage supplements for large families, medical care, a savings bank and a co-operative society.

Germany's Wilhelm von Ketteler, in the view of some deserving of 'the undying honour of having met the manifesto of the Communists with a program of Christian social reform that stands unsurpassed to this day', was an outspoken advocate of trade unions, producer co-operatives and other mutualist bodies.[17] His appointment as Bishop of Mainz in 1850 reflected the high standing that he enjoyed both locally and in Rome, for all that conservative Catholics on occasion denounced his sermons as 'socialistic-communistic impeachments'.[18] He was supportive of a role for the state in the bringing about social reforms, notable among them higher wages, reduced working hours, Sunday as a day of rest and the prohibition of women and children from working in factories, which many among his more critical co-religionists would have regarded as excessive.

'The new mission of Christianity', Ketteler wrote, 'is to free the world from this new slavery: pauperism'[19] He contributed significantly to the foundation of Ludwig Windthorst's Centre Party and drafting of the party's policy, and was elected to the inaugural Reichstag in 1870, albeit in circumstances where unease over incompatibilities between his role as a bishop and involvement in political disputes

---

16 Duncan, *The Church's Social Teaching*, 53.

17 Thomas. C. Kohler, 'In Praise of Little Platoons: Quadragesimo Anno (1931)', in George Weigel and Robert Royal (eds) *Building the Free Society: Democracy, Capitalism and Catholic Social Teaching* (Grand Rapids, MI: William B. Eerdmans Publishing Company, 1993) 35.

18 Duncan, *The Church's Social Teaching*, 32.

19 Eduardo Soderini, *The Pontificate of Leo XIII* (London: Burns, Oates and Washbourne, 1934) 161.

resulted in his resignation less than a year later. His key role in the development of Social Catholicism was acknowledged in a handsome reference to him by Pope Leo XIII as 'my great predecessor'.[20]

The Union of Fribourg, a group of adherents of Social Catholicism from different countries that met at Fribourg in Switzerland between 1885 and 1891, in turn drafted codes of social principles, declaring of them: 'The Church should recall the too-forgotten rules of her doctrine on the nature of property, the use of goods, and the respect due to the most precious of all goods, human life in the person of the poor'.[21] Cardinal Gaspar Mermillod warned Pope Leo in 1889 that 'Labour is treated as a mere commodity, the existence of the workers is at the mercy of the free play of material forces and the workers are reduced to a state that recalls pagan slavery'.[22]

Rerum Novarum and *Quadragesimo Anno*

The outcome ultimately of so extended an advocacy was the consolidation and codification by Leo of the Church's social teachings in his 1891 encyclical letter *Rerum Novarum*. The encyclical affirmed the right to ownership of productive property and its distribution on as widespread a basis as possible, condemnation of employers who exploited their workers, approval of trade unions and denunciation of Socialism in its Marxist or more extreme statist or centralist forms. An assessment by the prominent High Church Anglican scholar of the inter-war period, Maurice Reckitt, reads: '*Rerum Novarum* is the charter of Social Catholicism, and stands in that movement in the

20 Kohler, 'In Praise of Little Platoons: Quadragesimo Anno (1931)', 35.

21 Council of Fribourg 1886, Report to Pope Leo XIII, as quoted in Duncan, *The Church's Social Teaching*, 54.

22 Gaspard Mermillod, Letter to Pope Leo XIII, as quoted in Duncan, *The Church's Social Teaching*, 48.

same relation as the *Communist Manifesto* of Marx and Engels does to revolutionary socialism'.[23]

It also foreshadowed the principle of subsidiarity – the principle that higher levels of organisation should not assume on behalf of lower levels functions that the lower levels could perform for themselves – on which Leo's successor, Pope Pius XI, elaborated in another social teachings encyclical, *Quadragesimo Anno*, published in 1931 to mark the 40th anniversary of *Rerum Novarum*.

Quadragesimo Anno in its turn reads in part:

> The immense number of propertyless wage-earners on the one hand, and the superabundant riches of the few on the other, is an unanswerable argument that the earthly goods so abundantly produced in this age of industrialism are far from rightly distributed and equitably shared among the various classes of men. Every effort should, therefore, be made that at least in future a just share only of the fruits of production be permitted to accumulate in the hands of the wealthy, and that an ample sufficiency be supplied to the workman ... Unless serious attempts be made, with all energy and without delay to put them into practice, let nobody persuade himself that peace and tranquillity of human society can be effectively defended against the forces of revolution.

Nor was Pius XI's encyclical any less adamant on the indispensability of subsidiarity:

> Let those in power therefore, be convinced that the more faithfully this principle be followed, and the graded hierarchical order exist between the various subsidiary organisations, the more excellent will be both the authority and the efficiency of

23 Maurice Reckitt, *Faith and Society: A Study of the Structure, Outlook and Opportunity of the Christian Socialist Movement in Great Britain* (London: Longmans, Green & Co, 1932) 101.

> the social organisation as a whole, and the happier and more prosperous the condition of the state.[24]

Reaction

'First wave' Social Catholicism achieved its early high point, in France, with the foundation in 1895 by Marc Sangnier and fellow followers of the Thomist philosopher, Fr Alphonse Gratry, of their movement Le Sillon. Le Sillon - in English 'The Furrow' or 'The Path' - numbered at its peak some 500,000 predominantly young worker and student members, comprising in all some 2000 study circles or 'circles of Catholic education': 'Turning their backs on the old conservatism, members set about preparing Catholic youth to take part in the civic affairs of the republic'.[25] 'So long as we have monarchy in the factory, we cannot have the republic in society', Sangnier wrote.[26]

Even so, Le Sillon was for the time being the proverbial bridge too far, and a development for which the Church and Leo's immediate successor, Pius X, were as yet insufficiently prepared. For all the piety, zeal and deeply felt convictions of the reformers, obstacles arose, not least from the inconsistencies and about-faces on the part of the Vatican and insufficient episcopal support that Pius's anti-Modernist and Integralist outlook and approach in key respects so starkly exemplified. Pius – a supporter of credit unionism who encouraged the creation of credit unions in his own diocese and as pope endorsed them in the more advanced *caisse populaire* (credit union) form

24 Pius XI, *Quadragesimo Anno* (1931) 32–33.

25 Duncan, *The Church's Social Teaching*, 97.

26 Michael de la Bedoyere, *The Cardijn Story* (Milwaukee, WI: The Bruce Publishing Company, 1959) 29.

pioneered in Quebec by Alphonse Desjardins at the outset of the 20th century – nonetheless figures prominently in scholarly accounts as having 'instinctively mistrusted progressive endeavours … as wanting a change from Leo's more liberal policies towards "a certain reactionary policy" of Catholic defence and isolation'.[27]

Modernism, in the view of *The New Catholic Encyclopedia*, 'became a slogan to be applied to whatever was disliked in liberal Catholic thought, theology and politics'.[28] 'The bishops, for their part', writes Derek Holmes in his seminal *The Papacy in the Modern World*, 'were required to supervise the teaching given in seminaries and universities, and to establish vigilance committees to seek out Modernists and to counteract their teaching … Other measures included the imposition of an anti-Modernist oath on all candidates for ordination, on priests receiving faculties for hearing confessions or preaching and on professors in seminaries and universities'.[29].

By Cardinal Pietro Gasparri's account, Pius X 'approved, blessed and encouraged a secret espionage association outside and above the hierarchy, which spied on the members of the hierarchy itself, even on their Eminences, the Cardinals: in short, he approved, blessed and encouraged a sort of Freemasonry in the Church, something unheard of in ecclesiastical history'.[30] Its head within the Vatican Secretariat

---

27 Duncan, *The Church's Social Teaching*, 93. The endorsement was formalised by his naming of Desjardins in 1913 as a Commander of the Order of St Gregory the Great 'to reward him for his civil merit and contribution to Catholic social action'. As accessed 8/5/13 at http://www.desjardins.com/en/a_propos/profil/histoire/alphonse-desjardins.jsp.

28 J.J. Heaney, 'Modernism', in *The New Catholic Encyclopedia*, Vol 9, 994. As quoted in Duncan, *The Church's Social Teaching*, 95.

29 J. Derek Holmes, *The Papacy in the Modern World* (London: Burns & Oates, 1981) 271.

30 Holmes, *The Papacy in the Modern World*, 278–279. This secret organisation, named the *Sodalitium Pianum*, consisted of only about 50 members forming a network that denounced others as Modernists. Benigni (1862–1934) worked in the Roman Curia

of State was Msgr Umberto Benigni, who in later life 'joined *Action Francaise* before becoming an informer for Mussolini, supervising the Vatican mail on behalf of the Italian secret service'.[31]

Those suspected or denounced as Modernists included the future popes Benedict XV and Saint John XXIII, and even Manning's fellow convert, Cardinal John Henry Newman, is thought by some to have come under suspicion.[32] The prominent UK Catholic writer and MP Christopher Hollis characterises Pius X's suppression of modernism – 'his secret delations and vigilance committees' – as having employed 'methods that were essentially the methods of Dostoievsky's Grand Inquisitor'.[33]

An anecdote exposes the magnitude of the reversal. The biographer of Cardinal Hinsley – Archbishop of Westminster from 1935 until 1943 – has described how, as a young student in Rome in 1891, Hinsley awaited the publication of *Rerum Novarum* with 'restless longing':

> He arranged with the young Monsignor Merry del Val to receive a copy in the morning of its release from the Vatican Press. Merry del Val arrived with the Encyclical at the English College early on the morning of May 15. The young men spent the whole morning poring over *Rerum Novarum*, already thinking of it as the 'Workers' Charter' – the name soon to be given to it by general consent of the poor in every country.[34]

---

and in 1906 was promoted to the position of Undersecretary of the Congregation for Extraordinary Affairs, the forerunner of what later became the Section for States of the Secretariat of State. His influence waned under Pope Benedict XV.

31 Duncan, *The Church's Social Teaching*, 96.

32 William Buhlmann, *With Eyes to See: Church and World in the Third Millennium* (London: Oxford University Press, 1990) 21.

33 Christopher Hollis, *The Seven Ages: Their Exits and Their Entrances* (London: Heinemann, 1974) 107–108.

34 John C. Heenan, *Cardinal Hinsley* (London: Burns, Oates and Washbourne, 1944) 153.

Twenty years later, Cardinal Merry del Val, now Pius X's Secretary of State and Benigni's superior, was instrumental in the suppression by the Vatican of Le Sillon, and the rebuking of its close affiliate, de Mun's Catholic Association of French Youth (ACJF), for offences that admit interpretation as having been to take *Rerum Novarum* too seriously – namely, for 'the unreasonable enlargement of the domain of justice to the detriment of that of charity, and the subordination of the right of property to its use, usage being made into a function, not of charity, but of justice'.[35]

Cardijn

Meanwhile, Sangnier's insights lived on. Building in part on the example of Le Sillon's study groups and benefiting from the lessons of its demise, the young Flemish priest Joseph Cardijn founded in 1913 the League of Pius X, which in turn in 1920 became the Jeunesse Ouvrière Chrétienne (JOC or, in English, Y.C.W.). Its objective was to win back for the Church the working-class respect and confidence it had so largely forfeited, enable lapsed Catholic workers to recover their faith and secure the implementation of the encyclical's teachings. 'We have arrived at a decisive stage', Cardijn wrote:

> The working-class must accept responsibility; it must share in the running of industry and industrial concerns. ... There is no other means of progress, either for the Church or for all humanity, if we do not accept this: that the working-class must have an equitable share in the administration of production; that the working-class should accept its responsibilities for production.[36]

---

35 John McManners, *Church and State in France 1870–1914*, 170, as quoted in Duncan, *The Church's Social Teaching*, 99.

36 Josef Cardijn, *The Hour of the Working Class* (Melbourne, Vic: Y.C.W. National Headquarters, 1949) 20, 12.

Action should be '*with* the working class, *by* the working class, *for* the working class', and the working class should be enabled to take greater control of their own affairs.[37] The prayer recited for many years at the opening of Y.C.W. meetings reads in part 'May our souls remain in Your Grace today, and may the soul of every worker who died on labour's battlefield rest in peace'.[38]

The emphasis throughout was on formation – on the inculcation of an informed Catholic conscience and consciousness. The conceptual framework – 'Jocism', from Jeunesse Ouvrière Chrétienne – was formation through the organisation's 'Inquiry' or 'See, Judge and Act' approach, of enabling its members to apply moral principles within their workplaces and working lives. Raised to the cardinalate by Pope Paul VI in the aftermath of the Second Vatican Council (1962–1965), and currently like Arizmendiarrieta under considera-tion for canonisation, Cardijn believed that in modern conditions 'the ordinary man did not find his primary source of identity and interest within the parish, but in his employment and his economic class'.[39] The prominent South Australian Catholic Actionist, Paul McGuire, saw the life of the group as comprising three elements: 'It must pray together, it must study together, it must act together, and prayer, study and action should be the familiar life of the group from its first beginning. None should be deferred'.[40]

---

37 De La Bedoyere, *The Cardijn Story*, 31.

38 Val Noone, *'A New Youth for a New Australia': Young Christian Workers Around 1960*, Paper for the Australian Association for the Study of Religions, Australian Catholic University, Aquinas Campus, Ballarat, 6–9 July 1995. 6.

39 Colin H. Jory, *The Campion Society and Catholic Social Militancy in Australia 1929–1939* (Sydney, NSW: Harpham, 1986) 6. Cardijn and canonisation, as accessed 17/1/14 at http://www.cardijn.info/2013/12/cardijn-beatification-process.html.

40 Paul McGuire, 'Formation Technique' in John Fitzsimons and Paul McGuire, *Restoring All Things* (London: Sheed and Ward, 1939) 201.

A representative summary by an Australian Y.C.W. member of the day and subsequent long-time Y.C.W. co-operatives activist, Leon Magree, reads:

> If you saw a problem you judged whether that problem will start again; you saw a situation, you judged whether that situation was right or wrong having regard to the principles you were trying to adhere to: in other words was there a conflict between what you saw happening in your workplace or community compared with what you thought the situation should be? Then having judged there was something wrong you took action. That action might have been as an individual or it might have been some group action'.[41]

Briefed on the progress and prospects of the Y.C.W. by Cardijn in the Vatican in 1924, Pius XI responded 'At last! Here is someone who talks to me about the masses, of saving the masses'.

> Everyone else talks to me of the elite. What is needed is an elite in the masses, the leaven in the paste. The greatest possible work you can do for the Church is to restore to the Church the working masses which she has lost. The masses need the Church and the Church needs the masses ... A Church in which only the well-off are to be found is no longer our Lord's Church. Our Lord founded the Church for the poor. That is why it is necessary to restore to him the working masses.[42]

Jacques Maritain and the Church and Politics

As crucial to Catholic Action as its core values and distinctive approach were its constraints. As the Church's teachings made plain,

41 Leon Magree, as interviewed by Richard Raxworthy for the Australian Credit Union Historical Society Co-operative, Melbourne, 3 November 1991. Tape 1 Side A of three tapes. Transcript courtesy of the Australian Credit Union Archives, Sydney, 2007, 3.

42 De La Bedoyere, *The Cardijn Story*, 67.

there was to be no involvement by it in party politics. Condemning 'the opinion of those who mix up religion and partisan politics and make of them a confused unity, even to the point of declaring that men of another party are unfaithful to the Catholic name', Leo XIII wrote in the encyclical *Cum Multa* in 1882: 'This is to push political factions into the holy field of religion; it is deliberately to rupture fraternal harmony, and open the way to a disastrous amount of harm'.[43]

'Catholic Action ... neither must nor can enter politics for politics sake, we mean the political struggle, party politics', wrote Pius XI in 1924.[44] Catholic Action, Pius XII affirmed in 1940, 'is not and never will be a political organisation, but a chosen band showing good example and manifesting religious fervour'.[45] It was to be 'primarily a formative, educative action'.[46]

In Australia, the growth of Catholic-inspired co-operatives coincided with a furious debate about the role of the Church in society. The success of ANSCA director B.A. Santamaria's secret anti-Communist Catholic Social Studies Movement meant the Church in the early 1950s had direct influence in the Victorian Labor Party. Those Catholics who opposed Santamaria's understanding of the

---

43 Cited by Courtney Murray in *Theological Studies*, Vol XIV, June 1953, 202–203. As quoted in Xavier Connor, 'In Error on Church--State Doctrine: A Catholic Criticism' in Paul Ormonde (ed), *Santamaria: The Politics of Fear* (Richmond, Vic: Spectrum Publications, 2000) 152.

44 Luigi Civardi, *A Manual for Catholic Action* (New York, NY: Sheed and Ward, 1935) 34; and D.A. Benchy, *Church and State in Fascist Italy* (London: Oxford University Press, 1941) 497, as quoted in Kevin Peoples, *Santamaria's Salesman: Working for the National Catholic Rural Movement 1959–1961* (Mulgrave, Vic: John Garratt Publishing, 2012) 26.

45 Pius XII, Address to Members of Italian Catholic Action, 4 September 1940, in *Principles for Peace* 540, 685. As quoted in Connor, 'In Error on Church–State Doctrine', 153.

46 Civardi, *A Manual for Catholic Action*, 42.

relation of Church and politics relied heavily on the writings of the French philosopher and Catholic, Jacques Maritain (1882–1973).

A seminal passage from Maritain cuts through to the heart of the matter. It reads:

> The rule is not unity, but diversity. When the objective is the earthly life of men, when it concerns earthly interests and our temporal welfare, or such and such an ideal of the common good and the ways and means of realizing it, it is normal that the unanimity centre of the super-temporal order should be broken, and that Christians who communicate at the same altar should find themselves divided in the commonwealth. It would be contrary to the nature of things, and hence highly dangerous, to seek on this plane a union among Catholics which could be only artificial, and obtained either by a political materialization of religious energies (such as is too often seen in 'catholic parties' such as German *Centrum*) or by a weakening of the Christian's social and political energies, and a sort of flight from general principles.[47]

British Distributism

Meanwhile, in England, the Catholic Social Guild was formed in 1905 as a predominantly lay body, largely at the instigation of the Jesuit priest Charles Plater. Plater saw the reformist Guild as aiming 'not at control, but at enlightening ... Catholic social study in England' – as a body that 'does not associate itself with any one of the various policies open to Catholics, but leaves members free to select which they will'.[48] Guild members raised consciousness of social issues among Catholics, identified solutions consistent with

47 Jacques Maritain, *True Humanism* (London: Geoffrey Bles, 1938) 297–298.

48 Charles Plater, 'Retreats for Workers', in *Social Work for Catholic Layfolk* (London: Catholic Truth Society, 1911) 5, as quoted in Duncan, *The Church's Social Teaching*, 132.

the Church's teachings and relied for their implementation principally on the Labour Party and gradualist parliamentary reform.

A notably more radical outlook and approach characterised the Distributist Movement which arose shortly after the publication by the young Catholic writer Hilaire Belloc of his *The Servile State* in 1912. As the leading Anglo-Catholic and Christian Socialist Maurice Reckitt recalls of *The Servile State*: 'I cannot overestimate the impact of this book on my mind, and in this I was but symptomatic of thousands of others'.[49]

Belloc was assisted in his further development and promotion of the Distributist idea by his fellow writers Gilbert and Cecil Chesterton. A tribute to Belloc's leadership by Gilbert reads that the world might one day wake up and find 'a new democracy of Distributists':

> Now at the fountain of that river, at the root of that genealogical tree, your figure will stand in the history of England. You were the founder and father of this mission; we were the converts but you were the missionary ... you first revealed the truth both to its greater and lesser servants ... Great will be your glory if England breathes again.[50]

All three young men were former Socialists whose political schooling in and around the Socialist movements of the day was instrumental in enabling them to develop the Distributist doctrines through which they sought to give effect to the teachings of *Rerum Novarum*. Gilbert Chesterton wrote that 'It is my experience that the sort of man who does really become a Distributist is exactly the sort of man who has really been a Socialist. ... Mr Belloc had been

---

49 Maurice Reckitt, *As It Happened* (London: J.M. Dent & Sons, 1941) 107–108.

50 G.K. Chesterton, 'Open Letter to Hilaire Belloc', *The New Witness*, 27 April 1923, as quoted in Joseph Pearce, *Wisdom and Innocence: A Life of G.K. Chesterton* (San Francisco, CA: Ignatius Press, 1996) 324.

a Socialist; my brother had been a Socialist; I had been a Socialist'.[51] As defined by Cecil Chesterton:

> A Distributist is a man who desires that the means of production should, generally speaking, remain private property, but that their ownership should be so distributed as that the determining mass of families – ideally every family – should have an efficient share therein. That is Distributism and nothing else is Distributism. ... Distributism is quite as possible in an industrial or commercial as in an agrarian community.[52]

Responding to a claim by the best known Socialist of the day, George Bernard Shaw, that Distributism could not distribute a factory owned by a major engineering firm among the firm's workers – that it could not 'distribute Armstrong's works among Armstrong's men' – Cecil retorted:

> If Mr Shaw means, as I suppose he does, that it cannot distribute the ownership of the works, it might be as well to inquire first whether the ownership is not already distributed. I am writing far from books of reference but I must confess that I shall be surprised to learn that Armstrong's works are today the property of a single man named Armstrong. Perhaps they are the property of half a dozen Armstrongs, but I think the chances are that by this time they are the property of a limited company of some sort. That means that while the works are one the ownership is already widely distributed. I do not see why it should be harder to distribute it among Armstrong's men than to distribute it among a motley crowd of country clergymen, retired Generals and maiden ladies such as provide the bulk of the share list of most industrial concerns.[53]

---

51 G.K. Chesterton, 'Conversion and Conquest', *G.K's Weekly*, Vol XXII, No 566, 28 November 1935.

52 Cecil Chesterton, 'Shaw and My Neighbour's Chimney', *The New Witness*, 3 May 1917.

53 Cecil Chesterton, 'Shaw and My Neighbour's Chimney', 13.

And by Gilbert Chesterton's account:

> Even my Utopia would contain different things of different types holding on different tenures ... There would be some things nationalised, some machines owned corporately, some guilds sharing common profits, and so on, as well as many absolute owners, where such individual owners are most possible. ... Even while we remain industrial, we can work towards industrial distribution and away from industrial monopoly ... we can try to own our own tools ... In as far as the machine cannot be shared, it would have the ownership of it shared; that is, the direction of it shared, and the profits of it shared.[54]

Distributism was thereby pluralist and supportive of diversity and a mixed economy. Distributist values anticipated the E.F. Schumacher doctrine of 'small is beautiful'.[55] As has been seen, small shops were preferred to chain stores, smallholder farming to agribusiness, and self-employed craftsmen and small workshops with working proprietors or partnerships to larger enterprises and corporations.

For Gilbert Chesterton, tradition was central to the achieving of a Distributist future. Resonant for many with images such as of the 'mist procession' of British diplomat Robert Vansittart's memoirs or science fiction writer Arthur C. Clarke's 'Behind every man now alive stand thirty ghosts, for that is the ratio by which the dead outnumber the living', Chesterton's seminal 1908 book *Orthodoxy* characterises tradition as 'the democracy of the dead':

---

54 Gilbert K. Chesterton, *The Outline of Sanity* (London: Methuen & Company, 1926) 108, 151, 148.

55 See E.F. Schumacher, *Small is Beautiful* (London: Anthony Blond, 1973), and Barbara Wood, *E.F. Schumacher: His Life and Thought* (New York, NY: Harper and Row, 1984).

> Tradition means giving votes to the most obscure of all classes, our ancestors ... Tradition refuses to submit to the small and arrogant oligarchy of those who happen to be walking about.[56]

Co-operatives

Where ownership of productive property on an individual or small-scale basis was impractical, a mutualist or co-operative model of Distributism was preferred. As affirmed by the US Social Catholicism studies scholar Dermot Quinn:

> Co-operatives were essential to the Distributist ideal. They combined ownership, labour for profit, reward for initiative, a degree of self-sufficiency, elimination of waste (as in the duplication of equipment and the use of unnecessary middle-men), and a strong commitment to mutual self-help.[57]

Papal endorsement and approbation of co-operatives is longstanding and explicit. Pope Pius XII wrote: 'The small and average sized undertakings in agriculture, in the arts and crafts, in commerce and industry should be fostered and safeguarded. Moreover they should join together in co-operative associations to gain themselves the benefits and advantages that usually can be gained only from large organisations.' A message from Benedict XVI on the occasion of World Food Day in 2012 reads: 'The Church has always supported cooperatives, in the conviction that their activity is not limited only to the economic sphere, but contributes to the human, social, cultural

56 Robert Vansittart, *The Mist Procession: The Autobiography of Lord Vansittart* (London: Hutchinson, 1958); Arthur C. Clarke, *2001: A Space Odyssey* (New York: New American Library, 1968); Gilbert K. Chesterton, *Orthodoxy* (London: John Lane, The Bodley Head, 1908).

57 Dermot Quinn, 'The Historical Foundations of Modern Distributism', *The Chesterton Review*, 21, No 4, November 1985, 464.

and moral development of those who belong to them, and of the community of which they are part'.[58]

As Cardinal Archbishop of Buenos Aires, Pope Francis was supportive of Argentinian worker co-operatives including the Co-operative 20 de Diciembre which provides employment for survivors of human trafficking and slavery, and the Movimiento de Trabajadores which safeguards hundreds of Argentinians who, in the aftermath of the 2001 national economic crisis, made a living collecting cardboard from garbage cans. Congratulating worker owners of the Alameda co-operative on the occasion of its 10th anniversary in 2012, he commended them for helping to raise awareness of human exploitation and encouraged them to continue their fight for social justice.[59]

The causes and context of his support are plain: His 2013 apostolic exhortation *Evangelii Gaudium* reads:

> While the earnings of a minority are growing exponentially, so too is the gap separating the majority from the prosperity enjoyed by those happy few. This imbalance is the result of ideologies which defend the absolute autonomy of the marketplace and financial speculation. Consequently, they reject the right of states, charged with vigilance for the common good, to exercise any form of control. A new tyranny is thus born, invisible and often virtual, which relentlessly imposes its own laws and rules. Debt and the accumulation of interest also make it difficult for countries to realize the potential of their own economies and keep citizens from enjoying their real purchasing power. To all this we can add widespread corruption and self-serving tax evasion, which have taken on worldwide dimensions. The thirst for power and possessions knows no limits. In this system, which tends to

58 Benedict XVI, 2012, Message to Jose Graziano da Silva, director general of the United Nations' Rome-based Food and Agricultural Organization (FAO), for the occasion of World Food Day 2012.

59 'Pope Francis: His Fight against Social Injustice and Human Exploitation in Argentina', *Co-operative News*, 9 September 2013.

> devour everything which stands in the way of increased profits, whatever is fragile, like the environment, is defenceless before the interests of a deified market, which becomes the only rule.[60]

Addressing some 7000 members of the Confederation of Italian Co-operatives in February 2015, Francis urged them 'to look not only to the past, but also to the future ... It is a real mission that requires creative imagination to find forms, methods, attitudes and tools to combat the throwaway culture cultivated by the powers that support the economic and financial policies of the globalised world':

> We know in achieving a new quality of the economy, it is possible to enable people to grow in all their potential. A member of a co-operative must not be merely a worker but must instead always be a protagonist, and must grow, through the co-operative, as a person, socially and professionally, in responsibility. ... an enterprise managed by a co-operative must grow in a truly co-operative way, involving all. ... Cooperatives are not generally founded by great capitalists. ... In Italy certainly, but not only, it is difficult to obtain public finding to compensate for the scarcity of resources. The solution I propose to you is this: Unite with determination the right means for carrying out good works. Collaborate more with co-operative banks and businesses ... Money, placed at the service of life, can be managed in the right way by the co-operative ... *where capital does not rule over people, but people over capital.*[61]

Attributes

Co-operatives and other mutualist bodies are about resolute and principled households combining to bring about, through their shared

---

60 Francis, *Evangelii Gaudium,* Apostolic Exhortation, 47, para 56. As accessed 16/12/13 at http://www.vatican.va/evangelii-gaudium/en/index.html.

61 Francis, 'The Pope to Co-operatives' address, 2 March 2015, Vatican Information Service. Italics added and as accessed 7/3/15 at http://www.vis.va/vissolr/index.php?vi=all&dl=83025409-e567-235f-28cc-54f476.

efforts and enterprise, outcomes that would be unachievable for them in isolation from one another. They emerge consequent on unsatisfied needs, as a means whereby access is obtained to goods, services, shelter or security of employment that otherwise would be unavailable or unaffordable.

For example, the Rochdale Pioneers – the twenty-eight poor cotton weavers who established their Manchester co-operative store in 1844, and thereby gave rise to the modern consumer or retail co-operative movement – were responding to an unsatisfied need for affordable household necessities such as food and fuel. Friendly societies were a response initially to an unsatisfied need for funeral benefits, and later for unemployment benefits, sickness benefits, medical attendance and hospital care.

Access to affordable life assurance was offered by mutual life assurance societies, as was access to affordable home loans by housing co-operatives and building societies. Credit unions in their turn were at first a response to the need for affordable carry-on loans for smallholder farmers and later for the elimination of usurious 'pay day lenders' and access to affordable consumer finance. Agricultural processing and marketing co-operatives met a pressing need on the part of farmers to share in the value added to their produce beyond the farm gate.

Trade unions had their origin as mutualist bodies or co-operatives in the friendly society mould, and evolved over time as a means of enabling their members to obtain better working conditions and a just price for their labour. Labour parties such as in Australia, the UK and New Zealand in this sense owe their inception to co-operativism and mutualism. The one-time General Secretary of the UK Labour Party, Morgan Phillips (1902–1963), famously remarked that the party owed 'more to Methodism than to Marx', but the greater debt arguably is to the 'father of co-operativism', Robert Owen (1771–1858). Over time, national associations of mutuals and co-operatives emerged, which in turn gave rise to the International Co-operative Alliance and the World Council of Credit Unions.[62]

Internationally, co-operatives and mutuals constitute a major economic and social presence, as reflected in key performance indicators including 1000 million members, a $1700 billion turnover and jobs for some 196 million workers.[63] In the United States, co-operatives and other mutuals total some 130 million members and account collectively for two million jobs, $75 billion in wages and benefits and $500 billion in revenue. Reportedly, 'More Americans hold membership in co-operatives than hold shares in the stock market'.[64]

The UK's seven million member Co-operative Group – the former Co-operative Wholesale Society – today includes divisions respectively of Co-operative Food with 3000 retail outlets, Co-operative Travel with 450 travel agencies, Co-operative Funeral care with over 800 funeral parlours, Co-operative Pharmacy with nearly 800 branches, the Co-operative Bank with 342 High Street branches and 22 Corporate Banking Centres and Co-operative Legal Services as a national legal services provider.[65] Italy's Emilia Romagna region has some 7500 co-operatives, of which two-thirds are worker owned,

---

62 See, for example, W.P. Watkins, *The International Co-operative Alliance 1895–1970* (London: International Co-operative Alliance, 1970).

63 Richard Denniss and David Baker, *Who Knew Australians Were So Co-operative? The Size and Scope of Mutually Owned Co-ops in Australia*, Australia Institute Paper 10 (Canberra, ACT: The Australia Institute 2012) 2.

64 Marjorie Kelly, 'The Economy, Under New Ownership', *Yes! Magazine*, 19 February 2013.

65 Accessed 16/6/13 on the Co-operative Group website at http://www.co-operative.coop/corporate/about us/our businesses/.

and affiliation with France's worker co-operative federation totals some 2000 co-operatives with 40,000 employees.[66]

The Member–Management Relationship

Co-operatives and other mutualist bodies can exhibit the attributes of both businesses and social movements. The success of Evolved Distributism in the Mondragón mould is attributable to its having overcome in part – and potentially in its entirety – what agency theorists call 'the basic agency dilemma' of the relationship between those managing a co-operative and its members. Agency theory holds that how individuals and institutions behave socially and politically can be explained in terms of a series of 'contracts', where one party (the 'principal') commissions a second party (the 'agent') to act on the first party's behalf. The substance of the contract is the agreement by the agent or executive to comply with the wishes of the member or principal, who, in turn, agrees to provide the agent with a specified payment. The dilemma arises where compliance by the agent with the wishes of the principal does not occur or the proffered payment is not forthcoming.

As will be seen, the genius of Arizmendiarrieta lay in re-thinking co-operation on the Rochdale model so as to incorporate principles and structures that reduce – and perhaps ultimately eliminate – the basic agency dilemma, both within and between the Mondragón co-operatives. From the perspective of creating a more fair and efficient productive system where the principal is faithfully served and the agent is fairly compensated, what 'Evolved Distributism' in the

66 Hazel Corcoran and David Wilson, *The Worker Co-operative Movement in Italy, Mondragón and France*, Canadian Worker Co-operative Federation Research Paper 25. Accessed 8/7/13, at http://canadianworker.coop/files/CWCF_Research_Paper_International *16-6-2010*_fnl[1].pdf.

Mondragón mould is about is primarily the evolution – albeit as yet incomplete – of systems within which all principals are agents and all agents are principals.[67]

Social Movement Vulnerability

Conversely, Distributist and mutualist enterprises are vulnerable to failure in their social movement capacity. Consistent with social movement theory, the life cycle of a mutualist or Distributist enterprise may extend over as many as three stages. There is, in the first instance, a utopian stage where the urgency of the need and the vision and commitment of the founders energise their followers and bring the new entity into being; secondly, a stage where the enterprise assumes a more formal and institutional character in order to more effectively go about achieving its objectives; and, finally, a stage – usually referred to as the 'system' stage – where bureaucracy takes over, and the survival of the enterprise assumes precedence over its original intended purpose. Social movement theorists characterise the cycle in its entirety as comprising a 'generation–degeneration process'.[68]

What so many of the best-known examples of co-operatives and other mutualist enterprises – the major credit unions, agricultural co-operatives, mutual life assurance societies, permanent building societies and consumer co-operatives – now have in common with one another is the blind alley or 'Rochdale cul-de-sac' they have come to occupy, on having gravitated largely from the hands of their members to those of bureaucracies. In the absence of any meaningful

67 For co-operatives and agency theory, see Race Mathews, *Jobs of Our Own: Building a Stakeholder Society* (Annandale, NSW: Pluto Press, 1999) 10–12.

68 For co-operatives and other mutualist bodies as social movements, see Patrick Develtere, *Co-operative Development: Towards a Social Movement Perspective* (Saskatoon, SA: University of Saskatchewan Centre for Co-operative Studies, 1992).

measure of member involvement and participation, they have become for all practical purposes indistinguishable from their conventional commercial counterparts.

In so doing, they have in most instances wholly or in part forfeited their niche advantage over their competitors in terms of the principal–agent relationship. Moreover, recent experience suggests that the Rochdale cul-de-sac is not, as has been supposed, a stable condition which can be counted upon to continue indefinitely, but rather one of extreme fragility and precariousness. It invites either commercial failure as in the case of some major European consumer co-operatives – the one-time elite of the co-operative movement – or being taken over and looted either from without or within by predatory demutualisers.

Notable examples of third stage 'generation–degeneration' failure include the collapse and liquidation in 1998 of Germany's Co-op Dortmund-Kassel with 500,000 members, 350 supermarkets, sixteen department stores, 15,000 employees and an annual turnover of some 2.5 billion Deutschmarks. Once known as the 'Red Giant' of Austria's retail scene and with a membership at its peak of one in every four of the nation's population, Konsum Austria became bankrupt in 1995.

In 1997 Britain's giant Co-operative Wholesale Society – the oldest and biggest consumer co-operative in Europe, with 35,000 employees, over 500 stores, annual sales in excess of £3 billion and major subsidiaries in the Co-operative Bank and the Co-operative Insurance Society – narrowly escaped being demutualised by a corporate raider to whom it had previously sold substantial manufacturing assets.[69]

69 As accessed 8/7/13 at http://www.co-oppundit.org/a-new-cooperation-movement.html.

Following largely a failed IT project and the imprudent acquisition of a former building society, the bank was obliged in 2013 to secure a substantial injection of capital from private investors. The challenge historically is seen to have been to develop means by which the rise and fall cycle can be arrested at a point midway between its first and second stages, and concurrent high levels of member involvement and bureaucratic efficiencies thereby maintained.

Setbacks

British Distributism was centred around the weekly paper that appeared as successively *The Eye Witness*, *The New Witness*, *G.K.'s Weekly* and *The Weekly Review*, the Distributist League that was spun off from the paper, and the Catholic Rural Land Movement and its Land Association affiliates that were further spin-offs. Tragically, it withered on the vine with Gilbert Chesterton's death in 1936 and the outbreak of World War II three years later. And few setbacks can have been as crushing to Distributism or prejudicial to the morale of its adherents as the English Catholic hierarchy's turning its back in the late 1930s on so rare an example of practical, hands-on Distributism as the Catholic Rural Land Movement.

A summary of the thinking behind the Land Movement and its Catholic Rural Land Association affiliates by their principal spokesman, Harold Robbins, reads:

> If men were taught to farm, primarily to feed their families, secondarily to feed neighbours grouped in social communities round them, and only finally to market their surpluses co-operatively, it seemed not only would the marketing problem assume more modest proportions but the revival of social contacts would reverse the rural decline.[70]

70 Harold Robbins, 'A Land Movement', *GK's Weekly*, 3 August 1933, 349.

The Land Movement was accorded papal approval in 1933 in a letter over the signature of the Vatican Secretary of State – and future Pope Pius XII – Cardinal Eugenio Pacelli. Pacelli wrote:

> The Holy Father has heard with satisfaction of the progress already made by the five Catholic Land Associations of Great Britain, and prays this important work of restoring the sane and healthy life of the countryside may be abundantly blessed by God and result in a diminution of unemployment through the development of the agricultural resources of the country to the fullest possible extent. As an encouragement to persevere in this good work, His Holiness most gladly imparts his Apostolic Blessing to all who are engaged in helping to further this most praiseworthy enterprise.[71]

Unhappily, no comparable expressions of good will – much less more tangible support – were forthcoming from the Catholic authorities in England. The Land Movement and Associations effectively had to discontinue their activities when the hierarchy refused to authorise an annual nationwide collection to pay for the properties the trainees were ready to occupy.

Robbins commented bitterly that 'the Catholic authorities in England have never shown any other sentiment than embarrassment to have their principles stated so eloquently'. A more recent account acerbically concludes:

> Although the Catholic hierarchies were happy to support the initiative on the moral level, they were not prepared to back up that support on the practical level. It was a grievous misunderstanding of the true situation of society in that day. ... The answer was a categorical 'no'.[72]

---

71 Quoted in Harold Robbins, 'The Last of the Realists: G.K. Chesterton and his Work' Part III, in *The Cross and the Plough*, 15, No 3, Michaelmas 1948, 16.

72 Tobias Lanz, 'Introduction' in J. McQuillan and Others, *Flee to the Fields: The Founding Papers of the Catholic Land Movement* (London: Heath Cranton, 1934; repr Norfolk VA,

The divergence was over priorities, and rural resettlement was at best secondary in the eyes of the episcopacy to more pressing economic and pastoral concerns.

Antigonish

In the event, the Distributist idea did not die with Chesterton as many supposed, but rather had emigrated and was alive and well in the Antigonish Movement that was established in Nova Scotia in the late 1920s at the instigation of the Extension Department of the University of St Francis Xavier at Antigonish and the Distributist priests Moses Coady and 'Jimmy' Tompkins.

The basis of the Antigonish Movement was again formation on the Y.C.W. model, through adult education, Rochdale-style producer and consumer co-operation and credit unionism. Its aim was to enable local communities to become 'masters of their own destiny' and thereby enjoy 'the good and abundant life', by mobilising local and regional resources for regional economic development. Coady wrote:

> We start with simple things that are vital to human living and move on up the scale to the more cultural and refining activities that make life complete. Through credit unions, co-operative stores, lobster factories and sawmills, we are laying the foundations for an appreciation of Shakespeare and grand opera.[73]

'Surely it is the authentic voice of Chesterton', mused Maisie Ward in 1944, 'when Dr Tompkins says "Trust the little fellow", or

---

IHS Press, 2003) 10–11.

73 Moses Coady, *Masters of Their Own Destiny: The Story of the Antigonish Movement of Adult Education Through Economic Cooperation* (Antigonish, NS: Formac Publishing Company, 1980) 68.

Dr Coady declares "The people are great and powerful and can do everything"'.[74]

The magic and magnetism of Antigonish in its heyday is now insufficiently remembered or understood. As Coady's biographer, Michael R. Welton, so vividly recalls:

> Antigonish, now a rural town like so many others, graced by malls and fast-food outlets, glowed with a radiant light in the 1930s and 1940s ... For an evanescent historical moment, the Antigonish Movement captured the imagination of the world. Journalists, liberal-minded religious leaders, papal authorities, eastern seaboard intellectuals, professors, theologians, social reformers, wild-eyed dreamers, co-operative leaders and innocent youth came from far and wide to witness the 'miracle of Antigonish'. Hard minds and doubting hearts were transformed by the co-operative miracle as tourists witnessed rustic lobster factories springing up in communities with previously unremarkable histories.[75]

A 1987 study by Welton and Jim Lotz concludes that 'The Movement probably reached its peak in 1938–39'. It reads:

> In 1938, the Movement received official papal approval. In its Annual Report for the year ending 30 April 1939, the Extension Department noted that staff totalled eleven full-time members, seven part-time, and thirty additional staff in the fishing communities. The Annual Rural and Industrial Conference in August 1938 had attracted one thousand people. A Co-operative Institute gathering held after the Conference brought together two hundred educationists, clergymen, social workers and others, from thirty states in the United States and from every province in Canada. ... In the three Maritime Provinces, 19,600 people were enrolled in 2265 study clubs. At the annual

74 Ward, *Gilbert Keith Chesterton*, 446.

75 Michael R. Welton, *Little Mosie from Margaree: A Biography of Moses Michael Coady* (Toronto, ON: Thompson Educational Publishing Inc, 2001) 253.

> extension course held in February 1939, 136 people from the region had participated. In all, 342 credit unions had been established, and 162 other forms of co-operative organisation. In 1939, Father Coady's book *Masters of Their Own Destiny* appeared, and in this he articulated the philosophy of the Movement.[76]

If the Antigonish Movement ultimately asked more of consumer co-operation and credit unionism than they were able to deliver – if it succumbed ultimately to social movement theory's 'generation–degeneration cycle' – that in no way detracts from the energy its adherents devoted to their cause, nor from the short-to-medium-term alleviation of endemic poverty, the enhancement of human dignity and the restoration of hope that they accomplished, and the inspiration and encouragement they afforded for others after them and afar off.[77]

Mondragón

It remained for Arizmendiarrieta to bring an 'Evolved Distributism' to triumphant success at Mondragón. The Mondragón co-operatives are the fruit of Jocist formation in the Cardijn mould, in conjunction with the identification by Arizmendiarrieta of the fundamental flaws of Rochdale co-operation, and his game-changing insight that only work and property – as opposed, for example, to consumption or saving – are so central to the lives of ordinary people as to defeat the imperatives of social movement theory's 'generation–degeneration'

76 Jim Lotz and Michael R. Welton, '"Knowledge for the People": The Origins and Development of the Antigonish Movement', in Michael R. Welton (ed), *Knowledge for the People* (Toronto, ON: Oise Press, 1987) 107.

77 For a further extended discussion of the Antigonish Movement, see Mathews, *Jobs of Our Own*, 134–154.

cycle and provide the foundations on which enduring co-operatives and an ongoing Distributist social order can be built. In so doing, he endowed the Mondragón co-operatives with so great a flexibility and capacity to adapt to changing circumstances as for it to be said of them 'we build the road as we travel'.[78] A passage written a few days before his death in 1976 reads:

> Hand in hand, of one mind, renewed, united in work, through work, in our small land we shall create a more human environment for everyone and we shall improve this land. We shall include villages and towns in our new equality; the people and everything else: 'Ever forward'. Nobody shall be slave or master to anyone, everyone shall simply work for the benefit of everyone else, and we shall have to behave differently in the way we work. This shall be our human and progressive union – a union which can be created by the people.[79]

A New Paradigm

Evolved Distributism, as exemplified by Mondragón, is, in a sense, most usefully understood as the form in which Socialism of the mutualist, associative and communitarian kind originally embraced by Belloc and the Chesterton brothers has been re-born, following the well-intentioned but ultimately counterproductive flirtation with statism that so comprehensively distracted and diverted it for the greater part of the 20th century. Reminiscent of Le Sillon, it attests to the inextricability and indivisibility of economic and political democracy, and the inability of either to thrive indefinitely in the

78 Roy Morrison, *We Build the Road as We Travel* (Philadelphia, PA: New Society Publishers, 1991) 21.

79 Ormaechea, *The Mondragón Co-operative Experience*, 7. For an extended account of the history, principles, structure, governance and achievements of the Mondragón co-operatives, see Mathews, *Jobs of Our Own*, 179–231.

absence of the other. Echoing Sangnier and Cardijn, Evolved Distributism constitutes the genesis of a new paradigm of active citizenship and workplace empowerment, and the forerunner of new coalitions and alliances – of great new social movements – within which progressive parties provide the cutting political edge in conjunction with trade unions, local and regional communities and community groups.

In so doing, the triumphant success of the Mondragón co-operatives mocks the failure of 'First Wave' Australian Distributism to fulfil its promise.[80] For all the optimism of Maisie Ward's 1944 account, the Australian National Secretariat for Catholic Action and its affiliates and offshoots in their turn were not immune to shortcomings and vicissitudes including insufficiency of formation, mission creep or shifts in objective and strategic miscalculation. Already when Ward wrote, developments were underway which in little more than a decade were to relegate Distributist hopes seemingly to the status of an historical aberration or curiosity. 'We do not hold the encyclicals against you', a Communist spokesman reportedly once said to his Catholic counterpart, 'but we reproach you for scorning the encyclicals'.[81]

---

80 Salvador Antuñano, Address to the 'A Distributist View of the Global Economic Crisis' Conference, Oxford 2009, as quoted in Bernard Manzo 'Was Chesterton Right?', *Tablet*, 1 August 2009.

81 Brook W. Smith, *Jacques Maritain: Anti-Modern or Ultra-Modern?* (New York, NY: Elsevier, 1976) 92, as quoted in Bruce Duncan, *Crusade or Conspiracy: Catholics and the Anti-Communist Struggle in Australia* (Sydney, NSW: University of New South Wales Press, 2001) 398.

Chapter 2

CHURCH, STATE AND COMMUNITY: THE AUSTRALIAN CONTEXT

Arrivals and Aspirations

Australian Catholicism was born in chains, and spent the first hundred years of its existence trying to shed them and assert itself as a distinctive presence in a new land. In this, it was no different from others who settled what some were to come to regard as the true Great South Land of the Holy Spirit.

But Catholics also brought baggage to their new home – the legacy of longstanding enmities between British and Irish, Protestant and Catholic, the prosperous and the poor and those who held power and those who sought a share in it – that would colour their development and that of Australia well beyond that first century.

Many of the characteristics and controversies associated with the Church in Australia and its relationship with the wider Australian community in the early years of the 21st century can be traced back to those first 100 years of Catholicism on these shores. Prominent among them are the nature of authority, the place of religion in public life, local autonomy and global order, the absorption of different cultures and the role of the Church in educational and health care institutions serving a wider public.

Sydney priest and historian Edmund Campion records that the first Australian Catholics were lay people who arrived from England with the First Fleet in 1788. About one in ten of the 750 convicts and a few of the marines were Catholics, and about half the convict Catholics were born in Ireland. Eight days after the Union flag was raised at Sydney Cove on 26 January 1788 they joined everyone else in the colony at Australia's first church service, led by the Church of England chaplain, the Reverend Richard Johnson, who preached on the text 'What shall I render unto the Lord for all his benefits toward me'.

Campion's account continues 'The Catholic convicts who attended Johnson's service were not entirely dependent on him for religious sustenance':

> Like all migrants, they arrived with spiritual and intellectual luggage already acquired at home. Irish Catholicism before the Famine (1845–52) was a bewildering mixture of formal Catholicism, debased Catholic practices, family piety, superstition, magic and Celtic mythology. Catholic convicts brought this with them. Consequently, even without the ministration of priests, the Catholic faith survived in colonial Australia as a poem that gave life meaning or respite. It was a view of the world enabling one to sustain the present and hope for the future.[1]

Nor was it their faith alone that the Irish brought with them to Australia. Grievances from the Old World also accompanied them:

1 Edmund Campion, *Australian Catholics* (Ringwood, Vic: Viking/Penguin Books, 1987) 3.

> The conquest of Ireland had made them a landless people. In 1641, Catholics owned 59 per cent of the land; in 1688 22 per cent; in 1703 14 per cent; by 1788 about 5 per cent. The Protestant proprietors of Ireland maintained their hold on land through the Penal Laws, which kept the Catholic Irish as helots in their own country. When they came to Australia they carried this history with them and passed it on to their children.[2]

Inevitably not all the fallout from such adverse circumstances was benign. Interpretations of the early history of Catholicism in Australia are challenged by Campion's fellow historian, Patrick O'Farrell, as having been too deeply coloured by the popular conception of 'unfortunate Irish convicts, manly and courageous victims of political injustice and religious persecution, more sinned against than sinning'. In reality, O'Farrell writes, about four-fifths of the Irish convicts could be described properly as ordinary criminals, with about a third of them having had previous convictions.[3]

Tensions were apparent from the outset in that, whereas the English and Scots convicts were nearly all Protestants, the Irish were nearly all Catholics:

> So it was that the deepest chasm that existed within penal Australia was more specific than that between gaoler and prisoner; it was the bitter gulf between those who held power and authority, and Irish convicts. This obsessive antagonism between Anglo-Scots Protestant ascendancy and Irish convict Catholicism, established with the foundation of Australia, has been a central and persistent theme in the history of Catholicism's relations with its Australian environment. Its influence has been tragically corrosive.[4]

---

2 Campion, *Australian Catholics*, 6.

3 Patrick O'Farrell, *The Catholic Church and Community in Australia: An Australian History* (Kensington, NSW: NSW University Press, 1985) 3–4.

4 O'Farrell, Australian Catholics, 3–4.

So profound and persistent an estrangement and embitterment was to hamper the development of the Australian church repeatedly. 'Its twisted, shackled inheritance is epitomised in the circumstances of the first recorded Mass, which was celebrated for a congregation of prisoners in Sydney in May, 1803, under strict regulations drafted by Governor King and with police surveillance, by an Irish convict priest, transported – by mistake, it seems – for alleged complicity in the 1789 Irish rebellion', O'Farrell writes:

> The Governor's regulations stressed that the Catholics, so favoured by this 'extension of liberal toleration', must show 'becoming gratitude'; that assembly for Mass must never be the occasion of 'seditious conversation'; that the priest, Mr Dixon, was fully responsible for his congregation and must exert himself to detect and report any sign of disturbance or disaffection. This cautious toleration of Catholic worship had come fifteen years after the colony's foundation. It was withdrawn, in panic, the following year, and although Dixon, and after him Father Harold, exercised their ministry in a private capacity, it was not until 1820, another sixteen years, that Mass could be celebrated publicly again.[5]

Survival

Even so, in the absence of priests, laymen had emerged as spiritual leaders – a feature of the development of Catholicism in many parts of Australia. In Campion's view, what was noteworthy about Catholics in earliest colonial society was that, even without priests, the Catholic name did not disappear from sight:

> To say this is not to claims hothouse levels of piety; but neither does it refuse to acknowledge real achievements of lay Catholic

5 O'Farrell, *The Catholic Church and Community in Australia*, 1–2.

> faith. When the census was taken in 1828 there were about 10,000 Catholics in New South Wales. Of these, there were 374 adults, born in the colony, who declared themselves Catholics. This small group of Australian-born adult Catholics is highly significant: they are the products of settled family life and lay religious networks stretching back to the beginnings of the colony. Here was a pre-ecclesiastical Catholicism closely linked to the experience of being Irish. It survived and was nurtured mainly within family circles. At the very least, one must recognise a Catholic reality already in existence before regular priestly ministry began in Australia. The lay Catholicism which developed in Australia did not shun priests. On the contrary, it wanted a sacerdotal ministry. And, from time to time, there were priests here to minister to Catholics.[6]

In November 1817, an Irish priest, Jeremiah O'Flynn, arrived unannounced and celebrated Mass and administered the sacraments without permission. On being ordered out by Governor Macquarie he went underground, but was deported in May 1818, leaving behind the Blessed Sacrament in the home of a Sydney layman. It was not until October 1819 – more than fifteen years after King had imposed the ban on Mass being celebrated – that the Colonial Office informed Macquarie that two Catholic chaplains, Frs Philip Conolly and John Joseph Therry, had been appointed. 'Their arrival in Sydney Harbour on Tuesday, 3 May 1820, is seen by some as the beginning of formal Catholicism in Australia', Campion writes.[7]

Meanwhile, Conolly and Therry had to contend with Protestant harassment over the right to conduct marriages or burials or to visit members of their flock in Protestant-run hospitals and orphanages. A leading historian from the Protestant tradition, Ian Breward, notes

---

6 Campion, *Australian Catholics*, 9–10.

7 Campion, *Australian Catholics*, 13.

that 'Thrown on to their own resources, for their stipends were small, it is not surprising that they seemed contentious and money-conscious to their Protestant detractors':

> Even those who had little sympathy with the dominant Evangelical ethos of the colony were united in their dislike and suspicion of these Roman Catholic arrivals. It was widely believed that Britain's imperial greatness was bound up with the maintenance of the Protestant religion and the liberties it fostered. Contempt for the Roman Catholic Irish and resistance to their attempts to achieve equality were to remain an enduring theme in Australian history for more than a century.[8]

On a more affirmative note, Naomi Turner's two-volume study of the Australian laity reads that by 1820 'Catholics were so well accepted that no one saw anything unusual in the Governor of the settlement, Lachlan Macquarie, laying with grave courtesy the foundation stone of the first Catholic Church, while Francis Greenway and John Campbell, both Protestants, offered to be architect and treasurer respectively for the committee in charge of the project'.[9] In similar vein, in 1847 land for a Catholic church in the fledgling Melbourne suburb of Brighton was donated by a local Anglican, Jonathan Were.[10]

Benedictines

William Ullathorne, twenty-seven years old and a newly ordained English Benedictine priest, assumed office as Australia's Vicar-General in 1833, and in 1834 John Bede Polding, novice-master and

8 Ian Breward, *A History of the Australian Churches* (St Leonards, NSW: Allen & Unwin, 1993) 17.

9 Naomi Turner, *Catholics in Australia: A Social History*, Vol 1 (North Blackburn, Vic: Collins Dove, 1992) 3.

10 Breward, *A History of the Australian Churches*, 41–42.

sub-prior of the Benedictine monastery of Downside, became its first bishop. 'By 1838 Catholics could number among themselves people belonging to the high ranks of society as well as many emancipists achieving varying degrees of success within the community', Turner concludes.[11]

As the move towards responsible government progressed, Catholic dioceses – the first in a British possession since the Reformation – were established in Hobart and Adelaide in 1842, in Western Australia in 1845 and in Melbourne in 1847. Of the five bishops Polding appointed in the 1840s, three were Irish, Francis Murphy in Adelaide, John Brady in Perth and James Goold in Melbourne, and two English, Robert Willson of Hobart and Polding's coadjutor Charles Henry Davis.

With nine priests ministering Australia-wide to some 20,000 Catholics at the outset of his incumbency, Polding's goal was the creation of a Benedictine monastery, as 'the centre and form of Catholic life':

> He believed that the salvation of that sinful land lay in revealing to it the beauty of holiness: the ordered loveliness of religion would shine forth to the colonists in the exemplary lives of a monastic community which would manifest the ideal Christian life ... This vision, medieval in its concept of barbarism redeemed through the establishment of centres of monastic life and culture was, with Polding, more than hope. He was quite certain that, without the establishment of a Benedictine monastery 'We can do no good'.[12]

It was a forlorn hope, as was to be acknowledged two years later by Ullathorne, following his failure as Polding's emissary to obtain

11 Turner, *Catholics in Australia*, 3.

12 O'Farrell, *The Catholic Church and Community in Australia*, 44.

Benedictine monks, or at least English priests, for the Australian mission: 'To do anything Benedictine in the Colony is now out of the question … The Colony will become, of course, an Irish mission, and perhaps ought to be so'.[13] Breward sees Polding's forty-two-year ministry in Australia as a powerful reminder of how Catholicism's universal character was grounded in ethnic and cultural identities:

> English and Irish Catholicism were different, despite their common allegiances. Many Irish priests, religious and bishops were committed to an Irish imperialism which would transcend centuries of English oppression. Ullathorne saw the Irish future clearly. Polding did not. The later tensions among Australian Catholics came from competition between alternative visions and from disagreement about how the mission to Australia should be conducted.[14]

Education

Placing Anglicans on an equal footing with other Christian denominations including Catholics, Governor Richard Bourke's Church Act of 1836 achieved what Campion sees as having been 'a rough-and-ready equality between the main denominations'.[15] Less happily, it also gave rise to divisions over State Aid to churches and thereby the vexatious issue of funding for non-government schools which, as will be seen, were to persist well into the second half of the subsequent century.

> This question was being framed in such a way as to constitute, in the church's eyes, a fundamental menace to her mission. Essentially, the education question of the 1860s and 1870s

13 Quoted in O'Farrell, *The Catholic Church and Community in Australia*, 47.

14 Breward, *A History of the Australian Churches*, 30.

15 Campion, *Australian Catholics*, 27.

> came down came to this: will government money be withdrawn from any support of religious denominational education, and be devoted exclusively to a public educational system which would be free, compulsory and secular? ... This became the centre of what was probably the most passionate, fundamental and continuing ideological conflict in Australia's history, the Australian focus for a confrontation that was worldwide; between Catholicism and all those varieties of nineteenth century thought which came under the general heading of 'liberalism'.[16]

A representative take on the Church perspective by Campion's fellow historian-priest, James Murtagh, reads 'The older liberalism was still vaguely God-centred and retained a religious view of reality':

> But the new liberalism was man-centred and militantly secular. Secularism is the doctrine that morality should be based solely on regard to the well-being of mankind in the present life, to the exclusion of all considerations drawn from belief in God or in a future state. The spirit of secularism inspired the new liberalism, no longer revolutionary but evolutionary, and identified with capitalism, democracy and nationalism in a new faith in progress of a quasi-religious fervour. The older liberalism and the new were at issue in Australia's struggle over education.[17]

Despite the misgivings of some leading Catholic laity, sufficient numbers of the Catholic people fell in behind their priests and bishops to defend separate Catholic schooling even as the other churches largely abandoned their schools with the withdrawal of State Aid. In so doing, they elevated orders of priests, nuns and brothers to a

---

16 Campion, *Australian Catholics*, 27.

17 James G. Murtagh, *Australia: The Catholic Chapter* (Melbourne: The Polding Press, 1969 – a corrected reprint of the original 1959 edition) 94–95.

new status within the Australian Church. Referring to the Sisters of Mercy, the Brigidines, the Presentation Sisters, the Irish Christian Brothers, the Jesuits and the Marist Brothers, Breward writes:

> Their commitment to Catholic education, their willingness to put up with hardship and poverty, and the love and respect that many of them evoked gave Australian Catholicism a new direction and identity. The extent of the growth they made possible can be seen in Archbishop Thomas Carr's episcopate in Melbourne. Between 1886 and 1917, the number of pupils grew from 10,000 to 50,000.[18]

In Campion's view, 'Much church history is written around the personalities and activities of bishops – the reason is not hard to seek':

> On the level of living experience, however, there can be no doubt that the influence of religious sisters and brothers has been more penetrating. This is especially true of Australian Catholicism, whose central religious institution, the parochial (parish) school, was the creation of the sisters and brothers. … As early as 1860 Adelaide Catholics had said that they would not rest until their schools were in the hands of religious orders. This soon became mandatory elsewhere; so that by the end of the century wherever you went in Australia a Catholic school meant a school run by a religious order. … this is how the Catholic school system surmounted the challenge of the withdrawal of state aid. In 1880 there were 815 teaching sisters throughout Australia; by 1890 their number had passed the 2000 mark; and in another 20 years it would be more than 5000.[19]

In Melbourne, efforts had begun to bring in the Christian Brothers for primary education and a Jesuit college to open the way to 'governmental, mercantile and professional success'. In 1865 – twenty years after the arrival in South Australia of Austrian Jesuits

18 Breward, *A History of the Australian Churches*, 29.

19 Campion, *Australian Catholics*, 45–46.

with the colony's German farmers – two Irish Jesuit priests arrived in Melbourne and took over St Patrick's College in the shadow of East Melbourne's St Patrick's Cathedral.

Opening in Kew in 1878, Xavier College drew boarders from across Australia, and in the same year the Jesuits opened St Aloysius' College and Riverview in Sydney. In 1868, the Irish Christian Brothers came to Melbourne. Central to their vocation was the task of leading youth to God. Their scholastic aim was to prepare boys for the civil service examinations. Not without cause was it said that getting a job with the government was the key to security and a step up in life for sons of the working class.

Extra-curricular organisation – for men, women and children – reinforced the values imparted in church and classroom:

> Perhaps more than anything else in 19th century Australia – other than the Catholic school system – sodalities and guilds helped to maintain for considerable time a Catholic subculture within the total framework of society. These organisations were initiated by the clergy and a priest was always one of the organisers or supervisors of them. They provided ready-made social groups for Catholics, groups which celebrated occasions with picnics, sports days, balls or concerts. They even established local lending libraries.[20]

Social Concerns and Community Services

Intimations of widening social concerns had earlier on become evident. Ullathorne and Polding's incumbencies saw the Church articulate for the first time a view about the indigenous people who so largely had been dispossessed of their lands and hunting grounds. Ullathorne wrote in the 1830s: 'These poor people have often been

20 Turner, *Catholics in Australia*, 193.

treated by the convicts, at the out stations, with atrocious barbarity; who have been known to shoot them, as game for sport. … From these they have been initiated into more than our worst vices. The women have been shockingly treated. Where the European population is thickest, they are fast dying off'.[21]

In evidence to the NSW Legislative Council Select Committee on the Condition of the Aborigines in 1845, Polding ascribed the fall in the indigenous population to despondency at the loss of their lands. Asked how he knew, he replied remarkably: 'I am making myself a black, putting myself in that position, and taking all I know except that this is my country, that my father lived by pursuing the emu and the kangaroo, that I was driven away from my hunting grounds, that my children's tribes are subjected to the grossest barbarities'.[22]

Arriving with her officer husband from Madras in 1838 at the outset of an official assisted immigration scheme which over a fifty-year period was to bring out more than 200,000 settlers, nearly half of whom were Irish, Caroline Chisholm played a key role in drawing closer together the Church and the wider community:

> A convert to Catholicism, Chisholm had been brought up as an evangelical Anglican, with an evangelical's interest in social work. She thought the weakness in the government's scheme was that no one had found ways of encouraging new immigrants to go to the country, where their labour was needed. Instead, they stayed in Sydney, looking for work there. So she formed the habit of meeting each ship that came into the harbour and befriending girl immigrants in particular, for many of whom she found jobs. … To allay fears of unknown perils, she

21 Campion, *Australian Catholics*, 98.

22 Gregory Haines, Mary Gregory Forster and Frank Brophy (eds), *The Eye of Faith: The Pastoral Letters of John Bede Polding* (Kilmore, Vic: Lowden Publishing, circa 1977) 403–404.

> personally led convoys to new lives up country. No bushranger ever molested the Chisholm convoys. In her first year she placed more than 2000 persons, 1400 of them women. In six years she had placed 11,000 persons. ... Returning to England in 1846, she formed her own colonisation society, for which she won the support of Charles Dickens. She got conditions improved on outbound ships, made it easier for colonists to send money home, organised a missing friends bureau and answered thousands of queries about Australia.[23]

The year 1838 was notable also for the arrival of Australia's first religious sisters. Five Irish Sisters of Charity were recruited by Ullathorne, initially for an adult social work ministry and to teach religion in the Catholic school. In 1857 they opened Australia's first professional hospital, St Vincent's in Sydney. 'In a combative age St Vincent's was a centre of amity':

> From the beginning Protestant ministers attended members of their respective flocks there. Protestant tracts and Protestant bibles were made available by Protestant religious societies. In 1859 there was a storm when a priest removed Protestant bibles against the wishes of the sisters. Supported by the liberal laity, the sisters rode out the storm, although their superior, Mother de Lacy, went home to Ireland.[24]

Denied as the women might be of the authority vested by ordination, they could still wield power and influence in visibly Catholic institutions. In 1883, a further St Vincent's hospital was opened by the order in Melbourne.

In 1857, Polding founded an order in the Benedictine tradition, the Good Samaritans, to work with prostitutes. Its members also brought food and clothing to the poor, ran adult education programs

23 Campion, *Australian Catholics*, 23.

24 Campion, *Australian Catholics*, 36.

and visited the girls' reformatory on Cockatoo Island and the boys' training ships. Ten years later, a further order – the Sisters of St Joseph of the Sacred Heart – was founded in South Australia by Mary McKillop and the English priest Julian Tenison Woods.

Dedicated initially to the education of the poor, its activities were expanded over time throughout Australia, and to encompass delivery of a broad range of community services:

> The Sisters of St Joseph, the first order of nuns founded in Australia by an Australian, reflect at the religious level something of the egalitarian and democratic spirit, the sympathy and concern for the under-dog, the rejection of pose and display, which is the marked characteristic of Australian society. … Mother Mary McKillop emerges from the whole story as one of Australia's most gifted and saintly pioneer women, who reached secret heights of heroic holiness and even mystical experience. Her life's work was interwoven with the social and religious development of the country in its most critical and vital decades.[25]

In 2010 Mary McKillop was canonised as Australia's first saint.

Expansion

In what was to become Victoria, the 1836 census had shown only 14 Catholics living in the Port Phillip District out of a total population of 200. Meeting mainly in the house of Peter Bodecin, a zealous Frenchman who said the rosary and read litanies while the others present made the responses, these Catholics together with some Catholic soldiers petitioned Polding for a clergyman. With the arrival of the Franciscan, Patrick Geoghegan, as Victoria's first Catholic

25 Murtagh, *Australia: The Catholic Chapter*, 110.

priest in 1839, the pioneering situation was similar to that of Sydney, but without the convicts:

> Given that there was no convict class, in which Irish convicts were so prominent in New South Wales and Tasmania, the Catholics of Victoria were not so readily regarded as members of a different and inferior caste. Thus religious harmony prevailed in the infant Port Phillip community. With an ecumenism most remarkable, in 1839 Geoghegan praised religious toleration: 'To recognise the rights of everyone to worship God according to his conscience is a noble and enlightened principle'.[26]

In the event, the relative harmony was short-lived. Suspicion between Catholics and Protestants intensified in the face of an influx of dissenting ministers, many of whom such as the Presbyterian John Dunmore Lang were hostile to Catholicism, and as the colony moved towards self-government.

> That (Catholics) claimed rights and privileges which had previously been denied them had many Protestants nervous. Their fears were intensified by Pope Pius IX's reaction to the 1848 revolutions in Europe. Protestant arrogance and Catholic assertiveness could both be negative and sour, destructive of the very values which each claimed to be defending. Growing Irish migration roused the animus of Lang and led to his 1841 pamphlet *The Question of Questions*, which explored the likelihood of New South Wales becoming a Papal fief. Conversely, Irish priests worried about the corruption of Catholic girls by lustful Protestants, and the dangers of mixed marriages.[27]

Meanwhile, 'The decision by the Reverend J.D. Lang to stand in the Port Phillip election of June 1843 ended the period of religious calm':

---

26 O'Farrell, *The Catholic Church and Community*, 106–107.

27 Breward, *A History of the Australian Churches*, 41–42.

> In 1843, Lang decided he must stand against Edward Curr, a leading Catholic squatter, because it would be wrong for a Catholic to represent Melbourne. Lang's intervention was explicitly sectarian, deliberately anti-Catholic. So was the simultaneous formation of an Orange Lodge in Melbourne.[28]

By 1851, the year of separation from New South Wales, there were 18,014 Catholics recorded in the census, 5361 of them in Melbourne. Buoyed by the discovery of gold and the subsequent rush to exploit it, the overall population soared the following year to 338,000, of whom 87,000 were Catholics. The influx had the perverse outcome of doubling the number of Catholics while reducing their incidence as a proportion of the population to a quarter from what at an earlier stage of the colony had been a third.

As the strong Irish element in the miners' uprising at the Eureka Stockade on the Ballarat goldfields in 1854 and their preponderance among its casualties so plainly demonstrated, 'If Victoria's Irish Catholics were not religious radicals, they were radicals – or at least reformers – in political, social and economic affairs':

> By the end of the 1850s, the Victorian Catholic church had acquired enduring characteristics – exclusivist coherence, expressed in a spirit of self-reliant, indeed isolationist independence, a pugnacious suspicion of any criticism or hint of discrimination, a refusal to consider compromise, or concede any ground – and a growing emphasis on the importance of the Catholic school as preserver and bastion of the faith in a hostile world. These were characteristics of the Church in other states, but in Victoria they were particularly assertive.[29]

Polding's death in March 1877, and the sudden demise of his English Benedictine successor Roger Bede Vaughan in 1883, marked

---

28 O'Farrell, *The Catholic Church and Community*, 106–107.

29 O'Farrell, *The Catholic Church and Community*, 110–111.

the end of the Benedictine experiment in Sydney and entrenched the rule of Irish bishops in the See for the next half-century. Goold's death in Melbourne in 1886 and the accession to the See of a further Irishman, Thomas Joseph Carr, confirmed the new Irish ascendancy:

> The achievements of Polding and Vaughan may seem, in retrospect, very great. At the time, their deficiencies loomed much larger, especially to the Irish: tragically, dismayingly large. This was not so much a matter of what the Benedictine archbishops had actually done – although it was that too. Rather it was an Irish version of what might have been done under Irish episcopal rule. The Irish interpretation of Benedictine control came to this: if the Irish had full charge of the Australian church, more souls would have been saved, the church would be stronger, more extensive, more united. ... But the Irish clergy had much more than mere complaints; they had a vision of a spiritual empire. They would build, in Australia, a new, free Ireland, a religious realm in which the piety and fervour they knew so well in old Ireland experience an ennobling, transforming liberation, freed from the bitter weight of a persecuted history and the chains of British rule.[30]

The arrival of Polding's successor, Archbishop and soon to become Cardinal, Patrick Francis Moran, in Sydney in 1878 confirmed the giving way of an old order to a new. 'Not only were the colonies on the eve of great social and political changes, which called for enlightened Christian guidance, but the needs of the expanding Church demanded new vision and leadership', Campion's fellow historian priest James Murtagh concludes:

> The cardinal was brilliantly equipped for the task. He was acquainted with the history of Australia and the problems of the Catholic Church. During his 20 years in Rome he had lived through the stormy days of the revolutions of 1848 and studied

30 O'Farrell, *The Catholic Church and Community*, 194–195.

> in an atmosphere marked by growing preoccupation with the 'social question'. He was familiar with the rise of the Catholic social movement in Europe and was especially impressed with the progress in Germany. He understood, therefore, the true nature of the industrial conflict that was breaking over Australia.[31]

Nor was active encouragement from powerful allies at the most senior levels of the magisterium to be lacking, as the example of Manning's advocacy and the great Leonine social encyclical, *Rerum Novarum*, would so comprehensively now attest. The Secretary of the Royal Commission on the Housing of the Working Classes, to which Manning was appointed in 1884, wrote that 'If there had been some half dozen Mannings England would have run some risk of being converted to Christianity'.[32]

31 Murtagh, *Australia: The Catholic Chapter*, 116.

32 John F. Fitzsimons, *Manning: Anglican and Catholic* (London: Catholic Book Club, 1951) 116.

Chapter 3

THE PRECURSOR: HENRY EDWARD, CARDINAL MANNING

Origins and Attributes

Cardinal Manning's translation of *Rerum Novarum* and commentary on it in the *Dublin Review* were definitive for Catholics throughout the English-speaking world. Extended exposure to the suffering of the poor in the course of incumbencies as both an Anglican and a Catholic priest sensitised him to their predicament and the need for reform, including through co-operativist and mutualist institutions and measures. For him as for his counterparts, Cardinal Moran in Sydney and Baltimore's Cardinal Gibbons, it was axiomatic that the clergy should present to the laity and the secular state the social teachings of which they were bound to be observant. Their advocacy paved the way for the endorsement by the Church of the Distributism to which Belloc's *The Servile State* was so shortly to give expression, and which in its evolved form Mondragón would ultimately exemplify.

Manning championed striking workers and the right to strike, lobbied ministers for specific reformist measures and admired hands-on alleviation of the ravages of poverty such as were being undertaken by the Salvation Army under the direction of its leader General William Booth. He was scornful of those including fellow Catholics who opposed reform or were insufficiently supportive of it. And his episcopate became in all these respects a model and inspiration for fellow ecclesiastics who shared his outlook and aspirations, not least in Australia.

In England, Catholics and the Catholic Church were relative latecomers to the struggle against poverty. The recusant old Catholic families who had maintained their traditional loyalties to the Church throughout the centuries of its persecution were members predominantly of a country-keeping squirearchy, with minimal exposure to the urban poor or sympathy for their predicament. The Irish priests who welcomed or accompanied their refugee parishioners to England were preoccupied to the point of exhaustion with ministering to the spiritual needs of their explosively expanding congregations.

The focus of the former High Church Anglicans – in the view of some 'High Church malcontents'[1] – who had followed Manning and Newman into the Church of Rome likewise was largely on otherworldly rather than material concerns. Catholics were not necessarily immune to the conventional wisdom that, as the economic liberals of the day argued, poverty was the fault of the shiftlessness and other personal defects of the poor, or, as in the view of Malthus, to feed the poor was simply to increase their number, and thereby could not but be self-defeating.

Shortly before his death in 1892, Manning mourned an extensive inventory of omissions and inattention on the part of his co-religionists:

1 Andrew N. Wilson, *The Victorians* (London: Hutchinson, 2002) 140.

> The abolition of the slave and of slavery, and the persevering protests of the Anti-Slavery Society were cases in point, but, as far as I know, not a Catholic name shared in this. The whole temperance movement did not gain widespread Catholic support and it was a Quaker that made Father Mathew a total abstainer. The Act of Parliament to protect animals from cruelty was carried by a non-Catholic Irishman, as was the Anti-Vivisection Act. Both are derided, to my knowledge, among Catholics. The Acts to protect children from cruelty were the work of Dissenters. On these societies there is hardly a Catholic name. On the last, mine was for long the only one. So again, the uprising against the horrible depravity which destroys young girls – multitudes of ours – was literally denounced by Catholics – not one came forward. If it was ill done, why did nobody try to mend it? I might go on. There are endless works for the protection of shop assistants, overworked railway and tram men, women and children ground down by sweaters, and driven by starvation into the streets. Not one of the works in their behalf was started by us, hardly a Catholic name is to be found in their reports. Surely we are in the Sacristy?[2]

It was to Manning that the task of bringing the Church to a passionate sympathy and positive engagement with the poor had largely fallen. He was born to wealthy parents in 1808, raised in the Anglican Church and educated at Harrow and Oxford. His close friends at Oxford included the future Prime Minister, W.E. Gladstone. Manning's father – a prominent sugar merchant and one-time governor of the Bank of England, Lord Mayor of London and MP for Eversham – failed in business in 1831 while Manning was still at university. Manning is reported as having 'had the horrifying

2 Manning Papers, 'Diary for 1890, entry for 1 August', as quoted in Vincent A. McClelland, *Cardinal Manning: His Public Life and Influence 1865–1892* (London: Oxford University Press, 1962) 20–21.

experience of watching his father handing over his gold watch, the symbolic last possession of the bankrupt'.[3] It may be that the experience sensitised him to the essential fragility, transience and vulnerability of economic security and wellbeing that the poor also experienced, albeit in so exponentially greater a degree.

The family's financial embarrassment obliged Manning to consider briefly giving up becoming an Anglican clergyman, as had originally been his intention, in favour of a career in politics. Contemporaries saw him as having the makings of a Prime Minister, and Gladstone those of an Archbishop of Canterbury. In the event, faith prevailed over politics for Manning. Having been ordained as a deacon in 1832, he was appointed to a curacy at Lavington in West Sussex in January 1833, and succeeded his then future father-in-law, the Reverend John Sargeant, as rector there on Sargeant's sudden death four months later. His marriage to Caroline Sargeant was cut short by her death in 1837.

At the time of his conversion to Catholicism in 1851, he was Archdeacon of Chichester, and a man marked out for preferment to the highest offices of the Established Church. It was not to be. Following Cardinal Wiseman's reception of him into the Catholic Church, and his ordination as a priest three months later, he was sent to study at the Academia dei Nobili Ecclesiastici in Rome, and, on his return, became Wiseman's personal assistant. He was appointed provost of the Westminster Chapter in 1857, Archbishop of Westminster in succession to Wiseman following the latter's death in 1865, and a Cardinal in 1875.

3 Paul Johnson, Review of David Newsome, *The Convert Cardinals: J.H. Newman and H.E. Manning*, in the *Sunday Telegraph*, 26 December 1993. Reprinted in *The Chesterton Review*, XX, No 1, February 1994, 127.

As a Catholic, Manning was an ultramontane conservative in matters of faith, who served as the majority whip for the adoption of the doctrine of papal infallibility at the First Vatican Council in 1870.[4] He was also a social and political radical, whose passionate concern for the poor by far predated his admission to the Church or the high office to which it elevated him. Neither attribute was contradictory of the other. In the view of the US Social Catholicism studies scholar Dermot Quinn:

> Manning's ultramontanism and his Social Catholicism were not sequential but synchronous. He did not 'become' a friend of the poor, any more than he ceased being a friend of the pope. It was Manning's achievement to combine the two into an integrated Catholic identity.[5]

A UK scholar's assessment reads:

> For him nothing, no matter how trivial or weighty, could be divested of its theological significance. His Christianity extended to and embraced all states and conditions of human nature and existence. The remedy for social evil was an application into practice of the principles of Christianity.[6]

Empathy with the Poor

His empathy and sympathy for the poor were from the start a work in progress, dating from his seventeen-year incumbency at Lavington, and constantly increasing in their breadth, depth and passion

---

4 Ultramontane – literally 'beyond the mountains' – opinion within the Church upheld increasing Roman control and centralisation in policy and the appointment of bishops, as against those seeking to be wholly or in part free from papal direction. See Duncan, *The Church's Social Teaching*, 7–8.

5 Dermot Quinn, 'Manning, Chesterton and Social Catholicism', *The Chesterton Review*, XVIII, No 4, November 1992, 502.

6 McClelland, *Cardinal Manning*, 22.

throughout the subsequent stages of his life and ecclesiastic advancement. Of his initial exposure to rural poverty at Lavington, he wrote movingly in 1847:

> By the census it would appear that the average number in a family is five persons. Therefore our labouring poor were living, on an average of five persons, the father, mother and three children, on ten shillings a week. But this is the weekly average of only one person in a moderate household ... the father who works has a pound of pork in the week, it may be. The wives and children live on vegetables and bread, they keep a perpetual Lent ... We need no famines afar off to work on our charity.[7]

Championing the cause of the poor in Ireland in a letter to Lord Grey in 1868, he denounced the so-called Irish Land Question as 'a somewhat heartless euphemism' for 'hunger, thirst, nakedness, notice to quit, labour spent in vain, the toil of years seized upon, the breaking up of homes; the miseries, sickness, deaths of parents, children, wives; the despair and wildness of the poor when legal force, like a sharp harrow, goes over the most sensitive and vital rights of mankind'.[8] Rejecting the violence to which many among his Irish co-religionists were in desperation turning, he was fortified in a growing commitment to gradualist reform by the example of the Irish Land Acts whose culmination he did not live to witness, but which between 1870 and 1903 largely freed Irish smallholder farmers from the exactions of landlordism, by enabling them to secure title to their land.[9]

---

7 Henry E. Manning, *What One Work of Mercy Can I Do This Lent? A Letter to a Friend* (London: 1847) 10.

8 Manning to Lord Grey, 12 March 1868, as quoted in Georgiana Putnam McEntee, *The Social Catholic Movement in Great Britain* (New York, NY: The Macmillan Company, 1927) 58.

9 Respectively the Irish Land Acts of 1870 and 1881, and the Irish Land (Purchase) Acts of 1885 and 1903. The 1881 Act acceded to the Irish Land League's key demand

A letter to Gladstone in 1872 exemplified the increasingly practical and programmatic character of his concern and also his increasing impatience. It reads:

> Why cannot you do these things for the labourer? 1. Prohibit the labour of children under a certain age. 2. Compel payment of wages in money. 3. Regulate the number of dwellings according to the population of parishes, unions, counties or what you will: and prescribe the sanitary and other conditions necessary to the moral life of men by building acts. 4. Establish tribunals of arbitration in counties for questions between labour and land; thereby creating a public opinion which will control the arbitrary acts and wills of employers of the poor.[10]

In a lecture to the Leeds Mechanics Institute in 1874 he stated:

> If the peace, the purity of homes, the education of children, the duties of wives and mothers, the duties of husbands and fathers, be written in the natural law of mankind, and if these things are sacred beyond anything that can be sold in the market – then, I say, if the hours of labour resulting from the unregulated sale of man's strength and skill shall lead to the destruction of domestic life, to the neglect of children, to turning wives and mothers into living machines, and husbands into … creatures of burden … who rise up before the sun, and come back when it is set, wearied and able only to take food and to lie down to rest – the domestic life of men exists no longer, and we dare not go on in this path. … The accumulation of wealth in the land, the piling up of wealth like mountains, in the possession of classes or of individuals, cannot go on, if these moral conditions of

---

for the 'Three Fs' – Fair rent to be assessed by arbitration, Fixity of tenure, and Freedom for the tenant to sell his tenancy at the best market price. Edward Grierson, *The Imperial Dream: British Commonwealth and Empire 1775–1969* (London: Collins, 1972) 291.

10 Gladstone Papers, British Library, Manning to Gladstone, 26 December, 1872. As quoted in Shane Leslie, *Henry Edward Manning: His Life and Labours* (New York, NY: P.J. Kennedy and Sons, 1921) 349.

> our people are not healed. No commonwealth can rest on such foundations.[11]

And again in a Pastoral Letter in 1880:

> The inequalities of our social state, and the chasms which separate classes, the abrupt and harsh changes of soft and suffering lots, unless they are redressed by humility and charity, sympathy and self-denial, are dangerous to society and to our spiritual welfare. In London all these inequalities and evils are before us.[12]

His advocacy on behalf of the poor was at all times and stages matched by a comparable hands-on activism and preparedness to stand up and be counted. As a key Newman biographer, Sheridan Gilley, has noted of Manning:

> Well in advance of any Anglican bishop, he stepped forward to bless the Nonconformist, Joseph Arch, and his Agricultural Labourers' Union. He publicly defended 'The Dignity and Rights of Labour'. To the scandal of the respectable, including some of his own priests, he endorsed the journalist W.T. Stead's campaign against the horrors of the white slave trade in young girls, christened in Apocalyptic fashion, 'the maiden tribute of modern Babylon'; and, when Stead was goaled, he sent him his blessing. He moved the Mansion House resolution against the pogroms against Russian Jews, and extolled General Booth of the Salvation Army. He combined with Cardinal Gibbons of Baltimore to save the Knights of Labour from ecclesiastical censure. He wrote witheringly of English cruelty to children. He invited the land reformer, Henry George, and the trade

11 Henry E. Manning, 'The Dignity and Rights of Labour: A Lecture Delivered at the Mechanics' Institution, Leeds, on 2 January, 1874', in H.E. Manning, *Miscellanies* (3 Volumes) (London: Burns and Oates, 1888) Vol II, 94–97.

12 Henry E. Manning, *Lenten Pastoral Letter 1880* (Westminster Diocesan Archives). As quoted in Vincent A. McClelland, 'Manning's Work for Social Justice' in *The Chesterton Review*, XVIII, No 4, November 1992, 532.

> union leaders, Tom Mann and Ben Tillett, into the sacred precincts of Archbishop's House. He resolved the London Dock strike of 1899. With the reservation that he did not wish to lose the Irish Catholic members of the House of Commons, he approved Home Rule for Ireland. He demanded a just price for goods and a just wage for labour.[13]

And there was more. Claiming the same rights for labour as for property, Manning's 1874 Mechanics Institute in Leeds address – titled 'The Dignity and Rights of Labour' – foreshadowed in key respects the substance and spirit to which Distributism ultimately would give expression. It reads:

> I claim for labour the rights of property. There is no personal property so strictly one's own. The strength and skill that are in a man are as much his own as his life-blood; and that skill and strength which he has as his personal property no man can control. ... He can buy with it, and he can sell it. He can exchange it. He can set a price upon it. ... I claim for labour (and the skill which is always acquired by labour) the rights of capital. It is capital in the truest sense. ... Whatever rights, then, capital possesses, labour possesses.[14]

---

13 Sheridan Gilley, 'Manning and Chesterton', *The Chesterton Review*, XVIII, No 4, November 1992, 491. Arch's nascent National Agricultural Labourers' Union was effectively brought to its knees when an eighteen-week lockout in Suffolk cost it nearly £25,000 and caused many of the 2400 of its members involved to emigrate or move to other parts of England. Stead – a crusading journalist – challenged the practice of trafficking in children for prostitution by openly committing the offence and writing an article, 'The Maiden Tribute of Modern Babylon', which documented and denounced it. His three-month prison sentence was instrumental in bringing about the Criminal Amendment Act of 1885. Efforts by the Catholic Archbishop of New York, Patrick Corrigan, to ban the Knights of Labour – a largely mutualist body of working people with a strong commitment to establishing co-operatives as a means of bringing about a more equitable social order – on the grounds of their Socialist and Georgist sympathies were frustrated when Manning and Cardinal Gibbons of Baltimore convinced Leo XIII that to do so would be unjust and counterproductive. Gibbons and Manning were less successful in dissuading Leo from having George's works placed in the Index of Forbidden Books, although it was decided that the decision should be kept secret.

14 Manning, 'The Dignity and Rights of Labour', 81–85.

Rights of Labour

It followed in Manning's view that every labourer had a right to work or not to work, to determine for whom he would work, and where he would work, and to specify the wages upon which he could subsist. Labour collectively had a right not only to its own freedom, but to protect itself. He could conceive 'nothing more entirely in accordance with natural right and with the higher jurisprudence, than that those who have a common interest should unite together for the protection of that interest'.[15] The right to strike was on this basis inviolate.

In the aftermath of the major industrial disputes in the late 1880s, he foreshadowed a new order of workplace relations, expressive of the same profit sharing and perhaps industrial democracy that so shortly would come to characterise Distributism. He wrote:

> I have been thinking over the strike matters, and the more I think the more I am on the side of Labour. Labour and skill are Capital as much as gold and silver. Gold and silver are dependent on Labour and skill, but Labour and skill are independent *in limine*. The union of the two Capitals demands participation in the product. Wages are a minimised money representation of shares in product – that is, in profits. Silvertown gives 15 per cent to its shareholders and denies halfpence and farthings to its workers. This is more or less the state of the market at large.[16]

An instinctive mutualist, he had at even so early a point as his Lavington incumbency encouraged the development of village friendly societies as a means of enabling their members to make provision for illness or old age. Following representations from an 1887 London Co-operative Clothing Manufacturing Co deputation and advice

15 Manning, 'The Dignity and Rights of Labour', 87–88.

16 Manning to Lord Buxton, 16 November 1889, as quoted in Sydney Buxton, 'Cardinal Manning – A Reminiscence' in *Fortnightly Review*, 65, No 59, 591–592.

from Lord Ripon, who had linked Disraeli's 'Young England' thrust for social reform in the 1840s with co-operatives and the co-operative movement, he embraced the co-operativism that was to assume so central a significance for Distributism and extended the movement every possible support.[17]

In advance of most, he anticipated the impact of poverty on the national interest that was to loom increasingly in the minds of those whose sense of Empire and manifest Imperial destiny he applauded and shared. A prescient passage in 1890 reads:

> It is certain that the commercial prosperity of the country depends upon the manual skill and mental development of our workmen. And though our great productive supremacy has in times past been attained without systematic technical instruction, we can hardly hope to retain it in competition with foreign countries which are now systematically instructing their youth in the principles and practices of arts and manufactures. It is of absolute necessity that we keep pace with them in this also.[18]

Seminally for Distributism, Manning's callers at Archbishop's House included the twenty-year-old Hilaire Belloc. The inspiration and instruction that energised and guided Belloc in his development of Distributism were gained at Manning's feet. As he recalled in later life:

> It was my custom during my first days in London, as a very young man, before I went to Oxford, to call upon the Cardinal as regularly as he would receive me; and during those brief interviews I heard from him many things which I have had later occasion to test by the experience of human life. I was, it may be

17 McEntee, *The Social Catholic Movement in Great Britain*, 28.

18 Henry E. Manning, 'Diary for 1890, entry for 1 August', as quoted in Leslie, *Henry Edward Manning*, 350.

> said, too young to judge things so deep as sanctity and wisdom; but, on the other hand, youth has vision, especially on elemental things; and Manning did seem to me (and still seems to me) much the greatest Englishman of his time.[19]

An evocative assessment of the significance of their meetings by Belloc's early biographer, Robert Speaight, reads:

> The Cardinal's positive character and practical ability, his outspoken sympathy for the poor, his encouragement of Christian democracy, his crusade for social as well as political regeneration, met and influenced a mind stirred by radical theories of government. ... If he spoke of these things to Belloc, they must have sounded a tocsin to the boy's adventurous spirit. How challenging and turbulent they sounded! How remote from the stuffy, conventional round of the English Catholic families, so quiet and tenacious in their country-houses, so well-intentioned and so unaware![20]

Manning – now in the perhaps hyperbolic and overly Anglo-centric view of a recent biographer 'the doyen of the Catholic social movement that flourished in France under the leadership of Count Alfred de Mun and Léon Harmel' and even the 'leading social guru of European Catholics'[21] – affirmed in a letter to a congress in Liège in 1890 that harmonious relations between employers and employees would never be 'safely and solidly secured until the just and due proportion between profits and wages shall have been fixed, recognised, laid down, and publicly known to govern all free contracts between capital and labour'.[22]

19 Hilaire Belloc, *The Cruise of the 'Nona'* (London: Constable and Company Limited, 1925. This edition 1955) 54.

20 Robert Speaight, *The Life of Hilaire Belloc* (London: Hollis & Carter, 1957) 42–43.

21 Robert Gray, *Cardinal Manning: A Biography* (New York: St Martin's Press, 1985) 302.

22 Henry E. Manning, Message to the Congress of Liège, 2 September 1890. As quoted in Gray, *Cardinal Manning*, 304. Manning was to have attended the congress at the

The Dock Strike

When the London dockworkers under the leadership of Ben Tillett went on strike later the same year for an increase in their hourly wage from 5d to 6d, and a minimum payment equivalent to four hours wages for the casual workers taken on each morning, support was forthcoming even from as far afield as Australia, where the waterside workers and their allies raised some £30,000 to ensure that the strikers and their families would not go hungry.[23] In the rural centre of Ballarat alone, £1000 was donated.

Manning – described by Tillett in later life as 'the kindliest and greatest man it has been my good fortune to meet'[24] – mediated an acceptance of the increase between their leaders and the employers on terms that a meeting of the strike committee subsequently repudiated. Faced with a further deterioration in the long-running dispute which might well have resulted in widespread violence, he then arranged to speak personally at a subsequent committee meeting, with the effect that, as reported by one of those present, 'his eloquence carried the day; and when the meeting broke up, the strike was over'.[25]

The gratitude of the embattled workers and their allies, for a settlement that yielded them their just demand for 'the dockers' tanner', was expressed in an address that reads:

> When we remember how your Eminence, unasked and unsolicited, under the weight of four score years and two, came

invitation of Liège's Bishop Doutreloux, but declined consequent on his advanced age and instead sent his message, advocating, among other things, Sunday rest, freedom of association and arbitration, the limiting of children's and women's labour and an eight-hour day.

23 P.F. Donovan in *Labour History*, No 23 (Nov, 1972) 17.

24 Ben Tillett, *Memories and Reflections* (London: John Long, Limited, 1931) 91.

25 Henry H. Champion, '*Quorum Pars Fui*: An Unconventional Biography', in Leslie M. Henderson, *The Goldstein Story* (Melbourne, Vic: Stockland Press, 1973), 126.

> forward to mediate between masters and men; when we remember your prudent and wise counsels not to let any heat or passion or unreasonable view of the situation beguile us or lead us away from a fair point of view to our employers and ourselves; and when in fine we recall your venerable figure in our midst for over four hours in Wade Street School, listening to our complaints and giving us advice in our doubts and difficulties, we seem to see a father in the midst of a loving and well-loved family, rather than the ordinary mediator in the thick of a trade dispute.[26]

A painting of Manning presented by the dockworkers to the Ballarat unionists in appreciation of their support to this day hangs in the Ballarat Trades Hall Council chamber.

Manning wrote subsequently to Archbishop William Walsh in Dublin: 'We have been under the despotism of capital. The union of labourers is their only shelter'.[27] A letter he sent to a friend in 1890 reads:

> A clergyman said last week: The Dockers' Strike succeeded because the police did not do their duty; the Gas Strike has failed because the police did their duty. The freedom of contract is maintained by the truncheon. There is no justice, mercy, or compassion in the Plutocracy. There is my creed.[28]

Meanwhile, visitors welcomed by Tillett in his Dock, Wharf, Riverside and General Workers' Union office in the course of the strike and inspired by his example included the young Cardijn.

26 As quoted in Arthur Hinsley, 'Address at a Dinner Honouring the Dock Strike Leader, Ben Tillett, London, 21 October, 1936', *The Chesterton Review*, XVIII, No 4, November 1992, 624.

27 Manning to Walsh, 1 March 1890, Manning Papers, as quoted in Leslie, *Henry Edward Manning*, 376.

28 Manning to Buxton, 21 January 1890, Manning Papers, as quoted in Leslie, *Henry Edward Manning*, 376.

'Following Ben Tillett during his twenty-four years of trade union work, it seems there are two main ideas which had crystallised his aspirations, and like two stars had guided his efforts', Cardijn wrote in 1911:

> He wants to help first to create the strongest, the largest, the most united organization in which he wants the workers of the whole world to feel the solidarity of their interests and the unconquerable power of their union. Moreover, he wants for every worker in particular to carry out a work of personal education, a work of moral and intellectual uplift, so that each worker may feel the pressing need for more well-being and more justice.[29]

Rerum Novarum

Manning's career as a social reformer and friend of the poor now climaxed and fully came into its own with the publication of *Rerum Novarum* in 1891. Authorities differ as to whether his contribution was simply to instigate the encyclical by sheer force of advocacy and example, or also to involve himself actively in its preparation.[30] Leo XIII wrote to Manning in January 1891 that he was 'engaged in the consideration of … the care which touches you as to the condition of the working-men'.[31] A letter to Manning from Walsh in Rome

29 Marguerite Fievez and Jacques Meert, *Cardijn* (Preston Lancs: T. Snape & Co, ND) 27.

30 See, for example, the differing views of contributors to the Cardinal Manning Special Edition of *The Chesterton Review*, XVIII, No 4, November 1992. The drafting of *Rerum Novarum* was substantially delegated, most notably to the Jesuit priest Matteo Liberatore, but also to Cardinals Zigliara and Mazzella. For useful accounts of the drafting process, see John Molony, *The Worker Question: A Historical Perspective on Rerum Novarum* (Melbourne: Collins Dove, 1991) and Joseph N. Moody, 'Leo XIII and the Social Crisis' in Edward T. Gargan (ed), *Leo XIII and the Modern World* (New York, NY: Sheed and Ward, 1961) 75–79.

31 Manning Papers, Leo XIII to Manning 17 January 1891, as quoted in McClelland, *Cardinal Manning*, 159.

in March 1891 reported that 'The Holy Father ... spoke at great length to me about the coming Encyclical ... I think I can trace your Eminence's Influence in this as in many other things that I have noted here during this visit'.[32]

Bishop Hedley's eulogy for Manning at his funeral in 1892 noted that the encyclical 'owes something, beyond all doubt, to the counsels of Cardinal Manning'.[33] Manning's 1921 biographer, Shane Leslie, sees the encyclical as having shown signs of being based on Manning's Liège congress letter and demonstrating parallels between their respective wordings.[34] A 1962 study of Manning's public life and significance concurs that Leo had read Manning's Liège letter and been influenced by it.[35] By the account of Cardinal Hinsley – a successor of Manning as Archbishop of Westminster, and thereby well-placed to know – 'Pope Leo declared that one of his most famous encyclicals on the social question, *Rerum Novarum: On the Condition of Labour*, was really Manning's'.[36]

What is beyond doubt is that the encyclical was effectively the bestowal by Leo of his official blessing on such key elements of Manning's vision as affirmation of the right to productive property and its distribution on as wide a basis as possible, parity of esteem for labour and capital, condemnation of employers who exploited their workers, approval of trade unions, protection of the right to

---

32 Manning Papers, Walsh to Manning 24 March 1891, as quoted in McClelland, *Cardinal Manning*, 159.

33 John C. Hedley, Funeral Oration for Cardinal Manning 1892, as quoted in McClelland, *Cardinal Manning*, 160.

34 Leslie, *Henry Edward Manning*, 380.

35 McClelland, *Cardinal Manning*, 159.

36 Hinsley, 'Address at a Dinner Honouring the Dock Strike Leader, Ben Tillett, London, 21 October, 1936'. See also the letter by Francis Bywater in *The Chesterton Review*, XIX, No 4, November 1993, 579.

strike, self-help through co-operatives and other mutualist bodies and denunciation of Socialism in its Marxist or more extreme statist forms.

Manning – assisted by Walsh – was delegated with responsibility for the encyclical's translation into English. They were of the same mind as to the encyclical's significance. Walsh had previously championed arbitration as a means of resolving both smallholder tenancy and industrial disputes, along with new measures for the housing of the working classes and the provision of open spaces and recreational grounds. As with Manning in the dock strike, his interventions in the 1890 Builders Labourers strike and Great Southern Railway strike were instrumental in securing arbitrated settlements favourable to the workers. His biographer concludes that he and Manning:

> ... shared the encyclical's insistence that a chief duty of rulers was 'to provide equally for every section of the community by acting with unshakeable impartiality towards all', and the papal document might have almost had Walsh's abiding conviction in mind when it insisted that 'No one may outrage with impunity that human dignity which God himself treats with great reverence ... Man himself can never renounce his right to be treated according to his nature or surrender himself to any form of slavery of spirit'.[37]

Manning's aim was to ensure that the encyclical's message was fully understood and accepted by English Catholics, not least by lending the interpretation of it a distinctively English flavour. He was concerned that the encyclical's condemnation of Continental Socialism in its revolutionary, Marxist and more extreme statist forms

37 Thomas J. Morrissey, *William J. Walsh, Archbishop of Dublin 1841–1921: No Uncertain Voice* (Dublin: Four Courts Press, 2000) 209. For Walsh and reform more generally, see 188–209.

should not be misread as also referring to the distinctively mixed economy or mutualist models of Socialism to which most British Socialists so resolutely adhered.[38] The explicit affirmation of the right to strike that he ascribed to the encyclical may have exceeded its papal author's intentions.[39]

The task was undertaken with his customary vigour and disregard for opposition or obstacles. The commentary on the encyclical that he contributed to *The Dublin Review* in July 1891 gave eloquent expression to its condemnation of asymmetrical workplace power and destitution in the presence of abundance:

> By degrees, it has come to pass that working-men have been given over, isolated and defenceless, to the callousness of employers and the greed of unrestrained competition. The evil has been increased by rapacious usury, which though more than once condemned by the Church, is nevertheless, under a different form, but with the same guilt, still practised by avaricious and grasping men; and to this must be added the custom of working by contract; and the concentration of so many branches of trade in the hands of a few individuals, so that a very few rich men may have been able to lay upon the masses a yoke little better than slavery itself ... Starving men may be locked out with impunity. The hunger of their wives, the cries of their children, their own want of food, will compel them to come in. It is evident that between a capitalist and a working man there can be no true freedom of contract. The capitalist is invulnerable in his wealth. The working man without bread

38 McEntree, *The Social Catholic Movement in Great Britain*, 232, quotes a 1914 study of the opinions of eminent theologians, both English and Continental by Fr Plater as confirming that 'historically Pius and Leo had intended to condemn only the irreligious radical Socialism rampant in their day, "that universal and absolute Socialist communism which seeks to suppress all private property as being wrong or at least anti-social in itself"'.

39 See, for example, Leslie, *Henry Edward Manning: His Life and Labours*, 380: 'Manning, for instance, insisted on using the word "strike" and not a euphemism'.

> has no choice but either to agree or to hunger his hungry home. They forget that when thousands of women and children suffer while they are refusing to grant a penny more in wages, or an hour less of work, there is a wide field misery caused by their refusal, which prolongs a strike. It is then no private affair, but a public evil which excites the public condemnation.

It concluded 'For a century the Civil Powers in almost all the Christian world have been separating themselves from the Church. ... And now of a sudden they find that the millions of the world sympathise with the Church, which has compassion for the multitude rather than with the State or the plutocracy which has weighed so heavily upon them'.[40] With the publication of the encyclical, the foundations for Distributism were at last set squarely in place. It was an appropriate note with which to mark the culmination of a life that had been given over in so large a measure to the service of the dispossessed, and was now moving to its conclusion.

Last Days

That Manning's concern and compassion for the poor were appreciated and reciprocated was evident on his death in 1892. The crowds on the successive days of his lying in state and funeral – 'the most striking, certainly the most spontaneous demonstration of mass emotion in the capital during the late Victorian period'[41] – numbered more than 100,000. The funeral procession was four miles long. Leo XIII declared that 'A great light of the Church has gone out. I feel my

---

40 Henry E. Manning, 'A Pope on Capital and Labour: The Significance of the Encyclical *Rerum Novarum*', *Dublin Review*, July, 1891, 153–167.

41 Michael Straiton, 'The Cockney Cardinal', Opening Address at an Exhibition in Honour of the Centenary of the Death of Cardinal Manning and the Tenth Anniversary of the Papal Visit to Britain, Westminster Cathedral, London, in *The Chesterton Review*, XVIII, No 4, November 1992, 144.

own hour is at hand'.[42] Cardinal Capecelatro wrote in a posthumous tribute:

> I know none among Catholic Socialists (let the name be permitted me) braver than my late beloved friend Cardinal Manning, a social student fearless in speculation, effectual in enterprise ... Manning living as he did in the midst of the independent and tenacious English people, did not hesitate to put himself at the head of Christian 'Socialism' ... Temperance, arbitration, peace-making, public charity, had in him an eloquent, a persistent, a fearless advocate.[43]

A testimony to Manning's social influence by the Anglican Archdeacon Farrar reads:

> He has left behind him a great name and a great example, and it would be well for the Church of England, if she had one or two Bishops who would learn from him how a great ecclesiastic may win the enthusiastic confidence of the working classes, and stamp his influence on the humanitarian progress of the age.[44]

Sentiment within the English Church may have been less uniformly effusive. Manning's concern for the material wellbeing of the poor and overt association with their leaders and champions had been widely misunderstood, misrepresented or maligned in both clerical and lay circles, as being indicative variously of an idiosyncratic distraction or departure from the saving of souls, unseemly radicalism, waste of priestly time and perhaps lapse of priestly dignity and decorum. A scholarly, albeit perhaps not exhaustive, stocktaking of his detractors among fellow Catholics includes 'born Catholics who disliked the

42 Leslie, *Henry Edward Manning*, 495.

43 Alfonso Capecelatro, *Christ, the Church and Man* (St Louis, Miss: B. Herder, 1909) 73–74, as quoted in McEntee, *The Social Catholic Movement in Great Britain*, 257.

44 F.W. Farrar, in *Review of the Churches*, March 1892, as quoted in McClelland, *Cardinal Manning*, 21.

upstart convert, the Jesuits whom he had worsted in jurisdictional controversy, liberals and Anglo-Gallicans suspicious of his Ultramontanism, admirers of Cardinal Newman, and conservatives horrified by Manning's crusades for social reform'.[45]

As an early account of British Social Catholicism so pertinently observes:

> The pity is that such a man as Manning was not always greeted as a prophet by those who should have been his friends but became even an object of dislike as he preached his Social Catholicism, which has been called 'the most hateful of new doctrines to those faithful who look upon the Church as the guardian of their interests, and upon religion as the best safeguard of property'. Disquieted by what might be expected of them if they took to heart the views that he expounded, such as these went their way in sorrow – for they had great possessions.[46]

In the more acerbic view of some:

> The 'Old Catholics' were determined to resist, and looking for a rallying point for their cause they found it in John Henry Newman. In sympathy, taste, feelings and insularity Newman closely resembled the 'Old Catholics' and his name was used unscrupulously to thwart Manning's policies. Any opportunity for causing pain to the Archbishop was eagerly sought and used.[47]

Manning's friend and confidant in Rome, George Talbot – a papal chamberlain and major intermediary between the Church in England and the Pope – remonstrated with him as early as 1865 that 'Of course you must not neglect the poor, but many can do

45 Sheridan Gilley, *The Tablet*, 11 January 1992, as re-printed in *The Chesterton Review*, Cardinal Manning Special Issue XVIII, No 4, November 1992, 617.

46 McEntree, *The Social Catholic Movement in Great Britain*, 22–23.

47 McClelland, *Cardinal Manning*, 216.

that work; few have the influence you have – I may say no one – on the upper classes of Protestants'.[48] The leading Catholic journal of the day, *The Tablet*, commented in an editorial on the dock strike settlement in 1889 that 'Even in more sober quarters, there seems to be an uneasy feeling that it would have been better if the peacemaker had been another'.[49] Manning's successor, Cardinal Vaughan, himself of recusant origin, so much disapproved of his predecessor's dock strike and Temperance Movement involvements as to ascribe them after his death to an untimely onset of senile decay.[50]

Manning would have been unimpressed, impenitent and unapologetic. While attempting from the outset of his ecclesiastical career to reconcile the 'Old Catholics' to his social policies and priorities, he was adamant in resisting their efforts to deter him from his chosen course. In the face of the strictures and slanders of his critics, his 1891 *Dublin Review* article threw down the gauntlet:

> If any man would protect the world of labour from the oppression of 'free contracts' or 'starvation wages' he is a Socialist. So obscure from want of thought, or so warped by interest or class feeling are the minds of men.[51]

The apathy, inaction or opposition of those he saw as owing him their allegiance deeply disappointed and frustrated him, provoking as they did the rejoinder:

---

48 George Talbot, as quoted in Ida A. Taylor, *The Cardinal Democrat* (London: Kegan Paul, Trench, Trübner and Co., Ltd., 1908) 34.

49 *Tablet*, 14 September 1889, as quoted in Gray, *Cardinal Manning*, 310.

50 Herbert Vaughan, 'The Life of Cardinal Manning', *The Nineteenth Century*, February 1896, as quoted in Gray, *Cardinal Manning*, 312.

51 Manning, 'A Pope on Capital and Labour: The Significance of the Encyclical *Rerum Novarum*', 162.

> What are our people doing? Oh, I forgot, they have no time. They are examining their consciences, or praying for success in finding a really satisfactory maid.[52]

Vaughan in his turn was chided that 'He – Vaughan – was already a good Catholic and only needed to sit at the feet of General Booth to be a good Christian'.[53] It is unlikely that Manning would have been wholly unsympathetic with the characterisation of many among his fellow Catholics by one of their number in 1907 as being 'as completely unable to realise the fundamental change that has taken place in political, social and economic questions as were the French *noblesse* on the eve of the Revolution'.[54]

His mood as his life drew to its close was serene. A note taken in his last months provides a fitting epitaph. It reads: 'For more than fifty years I have lived among the poor people … I have seen and heard and known their wants, sufferings, hardships and the defeat of their petitions and hopes, and my whole soul is with them'.[55] And the impact of his example and inspiration was already apparent, in an obscure diocese on the far side of the world, where the Distributism for whose inspiration he was so largely responsible would in due course be taken briefly to heart.

---

52 Leslie, *Henry Edward Manning*, 485.

53 McEntee, *The Social Catholic Movement in Great Britain*, 152.

54 Leslie A. Toke in *The Catholic Mind*, Vol 5 (1907) 212, as quoted in McEntee, *The Social Catholic Movement in Great Britain*, 165.

55 Henry E. Manning, 'Cardinal Manning's Revised Edition of His Politics: An Autobiographical Note 1890', in E.S. Purcell, *Life of Cardinal Manning, Archbishop of Westminster* (Two Volumes), (London: MacMillan and Co, 1896) Vol II, 635.

Chapter 4

MORAN: 'THE RIGHTS AND DUTIES OF LABOUR'

For Sydney's Cardinal Moran as for Manning, instruction on Leo's message as on any other aspect of the faith was essentially a 'top down' process – a priestly prerogative, to which communicants in their turn owed an obligation in good conscience of attention and obedience. Three interwoven themes – *Rerum Novarum*, Federation and the labour movement – characterised the social and economic engagement of the Moran episcopate.[1] It was to the encyclical that he looked for the content of social reform, to Federation as the context most conducive to reform, and to the labour movement as the means by which reform might most usefully be driven forward.

Each theme was in turn spelled out in key public addresses, most notably on the encyclical in 1891, Federation in 1896 and the labour movement in 1905. His addresses attest to the radicalisation of his political and social attitudes in the course of his incumbency, as do also the less overt interventions in the public sphere that on occasion accompanied them.

1 For a useful historical account of evolution and usage of the terms 'Labor' and 'Labour', see Bede Nairn, *Civilising Capitalism: The Labor Movement in New South Wales 1870–1900* (Canberra, ACT: Australian National University Press, 1973) xii.

In the eloquent testimony of the future Archbishop Eris O'Brien, an intended author of a biography of Moran, but who died before it could be completed:

> The encyclical came at an opportune moment in Australian history. ... It gave Moran a Papal justification for intruding upon the social question in Australia. He took full advantage of the fact by expositions of the Papal teachings and fearlessly adapted this to Australian conditions. ... Ahead of his time, at least among the ecclesiastical leaders of Australia, he realised that the existing class war was a moral as well as a social problem which this nation had to solve and not merely check.[2]

Moran's initial public lecture on *Rerum Novarum* – delivered under the title 'The Rights and Duties of Labour', to a packed audience in Sydney's New Masonic Hall in August 1891 – embraced and articulated its insights in their entirety, with an eloquence, passion and wealth of information that rank it among Australia's finer feats of public interest oratory.[3] Consistent with the spirit of the encyclical and a clarion call for recognition of the predicament of the poor and rectification of their privation, the address favoured a broad spectrum of economic and social reform, including widespread ownership of productive property, profit-sharing, parity of esteem for labour and capital, worker representation in parliament, condemnation of employers who exploited their workers, approval of trade unions, arbitration of industrial disputes, protection of the right to strike, housing reform, self-help through co-operatives and other mutualist

---

2 Eris O'Brien, 'Cardinal Moran's Part in Public Affairs', *Royal Australian Historical Society Journal and Proceedings*, XXVIII, 1942, Part I, 21. O'Brien was at the time of writing a parish priest at Neutral Bay and former diocesan director of Catholic Action.

3 Patrick F. Moran, 'The Rights and Duties of Labour', *The Freeman's Journal*, 22 August 1891.

bodies such as the highly successful Hibernian Australasian Catholic Benefit Society and denunciation of Socialism in its more extreme statist forms. Building on the example of Manning's compassion and Leo's encyclical, Moran foreshadowed the Distributist agenda which Belloc's *The Servile State* would within little more than a decade introduce, fellow Australian bishops following in his footsteps would embrace, and ultimately in its evolved form would be implemented at Arizmendiarrieta's instigation in Mondragón.

'A Free Church in a Free State'

Elsewhere, Moran championed the resurgent Federationist sentiment of the day, and increasingly looked to Federation and the nascent Australian Labor Party (ALP) as key means of advancing the objectives of the encyclical. His stance was in neither instance reflective of any party political affiliation, but of his faith and of the social and economic conclusions and imperatives that he saw as stemming from it. As the church historian Patrick O'Farrell – no great admirer of Moran – concludes in his 1977 *The Catholic Church and Community in Australia: A History*, 'The stunning vision of a new religious world, free from the poison of old, hatred-ridden Europe, had its greatest prophet in Cardinal Moran'.[4] Moran saw his mission as the creation of 'A Free Church in a Free State'.[5] A federalist no less in the ecclesiastical than the national sphere, he introduced Plenary Councils of the Australasian bishops that met respectively in 1885,

---

4 Patrick O'Farrell, *The Catholic Church and Community in Australia: A History* (Melbourne, Vic: Thomas Nelson (Australia) Limited, 1977) 195.

5 Patrick Ford, *Cardinal Moran and the ALP: A Study in the Encounter between Moran and Socialism, 1890–1907: Its Effects upon the Australian Labor Party: The foundation of Catholic Social Thought and Action in Modern Australia* (Carlton, Vic: Melbourne University Press, 1966) 101.

1895 and 1905. In O'Brien's view, his practice of the federalism he preached helped to convince the Australian public that 'the Federal ideal was possible in politics as well as in ecclesiastical affairs'.[6]

In Australia as in Ireland, Moran's episcopate was notable for his close attention to the supervision and professional development of the local clergy, construction of new churches and expansion of parochial education.[7] He tirelessly championed the standing and prerogatives of the Church and the political and civil rights of its adherents, albeit on occasion to counterproductive effect, in as much as his rejection of overtures for interdenominational co-operation and at times intemperate criticism of other faiths gave rise to avoidable ill feeling and fanned sectarian prejudice.[8] A lifelong passion for learning and scholarship was reflected in his extensive body of historical research and writings on the Irish and Australian Churches, and the archival and archaeological interludes with which he interspersed his official duties.

He was unafraid to be unconventional. *The Bulletin* – the leading literary and political weekly of the day – caricatured him on its front page as 'the Chows' Patron' for his defence of Chinese migrants against racial prejudice and discriminatory legislation. He befriended Sydney's Jewish community and its Chief Rabbi with expressions of sympathy in the aftermath of the 1905 Odessa pogrom and his

---

6 O'Brien, 'Cardinal Moran's Part in Public Affairs', 16.

7 See, for example, O'Brien, 'Cardinal Moran's Part in Public Affairs', 26: 'In 1884 there were in the Sydney archdiocese 100 priests, 120 churches, 102 schools, 330 religious teachers, 11,000 pupils at all Catholic schools, and the Catholic population was 93,600. In 1911 there were 200 priests, 189 churches, 1600 religious teachers in schools, 336 schools, 24,000 pupils, and the Catholic population had grown to 175,000. It has been estimated, with what degree of accuracy I know not, that during Cardinal Moran's administration £2,000,000 was spent on buildings for ecclesiastical, charitable and educational purposes'.

8 Duncan, *The Church's Social Teaching*, 168.

criticism of French Catholic anti-Semitism as evidenced during the Dreyfus Affair. He pressed claims for additional support of missionaries in indigenous communities to which the majority of his fellow bishops were less receptive.

He embraced the women's suffrage cause that previously in Ireland he had as vigorously opposed, and was impatient with excessive censorship, as exemplified by the Index of Prohibited Books. His response when told of the removal of 2000 titles from the Index was that 'If I had had anything to do with it, they should have struck out 2000 more names'.[9]

His passionate devotion to Rome and strict adherence to papal teachings and doctrinal authority were matched by the no less fierce insistence on autonomy in local political judgement that he characterised as 'Religion from Rome, politics from home'.[10] He was unimpressed by the retreat from *Rerum Novarum*'s incipient Christian Democracy under Leo XIII's anti-Modernist successor. Following a day with the Vatican curia in 1902, he wrote from Rome 'Their ideas and ours run in quite different grooves'.[11]

Addressing seminarians in 1906, he counselled: 'Let us take a lesson from Ireland, in the past century there were a whole series of political events, bearing on the interests of the Church and in not one of those did the Catholics or clergy of Ireland ask Rome what course

9 Moran to Archbishop William Walsh, 29 May 1902, Moran Papers, as quoted in Philip Ayres, *Prince of the Church: Patrick Francis Moran 1830–1911* (Melbourne, Vic: The Miegunyah Press, 2007) 237. And see also O'Farrell, *The Catholic Church and Community in Australia*, 248.

10 Anthony E. Cahill, 'Cardinal Moran's Politics', *Journal of Religious History*, 15, 4 December 1989, 531.

11 Moran to Archbishop William Walsh, 29 May 1902, Dublin Catholic Archdiocesan Archives. As quoted in Cahill, 'Cardinal Moran's Politics', 531.

they should pursue'.[12] Responding to a papal directive to the bishops the following year, he established a committee to search for evidence of 'modernism', but concluded, perhaps unsurprisingly, that Australia had no cause for concern.[13]

His inclusion of the expatriate Victorian layman, P.S. Cleary – shortly to emerge as arguably Australia's first Distributist – among speakers at his 1909 Australasian Catholic Congress was reflective of both his commitment to the rich diversity of initiatives and experience that had preceded the encyclical or arisen from it and a heightened receptivity to the lay activism through which effect might be given to it. Erudite and eloquent, Cleary's congress paper, 'The Church and the Worker', recalled how 'The best modern methods of profit sharing and co-operation' had been fostered by Harmel in France, and Cardinal Agliardi had encouraged 'trade unions, co-operative and insurance societies and every movement to improve the condition of the workers'.[14] Co-operatives in Lombardy were busying themselves 'in collective buying of machinery and farming requisites, in loans to farmers at low interest, in stock insurance and so on'. In Belgium, the Boerenbond corporation had raised 'the Belgian farmer from an under-fed serf of the money-lender, to be the happiest and most independent landowner in Europe'.[15] Moreover, Cleary was in no doubt that the encyclical, to which the new mutualist and co-operativist measures so largely owed

12 Patrick F. Moran, 'Address at St Patrick's College, Manly 1906, 13 December', *Freeman's Journal*, 22 December 1906.

13 Anthony E. Cahill, 'Moran, Patrick Francis', in Bede Nairn and Geoffrey Serle (eds), *Australian Dictionary of Biography*, Vol 10: 1891–1939 (Carlton, Vic: Melbourne University Press, 1986) 580.

14 Patrick S. Cleary, 'The Church and the Worker: An Historical Sketch', *Proceedings of Third Australasian Catholic Congress*, held at St Mary's Cathedral, Sydney, 26 September (Sydney: 1909) 260–1, 265.

15 Cleary, 'The Church and the Worker', 264, 262–263.

their inception, marked no more than 'a stage in Social Reform, a new strategic point from which to start for a further advance'.[16]

Origins

Moran was the youngest of five children, born into a well-off family in Ireland in 1830. His mother died when he was fourteen months old, as did his father when he was eleven. His upbringing and education were completed in Rome, in the care of his maternal uncle, the then Rector of the Irish College and future Cardinal, Paul Cullen. The conservative Cullen – 'an ecclesiastical autocrat, reactionary and pro-English in politics'[17] – became his orphaned nephew's key mentor and formative influence, tutoring him in the intricacies and exigencies of ecclesiastical governance and administration and assisting his advancement.

The circumstances of the day were unconducive to any precipitate or precocious adoption of the radicalism of his Australian incumbency, exposing him as they did to the turmoil and upheaval attendant on nationalist struggles for unity and independence:

> As a student, he witnessed the excesses of the revolution of 1848. Mazzinian nationalists and radical revolutionists assassinated the Prime Minister of the Papal States, forced the Pope to flee from Rome, dispersed the Jesuits, searched the Irish College for counter-revolutionaries, and replaced the Pope's temporal rule by a Roman Republic. Later, with the restoration of the Pope, French troops were quartered in Irish College buildings. In 1859–60 Moran saw the Piedmontese nationalists take over the Papal States and incorporate them in United Italy. Returning to

16 Cleary, 'The Church and the Worker', 269.

17 O'Farrell, *The Catholic Church and Community in Australia*, 220.

> Ireland in 1866, he saw fresh evidence of violence erupting all around him.[18]

The effect was to leave him for the rest of his life 'trying to come to terms with the continually evolving pattern of social reform, inhibited as he was by those early experiences of revolutionary violence and yet increasingly convinced of the need for a reformist movement'.[19] He was awarded his doctorate in 1862 by an admiring panel that included the future Pope Leo XIII. He was ordained as a priest the following year, and held positions in Rome as Vice-Rector of the Irish College and Professor of Hebrew in the Propaganda College, before returning to Ireland as Cullen's private secretary with the rank of monsignor in 1866.

Like Manning, he was an ultramontane conservative in matters of faith who became – albeit over a more extended period than Manning – a social and economic radical. Both were present at the First Vatican Council in Rome in 1869, which Moran attended in his capacity as Cullen's secretary. Majority support for the Council's adoption of the doctrine of Papal Infallibility was marshalled by Manning on the basis of a proposal from Cullen that Moran is thought to have drafted.[20] The contact was maintained, and Moran may not have been uninfluenced by his older and more senior colleague's increasingly impassioned Social Catholicist convictions and advocacy.[21]

18 Luscombe, *Builders and Crusaders*, 104.

19 Luscombe, *Builders and Crusaders*, 105.

20 For a representative account of the episode, see Ayres, *Prince of the Church*, 50–54.

21 They had been in touch with one another at least as far back as 1862, and, following Moran's appointment to Australia, he called on Manning while passing through London in 1884 and 1888.

Ossory and After

Moran was appointed as Coadjutor Bishop of Ossory in Ireland in 1872, and succeeded the incumbent, Bishop Edward Walsh, on Walsh's death four years later. Enthusiasm for his advancement within the local hierarchy was not necessarily universal or unrestrained. The strengths that were to characterise his Australian episcopate were yet to become evident. The Cullen connection was no longer wholly to his advantage, tarnishing him as it did in the minds of some among his episcopal colleagues with a Cullenite concern for the preservation in Ireland of the power and influence of Rome and antipathy for the nationalist cause to which he in neither case any longer wholly subscribed.

The upshot was to render Moran in some circles 'highly unpopular'. As O'Farrell reports:

> Nor was he given much credit for ability or real importance. For this, his personality was also in part to blame. Orphaned young, and living from the age of twelve in ecclesiastical institutions, Moran lacked warmth. He was reserved and shy, seldom even raising his eyes, never his voice. He had a habit of joining his hands in front of him, and rubbing them together softly. His whole demeanour spoke of stern, unruffled ecclesiastical taciturnity. As Walter McDonald reminisced of him at Kilkenny: 'He was a Churchman born, very much respected, a good deal feared, but little loved'. Volatile personalities could not stomach him at all. Archbishop Croke, of Cashel, dismissed Moran contemptuously as 'some cold and colourless ecclesiastic'. True, the nationalist Croke had a hearty dislike of Moran's politics – or lack of them. But Cardinal McCabe, who, like Moran, fought shy of popular politics, also had a low opinion of him. Simply on grounds of ability, Moran's reputation was not

> high. Cardinal Manning, in England, rated his ecclesiastical abilities as no more than ordinary.[22]

So dismissive a judgement of Moran by his peers was premature. Unbeknown to his detractors within the hierarchy, the episcopal ugly duckling of their imagining was undergoing a quiet metamorphosis, whose magnitude and significance it remained for a new phase in his life and advancement to fully reveal. The man, the hour and a new land awaited one another.

Like Manning, Moran was appalled by the suffering of the Irish poor, but as resolutely as Manning rejected violence as a means of alleviating or eliminating poverty, and favoured gradualist change such as the successive Irish Land Acts had begun to deliver. Commissioned by Pope Leo XIII in 1888 to report privately to him on conditions in Ireland, he denounced the 'legal injustice' of British rule with a fervour that some in Rome held to his discredit, as intemperate and unhelpful. As the religious history scholar A.E. Cahill, like O'Brien deceased before his intended biography of Moran could be completed, has noted: 'His famous step-uncle would not have written with the passion – and the frankness – of Moran's report'.[23]

For all that doubts as to Moran's nationalist credentials may have lingered within the hierarchy, they in no way inhibited his fellow members from availing themselves of his diplomatic skills and Roman contacts in the face of crises, such as when in January 1881 a papal letter publicly censuring the land movement was seen to be 'insufficiently harsh to please England, too harsh for the Catholics of

---

22 O'Farrell, *The Catholic Church and Community in Australia*, 230. For McDonald's assessment in full, see Ayres, *Prince of the Church*, 122–123.

23 Moran to Leo XIII, 21 October 1888, as quoted in Cahill, 'Cardinal Moran's Politics', 530.

Ireland and written at the behest of pro-English agencies', or later the same month a rumoured prospect of diplomatic ties between Britain and the Vatican gave rise to fears that 'Whitehall would represent Ireland in Rome'.[24] He was repeatedly an agent or intermediary for the expatriate Irish episcopate within the NSW church, in negotiations with Rome consequent on their differences with the English ascendancy of the day, as exemplified successively by his Benedictine predecessors, Archbishops John Polding and Roger Vaughan.

This familiarity with the affairs of the colonies now stood him in good stead.[25] Chosen to head the Australian hierarchy as Archbishop of Sydney in succession to Vaughan in 1884, his arrival in his antipodean diocese attracted 'a tumultuous festive welcome, estimated to involve 100,000 people on harbour steamers gay with bunting, at the wharf, and lining the route to the Cathedral'.[26] Setting foot for the first time on Australian soil, he unhesitatingly proclaimed his intention to be 'an Australian among Australians'.[27] He was raised to the Cardinalate the following year, and shortly also became the Pope's Apostolic Delegate. Returning to Australia from Rome in the aftermath of his elevation, he was accorded a further rapturous reception.

24 Ayres, *Prince of the Church*, 104.

25 Notable examples included his preparation on behalf of Archdeacon McEncroe in 1859 of a petition to the Vatican calling for the creation of new Australian Sees for Irish bishops, and a request for his intervention five years later to secure an Irish bishop for the new Goulburn See in preference to an English appointee as favoured by Polding. For detailed background to the rivalry between the Irish and English interests, see, for example, O'Farrell, *The Catholic Church and Community in Australia*, 195–225.

26 O'Farrell, *The Catholic Church and Community in Australia*, 231.

27 Luscombe, *Builders and Crusaders*, 105.

The Maritime Strike

The arrival of a new era in the willingness of the Australian Church to stand up for its predominantly working class and underprivileged adherents was signalled by Moran's response to the 1890 maritime strike. Like Cardinal Manning in the previous year's London dock strike, Moran sided squarely with the workers, asserting in a groundbreaking press interview that they had based their claims on right and reason, and were fully justified in their call for fairer wages, and proposing that a conference should be called to resolve the impasse with the employers through negotiation.

The strikers in their turn reciprocated, responding to the Mercantile Marine Officers' Association call for 'Three Cheers for the Cardinal' as they marched 10,000 strong past St Mary's Cathedral, on their way to a mass meeting in the Domain Gardens.[28] A Presbyterian strike leader, Duncan Ross, wrote in a Sydney newspaper at the height of the dispute that the only true friends of the masses were 'the Roman Catholic hierarchy, as in the days when Stephen Langton, the Cardinal-Archbishop of Canterbury, wrested the people's liberties from King John by making him sign the Magna Carta'.[29]

When the strike failed in the face of an obdurate refusal on the part of the employers to compromise or settle for less than the crushing of their unionist adversaries, Moran congratulated the defeated and despairing workers for having maintained an 'admirable order' reflective of 'their stern determination to maintain their case, despite the terrible odds arrayed against them', so that 'the rights and dignity of labour were never so clearly set before the people'.[30] It was an apt

28 Ford, *Cardinal Moran and the ALP*, 74.

29 Murtagh, *Australia: The Catholic Chapter*, 118.

30 *Catholic Press*, 21 May 1903, as quoted in Luscome, *Builders and Crusaders*, 114.

and instructive prelude and curtain-raiser for his great Masonic Hall address on *Rerum Novarum* the following year.

Contemporary accounts capture the intensity of public interest in the address. 'Though contrary to the rule in Sydney high prices were asked for the tickets', the Catholic *Freeman's Journal* reported, 'the body of the hall was completely filled, while the large gallery at a shilling admission was crowded'.[31] The chair was taken by the prominent MLC and president of the recently concluded Royal Commission on strikes, Andrew Garran, and other MPs present included the Opposition Leader, George Dibbs, the Postmaster-General, Daniel O'Connor, the future Prime Minister, Edmund Barton, and most of the thirty-five recently elected members of the Parliamentary Labor Party. The dramatic conclusion to Moran's remarks reads:

> I do not think there is any wrong to be redressed which in a free country may not be reached by the just laws of the land, but if, to remedy a manifest injustice and redress the crying hardships under which a great majority of the people are oppressed, a revolution may be necessary, then I say a revolution for me will have no terrors.[32]

Recession

Added urgency was imminent. Moran's delivery of his address coincided with the onset of a crippling recession and near collapse of

31 *Freeman's Journal*, 22 August 1891.

32 Albeit a bloodless revolution, as exemplified in his view by the entry into Rome of Constantine's legions 'with the banners of the Cross unfurled in triumph', or the extortion of Magna Carta from the King by the barons at Runnymede. *Freeman's Journal*, 22 August 1891.

the colonial economy. As Brian Fitzpatrick recounts in his seminal *The Australian People 1878–1945*:

> A fifth of the 'the people's' building societies of 1890 had closed their doors before 1893, and those remaining in 1892 lent only an eighth of their 1888 advances. Of 1154 business companies formed in the six years to mid-1893, more than a third, with nearly ten million pounds paid up capital, were 'defunct' (the startled statistician's word) by the end of that year. Lugubrious thousands saw their income and capital shrink and even vanish in this calamitous liquidation, or in the failure of the land banks. A score of these last in Sydney and many more in Melbourne closed their doors in the eight or nine months of 1891–2 with liabilities of £25 millions. Nearly £15 million of this was depositors' money. And when a baker's dozen of banks of issue went into 'reconstruction' in a single month of 1893, they owed their depositors no less than £72 millions.[33]

The impact of the downturn was devastating. Jobless urban workers joined a mass exodus in frequently fruitless search of new livelihoods in country districts, or as fossickers on the West Australian gold fields. The dependents they left behind them made ends meet as best they could, or turned for relief to the over-stretched benevolent societies and charities of the day. Middle class casualties of the 'changed conditions of the colony' – including in particular older or single women – went hungry in preference to the stigma of accepting charity.[34] A contemporary account reported 'over twenty thousand houses to let in and around Melbourne':

---

33 Brian Fitzpatrick, *The Australian People 1878–1945* (Carlton, Vic: Melbourne University Press, 1946) 220.

34 Melbourne Ladies Benevolent Society, *Forty-Eighth Annual Report*, 1894, and *Illustrated Australian News*, 1 May 1894, as quoted in James Grant and Geoffrey Serle, *The Melbourne Scene 1803–1956* (Carlton, Vic: Melbourne University Press, 1957) 211.

> Many of these houses will go to ruin. Vagabonds go round to the empty tenements and strip them of everything portable. They break into houses and remove the fixtures, and even piping is not safe from them, as they tear it up and sell it for old lead. Coppers are coolly carted away; and I have seen houses literally stripped of everything by these thieves. ... The scarcity of employment drove men, who would otherwise have been honest, to desperation.[35]

Moran's response was to intensify the articulation of his aspirations and concerns. Having affirmed and amplified the teachings of *Rerum Novarum* in terms of so categorical and uncompromising a character – and wherever possible extending relief and comfort to the needy among his co-religionists through the numerous parish organisations and other lay bodies such as the St Vincent de Paul Society, the Australian Holy Catholic Guild and the mutualist Hibernian Australian Catholic Benefit Society that his incumbency had seeded or fostered[36] – he now also became more overtly sympathetic to the labour movement and outspoken in his advocacy of the federalism that was so logical a corollary of his outspoken Australian nationalism and hopes for a solution to the festering social problems whose gravity the recession was so cruelly worsening.

His advocacy of Federation was appreciated and applauded, even in unlikely quarters. As the NSW Premier of the day, Sir Henry Parkes – no friend of the Church – acknowledged in an 1894 parliamentary tribute to supporters of the Federalist cause:

35 Nathan Gould, *Town and Bush* (London: George Routledge, 1896) 122–123.

36 Bodies such as the Society of St Vincent de Paul apart, 'At the end of his career the Catholic charitable institutions in Sydney comprised nine hospitals, eight orphanages, eight industrial or specialised schools, and seven institutions for the blind, mentally affected and other classes of unfortunate people'. O'Brien, 'Cardinal Moran's Part in Public Affairs', 15.

> There is another person who is an entire stranger to me, and, I should think, a gentleman who has no very high opinion of me, whose services I should acknowledge. Of all the voices on this question, no voice has been more distinct, more full of worthy foreshadowing of the question's greatness and more fraught with a clear prescience of what is likely to come as a result of Federation, than the voice of this eminent prelate.[37]

Parkes told his parliamentary colleague, B.R. Wise, that Moran's advocacy of Federation had 'swayed thousands whom the politicians could not have reached'.[38] Wise for his own part wrote to Moran in the aftermath of the acceptance of Federation, expressing 'his deep gratitude to His Eminence for his outspoken, courageous and unselfish utterances on this great question'.[39]

'Always a Labour Man'

Moran wrote to the ALP federal minister Hugh Mahon in 1904 that 'I have been myself always a labour man'.[40] He saw the ALP as being the closest in spirit of the parties to *Rerum Novarum*, and the most likely of them to in some degree give effect to the encyclical's teachings. It was also the party to which the overwhelming majority of his predominantly under-privileged co-religionists looked for understanding and alleviation of their predicament. It was the ALP that he singled out for praise as 'the only party above religious

37 New South Wales *Hansard*, 13 November 1884, Folio 2194/5.

38 Bernard R. Wise, *The Making of the Australian Commonwealth* (1913. This edition is a digital text sponsored by the New South Wales Centenary of Federation Committee, University of Sydney Library, 144. Accessed 5 February 2008).

39 As quoted in Ford, *Cardinal Moran and the ALP*, 235.

40 Moran to Hugh Mahon, 1 May 1904, as quoted in Cahill, 'Cardinal Moran's Politics', 531, and characterised by him as 'a letter that Moran knew would be circulated in the new Labor cabinet'.

prejudice'.[41] The Liberal Party and the ALP represented in his view 'two phases of the same liberal idea, the Labor Party being the more advanced'.[42]

He supported further strikes including the 1903 Victorian railways strike and the 1909 NSW miners' strike. He backed the ALP at the 1904, 1906 and 1910 federal elections and addressed meetings in three states in support of the federal ALP's 1911 referendum bid for powers to regulate workplace relations and trade and commerce, and nationalise corporations that the parliament declared to be monopolies.

When shortly before his death in 1911 the NSW ALP government of the day faced defeat with the likely resignation of a Catholic MP, he counselled the prospective defector to such salutary effect that 'A very few words set him right'.[43] The ALP increased its majority at the subsequent elections and retained office for a further five years. The key historian of the party's NSW branch, Graham Freudenberg, sees its early success as having been owed 'a lot more to Cardinal Moran at St Mary's Cathedral, Sydney, than to Karl Marx at the British Museum, London'.[44]

The convergence of his social and economic concerns and aspirations with those of the ALP was in no sense instantaneous or without its setbacks and vicissitudes. Throughout much of the 1890s he and the party circled one another in a process of mutual appraisal, in which each sought to satisfy itself of the other's intentions and merits, Moran for his part seeking certainty that the ALP was, as he supposed, free

41 Moran as quoted in Nairn and Serle, 'Moran, Patrick Francis' 580.

42 Patrick F. Moran, 'Cardinal Moran: An Observer of the Times', *Advertiser* (Adelaide), 27 March 1911.

43 Moran Papers, 29 July 1911, as quoted in Cahill, 'Cardinal Moran's Politics', 526.

44 Graham Freudenberg, as quoted in Edmund Campion, 'Were Irish & Catholic Synonymous?' *Tintéan*, March, 2008.

of the taint of the 'extreme Socialism' that *Rerum Novarum* had so comprehensively anathematised and he personally execrated, while the party in its turn overcame the lingering suspicions of numbers of its leaders and adherents that, as so frequently in Europe and the Central and South Americas, the Church would side with the rich, privileged and powerful against the downtrodden and destitute.

And their differences may have been less great than sometimes has been supposed. Suggestions by some – most notably Fr Patrick Ford in his 1966 *Cardinal Moran and the ALP: A Study in the Encounter between Moran and Socialism 1890 to 1907* – that Marxism was Moran's major concern are now seen widely as having been a superimposition on the 1890s of the Cold War and ALP Split passions and preoccupations of half a century and more later. Moran's biographer concurs with Cahill that 'It is unpersuasive to present him as a crusading anti-Marxist given that he quotes Marx just once (on the social consequences of capitalism) and never actually refers to him'.[45] A scholarly review of Ford's book characterises the author as having made Moran 'too alarmist in the 90s to be the same man who ridiculed notions of a Socialist threat a few years later'.[46] Nor has the episode lacked unintended consequences. As Cahill concludes, 'Uncritical acceptance of Ford's argument has resulted in Moran's appearance in a recent study as a symbol of clerical reaction in defence of capitalism'.[47]

Even so, misunderstandings and instances of working at cross-purposes were not infrequent, as when Moran's candidature for the

---

45 Ayres, *Prince of the Church*, 170.

46 Bruce Mansfield, *Politics*, 1, No 2, November 1966.

47 Cahill, 'Cardinal Moran's Politics', 529, referring to Buckley, Ken, and Wheelwright, Ted, *No Paradise for Workers: Capitalism and the Common People in Australia, 1788–1914* (Melbourne: Oxford University Press, 1988) 12, 154. Cahill notes that: 'The relevant references all cite Ford'.

NSW delegation to the 1897 Federal Convention not only resulted in his own defeat and fanned sectarian sentiments, but also, by splitting the Catholic vote, denied the ALP the representation that it might otherwise have anticipated, and the Convention the benefit of its input. Rapprochements in each case followed. By the turn of the century his doubts had been resolved and his reservations satisfied.

Attitude to Socialism

His new certainties were reflected in an interview for the French magazine *L'Univers* in 1902. Asked by his interviewer 'But has not the Labor Party been formed through a vile antagonism against capital? Does it not likely give rise to unpleasant forebodings?', Moran answered in the trenchant tone and terms with which many throughout Australia had become familiar:

> Decidedly not. Our Labor Party does not cherish any vague theories, any ambiguous and high-sounding formulae. Its object is precise reforms, and concrete measures in favour of the toiling masses. ... If we showed aversion to the labour movement we would drive the toiling masses from the Church, which would become unpopular, but do not imagine that our sympathetic attitude towards this movement is one of opportunism, or that it is a kind of apostolic manoeuvre. No! It is with our whole heart that we sympathise with the rise of the people. We wish always to elevate the people more and more, and everything that will advance (them) will most assuredly meet our greatest and most heartfelt sympathy.[48]

48 Patrick F. Moran, 'Un Entretien avec S. Em. Le Cardinal Moran', *L'Univers* (Paris), 15 June 1902. Translation as in *Catholic Press*, Sydney, 16 August 1902.

His address to the 1905 Annual Breakfast of the Irish National Foresters Benefit Society in Sydney – delivered at the height of a heated political controversy, and in Cahill's view 'the most important' of his 27-year Australian incumbency[49] – gave detailed expression to what was now his settled position. Initially, a Catholic delegate to the 1905 Political Labour Leagues conference in Sydney had written in a letter to the weekly *Catholic Press*, a competitor of the longer established *Freeman's Journal*, that a statement of principles adopted by the conference was proof positive that the party was Socialist in the sense that *Rerum Novarum* had so explicitly condemned, and that a new body should be formed to reverse the conference's decision. That the letter appeared as a front page article under the banner headline 'Labour Party Now Undisguised Socialists', and was accorded editorial support equating the party's aims with those of the German Social-Democratic Party's Ehrfurt program, ensured that its allegations would become as much an issue of party political as of Church significance.

The secular press seized on the allegations to berate and belittle the ALP, as did also the anti-Labor Prime Minister of the day, Sir George Reid, in announcing that the party had 'thrown off the mask' and exposed 'the party's soul', and accordingly he would lead a nationwide campaign in the cause of anti-Socialism.[50] Opinion among Catholics was divided, with the *Freeman's Journal* offering 'an unequivocal defence of the Labour Party and the new Objective',

---

49 Anthony E. Cahill, 'Catholicism and Socialism – The 1905 Controversy', *Australian Journal of Religious History*, No 1, 1960, 93.

50 Cahill, 'Catholicism and Socialism', 94.

and condemning its co-religionist competitor for 'a "scare issue" for which no justification could be found in the actual state of the party'.[51]

Moran would have none of it. His address cut through the morass of misinformation and confusion to devastating effect, repudiating 'completely and entirely' the actions of those who attributed Communist or extreme Socialist principles to the ALP:

> There are some gentlemen who would call themselves Socialists. Well, I don't like the name of Socialism, but, then, what's in a name? If gentlemen assume the name of Socialists while they are repudiating all that is fallacious and deceitful in the principles of Socialism, then they are quite within their rights in assuming that name. For my part, I do not like it, for the reason that in the English-speaking world of today Communism and Socialism are partially convertible terms, and no one in his senses would look to its maxims as a source of blessing and peace to society at the present hour. But if men in the advancement of their political interests choose the name of Socialists, I say again what's in a name if the false maxims of Communism are not adopted by those men?

And sterner strictures were to follow. Moran had not finished with those he saw as exploiting the encyclical for party-political advantage. Addressing the 25th Annual General Meeting of the Hibernian Australian Catholic Benefit Society a few weeks later, he called on those present not to be deterred or distracted from making their country great among the nations of the earth and fit to carry out its great destiny:

> Let them not be led away by any cries of 'Socialism' meant only to alarm. He had been unable to find this much-talked-of Socialism. There was an academic Socialism in the old country, and opponents of reform used its name by way of grasping at the

51 Cahill, 'Catholicism and Socialism', 93.

> last straw. When Mr Gladstone had proposed to disestablish the Church of Ireland he was met with cries of 'Socialism'. But he had gone on and succeeded, and no terrible results had followed, and the country was more prosperous than ever before. And so with the settlement of the Irish land question – again the cry had been raised. But the work had been done, and the abyss between landlord and tenant bridged. Let all work together to secure the rights of the people, and be terrified by no political will-o'-the-wisp.[52]

Refuted and rebuked from so unexpected a quarter as the Church, Reid cited *Rerum Novarum*'s denunciation of extreme Socialism as 'the considered warning of the great head of a great Church', and declared that Moran's defence of the ALP was contradictory of papal pronouncements:

> The alliance between Cardinal Moran and the Labor-Socialists is of a most extraordinary character, because the latter have never disguised their Socialistic principles and the most eminent Prelates of the Church to which I refer have become the strongest opponents of Socialism. We may be sure an alliance between two such parties, working upon an arrangement of 'support in return for concessions' constitutes one of the gravest of dangers in Australian politics today.[53]

Moran was not for turning. His ripostes ridiculed Reid as 'a tilter at windmills'.[54] O'Brien's magisterial analysis of the fracas characterises Moran and Reid as having been 'one of them bent on crushing Labour and the other equally determined to justify Labour to the utmost possible extent':

---

52 Patrick F. Moran, 'Speech by the Cardinal', *Daily Telegraph*, 15 March 1905.

53 *Daily Telegraph*, 11 January 1907.

54 O'Brien, 'Cardinal Moran's Part in Public Affairs', 23.

> Moran clearly differentiated the varying degrees of socialism then existing, emphasising that the Pope clearly had in mind the anarchical and communist types that existed on the continent. He maintained that the objectives of the Australian Labour Party were clearly not of this type, but were democratic and sought to remove those social anomalies of capitalist domination which the Pope had specifically condemned, and which Reid conveniently ignored in the Encyclical which he was then exploiting. ... The Cardinal usefully intervened on behalf of the Australian Labour Party at a moment that was fateful in its destiny.[55]

Radicalism and Resistance

Meanwhile, an increasingly radical advocacy and explanation of the encyclical, its concern for the poor and the measures necessary for their relief remained a frequent theme in Moran's innumerable addresses and interviews. He applauded the kind of democracy 'that had once been a synonym for violence and encroachment on the rights of others' and had now become 'a source of blessing for all mankind'.[56] He warned against those who would 'place the wealth and comforts of a country in the pockets of the few'. He urged NSW's newly enfranchised women to ensure through their votes that even the poorest within the community should enjoy all the comforts that the Holy Father had in *Rerum Novarum* told them was 'a right to which all might aspire'.[57]

He endorsed, subject to the observance of 'fundamental principles', the sweeping away of monopolies and the nationalisation of 'every

---

55 O'Brien, 'Cardinal Moran's Part in Public Affairs', 23.

56 Patrick F. Moran, 'Consecrated by the Cardinal at Armidale', *Freeman's Journal*, 9 May 1903.

57 Patrick F. Moran, 'Australian Women and the Franchise', *Freeman's Journal*, 23 May 1903.

bit of land as far as you please'.[58] Increasingly as much a centralist as a federalist, he argued that, subject to the maintenance of state governments 'for purely local interests', 'There should be one powerful Government for Australia ... We should strengthen the hands of the Federal Parliament and give it all the support it needs'.[59]

As with Manning, none of this meant that Moran's social and economic priorities were not sometimes resented or resisted. As early as 1902, numbers of his fellow bishops were critical of him for what they saw as his pursuit of social reform at the expense of their demands for 'educational justice'.[60] His 1905 denial that the ALP's platform made it unacceptable to Catholics offended not only Reid but also such prominent laymen as the influential editor of the *Catholic Press*, J. Tighe Ryan, who had editorialised in Reid's favour. Moran's advocacy of the 'Yes' case at the ALP government's 1911 reference of powers referendum prompted anxious requests from Cardinal Gibbons of Baltimore and Archbishop John Ireland of St Paul, for clarification of US press reports to the effect that the party responsible for the referendum had drawn the majority of its members 'from the ranks of the Socialists', and yet had received 'the bulk of the Catholic vote'.[61]

The wealthy Sydney Catholic Thomas Donovan may have reflected the sentiments of numbers of the better-off among his co-religionists when, following Moran's death, he wrote to the then Abbot of Downside and soon to be Cardinal, Francis Aidan Gasquet, that

58 Patrick F. Moran, 'Fundamental Principles of the Catholic Citizen', *Freeman's Journal*, 18 November 1905.

59 Patrick F. Moran, 'Cardinal Moran: An Observer of the Times', *Advertiser* (Adelaide), 27 March 1911.

60 Cahill, 'Moran, Patrick Francis', 580.

61 Cahill, 'Cardinal Moran's Politics', 528.

'relief has come to many a sore heart' and Moran's 'firebrand' politics should be buried with him.[62] Donovan's complaints may not have fallen on deaf ears. Gasquet had previously characterised Moran as 'an aged Cuckoo, who having got possession of a Benedictine nest has always tried to ignore the work of his Benedictine predecessors'.[63]

And historians too may have given Moran less than his due. Would the Moran of O'Farrell's strictures, who 'left to himself ... thought in unrealistic vaguenesses, pious sentiments, attempts to please everybody and cautious platitudes' and whose pronouncements lacked 'either originality or clear practical application', have aroused so passionate an antipathy on the part of a co-religionist as that exhibited by Donovan?[64] Or have attracted so passionate an approbation as was expressed following his death by the ALP leaders whose cause his support had so boldly advanced? Or have inspired the President of Australia's newly created Arbitration Court, Henry Bournes Higgins, to incorporate the encyclical's concept of a just wage – a wage sufficient to support a wife and three children 'in reasonable and frugal comfort as understood by a civilised community' – in his seminal 1907 Harvester Case judgement? And might not O'Farrell's censure of Moran for a supposed lack of interest in the nuts and bolts of reform have missed the point that it was a specifically moral and ethical guidance that his priestly office was called upon to provide?

Tributes

No such reservations or recrimination troubled the rank and file of Catholics, and well-wishers of other faiths or none, who turned out,

62 Cahill, 'Cardinal Moran's Politics', 526.

63 O'Farrell, *The Catholic Church and Community in Australia*, 244.

64 O'Farrell, *The Catholic Church and Community in Australia*, 280.

reportedly some 250,000 strong, for Moran's funeral. Fittingly, the most heartfelt tribute may well have been that of the NSW ALP Leader of the day, William Holman:

> To say that the death of the Cardinal will throw many thousands of his Church throughout Australia into deep affliction is only to present in a very feeble way the loss which the removal of his great figure represents. The Cardinal was not only a great Churchman, but a great statesman. During the latter years of his life, when the combative spirit which pre-eminently distinguished him at an earlier date, had a little subsided, I don't think there could have been found any to doubt that his great powers were uniformly exerted to the advantage of Australia.[65]

Even so, for all Moran's championing of *Rerum Novarum*, the extent to which the encyclical's significance and content were internalised elsewhere in the local hierarchy or there was awareness of them at the parish level may not have been profound. A relevant anecdote from John Molony – Emeritus Professor of History at the Australian National University and a former priest and Young Christian Workers chaplain at Ballarat – reads:

> Many years ago, Bishop Basil Roper told me a story of an event in his life which he much regretted. Before the First World War he was a young priest at the cathedral presbytery in Ballarat. One day, he was called to the parlour where a young man awaited him with a small document in his hand. It was a copy of *Rerum Novarum* and the young man wanted the priest to explain its contents to him. The priest was forced to tell him that he could not do so because, although he was aware of Leo's encyclical, he was unable to explain it as he had never studied it. The young man went away unsatisfied, according to the bishop, and ceased from that day to interest himself in the social teachings of the Church to which he belonged. It was regrettable because he was

65 As quoted in O'Brien, 'Cardinal Moran's Part in Public Affairs', 25.

> James Scullin, who, later, in the very week of the Wall Street crash in New York in 1929, became the first Catholic prime minister of Australia.[66]

Roper's point about the absence of adequate instruction or encouragement of parish priests in the passing on of the encyclical's teachings to their parishioners was well taken, but he judged himself too harshly. In reality, Scullin's interest in the Church's social teachings was undeterred. The enlightenment that he had been denied at the presbytery door was pursued instead through widespread reading that included the Distributist weeklies, the *Eye Witness* and the *New Witness*. Articles by Belloc were reprinted in the Ballarat newspaper, the *Ballarat Echo*, which he edited from 1913 until 1922, and his biographer sees the encyclical as having influenced him on questions of social justice. A conviction politician whose world-view synthesised to his satisfaction the values respectively of Distributism and Socialism in its predominantly co-operativist or communitarian forms, it was his strong view that 'If Christians don't try and lead the workers, the atheists and agnostics will'.[67] And the quality of his leadership was in due course to be sorely tested, as the ineffectuality of his government in the face of the rigours of the Great Depression and its ultimate overthrow from within would shortly demonstrate.

66 Molony, *The Worker Question*, 191.

67 Duncan, *The Church's Social Teaching*, 203; John R. Robertson, 'Scullin, James Henry (1876–1953)', in Serle, Geoffrey (ed), 1988, *Australian Dictionary of Biography*, Vol II: 1891–1939, 554; Kevin T. Kelly, 'Scullin', *Canberra Historical Journal*, September 1975, 106.

Chapter 5

MANNIX: THE MAN

Attributes

With Moran's death, clerical championing of *Rerum Novarum* largely gravitated from Sydney to Melbourne, where the President of Ireland's Royal Catholic College at Maynooth, Dr Daniel Mannix, was appointed as coadjutor bishop to the ailing Archbishop Carr in 1912, and succeeded to the See on Carr's death five years later. Their respective outlooks and approaches differed on the key issue of how best the substance of the encyclical should be promulgated and its objectives achieved. Mannix's vision was the more inclusive. He saw *Rerum Novarum* and subsequently *Quadragesimo Anno* – the 1931 encyclical of Pope Pius XI, which, as its title suggests, marked the 40th anniversary of Leo's document – as being an enfranchisement of the laity, with whom responsibility properly rested for the interpretation of their precepts and the application of them to their lives and civic responsibilities.

An outspoken advocate of co-operatives from as early a point in his career as his 1890s inaugural secretaryship of Maynooth's alumni union, and ultimately also of Distributism, he thanked the Y.C.W. co-operators at a 1954 communion breakfast for 'having done something worthwhile to improve the lot of the working man':

> Though the Y.C.W. has been working for only a comparatively few years, it has done wonderful things. By the co-operatives started here, houses have been built and furnished, insurances taken out on the houses and furniture, all on most reasonable terms and with the most absolute security. Credit co-operatives have been established and are spreading.[1]

For half a century the prospects for implementation of the encyclicals, and the degree of formation needed to give effect to them, waxed and waned in concert with his priorities, and ultimately were defeated by them. A necessarily extended account captures something of the qualities that caused his legacy to be one of a divided Church and a shattered Labor Party. Had he made way a decade earlier for his coadjutor, Archbishop Justin Simonds, much grief may have been averted, and he would be remembered more kindly.

Over time, lesser and larger degrees of lay autonomy and empowerment were to become defining attributes of the respective Sydney and Melbourne diocesan cultures, with far-reaching implications for the greater divergences that were to so extensively estrange them from one another in and beyond the mid-20th century. State Aid for the Church's schools, Irish ties, the encyclical, opposition to Communism and enfranchisement of the laity were defining attributes of the three phases – disappointment, hope and again disappointment – that comprised the socio-political sphere and cycle of his incumbency. The fortunes of the episcopate and those of the struggle to give effect to the Church's social teachings and Distributism were inextricably intertwined.

---

1 'Dr Mannix – Tribute from Y.C.W. Co-ops', *The Co-operator*, 4, No 3, November–December 1963, 1–2.

Mannix from the outset outshone Sydney's colourless Archbishop Michael Kelly – in the view of some 'this mitred mediocrity'[2] – to become the public face of Australian Catholicism and hero of its mainly Irish and working-class adherents. O'Farrell characterises him as having personified 'Confrontation, challenge, conflict':

> For half a century, from 1913 to 1963, Mannix, as Archbishop of Melbourne, faced Australia with Catholic principles as he saw them, often amid a blaze of controversy. Here was another Catholicism, that which aggressively accepted a role as a standing scandal in the eyes of the world. Moran's search for peaceful harmony gave way to Mannix's rigorous pursuit of principle. Assertion replaced amiability as the Catholic mode of social behaviour.[3]

An austere and even aloof manner belied the intensity of his commitment to pastoral care and aversion to injustice. While a strict disciplinarian in his Maynooth days, his preference in the exercise of his authority within his diocese was for indirection – to err on the side of diversity and guide rather than confront or command.

The impression he made on his clergy was 'one of deep spirituality and firm regard for the religious duties of the priestly life'.[4] His parishioners saw him as 'a person of great humanity and simplicity', and even critics among them could be laudatory.[5] In the eyes of a prominent layman who differed from him on significant issues, 'the Australian Church had perhaps never had so commanding a

2 Edmund Campion, 'Were Irish & Catholic Synonymous?', *Tintéan*, March 2008.

3 O'Farrell, *Catholic Church and Community in Australia*, 298.

4 O'Farrell, *Catholic Church and Community in Australia*, 304.

5 B.A. Santamaria, *Daniel Mannix: The Quality of Leadership* (Carlton, Vic: Melbourne University Press, 1984) 158.

personality, so evident a leader'.[6] Another recalls him as 'the most impressive man I have ever met'.[7]

Nor was it within his own communion alone that he was held in high regard. A tribute, reflective of public esteem for his persuasive powers and common touch at its peak, appeared in the Melbourne *Argus* on the occasion of his episcopal Silver Jubilee in 1937. The accolade was the more impressive by reason of its source, as the newspaper had in earlier years been among his more vociferous critics:

> One man, of all those in Victoria today who have the gift of being able to express opinions in public, who never fails to carry his audience with him, is Archbishop Mannix, one of the best known public figures in this State. ... Scholar, classical student, philosophic thinker, deeply read in the sciences and arts, Dr Mannix has never, since he first spoke in public in Victoria, said anything the meaning of which was not obvious to the least literate man and woman who have heard him. ... Therein lies his power. Scorning the higher flights of oratorical fancy that come so easy to the lettered few, he speaks his message straight to the everyday worker. And so the excitement which his dynamic personality rouses gives way, as he talks, to acquiescence, then keen response and to quickened interest, for as he throws out one simple idea and then another, the audience forgets the formality of the occasion. He not only speaks to the toilers; they feel that he says for them what they cannot say for themselves.[8]

Education was for him the key to enabling Catholics to take their rightful role in society and share in its benefits on an equitable basis. The securing of State Aid was from the outset the issue that he prioritised above all others. His encouragement of young Catholics

6 Vincent Buckley, *Cutting Green Hay: Friendships. Movements and Cultural Conflicts in Australia's Great Decades* (Ringwood, Vic: Penguin Books, 1983) 140.

7 Max Charlesworth, *Church, State and Conscience* (St Lucia, Qld: University of Queensland Press 1973), xi.

8 *Argus*, 18/12/37.

to undertake tertiary education and his facing down of proposals for a confessional university in favour of the opening of Melbourne University's Newman College in 1918 were among his most enduring achievements. Provision for the training of priests followed, with the foundation in 1923 of the Corpus Christi seminary at Werribee. Public subscriptions of £60,000 on the occasion of the Diamond Jubilee of his ordination in 1950 endowed Mannix travelling scholarships for aspiring Catholic academics, including some who were critical of him. When new challenges to the Church's social teachings arose in the face of the economic and political exigencies of the 1930s, a generation of Catholic graduates and younger priests were at hand to respond to them.

Rerum Novarum

Rerum Novarum and the 'one big thing' of a more widespread ownership of productive property mattered to him. The encyclical's critique of Capitalism and intimations of an alternative social order informed and inspired him in his delivery of impassioned addresses at the height of World War I and the campaign against conscription in 1917, and again during the Great Depression of the 1930s. His onslaught on the system he held responsible for both the war and the Depression's impoverishment, misery and humiliation of so large a proportion of his co-religionists was explicit, inflammatory and unrelenting.

'The War', he wrote in his distinctively Distributist foreword to the first issue of the new Catholic monthly *Australia* in 1917, 'had made men and women think much and think hard':

> They would not cease thinking when the war was over. They would not be satisfied to be cogs in a wheel. More and more

> they would try to control the industries in which they were engaged. It would be hard to convince them or convince anyone that they were not entitled to industrial control as they were to political power. The people were just now in the temper to assert themselves – politically, socially and industrially. And if they were to move along safe lines it was never more necessary than it was now that the public mind should be leavened by Catholic principles.[9]

Responding to the Seamen's strike in 1919, he queried whether 'any of the sneering critics would undertake to balance the family budget on the strikers' wages and at the present cost of living':

> Would they live in the conditions, in the holds, or in the slums, on sea or land, in which the strikers had been living? If they themselves were the workers, would they patiently bear their lot in the face of all that was said about the profiteers, and especially about the shipping interests? People's sympathy was asked for the man who, owing to the strike, had to change his hour of rising or be content with a cold breakfast! What about the women and children who had to be thankful if they had any kind of breakfast, hot or cold? The sooner people understood that the worker must get, not just a living wage, but a fair share of the wealth he produced, the better.[10]

'All over the world', he told the Annual Conference of the Hibernian Society in October 1931, 'people were experiencing a very anxious time':

> They were only now beginning to realise how wise Pope Leo XIII was when he told the world, about forty years ago, that if radical change were not made in society, much trouble, and even revolution, might have to be faced. There was more

---

9 Frank Murphy, *Daniel Mannix: Archbishop of Melbourne 1917–1963* (Melbourne, Vic: The Polding Press, 1972) 63–64.

10 As quoted in Edwin J. Brady, *Dr Mannix: Archbishop of Melbourne* (Melbourne, Vic: The Library of National Biography, 1934) 129–130.

> unemployment in the world than had ever existed before, and people were worse off than when slavery existed. Slave owners had to feed, clothe and look after those subject to them, but many who called themselves free men today had scarcely anybody to look after them. Until the unemployment problem was solved, the world would never be at rest.[11]

'The existing system', he had concluded by 1932, 'was undoubtedly a fiasco, a tragedy and a failure'.[12]

Politics

Like Moran, he favoured the ALP as the more likely of the major parties to respect and reflect the encyclical's teachings. He was dismissive of the anti-Labor parties of the day as promising no redress of Catholic grievances or fulfilment of their hopes, and asked and expected nothing of them. His underlying social democratic, liberal and labour movement sympathies were exemplified by his support for striking police in their 1923 dispute with the Victorian Government, denunciations of inequality, advocacy of the abolition of capital punishment and endorsement of the federal government's 1944 referral of powers referendum and its bank nationalisation referendum three years later.

He was insistent on the right and responsibility of women to participate to the full in politics and public affairs, wrote in sympathy to the president of the Melbourne Hebrew Congregation in 1933 over the treatment of the Jews by the Nazis and applauded the admission to Australia of Jewish refugees, condemned the dropping of the atomic bomb on Hiroshima in 1945 as 'immoral and indefensible', supported

11 Brady, *Dr Mannix*, 244–245 .

12 *Advocate*, 8 December 1932.

Evatt's defence of small power interests at the 1945 San Francisco conference, and in 1948 favoured tempering of the White Australia policy through the adoption of an entry quota for Asian migrants. He voted 'No' at the Menzies government's 1951 Communist Party dissolution referendum, and pleaded with President Eisenhower in 1953 for a reprieve from execution for Julius and Ethel Rosenberg, following their conviction for passing atomic secrets to the Soviet Union.

Denouncing both Communism and Capitalism with equal vehemence, he welcomed the championing by the nascent Campion Society in the 1930s of 'Third Way' proposals for a Distributist Catholic social order. He was instrumental in securing the adoption by his fellow bishops of the society's proposals for the establishment of the Australian National Secretariat for Catholic Action (ANSCA), and through it of Distributism as in all but name the social and economic philosophy of the Australian Church. Asked as was famously Cardinal Newman 'Who are the laity?', he likewise would have replied 'The Church would look foolish without them'.[13]

Dragon's Teeth

Not all aspects of his episcopate were as benign. In the years immediately subsequent to his arrival in Australia, he sowed dragon's teeth of divisiveness, whose dark progeny for the rest of his life returned to haunt and harass him. Consistent with Irish precept and practice, his approach was 'Religion from Rome, politics from home'. His approach to Canon Law has been characterised in a friendly quarter as 'not easy to define': 'The few letters that remain in the

13 Meriol Trevor, *Newman: Light in Winter* (London: Macmillan, 1962) 201.

Dublin archives reveal a thorough knowledge of the content, but a glimmer of disdain comes through. In Australia he largely ignored it'.[14] A key scholarly account sees him as having 'never made any distinction between politics and religion' – as having grown up 'to see political action as a means to attain religious objectives'.[15] In so doing, he was neglectful of theological discourse on limits to the Church's involvement in politics dating back at least to the French Dominican, John of Paris, in the 14th century, and the need to distinguish clearly between Maritain's 'Catholic Action' and 'action by Catholics'.

Signposts to future difficulties from the start abounded. He at no stage of his long incumbency was averse to coercing the ALP in the hope of securing concessions from it, falling out with the party when it disappointed him or countenancing and inciting permeations, penetrations and ultimately a would-be takeover of it. O'Farrell notes in a pregnant aside that 'It must be an interesting point of speculation whether or not Mannix saw in the conscription split of the Labor Party a providential means of securing the more Catholic, more Christian Labor Party he so ardently desired'.[16] A study of lay activism in Victoria characterises him as having set out in the aftermath of the war to establish an overtly Catholic political party, only to be deterred by the failure of the Catholic Federation in NSW to gain support for its all but confessional Democratic Party at the 1920 and 1922 state elections, despite the intentions of the author of its platform, P.S. Cleary.[17]

---

14 Walter A. Ebsworth, *Archbishop Mannix* (Armidale, Vic: The Graphic Workshop, 1977) 64.

15 Colm Kiernan, *Daniel Mannix and Ireland* (Morwell, Vic: Alella Books, 1984) 8.

16 O'Farrell, *Catholic Church and Community in Australia*, 329.

17 Cecily Close, *The Organisation of the Catholic Laity in Victoria 1911–1930*, MA Thesis, Department of History, University of Melbourne, 1972.

His relations with the Vatican were frequently strained, and his clashes with its local representatives endemic. In championing the 'No' vote at the 1916 and 1917 conscription referenda he disregarded the ruling by the Apostolic Delegate of the day, Archbishop Cerretti, that conscription was a political question and accordingly the Church would not have a policy on it.[18] Responding to Cerretti's edict, he invoked his right as a private citizen to voice his opinions. Dressing as he did in each instance in his episcopal clothing and speaking from the same platforms and at the same official events as in his episcopal capacity, the distinction was unpersuasive. A precedent was set, from which ultimately the Church was only with great difficulty and agony of conscience extricated.

The sole supporter among the world's bishops of the republican insurgency that followed on the 1921 Anglo-Irish Treaty and the establishment of the Irish Free State, he visited Ireland in 1925 against the express wishes of the local hierarchy, whose members then ostracised him throughout his stay and boycotted his meetings.[19] And Rome was no more ready than the hierarchy 'to accept every expression of his support for the Republican cause as being in harmony with his ecclesiastical role'.[20] In 1934, Cerretti's successor, Archbishop Filippo Bernardini, wrote to him 'in accordance with instructions received from the Holy See', requesting that 'in the future you would cautiously avoid public discussions or "statements" which could be evilly interpreted and used by those who, from a division of minds, or from a religious disturbance of the noble Irish

18 *Catholic Press*, 5 October 2016.

19 For an extended account of the episode, see Kiernan, *Daniel Mannix and Ireland*, 185–202.

20 B.A. Santamaria, *Daniel Mannix: A Biography* (Carlton Vic: Melbourne University Press, 1984) 141.

nation, have every thing to gain'.[21] Mannix gave him short shrift. 'I was an Irishman before I was an Archbishop', he declared, 'And I remain an Irishman in spite of the fact that I am an Archbishop'.[22]

Panico

Relations with Archbishop Giovanni Panico, who succeeded Bernardini as Apostolic Delegate in 1935, were no less fraught. As recalled in 1955 by the prominent lay Catholic and then Deputy ALP Leader, Arthur Calwell, 'There was bad blood, real bad blood, between Panico and Mannix, and I've got the whole story from Mannix's lips'.[23] Panico's brief from Rome was to secure a more rapid transition from an Irish to an Australian-born hierarchy, and in the process curb Mannix's influence and perceived intransigence. In his view, the devices which some of the Bishops had utilised to secure acceptance by the Holy See of their nominees 'has not always been the cleanest', and a definitive break with past practice was required.[24] Nor was he averse to an at times peremptory exercise of his prerogatives, or wedded to avoidable consultation.

Neither on Panico's replacement of the long-serving Michael Sheehan as Kelly's Coadjutor with Norman Gilroy in 1937 nor on the appointment in 1942 of Justin Simonds as Mannix's Coadjutor was notice of his intentions given to the local hierarchy or their

21 Bernardini to Mannix, 11 January 1934, as quoted in Santamaria, *Daniel Mannix*, 143.

22 *Catholic Bulletin*, 1921, Vol XI, 679. As quoted in Kiernan, *Daniel Mannix and Ireland*, 154.

23 Calwell to E.J. Ward, 9 February 1955, Calwell Papers, as quoted in Colm Kiernan, *Calwell: A Personal and Political Biography* (Melbourne, Vic: Thomas Nelson [Australia]) Limited) 1978) 191.

24 Panico to Fumasoni-Biondi, 5 October 1937, as quoted in Santamaria, *Daniel Mannix*, 183.

consent sought. 'We can only express our regret', the bishops wrote to Sheehan, 'that, before your resignation took effect, we, your colleagues, who know you best, had no opportunity of trying to alter your decision'.[25] As recalled by Simonds of Panico's notification of him of his appointment, 'I asked him whether Dr Mannix had been informed, but was told this was not my affair'.[26]

Panico's intention was unambiguous: 'To make such an appointment without any prior discussion whatsoever with one who was by universal consent the most outstanding of all Australian bishops was, and was meant to be, slighting'.[27] In the event, his hopes for Simonds were frustrated by Mannix's exceptional longevity. It was not until his death in 1963 that the See finally passed to Simonds, who already was in poor health, and died four years later. Passing the archiepiscopal residence 'Raheen' in the course of the 21-year hiatus that he came to regard as his 'apprenticeship', Simonds reportedly remarked to a guest, 'That's my house, but I can't get vacant possession'.[28]

Panico stated in an address on the occasion of the diocesan centenary in 1948 that he 'looked forward to the day when every Bishop in Australia would be an Australian'. Mannix responded 'I would like to say to the Apostolic Delegate that I look forward to the day when the Apostolic Delegate will be an Australian'. Nor were all the consequences of their mutual antipathy intentional or immediately apparent: 'Whatever Panico's policy signified for the purely ecclesiastical aspects of the Church's administration its consequences for the lay movement had the effect of a delayed time-bomb'.[29] An elderly

25 *Tribune*, 1 July 1937.

26 Santamaria, *Daniel Mannix*, 186.

27 Santamaria, *Daniel Mannix*, 185.

28 Santamaria, *Daniel Mannix*, 187.

29 Santamaria, *Daniel Mannix*, 189.

Irish cleric reportedly on reading the news of Gilroy's elevation to the cardinalate 'flung his newspaper to the ground and roared "So the dago's pup has got it, after all"'.[30]

Metastases

By 1954, Mannix's central and over-riding objective of State Aid appeared to have all but been achieved, with its adoption by the ALP Federal Conference in 1951 as party policy. All that was required of him was to wait on the election of the ALP governments that would enact it. At a crucial juncture, he was advised by Santamaria that control of the party was likely to pass shortly into the hands of the covert Catholic Social Studies Movement (CSSM) in whose creation and empowering with spurious ecclesiastical sanction and authority his support had been decisive.[31] And hubris prevailed, to the enduring detriment of the Church, the party, the national interest and his place in history.

Faced subsequently with an adverse ruling by the Vatican on the party political involvement of Church agencies to whose creation and preservation he had made so major a contribution, he responded 'Rome has blundered again'.[32] Others were unconvinced. In Molony's view, Mannix 'must be regarded as the principal actor in betraying the mission of the Church by directly fostering its activity on the political arena in Australia. … From the time of his arrival in Australia,

30 Brennan, *Dr Mannix*, 316.

31 See, for example, Santamaria to Mannix 11/12/1952 in Patrick Morgan, *B.A. Santamaria: Your Most Obedient Servant: Selected Letters 1938–1996* (Melbourne, Vic: The Miegunyah Press in Association with the State Library of Victoria, 2007) 73–79, and Santamaria to Colin Clark 16/6/1953, in *BAS Correspondence with Colin Clark 1946–65*, BAS Archives 1953: s5b3f7, Melbourne, State Library of Victoria.

32 James Griffin, 'Daniel Mannix', in G. Serle (ed), *Australian Dictionary of Biography*, Vol 10: 1891–1939 (Carlton, Vic: Melbourne University Press, 1986) 398.

Dr Mannix had never shown evidence of having a tender conscience in this vital matter and his conviction on the danger to Australia of the Communist menace further clouded his judgement'.[33]

His obduracy metastasised to his own and the Church's disadvantage. Having secured so central and significant a role for Social Catholicism and Distributism within the Church as the Campions and ANSCA exemplified, he also was central to their demise. The responsibility in this respect was not his alone. It was shared by numbers of his senior clergy and fellow bishops, some of whom concluded subsequently that their confidence in him had been misplaced.

Britain

Ardent and visceral as were Mannix's Irish affinities and aversions, he was largely insensitive to the no less passionate ties of majority opinion to Britain. Identification with Britain and the British Empire was perhaps more pervasive and passionately felt in Australia than in Britain itself. From Britain's history stemmed 'the vision, the grandeur and the glorious past that Australians were not able to find in their own beginnings'.[34] The Empire was felt to constitute 'an international brotherhood of free "British" nations across the seas who, led by Britain, would defend them against any threats, especially from Asia'.[35]

33 John Molony, 2008, Notes for his presentation to the 'Meeting the Show' Santamaria panel discussion, State Library of Victoria, 26 August 2008. Copy by courtesy of the author. Molony recalls in his address that he 'received the sacrament of Confirmation at Mannix's hands', knew him personally, revered and 'in considerable measure' still reveres him.

34 Mark McKenna, *The Captive Republic* (Melbourne, Vic: Cambridge University Press, 1996) 206–207.

35 Eric M. Andrews, *The Anzac Illusion* (Melbourne, Vic: Cambridge University Press, 1994) 5. McKenna, *The Captive Republic*, 206–207.

He was in all these respects out of step and sympathy with the conventional wisdom of an entrenched attachment to Britain. He opposed immigration in the 1920s and 1930s when more than three-quarters of the assisted migrants were English or Scottish Protestants, and welcomed it in the postwar period when the massive influx of predominantly Southern European newcomers increased the proportion of Catholics to overall population from its prewar level of around 17.5 per cent to 20.7 per cent in 1947 and 27 per cent in 1971.[36]

His at times ambiguous or hostile assessment of the righteousness of Britain's role in World War I, perceived sympathies with Irish insurrectionism and opposition to conscription caused him to be assailed severally for disloyalty, sedition, subversion and High Treason, not least by numbers of the more prominent or affluent among his co-religionists. Those disassociating themselves publicly from his views included Catholics of the stature of Mr Justice Heydon, Mr Justice Gavan Duffy, Sir Thomas Hughes and the Lord Mayor of Sydney, R.D. Meagher.[37]

Heydon wrote of Mannix's opposition to conscription that 'The Catholic Archbishop of Melbourne has shown himself to be not only disloyal as a man, but – and I say it emphatically, archbishop though he is, and simple layman though I be – untrue to the teachings of

36 William J. Newland, *Mannix Depression: Challenging the Biographies' 'Mannix Legend' with an Examination of Archbishop Daniel Mannix during the Great Depression Period*, Batchelor of Arts (Honours) Thesis, University of Melbourne, 2005, FN 94, 20–21; James Jupp, *Immigration* (South Melbourne, Vic: Sydney University Press in Association with Oxford University Press, 1991), 58–60; Frank Lewins, 'Continuity and Change in a Religious Organisation: Some Aspects of the Australian Catholic Church', *Journal for the Scientific Study of Religion*, 16, No 4, 371; O'Farrell, *Catholic Church and Community in Australia*, 404.

37 O'Farrell, *Catholic Church and Community in Australia*, 331.

the church, of which by his office he should be a guardian'.[38] Hughes accused him of having 'advised Irishmen to take advantage of England's extremity and stab her in the back while her whole energies were absorbed in fighting for the civilisation of the world'.[39] When a deputation of the disaffected laity sought to put their concerns to Carr, he referred them to Mannix who in turn refused to receive them. Heydon, he remarked, was 'a second or third class judge ... who could not have got as many to listen to him as would have filled a lolly shop'.[40]

And opinions of Mannix in the official circles of the day were no less hostile. His conduct, noted the Head of the recently formed Australian Counter-Espionage Bureau, Major George Stewart, in 1918, 'would not have permitted him to have lived in Berlin more than twenty-four hours after the mildest of his utterances in this country ... He has been the most disturbing element this country has ever seen: clever, cunning, and untrustworthy in anything and everything which concerned the rights of the Empire'.[41]

A memorandum on Mannix was prepared by the Prime Minister's Office at the request of the British Government, in the aftermath of the arrest of seven members of the Irish Republican Brotherhood in Australia in 1918. It reads:

> In order to appreciate the full significance of this latest development it is necessary to review the events that have led up to

---

38 *Age* 19/1/1917.

39 *Argus* 26/1/1917.

40 O'Farrell, *Catholic Church and Community in Australia*, 330–331.

41 Reverend Dr D. Mannix (Anti-Conscription and Anti-British Utterances: Sinn Feiner, ANA A8911/1, Control symbol 240). Stewart to Hall, 30 January 1918, as quoted in G. Calderwood, 'A Question of Loyalty: Archbishop Daniel Mannix, the Australian Government and the Papacy, 1914–18', *Australasian Studies*, 17, No 2, Winter 2002, 74.

> it. This can best be done by following the history of one man who is the acknowledged leader of Sinn Fein in Australia. This man declared that 'he was a Sinn Feiner and was proud of the fact'. His name is Daniel Mannix and he is Archbishop of Melbourne and the head of the Roman Catholic Church in Victoria. Because he holds this position he is still at large in Australia. Had anyone else dared to say the things he has said, he would have been interned or deported long ago.[42]

The British Foreign Secretary, A.J. Balfour, advised the Australian Prime Minister of the day, W.M. Hughes, at the height of the conscription controversy that 'remonstrances' had twice been addressed to Mannix from Rome, albeit 'apparently with little or no effect'.[43] Cardinal Pietro Gasparri confirmed that 'repeated recommendations' had been made to the Archbishop, 'most especially those sent to him through the *Sacra Congregazione di Propaganda*.[44] Responding to reports of a suggestion by a troubled King George V at the height of the post–World War I Irish turmoil that Mannix might usefully be transferred from Melbourne to Rome, Cardinal Francis Gasquet reportedly retorted 'God forbid'.[45]

He was seen increasingly to be a source of discord, turning public opinion against Catholics and Catholics against one another, and causing ill feeling among the bishops. Even so, the costs of removing or reining in so popular an incumbent seemingly were judged to outweigh its advantages. If so, it was an excess of prudence or failure

42 Foreign Office: Legation, Vatican: General Correspondence. Correspondence Received I. Sinn Fein in Australia, 23 July 1918, TNA FO 380 17 1918, as quoted in Calderwood, 'A Question of Loyalty', 68.

43 Arthur J. Balfour. to William A. Hughes, 26 June 1918, Calwell Papers, as quoted in Kiernan, *Daniel Mannix and Ireland*, 122.

44 Cardinal Gasparri to Count J de Salis, 26 July 1918, Calwell Papers, as quoted in Kiernan, *Daniel Mannix and Ireland*, 124.

45 James Murtagh, Interview with the Hon Arthur Calwell, 1 February 1970. Murtagh Papers, Melbourne Diocesan Historical Commission.

of nerve that the Church would have recurrent cause to regret, not least in the turbulent decade immediately prior to his death in 1963.

Origins

He was born to Timothy and Ellen Mannix at Charleville in County Cork in 1864, as the first of eight children, three of whom died in infancy and a fourth from tuberculosis in early manhood. Timothy Mannix was a tenant farmer, whose 'Deerpark' holding increased over time from 100 to 135 acres.[46] He was well off relative to most of his neighbours and served on the Board of Guardians in nearby Kilmallock, and as a prominent local activist and office-bearer in the increasingly militant Irish Land League. He chaired the 1880 meeting, attended by 'not less than 10,000 persons', at which the League's Charleville Branch was formed, and was the Honorary Secretary for the gathering at nearby Michelstown later the same year, where a crowd of some 20,000 heard the League's founder, Michael Davitt, speak.[47]

He and his wife were ambitious for their children. Their education was encouraged to such effect that one of the future archbishop's brothers, Patrick, studied medicine and another, Michael, law, and their surviving sister, Mary, completed finishing school at a Paris convent. A reputedly happy home and a loving – albeit perhaps also domineering – mother endowed Mannix with resolute self-assurance, and a confidence in his capacity for sound judgement that at times

46 Title to the Mannix farm was finally secured for the family in 1903, through a loan that Daniel Mannix negotiated on its behalf through the Munster and Leinster Bank at Charleville. Document, Mannix to Michael Cagney, 3 February 1906, Cagney Papers. As quoted in Kiernan, *Daniel Mannix and Ireland*, 29.

47 *Cork Examiner* 19/4/1880, 27/9/1880, 11/10/1880, 17/11/1880, as quoted in Kiernan, *Daniel Mannix and Ireland*, 5–6.

was misplaced. In reality, the relationships within the household may have been less simple, and not necessarily for all the siblings as benign. Patrick Mannix in later life abandoned his faith to embrace rationalism, married a Protestant and is recalled as having in his Will perpetrated 'the typical 18th century Rationalist act of defiance and disbelief in resurrection, directing that his remains be cremated'.[48] The family farm passed to the remaining brother, Timothy Jnr, but failed financially, consequent on 'drink and mismanagement'.[49]

The daily routine for the young Daniel – 'buried in his books, but never to the point that, on returning home to an early evening meal, he did not play his part in the domestic economy of the family home' – was 'physically hard but satisfying': 'It meant a 5 o'clock rise, even in the rigorous Irish winter. As late as his 90s, Mannix recalled 'the ice which covered the buckets of water outside the house, the need to hurry over his evening meal so that he could herd and supervise the cows which his mother would milk, with himself lending a hand'.[50]

While shielded in part by his family's relatively comfortable circumstances, he was a witness at first hand to the suffering that prompted so massive and sustained an exodus of his fellow country-men in search of new homes and hopes, predominantly in the United States, Canada and Australia. Memories of the devastating 1845–1851 Famine were still raw and embittered. As a child, he would have had told to him how a Charleville unit fought with the Fenians in their abortive 1867 insurrection – would perhaps, as in the view of an at times overly excitable biographer, 'have thrilled to see in the local forge the pikes of the Fenian heroes used against the cavalry, and

---

48 Ebsworth, *Archbishop Mannix*, 7.

49 Griffin, 'Daniel Mannix', 399.

50 Santamaria, *Daniel Mannix*, 17.

heard no doubt imaginative accounts of how the pikemen fought, cutting with the keen-edged hatchet part of the pike the horseman's reins while wreaking vengeance on the rider with the long-stabbing blades'.[51]

As a sixteen-year-old schoolboy, he was present with his schoolmaster and classmates at the foundation by the Land League of its Charleville Branch, and attended its Michelstown rally. He was seventeen and still living at home when violent protests in the face of failing harvests, renewed fears of a return of the Great Hunger and a further wave of evictions prompted the enactment by the Irish Secretary of the day, W.E. Forster, of legislation – the 1881 Coercion Act – that suspended habeas corpus, banned meetings, authorised police to enter and search premises at any hour, authorised imprisonment on suspicion and filled the jails to overflowing. Three local farmers who were shot in an attempt by police to break up a proscribed Land League meeting in Michelstown in 1887 – reported widely at the time as the 'Michelstown Massacre' – may well have been family friends and known personally to him.

He was to recall in later life hearing from his father how 'almost every year' throughout the previous century had brought with it a new Coercion Act.[52] Incidents of so grim a character as the 'Michelstown Massacre' and the example of Timothy's nationalist sentiments and Land League affiliations were not lost on him. He 'learnt from his observation of the Land League agitation between 1870 and 1903 to integrate his politics and his religion'.[53] The focus of his hopes for Ireland and preferred means of achieving their fulfilment evolved

51 Ebsworth, *Archbishop Mannix*, 36

52 Ebsworth, *Archbishop Mannix*, 18.

53 Kiernan, *Daniel Mannix and Ireland*, 19.

and radicalised over time. He was a champion successively of land tenure reform, Home Rule and ultimately a passionately separatist and insurrectionary republicanism.

He entered the local parish school when he was six, and was a student successively at the Charleville Christian Brothers' school, the Kilfinane Latin School, the Charleville Latin School and finally St Colman's College in Fermoy, where he was awarded the scholarship that enabled him to study for the priesthood at Maynooth. His gratitude to his teachers was unreserved. Addressing a Melbourne audience in 1913, he recalled that 'I owe my early education to the Sisters of Mercy'.[54] An audience of Christian Brothers and their pupils later the same year was assured by him that 'There is a very special reason why I should feel at home with you, for, as you remind me, I am an old pupil of the Christian Brothers'.[55] The at times intemperate criticisms that he directed at government schools in the course of his episcopacy may have owed something to the fact that he had had no direct experience of them.

Maynooth

His academic prowess gained him repeated distinctions, and he served for a year as Maynooth's Head Prefect. Following his ordination as a priest in 1890 and a further year's postgraduate study, the college appointed him to its junior Chair of Logic, Metaphysics and Ethics. He became its Professor of Higher Philosophy in 1893, and the following year Professor of Moral Theology. He edited the Moral Theology section of the *Irish Ecclesiastical Review*, instigated the inception of the Maynooth Union of college alumni in 1895, and,

54 *Advocate*, 5/4/1913.

55 *Advocate*, 12/4/1913.

as the Union's inaugural secretary from 1896 to 1903, saw paid up membership increase to some 700 within two years of its inception.[56]

He was instrumental in broadening the Union's initial theological and philosophical preoccupations to encompass more pressing socio-economic concerns. Anticipative of future Distributist sympathies and convictions, his report to the 1897 Annual General Meeting – attended by some 250 priests and bishops[57] – recommended that topics for future discussion should include 'the co-operative movement and the priest's relation to it; the temperance movement ... the better housing of the poor ... the work-houses and their management; the nursing of the sick ... and a hundred such subjects'.[58]

His 1901 Maynooth Union paper 'Have We Solved the Land Problem in Ireland?' reads:

> I am tempted to think that England might be really a greater and more powerful nation today if she had not sacrificed her peasantry in order to push her manufactures. Already England has had to take anxious thought for her food supply in the event of war. She has reason to regret the strong, vigorous tillers of the fields, the strength of her armies in war, and the sires of a virile, healthy people.[59]

It was a foretaste of the distinctively agrarian preoccupations – in the view of some 'agrarian utopianism'[60] – to which many among his closer Distributist protégés and associates were to devote extended and at times disproportionate advocacy.

---

56 Kiernan, *Daniel Mannix and Ireland*, 24.

57 Kiernan, *Daniel Mannix and Ireland*, 24.

58 G. Brendain, 'Memories of Mgr Mannix', *Austral Light*, XIII, No 9, September 1912, 716.

59 Brendain, 'Memories of Mgr Mannix', 717.

60 Mark Finnane, *J.V. Barry: A Life* (Sydney, NSW: University of New South Wales Press, 2007) 185.

He was appointed Vice-President of Maynooth in June 1903, and elected to its presidency on the death of the incumbent, Dr Gargan, in October. His nine-year tenure of the office was notable in particular for the college's upgrading of its academic standards and acceptance as a Royal University of Ireland affiliate. It was now obligatory that students should gain a three-year liberal arts degree before proceeding to their priestly studies.

Less happily, his intense focus on lifting academic standards at Maynooth entailed a corresponding relegation of Irish language studies at the college from a compulsory to an elective status. Dissension arising from the changes resulted in an acrimonious breakdown of relations with the college's resident Irish language expert and advocate, Professor Michael O'Hickey, which culminated with O'Hickey's dismissal. O'Hickey then appealed to Rome. The case was referred to the Vatican's Rota canonical tribunal, where it stalled, suppurated and was still unresolved when he died in 1916, unreconciled and affirming to the last 'I withdraw nothing; I apologise for nothing'.[61]

The imbroglio earned Mannix the animosity of powerful figures within the nationalist movement, such as the Gaelic League's Patrick Pearse. Pearse – later to be executed for his part in the 1916 Easter Uprising – queried in the League's journal 'Are priests from the college of O'Growney to preach in the language of Queen Elizabeth from altars round which only *Gaedhilgeoiri* (Gaelic speakers) kneel?':

> With most Irishmen we had hoped much from Dr Mannix's energy, progressiveness, clear-sightedness and broad national

61 Michael P. O'Hickey, 'Statement Concerning the Dismissal of the Rev Dr O'Hickey from the Irish Chair of St Patrick's College, Maynooth, 15/12/1909', in P.E. MacPhinn, *Ant-Athair Miceal P O h-Iceadha* (Dublin: 1974) 232, as quoted in Kiernan, *Daniel Mannix and Ireland*, 95.

> sympathies. Can it be that where Irish Ireland had hoped to find a friend she has found an enemy?[62]

In calling into question the wisdom of O'Hickey's dismissal, the case also raised doubts as to Mannix's judgement in having allowed the deliberations to drag on so long without achieving a resolution, and perhaps offended members of the hierarchy whose sympathies were with O'Hickey, or who were embarrassed by the adverse publicity that his appeal attracted.

Their unease is seen by some to have been unconducive to his prospects for a local preferment. In particular, Dublin's influential Archbishop William Walsh – 'a champion of Irish language studies and close friend of O'Hickey' – is thought to have concluded from the O'Hickey affair that Mannix's outlook was 'too simplistic for Ireland approaching Home Rule where militant nationalism was overtaking the parliamentary movement' and that he 'would function better in Melbourne than in Ireland'.[63] Walsh was a conspicuous absentee from Mannix's consecration. In the view of Sir Shane Leslie, author of a notable early biography of Manning, and well known to Mannix, 'Dr Mannix was appointed to Melbourne to get rid of him'.[64] If so, Ireland's loss was Australia's gain, as – among other things – the vigorous advocacy by Melbourne's new archbishop of the Church's social teachings and ultimate endorsement of Distributism would so comprehensively attest.

---

62 Ebsworth, *Archbishop Mannix*, 85.

63 Kiernan, *Daniel Mannix and Ireland*, 64.

64 Ebsworth, *Archbishop Mannix*, 120–121.

Chapter 6

MANNIX: THE EPISCOPACY

Departure

The attainment by Maynooth of its status as an affiliate of the Royal University of Ireland marked 'the moment when Mannix was available for a different type of service to the Church to which he had subordinated all his abilities'.[1] His reputation had by then preceded him to Australia. He had had Carr to speak on Catholic education in Victoria for the Maynooth Union in 1898, and gained Moran's good opinion through his preparation at the Cardinal's request of papers – 'the riches to be found in the three volumes of transactions'[2] – for the three Australian Catholic Congresses that took place between 1900 and 1909. By the account of Moran's secretary and confidant, Msgr O'Haran, in 1917: 'Our late beloved Cardinal Moran said of Dr Mannix long before he came South that, in his opinion, Dr Mannix was destined to do great work for the Australian Church, for, added his Eminence, "he is a born leader of men"'.[3]

1 Santamaria, *Daniel Mannix*, 31.

2 *Advocate*, 3 August 1912.

3 *Advocate*, 8 December 1917.

With the concurrence of his senior diocesan priests and fellow bishops and Moran's blessing, Carr revisited Ireland in 1908 to inquire of the hierarchy whether Mannix might be considered for the position of Coadjutor Archbishop, with the right of succession in Melbourne. The Irish *Weekly Freeman* reported in August 1912 that the name of Maynooth's president had headed the list of nominees submitted by the Melbourne Chapter to the Holy See. The Vatican advised Mannix of his appointment on 6 October 1912 to seemingly general satisfaction, albeit also to the disappointment of well-wishers who had hoped to see him succeed Walsh as Archbishop of Dublin. Cardinal Michael Logue – like Walsh seen by some to have been unsympathetic to Mannix[4] – declared on the occasion of his consecration in an address perhaps not wholly devoid of irony, 'We are placing the Church in Australia under a deep debt of gratitude for exporting Mgr Mannix to it'.[5]

Mannix was a reluctant but acquiescent appointee. Severance at the age of forty-nine from family, friends, the familiar surroundings and routines of Maynooth and the hope of appointment to a senior Irish See such as Dublin or Armagh was as unforeseen as it was unwelcome to him. As he was to recall in 1920, 'he did not seek his position in Australia ... he was sent without being consulted'.[6] A key account of the period characterises him as having 'neither expected nor wanted an appointment outside Ireland', and seeing the posting to be 'unjust and wrong-headed'.[7] A close associate concludes that 'His deepest instincts were opposed to the final break with family and

4 Ebsworth, *Archbishop Mannix*, 120–121.

5 Brennan, Dr Mannix, 69.

6 *Advocate*, 25 May 1920; *Irish Independent*, 6 July 1920, as quoted in Kiernan, *Daniel Mannix and Ireland*, 94.

7 Kiernan, *Daniel Mannix and Ireland*, 66, 195.

country represented by the Melbourne appointment'.[8] 'It was a great sorrow and a great wrench', he told a predominantly Irish audience shortly after his arrival in his new diocese, 'to turn my face away from my own dear country and from my own kindred. A hundred bonds stronger than steel bound me to the dear old land from which many of you, like myself have come'.[9]

The Rector of the Irish College in Rome, Mgr O'Riordan, counselled him against acceptance on the grounds that there were more important things for him to do in Ireland.[10] He was reluctant to forego contributing to the reconstruction and revitalisation of Ireland that he expected to follow on the enactment of the Asquith government's Home Rule legislation. 'It was a hard – almost a cruel thing, humanely speaking – to ask me to leave the land of my birth at the present time', he recalled on the occasion of his welcome to the West Melbourne parish that was to be his new home, 'For, through all the years I can remember, the Irish people have been journeying, as it were, through the desert, and, at last, when the promised land of freedom is in sight, I am called by the Holy Father to leave my country and my people'.[11] Priestly loyalty and obedience prevailed upon him to agree, but not without uncertainty, grief and trepidation. Asked by an uncle whether he might not decline to take up the appointment, his response was peremptory: 'I'll do whatever the Pope says, and no more about it'.[12]

---

8 Santamaria, *Archbishop Mannix: His Contribution to the Art of Public Leadership in Australia*, 6.

9 *Advocate*, 29 March 1913.

10 Michael Gilchrist, *Wit and Wisdom: Daniel Mannix* (North Melbourne: Vic: Freedom Publishing, 2004) 10.

11 *Advocate*, 5 April 1913.

12 Recollections of a first cousin, Mrs Cagney of Meanus, Croom, County Limerick, as quoted in Santamaria, *Daniel Mannix*, 39.

And it may not have been wholly coincidental that the announcement of the appointment was followed by a flare-up of his recurrent bronchitis and an attack of pneumonia 'sufficiently serious to create anxiety and warrant the issue of medical bulletins', or that his initial reaction to the summer heat on his arrival in Australia was to wonder whether he might not be unlikely to survive other than briefly in so unfamiliar and inhospitable an environment.[13]

Melbourne

'I can remember', he acknowledged, 'driving about the streets of Adelaide and feeling the heat rising from the ground; and I said to myself (to nobody else of course): "I shall never be able to live in this country"'.[14] And conditions in Melbourne were no less oppressive. A woman bystander who witnessed his welcome in St Patrick's Cathedral in Melbourne told him years later that he had 'looked so sick she believed he would be dead in six months'.[15] The impression left on another of those present was to similar effect: 'He looked like a very sick man, like a consumptive. ... The general opinion of people at the time was that he would not live long'.[16]

Nor was it disappointment and indisposition alone that troubled him. By his own admission, he 'came out here untried and inexperienced ... knowing little about Australia and scarcely anything at all about Australians'.[17] Nothing in his previously cloistered academic experience had prepared him for the radically different and to

13 Santamaria, *Daniel Mannix*, 40.

14 *Advocate*, 16 June 1960.

15 Kiernan, *Daniel Mannix and Ireland*, 75.

16 Ebsworth, *Archbishop Mannix*, 114.

17 Ebsworth, *Archbishop Mannix*, 315, and *Advocate*, 20 May 1920.

him deeply unsettling setting and circumstances in which he now found himself, or the alacrity with which he was required to adapt to them and the expectations that were invested in him. Too crushing a burden of insufficiently examined Irish assumptions accompanied him.

The urgency he imparted to the State Aid issue may not have been wholly unrelated to an expectation or hope that his unwanted exile might be less protracted if the impasse over education could be overcome. As noted by the Irish historian Dermot Keogh, 'It is certain that he had not abandoned the idea of returning to an Irish see. ... His desire to minister again in Ireland was very much to the fore'.[18] It was only with his shunning by the Irish hierarchy in the course of his 1925 visit that reality finally dawned, with the realisation that 'Neither Irish church nor Irish state wanted him back' and whatever hopes of being translated back home he may have entertained had 'vanished completely'.[19]

In the view of a perceptive biographer, Niall Brennan – son of the prominent Scullin government minister Frank Brennan, and brought up in a household where Mannix was a frequent visitor – 'Mannix could not comprehend the notion of a sincere Protestant; he saw only the Church and its enemies'.[20] Others characterise him as having regarded hatred of Catholics by Protestants 'with their unfilled churches and babel of doctrines' as being inevitable; hence, he limited the character and quality of his intercourse with them to 'courtesy, never fraternisation' and declined to enter their churches.[21]

18 Dermot Keogh, 'Mannix, De Valera and Irish Nationalism' Part 2, *Australasian Catholic Record*, July 1988, 349.

19 Keogh, 'Mannix, De Valera and Irish Nationalism', 349.

20 Brennan, *Dr Mannix*, 83.

21 Griffin, 'Daniel Mannix', 402.

He too hastily and uncritically assumed communions other than his own to comprise as cohesive, oppressive and implacably anti-Catholic an ascendancy as in Ireland, Catholics to be as discriminated against as in Ireland, and the obsessively outspoken anti-Catholicism of fringe Protestant groups to be of a significance comparable to that of 'the traditional persecutors of the Church whom he had known so well back home in Ireland'.[22] He was unprepared for the lesser capacity of the Australian than the Irish Church to influence the political affiliations and voting intentions of its adherents, or the alarm and resistance to which attempting to do so would give rise in the wider community.

And there was more. His unfamiliarity with the state's history and institutions rendered him prone to avoidable and at times egregious errors of fact and interpretation that with greater patience and prudence he may not have perpetrated. References such as to Catholic children who accepted government school scholarships as 'little bribed renegades' and to the schools themselves as 'sinks of iniquity' were as unjust as they were unbecoming to him.[23] He was averse to the admission of error. Brennan concludes that 'The grand implication of all this, that Australia was, in its raffish way, a tolerant and not a bigoted society, eluded him altogether'.[24]

Controversy

A measure of his unease for his new surroundings was evident in an address in 1917. It reads:

---

22 Brennan, *Dr Mannix*, 78.

23 *Argus*, 20 October 1913, and Brennan, *Dr Mannix*, 89.

24 Brennan, *Dr Mannix*, 79.

> I do not remember that up to the time I came to Australia I ever took part in controversy of any sort or description. The reason for the change that has come over my habit of life must be that in the old countries I had never come into close official contact with people like some of those I have met since I came to Australia. Some of these people think because they can abuse me on six days of the week – I can get in a word only once a week or once a month – that in the end they will reduce me to silence. They are very much mistaken.[25]

Uncertainties and insecurities of so marked a magnitude engendered in him a pattern of pervasive over-compensation and exaggeration. Carr's biographer, Fr Thomas Boland, sees an outwardly unswerving public support for Mannix on Carr's part as having masked an inner discomfort with what he came to regard privately as his coadjutor's excesses. 'Mannix', he writes, 'fed the crowds who flocked to hear him, and in turn was nourished by their reaction. He was captive to his own cutting wit, and he did not measure the hurt that it did to those on whom he exercised it'.[26] O'Farrell in similar vein sees Mannix as having by his own admission 'tended to confront all situations with an acerbity, which if he might regret, he did not always suppress'.[27] Carr's nurse, Margaret Green, characterises Carr as having come to inquire consistently on the mornings following Mannix's Sunday addresses 'What did he say yesterday – anything outrageous?'.[28] Nor would Mannix himself necessarily have regarded such strictures as undeserved. Duhig's Coadjutor, Archbishop Patrick

---

25 *Advocate*, 14 April 1917.

26 Thomas P. Boland, *Thomas Carr: Archbishop of Melbourne* (St Lucia, Qld: University of Queensland Press, 1997) 377.

27 O'Farrell, *Catholic Church and Community in Australia*, 333.

28 James Murtagh, Interview with Father John O'Donnell, 5 May 1969, Murtagh Papers, Melbourne Diocesan Historical Commission.

O'Donnell, recalls him as regretting in later life that he had caused Carr 'much anxiety'.[29]

His surprise that his aggressive approach should have provoked responses in kind was itself surprising, and in part indicative of his unpreparedness for the onerous and unfamiliar responsibilities that had been thrust upon him. Disaffected, disorientated and physically debilitated – 'weakened in health and saddened in spirit'[30] – he committed prematurely to strategies that with more forethought and fewer distractions he may have seen to be imprudent, inflexible, ill-advised and leaving him with insufficient room for manoeuvre in the event of unforeseen contingencies.

By the time the magnitude of his miscalculation became apparent to him, major setbacks to his stated objectives, the Church's standing and the wellbeing of ordinary Catholics, had been incurred. By Brennan's account, 'An elderly lady looked back on it all and said: "He should have spent twelve months just soaking up the atmosphere". Another added: "He said too much too soon"'.[31]

State Aid

State Aid set the pattern to which the pursuit of his subsequent causes conformed. Logue had highlighted in his consecration address the expectation of Mannix that he would make achieving a just resolution of the State Aid impasse – in the view of some, 'the oldest, deepest, most poisonous debate in Australian history'[32] – his major priority:

29 O'Donnell to Murtagh, 1969, Murtagh Papers, Melbourne Diocesan Historical Commission.

30 Kiernan, *Daniel Mannix and Ireland*, 66.

31 Brennan, *Dr Mannix*, 85.

32 Graham Freudenberg, *A Certain Grandeur: Gough Whitlam in Politics* (South Melbourne, Vic: Macmillan, 1977) 24.

'The question of education was a great question at the present day, and his Eminence didn't believe that within the four seas of Ireland or the British Empire an ecclesiastic existed who was better prepared and qualified for that great work'.[33]

Carr's intentions were unambiguous. He had chosen Mannix for his Co-adjutor 'as one experienced in education and aggressive in achievement'.[34] Melbourne's leading Catholic layman of the day, Dr A.L. Kenny, now emphasised, in welcoming Mannix on behalf of the laity, 'the cruel and unjust discrimination against Catholics in Australia in the denial of aid to their schools'.[35] His address continued 'You have been entrusted with responsibilities by the British government in educational matters. We express the hope that you will do something about our educational problems here'.[36]

The initial endeavour by the Australian colonies to extend access to education through the provision of subsidies to denominational schools on specified conditions is summed up by a key labour movement historian as having 'pleased nobody, neither the Protestant Ascendancy, the emerging secular humanism, nor the Catholic hierarchy'.[37] Faced in the 1860s and 1870s with the inability of the respective communions to agree on an acceptable formula for moving ahead, the governments of the day reacted with the enactment of legislation for the establishment of government schools on the principle that education should be 'free, compulsory and secular'.

The new measures in their turn were condemned by the Church in terms that were not notably moderate or conciliatory. An 1879

---

33 O'Farrell, *Catholic Church and Community in Australia*, 303.

34 Boland, *Thomas Carr: Archbishop of Melbourne*, 370.

35 Ebsworth, *Archbishop Mannix*, 114.

36 Brennan, *Dr Mannix*, 77.

37 Freudenberg, *A Certain Grandeur*, 24.

pastoral letter over the signatures of the Archbishop Vaughan and NSW bishops reads:

> Education without Christianity is impossible: you may call it instruction, filling the mind with a certain quantity of secular knowledge, but you cannot dignify it with the name of education; for religion is an essential part of education; and to divorce religion or Christianity from education is to return to paganism and reject the Gospel of Jesus Christ. Thus it is that the Church condemns, with marked emphasis, those schools, and that method of teaching in which the religious is divorced from the secular. She knows that instruction is not education and that a system of national training from which Christianity is banished is a system of practical paganism, which leads to corruption of morals and loss of faith, to national effeminacy and dishonour. ... We condemn them, first, because they contravene the first principles of the Christian religion; and secondly, because they are seed-beds of future immorality, infidelity, and lawlessness, being calculated to debase the standard of human excellence and to corrupt the political, social and individual life of the citizens.[38]

In the event, confusing the merits of the case for State Aid with so vituperative a vilification of the schools that catered for the overwhelming majority of the community's children – and by implication the one in every four of their teachers who were Catholics[39] – exacerbated the resistance it was intended to overcome.

Mannix out-Vaughaned Vaughan. His challenge and call to arms on the issue were set out in a response to his welcome in the Cathedral in 1913, in an address that – uncharacteristically and perhaps uniquely – he delivered from a prepared text. 'From the Catholic standpoint',

---

38 Roger B. Vaughan, *Pastorals and Speeches on Education* (Sydney, NSW: Edward F. Flanagan, 1879) 4, 11.

39 O'Farrell, *Catholic Church and Community in Australia*, 187.

it reads, the unequal treatment meted out to them in the schools is 'as far as I can judge, the one great stain upon the statute books of this free and progressive land':

> Long before he had ever thought that the education question of Australia would have for him the practical interest that it had today, he had wondered that a problem that had been solved, with greater or less success, in many of the old countries, had found no satisfactory solution – no attempt even at a solution – in any of the States of this great democratic land, in which freedom and fair play for every good citizen are claimed to be the very life breath of the Constitution ... Catholics did not expect the impossible. They only wanted fair play from any statesman or party who would come out to meet them and treat with them on the borderland of reason and just concession.[40]

The address – characterised variously as his 'manifesto', 'the most remarkable speech of his career' and 'this harbinger of greater barrages to come'[41] – signalled his rejection of Establishment overtures for conciliation and co-operation as reflected in *The Argus*, to the effect that:

> It is not only within his own communion that the ripe scholarship and rich educational experience of a man like Dr Mannix, the new Roman Catholic Coadjutor Archbishop of Melbourne, are understood and appreciated. His attainments, apart from all other considerations, must make him a welcome addition to the intellectual life of Victoria. He comes here with an established reputation, since he has not only been the head of a great college for the training of Roman Catholic clergy, but also a member of

40 *Advocate,* 29 March 1913. Mannix habitually spoke *extempore*, and destroyed his correspondence in an act that Carr's biographer, Fr T.P. Boland, characterises as 'criminal'. Thomas P. Boland, 'The Growth of Australian Catholic Historiography' in *Journal of the Australian Catholic Historical Society*, January 2006. Accessed 21/6/2013 at htpp://www.accessmylibrary.com/coms2/summary_0286-33678441_ITM.

41 Kiernan, *Daniel Mannix and Ireland*, 76–77, and Brennan, *Dr Mannix*, 78.

> University Governing Bodies in Ireland. It will be to the public's advantage if his ability and knowledge can be made available in all possible ways for the whole instead of being restricted to the service of one section alone.[42]

It was an opening whose loss he may on reflection have regretted. In the view of some 'That a newly-arrived Catholic archbishop should devote himself to "National Education in the highest and widest sense of the term", granted the actual condition of Catholic schools in 1913, could only have been regarded as an essay in fantasy or cynicism'.[43] But was it necessarily so intended? And might not it more usefully have been taken at its face value and explored? *The Argus* for its part was in no doubt as to the downside. Its commentary continued:

> From the addresses presented to him on Sunday, and his own reply to them, it is to be feared that the question of separate schools for primary education may prove an obstacle to his cooperating as fully as he might in work outside exclusively Roman Catholic institutions. If that be the case, it will, we believe, be a loss to the State and his own Church.[44]

The Catholic Federation

Mannix would have none of it. By his own account, 'he had not come here to court popularity'.[45] And a predominantly lay ally amenable to his outlook and approach was at hand, in the Australian Catholic Federation. The Federation's inception preceded his arrival, but he embraced it and for a time made it all but his own. Its office-bearers

---

42 *Argus*, 27 March 1913.

43 Santamaria, *Daniel Mannix*, 46–47.

44 *Argus*, 27 March 1913.

45 *Advocate*, 17 March 1917.

had at the time of his appointment written congratulating him on the brief for the securing of State Aid with which he had so comprehensively been entrusted. He had replied in terms pregnant with the prospect of future turmoil: 'I hope to have later on many opportunities of proving my whole-hearted sympathy with the objects for which the Federation has been established, and of helping to realise those objectives according to the measure of my ability'.[46]

The Federation's paramount objective was stated as being justice for Catholic schools and relief for Catholics from double taxation. As well, its Constitution specified it to be for 'the mutual support and advancement of Catholic societies; the dissemination of Catholic literature; the safeguarding of Catholic education; the expression of Catholic opinion on social and public questions affecting Catholic interests'. It was to stand also 'for the Christian life of the nation; for the proper observance of Sunday; for the Christian education of youth; for the repression of intemperance; for the sanctity and indissolubility of Christian marriage; and for the suppression of indecent and infidel literature'.[47] The motto proposed for it was 'In Things Essential, Unity; in All Things Charity'. Its manifesto reads:

> Why should not we be one in organization? Why should not Catholics march to their glorious goal of human betterment with the ordered steps of a disciplined regiment rather than with the hustling and jostling of a disorganised multitude? ... People of one mind must unite their strength or go under.[48]

Its strategy for securing State Aid was put bluntly by Dr Maurice O'Reilly, President of St Stanislaus College in Bathurst and seen

46 Ebsworth, *Archbishop Mannix*, 100.

47 *Advocate*, 4 November 1911.

48 O'Farrell, *Catholic Church and Community in Australia*, 187, 300.

widely as the Federation's 'most spectacular public advocate'. O'Reilly stated in 1913 that, for the first time in at least twelve years, he would not be voting Labor:

> I have not the control of any vote except my own, but I am in the market every time. If I approach two political candidates, and one man gives me better terms than the other does, then I will make a deal with the man who will give me better terms, and to that extent I am on the market. ... You might say to me, then, I am a deserter from the cause of Labor. I say 'No, I am not because Labor, as I take it, must be built upon a proper idea of true democracy'. I won't believe that any man who says 'No' to the justice of the moderate demands made by the Catholics is a friend of Labor.[49]

At the 1913 elections in NSW and again the following year in Victoria, Catholic voters were urged to vote selectively for ALP candidates who undertook to support State Aid, and against those who opposed it. When the election outcomes in both states showed the Federation's estimates of the willingness of Catholic voters to detach themselves from their ALP affiliations at its behest to have been mistaken, new tactics were adopted. A Catholic Workers' Association was established to achieve through penetration and permeation of the party the support for State Aid that external pressure had so signally failed to deliver, but with no greater success.

The ALP leadership of the day was not for turning. While affirming his strong belief in religious education, the staunchly Catholic future Prime Minister, James Scullin, opposed committing the party to the provision of State Aid, on the grounds that it would 'entirely disrupt the Labour Movement' and 'divide men and women

---

49 H.V. Evatt, *Australian Labour Leader: The Story of W.A. Holman and the Labour Movement* (Sydney, NSW: Angus and Robertson, 1945) 332.

who are otherwise agreed on economic principles which have been a greater financial gain to Catholic workers than twenty such grants as is being asked would be'.[50] It was unsurprising that the difference of opinion should have arisen. The issue was one of what properly was due to Caesar and what to God.

Mannix was at the forefront of the agitation throughout, speaking out in support of the Federation and the Association and rallying and reassuring their leaders in the face of their setbacks and disappointments. His sentiments prior to the Victorian elections echoed and amplified those of O'Reilly in NSW. 'People', he urged, 'especially if they are in a minority, never got anything by taking things quietly. They could not always turn the other cheek'. The General Election, in his view, would be the time for the Federation 'to take its turn at twisting the screw'.[51] All Catholic eyes were at present on Victoria, 'where, for the first time in our history, the anti-Catholic candidate is being really fought by Catholics, and where even a Labour ticket, wildly flourished, will not save him'.[52]

Subsequent to the 1913 and 1914 electoral setbacks, he warned repeatedly that Catholic Labor men should 'bestir themselves to save the Labor Party from disaster'. The Catholic Church, he asserted, 'was an organization which, in the past, whenever religion was threatened or conscience violated, had supported, and, if need be, selected, candidates for Parliament, and he could tell the Political Labour Conference that in similar circumstances in the future it would do the same again'.[53] Catholics did not want war either in state

---

50 Robertson, *J.H. Scullin*, 40.

51 *Advocate*, 25 October 1913.

52 O'Farrell, *Catholic Church and Community in Australia*, 312.

53 O'Farrell, *Catholic Church and Community in Australia*, 313.

or in federal politics, but 'if any State party made war upon them they would leave no stone unturned to defeat that party everywhere it showed itself'.[54] Until the Education Act was so amended as to relieve Catholics of the unjust and intolerable education burden which they now bore, there would never be 'an election in Victoria in which the Federation will not do its utmost to oppose and defeat the enemies of justice and fair play'.[55]

It was not to be. The campaign culminated with the establishment by the Catholic Federation in NSW in 1919 of the all but confessional Democratic Party, and its crushing defeat at the 1920 and 1922 state elections. The outcome was an unprecedented upsurge of sectarian sentiment that setbacks to Home Rule in Ireland and controversies over the war and conscription shortly conflated and compounded, to disastrous effect.

Ireland

The deferral by the Asquith government of Home Rule for Ireland at the outset of the war in turn saddened and angered Mannix, who had maintained his faith in the government's promises, in the face frequently of arguments to the contrary on the part of his possibly more hard-headed nationalist compatriots. Home Rule legislation enacted by the Asquith government in 1911 was challenged and subverted, most notably by the prominent Tory MPs Edward Carson and F.E. Smith, who incited opposition to it within Ulster and the British Army around the slogan 'Ulster Will Fight and Ulster Will Be Right'. Their plainly seditious campaign culminated with the 'Curragh Mutiny', whereby army officers threatened to resign their

54 *Catholic Press*, 5 May 1915.

55 *Advocate*, 5 December 1913.

commissions rather than enforce the legislation and drilled volunteers in preparation for the anticipated hostilities. At the outbreak of war with Germany, the government caved into its Ulster adversaries, with the announcement that the implementation of the legislation would be deferred for the duration of the conflict. Carson shortly became a member of the War Cabinet. Smith retained the status in public life that in due course also brought about his elevation to the ministry and the peerage, and the mutinous commanders were spared the court martials that their conduct had so richly merited.

While not overtly opposing the war, Mannix was critical of the justifications offered for it and their inconsistencies. If its purpose was to defend the freedom of small nations such as Belgium, why should not freedom be granted equally to Ireland – was it wrong 'to suggest that when England claims to be fighting for Belgium and other small nations, that she should put her own house in order and do justice to Ireland?'.[56] Was not Ireland in reality 'a little Belgium'? Was not the war less a struggle for ideals than in reality what he characterised to widespread public outrage and denunciation as 'just an ordinary trade war?'.[57] When in 1916 the leaders of Sinn Fein's 'Easter Uprising' were summarily executed, he demanded to know in what respect theirs had been a greater treason than that of the 'Curragh Mutineers'. And by what travesty of justice had either the conspirators not been similarly punished, or the lives of the Easter rebels spared?

Conscription

Meanwhile, the fracas over the 1916 and 1917 conscription referenda deepened his disaffection. As over State Aid and Ireland, he was

56 *Advocate*, 17 March 1917.

57 *Advocate*, 3 February 1913.

in the forefront of the agitation against conscription and its foremost advocate in the Prime Minister of the day, W.M. Hughes. Campaigning initially for the 'No' case in 1916, his focus was on mobilising opposition among Catholics, primarily through addresses at Catholic gatherings that were disseminated widely by his diocesan weeklies, *The Advocate* and *The Tribune* and picked up from them by their Church counterparts in other states. Conscription, he argued, was 'a hateful thing' and 'almost certain to bring evil in its train'. Australians were 'a peace-loving people' who would 'not easily give conscription a foothold'.[58]

Following Hughes's defeat at the 1916 referendum, he and his fellow pro-conscription MPs were expelled by the ALP for their perceived disloyalty and disregard for the party's policy and rules, but carried on as a National Labor government with Liberal Party support, until their re-election in 1917 and merger with the Liberals in the newly formed National Party. The Split in Labor's ranks effectively enabled anti-Labor governments to retain office under the National Party banner until their defeat by Scullin in 1929, and thereafter as the United Australia Party from 1932 until 1941. And the outcome for the ALP at the state level was no less disadvantageous, with South Australia's Vaughan Labor government becoming the Vaughan anti-Labor government, NSW's Labor Premier Holman forming an anti-Labor Ministry and the Tasmanian Labor Premier's defection ushering in seven-and-a-half years of anti-Labor rule.

Voters at the elections subsequent to the government's referendum defeat were warned by Mannix that returning it to office would result in the question being re-introduced. There was 'but one issue at the

58 *Advocate*, 23 September 1919.

coming election' and that was conscription: 'Those who had failed in October want to try again'.[59] In his view, 'the two parties were simply and solely conscriptionists and anti-conscriptionists'. Anybody who denied it was 'only attempting to throw dust in the eyes of the Australian people', and, in his judgement, every man who voted for Mr Hughes was 'voting for another referendum of the people of Australia on conscription'.[60] He was opposed to conscription and would vote against another referendum, but it was his intention also to vote against the Prime Minister at the present election 'in order to prevent, if I can, another referendum'.[61]

Faced in the aftermath of the government's re-election with the foreseen re-submission by Hughes of the question, he assumed a national profile and a broader appeal as much to Protestant as to Catholic voters, that again contributed significantly to the government's failure to achieve its intended outcome. He was, he said, doing his 'humble part to bring Catholics and Protestants together to defend Australia's freedom'.[62] The greatest enemies of Australia had been 'those who introduced Conscription in the first place, and plunged Australia into the turmoil of a referendum on that question'.[63] The question of conscription was 'not a Catholic question, nor an Irish nor an English question', but 'purely and simply an Australian question'.[64] On the conscription issue, the people were asked to put the Empire first and Australia second. He would ask

59 *Advocate*, 28 April 1917.

60 *Argus*, 23 April 1917.

61 *Argus*, 23 April 1917.

62 Cyril Bryan, *Archbishop Mannix: Champion of Australian Democracy* (Melbourne, Vic: 1918) 159.

63 As quoted in Brady, *Dr Mannix*, 78

64 Bryan, *Archbishop Mannix*, 153.

them to put Australia first and the Empire second'.[65] In the event, the government's proposal was again defeated.

'A Prisoner of War'

With the cessation of hostilities in 1918, Ireland reasserted its claim on his attention. The bloody repression of Irish resistance at the hands of the Lloyd George government and its 'Black and Tan' irregulars heightened his disaffection. In addresses overseas in 1921 and again in 1925 he electrified predominantly Irish audiences with his denunciations of British misrule. 'Ireland', he told an audience in Omaha, Nebraska, in 1921 'is ruled by an alien nation':

> When your fathers fought it was against England. Ireland has the same grievance against the same enemy only ten times greater. I hope Ireland will make a fight equally successful. England was your enemy; she is your enemy today; she will be your enemy for all time. England is one of the greatest hypocrites in the world. She pretended to be your friend in the war. Now the war is over she tells you to mind your own business.[66]

Removed under arrest from the vessel carrying him to Ireland by British authorities fearful that his appearance there 'would assuredly have resulted in increased bloodshed', he remonstrated in an address at Harrogate that he was by profession a man of peace, but the British Government had made him 'a prisoner of war': 'Since the Jutland battle the British navy had not scored a success comparable to the capture of the Archbishop of Melbourne without the loss of a single British sailor. ... When a little while more has passed I venture to

65 *Argus*, 12 November 1917.

66 *The Times*, 16 July 1920; *Tablet*, 24 July 1920. As quoted in Kiernan, *Daniel Mannix and Ireland*, 148.

think that they will come to regret, and very deeply, the day they captured me off the coast of Ireland'.[67]

In the aftermath of the 1921 Anglo-Irish Treaty's conferral of dominion status on Ireland – albeit an Ireland from which Ulster had been excised – he alone among the bishops sided with Eamon de Valera's Sinn Fein republican insurgents against the nascent Free State government, in the civil war that divided the nationalist movement and pitted its adherents against one another. His stand placed him on a collision course with the Irish hierarchy, whose members had issued a Pastoral Letter denouncing the insurgency.

> ... a section of the community, refusing to acknowledge the Government set up by the nation, have chosen to attack their own country as if she were a foreign power ... they carry on what they call a war, but, which, in the absence of any legitimate authority to justify it, is morally only a system of murder and assassination ... killing in an unjust war is as much murder before God as if there were no war ... All those who, in contravention of this teaching, participate in such crimes are guilty of the gravest sins, and may not be absolved in Confession, nor admitted to Holy Communion, if they purpose to persevere in such evil purposes. ... We, each in his own diocese, hereby forbid, under great pain of suspension ipso facto, reserved to the Ordinary, any priest to advocate or encourage this revolt.[68]

Mannix was unmoved. His Sinn Fein affiliations were now open and unapologetic. Not only was he by his own admission a Sinn Feiner, but so also in his opinion was 'Every Australian worthy of

67 *Irish Independent*, 16 August 1920. As quoted in Kiernan, *Daniel Mannix and Ireland*, 147.

68 Michael, Cardinal Logue, 1922, *Pastoral Letter*, 3–7, as quoted in Keirnan, *Daniel Mannix and Ireland*, 188–189.

the name ... an Australian Sinn Feiner.'[69] He would not, he told audiences in the course of his controversial visit to Ireland in 1925, have signed the Treaty and he 'sided with de Valera in his stand for full freedom'.

Mistrust and Mutual Antipathy

Even the defeat of conscription proved to have been a Pyrrhic victory. Partisan or sectarian as may have been much of the denigration of Mannix, it in no way exaggerated or misrepresented the hostility towards him on the part of many – perhaps most – within the community who were 'neither bigots nor normally opposed to others practising whatever religious observances they wished', but whom his aggressive politicisation of the Church over State Aid, the war, conscription and Ireland had deeply affronted and alarmed.[70] The mistrust and mutual antipathy within a society divided predominantly along lines of faith was palpable:

> The feeling on both sides of the prolonged warfare between the Protestant and Catholic forces in Melbourne crept unpublicised, but never unfelt, into Federal and State government departments, into board rooms, into Trade Union councils, into the media of mass publicity. Like an invisible, undiagnosed cancer, it ate into the communal life and development of the Melbourne community, with repercussions throughout the land.[71]

Brennan's account captures the sour flavour of the times: '"You could not get a job without being asked your religion", a contemporary

69 *Catholic Bulletin*, 1921, XI, No 37, as quoted in Kiernan, *Daniel Mannix and Ireland*, 160; *Advocate*, 1 December 1921.

70 Rohan Rivett, *Australian Citizen: Herbert Brookes 1867–1963* (Carlton Vic: Melbourne University Press, 1965) 69.

71 Rivett, *Australian Citizen*, 373.

said. "You could see it in the newspapers", said another – "Prot only need apply"'.[72] The young lawyer and future anti-Labor prime minister, Robert Menzies, characterised Mannix as a 'cunning, sinister ... national menace'.[73]

Immoderation had the upper hand, as the example of the prominent Deakinite Liberal and influential businessman, Herbert Brookes, so amply attests. Brookes – son-in-law of the former Prime Minister Alfred Deakin and by his biographer's account initially an undogmatic Anglican and 'deeply Christian, but no churchgoer' – saw himself as having been provoked 'to devote himself to the work of defending the Loyalist and Protestant creed from what he now conceived to be a frontal challenge from Sinn Feinism within the Roman Catholic Church in Melbourne as led by Dr Mannix'.[74] An entry from his diary in 1918 reads: 'Every thing we hold dear for our children's sakes is at stake. The genius of England, Scotland and Wales for freedom, justice and fair play is challenged, is endangered. If we want to assure it for our children and our children's children it can only be at the price of sleepless nights and eternal vigilance'.[75]

The Citizens' Loyalist Committee – later the Loyalist League – for whose foundation the same year he was largely responsible waged through its journal *The Vigilant* well into the 1950s 'an unceasing and unrelenting campaign of denunciation, exposure and hostility against the Archbishop, his principal aides and supporters and such wealthy and colourful associates as John Wren': 'It fastened onto all the most controversial and anti-Protestant statements by Catholic

72 Brennan, *Dr Mannix*, 85.

73 As quoted in Michael Gilchrist, *Daniel Mannix: Priest and Patriot* (Melbourne, Vic: Dove Communications, 1982) 49.

74 Rivett, *Australian Citizen*, 69.

75 Rivett, *Australian Citizen*, 69–71.

spokesmen inside and outside Australia. It publicised, to men who had an assured audience every Sunday, every action of Dr Mannix or his Church which in the view of *The Vigilant*, could damage Australia or the British Empire'.[76]

The Catholic Federation, the Catholic Workers' Association and the Democratic Party had faded away, but their legacy of suspicion survived them. An ALP shattered, squabbling and impotent in the aftermath of the defection of Hughes and his conscriptionist followers was incapable – even if it had been so inclined – of fulfilling the hopes that Mannix had invested in it. State Aid was no closer to being achieved than at the time of his arrival. The unity and solidarity of the Catholic community is held by some to have been reinforced, but to what if any degree had they previously been deficient? Was the supposed gain a solution in search of a problem? Catholic representation had doubled among Labor MPs from 25 to 50 per cent while remaining static at around 25 per cent of the overall population, but to what advantage?[77] And what seeds of future miscalculation had been planted? And at what cost?

An Uneasy Standoff

Tensions of such intensity as Mannix's mass rallies and the inception of Brookes's Loyalist Committee so nakedly exposed could not be sustained indefinitely. Confrontation was replaced shortly by an uneasy standoff – in the eyes of some 'the institutionalising of the Catholic–Protestant division'[78] – that persisted into the 1950s. The

---

76 Rivett, *Australian Citizen*, 71.

77 Robert Murray, *The Split: Australian Labor in the Fifties* (Melbourne, Vic: Cheshire, 1970) 26.

78 O'Farrell, *Catholic Church and Community in Australia*, 352.

point of mutual exhaustion was marked with the failure of the attempt by the conservative NSW government in 1925 to outlaw Church constraints on marriages between non-Catholics and Catholics. Archbishop Kelly remarked in the aftermath of the final furore, 'It is all over now. Let us go ahead building our schools and with the marriage laws of our Church'.[79]

Ireland's cause too had forfeited much of its ardour in the face of the falling out of the nationalists with one another and the onset of the civil war. Bathurst's Dr O'Reilly may have expressed the sentiments of many when he wrote in 1927, 'As to poor old Ireland and how she stands, like most Irishmen abroad, I can hardly pretend to be interested. Possibly I had idealised too much and have thus made more painful than needs be the inevitable disillusion'.[80] 'I am completely disillusioned', mourned Archbishop Barry, 'This is not the Ireland of my youth and my dreams'.[81]

'Peace reigned', O'Farrell concludes, 'but it was a peace of exhaustion and of segregation':

> Protestants had become convinced that Catholics were, in Herbert Moran's vivid phrase, 'a breed apart, fire-branded like travelling stock in a strange country', suspect and menacing. Catholics believed that Protestants were hostile bigots determined to exclude and demean them. Social as well as religious segregation was an arrangement satisfactory to both parties.[82]

By Brennan's account, 'Had Mannix gone to his eternal reward in 1913, he would have been written off as a prelate of little consequence

79 O'Farrell, *Catholic Church and Community in Australia*, 352.

80 O'Farrell, *Catholic Church and Community in Australia*, 345.

81 O'Farrell, *Catholic Church and Community in Australia*, 346.

82 O'Farrell, *Catholic Church and Community in Australia*, 352.

and less taste'.[83] An assessment of his episcopate at any stage prior to the Great Depression would have had little reason to be more affirmative. In taking up more causes than his political capital could support, he had achieved unqualified success in none of them. His strategies were in tatters, and his hopes largely reduced to ashes. Even so, adversity could also give rise to opportunity, as new allies and initiatives in the struggle to give effect to the Church's social teachings would so shortly demonstrate. The coming of age of the lay social apostolate – the flowering of Catholic Action as properly so understood, through which he was shortly to meet the young Francis Kevin Heathcote Maher, together with the younger still Bartholomew Augustine Santamaria – was at hand.

83 Brennan, *Dr Mannix*, 85.

Frank Maher
(Melbourne Diocesan Historical Commission)

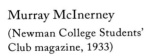

Murray McInerney
(Newman College Students' Club magazine, 1933)

Gerard Heffey

(Courtesy of Peter Heffey and Marilyn Puglesi (Heffey))

Denys Jackson

(Melbourne Diocesan Historical Commission)

Kevin T. Kelly,
University of Melbourne,
9 April 1932
(Courtesy of the Kelly family)

Kevin T. Kelly, R.A.N.V.R. and Mr John Ginnane, LLb, Melbourne, circa 1942–1943. Kelly and Ginnane compiled *The Catholic Worker* magazine's *Design for Democrats: The Autobiography of a Free Journal by 25 Men*.
(Courtesy of the Kelly family)

Early members of the Campion Society on a walk, circa 1934.
Left to right: Fr William Hackett S.J., Kevin T. Kelly, Ken Mitchell, Frank K. Maher, William Knowles; and in the foreground, Arthur Adams.
(Courtesy of the Kelly family)

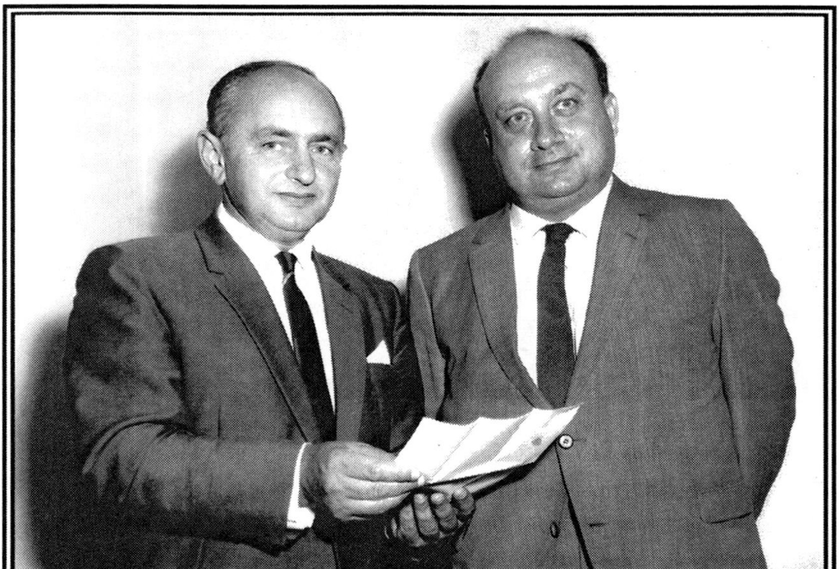

B.A. Santamaria and Frank Knopfelmacher
(*Santamaria: A Most Unusual Man* by Gerard Henderson, courtesy of the author)

Ted Long
(Courtesy of the Long family)

Frank McCann
(Melbourne Diocesan Historical Commission)

Leon Magree
(Courtesy of the Magree family)

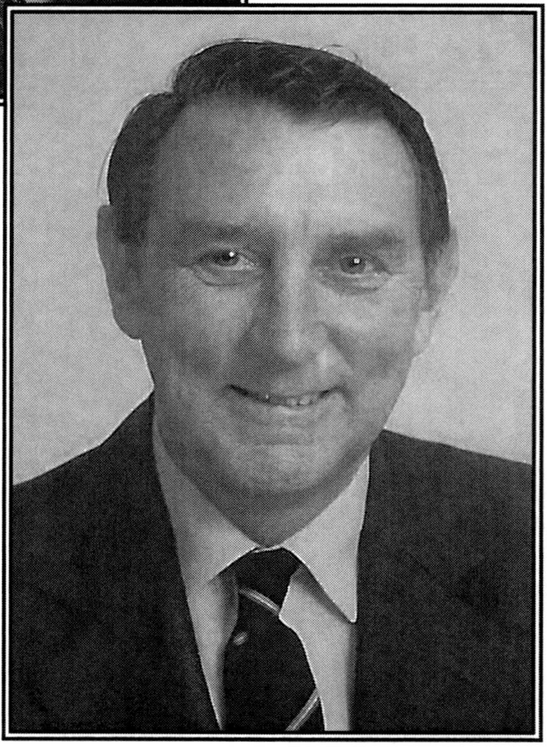

Bob Maybury
(Courtesy of the Maybury family)

Opening of the Y.C.W. Trading Co-operative offices and show room in A'Beckett Street, Melbourne, 27 July 1960.
Left to right: Archbishop Justin Simonds, Fr Kevin Twomey, Melbourne City Councillor, Ted Long, Arthur Carter.
(Courtesy of the Magree family)

The Y.C.W. Trading Co-operative Store
(Australian Credit Union Archives)

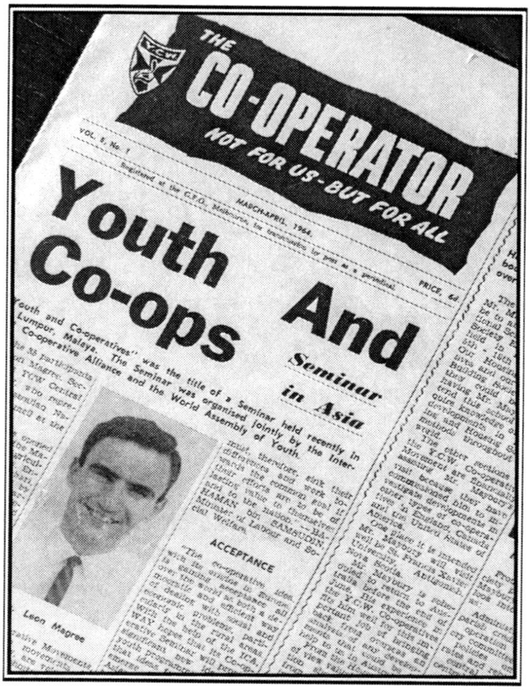

The Y.C.W. Co-operative Trading Society magazine *The Co-operator*, March–April 1964
(Courtesy of the Magree family)

Archbishop Mannix congratulates Ted Long and Frank McCann on the Y.C.W. Co-operative Trading Society store project.
(Courtesy of the Puglesi family)

Ninth Annual Meeting of the Association of Catholic Co-operative Credit Societies, 1966. Left to right: David Manjiviona, John Bredhauer, John Cooney, Arthur Otis, Leon Magree, Tom Stubbs, Arthur Carter, Vin Barca.
(Australian Credit Union Archives)

Attendees at the annual Victorian Credit Co-operatives Association Training School, Warburton, 27 March 1971.
(Australian Credit Union Archives)

Arizmendiarrieta: The Republican soldier prior to his imprisonment and intended execution by Franco's Nationalist forces in 1937.
(*TUlankide*)

Arizmendiarrieta: The young priest on his arrival in Mondragón, 21 April 1941.
(Arizmendiarrieta Kristau Fundazioa)

Arizmendiarrieta: Inspiration, guide and mentor of the Mondragón Co-operatives.
(Collage by John Best, central image courtesy *TUlankide*)

Industrial democracy in action: worker-owners in session at the Mondragón Co-operatives Congress.
(*TUlankide*)

Chapter 7

FRANK MAHER AND THE CAMPION SOCIETY

Hard Times

The onset of the Great Depression in 1929 and the downfall in 1932 of Australia's first government to be headed by a Catholic Prime Minister, James Scullin, and with Catholic majorities both in the Cabinet and among its MPs revived and intensified Mannix's wartime antipathy towards Capitalism and enhanced his Distributist sympathies, while at the same time diminishing such confidence as he may have retained in the capacity of the ALP and the party system to bring about significant change. The effect was to render him more open to the nascent lay activism among elements of the new generation of Catholic graduates whose education and formation he had so comprehensively encouraged and nurtured.

The outcome was the foundation of the Campion Society in 1931 and in 1938 of the Australian National Secretariat for Catholic Action (ANSCA). Mannix embraced the Campions as 'the flower and fruit of the Australian Catholic school system' and secured the adoption by the Bishops of their proposal for the Secretariat.[1] A key

1 Gerard Henderson, *Mr Santamaria and the Bishops* (Sydney, NSW: Hale and Iremonger, 1982) 11.

assessment of the significance of the society by its historian, Colin Jory, reads:

> For some years, from 1931 to 1938, it exerted an influence unparalleled by that of any other Catholic lay association in Australian history. Indeed, it is doubtful if anywhere in the world there existed an entirely lay-led organization which could boast a comparable record of achievement.[2]

The prominent UK-based Australian layman and publisher, Frank Sheed, affirmed to similar effect at a Campion Society dinner that he 'was aware that he was addressing the like of whom did not exist in any other part of the world'.[3] So largely was ANSCA staffed by society members in both paid and voluntary capacities that 'for some time the distinction between the two bodies was merely nominal'.[4]

Events and circumstances at the point of the society's inception were unconducive to passivity or inactivity. Scullin and his ministers were in office, but effectively powerless to properly exercise their prerogatives or discharge their responsibilities. A hostile Senate and implacably obstructionist financial institutions frustrated their every move:

> They were bound and gagged: the federal ALP government couldn't borrow money, they couldn't control monetary policy and they couldn't provide money for the unemployed. As things stood, they were powerless to mitigate, let along halt, the Depression.[5]

---

2 Colin H. Jory, *The Campion Society and Catholic Social Militancy in Australia 1929–1939* (Sydney, NSW: Harpham, 1986) 121.

3 Gerard Heffey, *Campion Reflections* (Unpublished memoir, 1990, Bruce Duncan Papers) 19.

4 Jory, *The Campion Society*, 93.

5 Ross Fitzgerald, *'Red Ted': The Life of E.G. Theodore* (St Lucia, Qld: University of Queensland Press, 1994) 239.

Within days of the ALP's election triumph in October 1929, the Wall Street Crash had ushered in the Depression. By Christmas, unemployment had risen by a third, to 12.9 per cent.[6] At its peak in 1931–32, 35 per cent of all wage and salary earners were unemployed.[7] Those hardest hit were the unskilled workers who could least afford it. Relief measures were meagre in the extreme or unavailable. Dole payments were disbursed in the form of food or 'rations' tickets. Single men had weekly allocations of tickets to the value of five shillings. The entitlement for a married man with three children was 16 shillings and three pence – subject to the proviso that no more than an additional 30 shillings were earned. A further requirement was that all assets apart from a minimum of clothing and furniture had to be sold, in order for applicants to qualify for official relief.[8]

Relief depots had become an established feature of the Australian scene, as had other manifestations of the overall immiseration: 'Destitute men knocked on many a householder's door, begging for a job or despairingly trying to sell some handmade kitchenware. Some tramped the road or jumped the train in a forlorn search for work, or camped degradingly on the outskirts of towns or cities in mushroom villages of galvanised iron and hessian shanties'.[9] The then secretary of the Newman Society and future Campion Society president, Murray McInerney, witnessed at the outset of the Depression 'unemployed

---

6 Colin B. Schedvin, 'The Long and Short of Depression Origins', in Robert Cooksey (ed), *The Great Depression in Australia* (Canberra, ACT: Australian Society for the Study of Labour History) 4.

7 C. Forster, 'Unemployment and the Australian Economic Recovery of the 1930s', in R.G. Gregory and N.G. Butlin (eds), 'Recovery from the Depression: Australia and the World Economy in the 1930s' (Melbourne, Vic: Cambridge University Press, 1988) 309.

8 Cannon, *The Human Face of the Great Depression*, 92–95.

9 Robertson, *Scullin*, 338.

men lining up outside the Public Library waiting for its doors to open at 10:00am so they would have the shelter and warmth of the large Reading Room under its Dome'. 'And I had seen, on the bricks of the boiler room chimneys of the Royal Melbourne Hospital the grease marks from the coats of the unemployed as they sought warmth by standing against those bricks', McInerney wrote.[10]

The writer Alan Marshall joined 'a queue of starving men in an alley beside an Elizabeth Street hotel', where shortly:

> A door opened, and a man carrying a rubbish tin appeared. He up-ended it, and tipped the day's kitchen slops on the ground. The man at the head of the queue divided the semi-liquid mass into portions with his bare hands. Each person stepped forward to shovel his share into an old newspaper, before slinking away to consume it in silence.[11]

And there was no solace for Mannix in the failure of his co-religionists within the government to observe the unity and solidarity among themselves that he had so consistently from the outset of his episcopate sought. Catholics had proved to be no less prone than others in the wider community to the dictates of class and economic self-interest, nor less resistant in their diverse political opinions and affiliations to external direction. Following months of external pressure and internal dissension, key ministers – 'each man devout and with some claims to real spiritual depth'[12] – turned on one another and tore the government apart.

The financially ultra-orthodox advocate of budget restraint J.A. Lyons defected with four followers from his co-religionist Scullin on 13 March 1931, and on 7 May merged with the Nationalists

10 Murray McInerney, 'Memoir' (Unpublished memoir, 1987, Bruce Duncan Papers) 1.

11 Cannon, *The Human Face of the Great Depression*, 94.

12 Luscombe, *Builders and Crusaders*, 158.

to form the United Australia Party (UAP) and become its leader. The Catholic J.A. Beasley and five fellow supporters of the debt repudiation or re-scheduling policies of the fiery NSW Premier J.T. Lang shortly followed the example of the Lyons faction's desertion, to sit separately as the 'Lang Labor Party'.

On 25 November 1931, 'Judas Joe' Lyons and 'Stabber Jack' Beasley joined forces to bring down the government over its rejection of demands by Beasley for a formal inquiry into the distribution by the Treasurer of the day, E.G. Theodore – likewise a Catholic – of unemployment relief. At the elections on 19 December, six ALP ministers including Theodore and Chifley were defeated, and UAP candidates won 56 of the 75 House of Representatives seats.

The circumstances of the debacle held out little hope that Catholics in any future government could any more be relied upon by reason of their shared faith to act in concert with one another. Scullin, Lyons and Beasley had each headed their respective factions within the government and taken them on their disastrously divergent courses of action on wholly political grounds, and without regard for any shared values, interests or obligations to which religion might have been thought to direct their attention.

The ALP had once again relegated itself to the political wilderness, for a further decade until the formation of its wartime government in 1941. Mannix and the Church again had little to show for their largely unswerving support of the party, and once more, as following the Conscription split, could look forward to none in the further protracted period of Opposition that now lay ahead of it. Nor, for all that the staunchly Catholic Lyons was now Prime Minister in Scullin's place, was anything to be expected from the 'hard-faced men' of his otherwise monolithically Protestant incoming UAP administration.

And it was inwards, to such substitutes or supplements for purely party political remedies as the Church's social teachings might offer, that attention increasingly now turned.

Frank Maher

The Campion Society's founder was the young Catholic lawyer, Frank Maher. His socio-political outlook and dedication to social reform were shaped and driven by the convergence of his faith with his exposure in the course of his upbringing and education to World War I and its aftermath.[13] War, poverty and the rise of Communism fired him with a commitment to bringing to fruition through Distributism the vision of an alternative social order that Leo XIII's encyclical *Rerum Novarum* had outlined in 1891 and in 1931 Pius XI's *Quadragesimo Anno* elaborated.

In common with his fellow Campions, he was excited by ideas and relished argument. His imagination was captured by the rebuttal of the Whig interpretation of history by writers associated in varying degrees with the English Catholic Literary Revival, and he adopted their narrative of the Reformation as the turning point from which the injustices of the Enclosures and the Industrial Revolution had stemmed. The Distributists among them endowed him with a coherent political philosophy, to which in his turn he imparted a distinctively Australian character. A major and enduring focus of his attention was on the development of practical measures for securing specific objectives, including in particular the central Distributist tenet and 'one big thing' of a more widespread ownership of productive property and the right of workers to share

13 James G. Murtagh, 'Australia Comes of Age: A Sketch-portrait of a Continent Commonwealth', *Commonweal*, 9 January 1942, 289.

in the ownership and control of their workplaces and the profits from their labour.

Maher's 1938 ANSCA pamphlet *For Social Justice* read that 'The plan proposed for Australia by those who are immersed in the study of Catholic social principles is ownership by all the workers':

> This is not an idealistic scheme which cannot be reduced to practice. In industry the system of democratic control can be begun by the inauguration of vocational groups ... This can be followed by a scheme of co-operative control, by which the workers shall be shareholders in the industry in which they are operating. This does not simply mean profit sharing. It means that, as in every other company, the workers can elect their own directors, and these directors will share in the control of the industry in question.[14]

Arguing in his 1944 ANSCA pamphlet *Self-Government for Industry* for the interim and transitional measure of the formation of Industrial Councils, he wrote that 'The Industrial Council will operate most satisfactorily only when a far greater proportion of men than now are running their own businesses':

> Though our present plan is not directly concerned with ownership, we look forward to their slowly building up a feeling of confidence and initiative among the workers so that they will 'set up their own' – and incidentally be protected by the Industrial Council against that species of unfair competition that bears so hard on the small man today.

Where businesses were too big to be run by one man, his Catholic Social Guild pamphlet *An Introduction to Social Principles* argued, small men were 'learning that they could gain splendid results through co-operatives':

---

14 F.K.H. Maher, 'For Social Justice', *Australian Catholic Truth Society Record*, 125, 10 February 1938, 24.

> There are Co-operative Banks or Credit Unions, which lend money to their members at low interest rates. There are Co-operative Businesses, in which men with little capital can invest and share the profits among themselves. There are Co-operative Housing Societies, which help poor people to own their own homes. Groups of manufacturers or shopkeepers or fishermen can combine in many ways and compete with chain stores or big companies. Groups of workers can buy shares in the firm in which they are employed.[15]

Aptitude and inclination ideally suited Maher to bringing together the initially small circle of predominantly young graduates from whose discussions the society's foundation stemmed. A contemporary account recalls him as 'the right man in the right place at the right time':

> He had a capacity for listening to everyone in a quiet, receptive way. He made everyone feel they were special. He had a habit of never directly opposing any point of view by saying words like 'but don't you think, etc, etc' or 'although it might, etc, etc'. This custom had the effect of turning what could have been a debate into a discussion of all points of view ... There was never a split in the Society, and no one ever thought of opposing Frank for President. He was everyone's friend.[16]

He was born in 1905. His grandparents were farmers from the west coast of Ireland, who took up a property outside Albury in the second half of the previous century. Unfitted by a leg injury for work on the farm, his father married the daughter of a bank employee and rose through the ranks of the Victorian public service to a senior position. Maher in his turn became the first of the family to have a

15 F.K.H. Maher, *An Introduction to Social Principles* (Carnegie Vic: Catholic Social Guild and Renown Press, ND) 61.

16 Heffey, *Campion Reflections*, 20.

tertiary education and a professional career. A lifelong friend and close associate characterises him as having been unsuited for his chosen career as a solicitor, and 'eventually found his true metier as a University Lecturer at Melbourne University, which bestowed on him a Doctorate of Laws ... The tennis court and the senior common room were his appropriate forums ... He was a good speaker, had a first class intellect, was musical and could play the piano'.[17]

His prowess as a student at De La Salle Malvern and subsequently St Kevin's College was rewarded with a residential scholarship at Newman College for the three-year period from 1925 to 1928, on which he was to look back ultimately as the happiest in his life. He was employed by the university in its registry office reportedly for £1 a week, debated for its teams in intervarsity and international competitions and revived old friendships and formed new ones as a Newman Society member.

He gained Honours in History and Economics in the first stage of his Arts/Law course and was awarded a Wyselaskie Scholarship for Economics, but abandoned full-time study for a brief sojourn as a graduate executive with the Shell Company and subsequently a Jesuit novice in Sydney which also shortly was discontinued. Aged 25 on his return to Melbourne in 1930, he worked as a temporary teacher at the Seymour High School before taking up a position the following year at St Kevin's College and resuming his law course on a part-time basis.

Fostering Catholic Intellectual Life

Deeply conscious of the intellectual backwardness of Australian Catholicism, he was avid also for an opportunity to assist in remedying

17 Heffey, *Campion Reflections*, 20.

it. Efforts to foster Catholic intellectual life were not new to Victoria. Examples had abounded. The Catholic Federation experience apart, the Victorian Catholic Young Men's Societies' Union as far back as 1888 established the *Catholic Magazine* as a quarterly journal whose convert editor, the literary-minded and English-born Benjamin Hoare, was also a leader writer for *The Age* newspaper. It was succeeded in 1892 by the long-running independent Catholic monthly, *Austral Light*, which sought to provide 'in the front rank of literary beacons, a lamp of light over the semi-darkness that covers the deep of human thought and human speculation', and survived until 1920.

The Australian Catholic Truth Society was formed in 1904, as a means of producing monthly pamphlets on topics of interest to Catholics, as was a Newman Society six years later to promote discussion among Catholic graduates and undergraduates. The Social Study Club that the Catholic Federation established in 1913 was succeeded in 1916 by a Leo Guild with similar objectives. Consciousness-raising on social issues and the Church's response to them became a key feature of the Catholic Women's Social Guild (CWSG) that was formed the same year by the Jesuit priest William Lockington, and the annual Winter Lectures program at the Cathedral Hall in Fitzroy whose inauguration Lockington also initiated. The Leo Guild in turn gave birth in 1917 to the further journal *Australia: A Review of the Month*, but by 1923 activities other than on the part of the Catholic Truth Society and the CWSG were largely moribund.

Intimations of a turn for the better emerged with the founding by the expatriate Irish priest William Hackett SJ of the Central Catholic Library in 1924. Hackett saw Australian Catholics as having 'so long been deprived of the opportunity to engage their intellectual powers that the wish to do so had now to be created'.[18] Like Mannix, he was an outspoken supporter of lay activism: 'Laymen do well when they are given their head. I don't believe in treating them as schoolboys or slaves. They are not my inferiors'.[19] A circuit breaker was required to correct the imbalance and unleash the latent energies of an informed and empowered laity.

His library adopted the model introduced in Dublin earlier the same year by his fellow Jesuit, Stephen Brown: 'A centre of Catholic thought, a well-spring, however modest its present beginnings, of information and inspiration regarding every subject that concerns our Faith'.[20] Housed initially in a room at the Catholic Federation's office, it moved in 1926 to premises of its own in the Orient Line Building in Collins Street, where the walls were hung with framed portraits of the Catholic Literary Revival giants and founder Distributists: 'G.K. Chesterton, Hilaire Belloc, Maurice Baring and others whose writings were new and exciting in the 1930s'.[21] The number of books held increased between 1923 and 1930 from an initial 740 to some 10,000, of which all but 2000 were non-fiction. Circulation increased by 1930 to 24,000 and by 1938 to 60,000. Nor was it Catholic authors alone whose books Hackett added to his collection – 'else', as remarked by an impressed visitor in 1930, 'we die of in-breeding'.[22]

---

18 O'Farrell, *The Catholic Church and Community in Australia*, 317.

19 O'Farrell, *The Catholic Church and Community in Australia*, 317.

20 Stephen J. Brown, *A Catholic Library for Dublin*, 307–308, as quoted in Ursula L. Bygott, *With Pen and Tongue: The Jesuits in Australia 1865–1939* (Carlton, Vic: Melbourne University Press, 1980) 216.

21 Brenda Niall, *The Riddle of Father Hackett: A Life in Ireland and Australia* (Canberra, ACT: National Library of Australia, 2009) 167.

22 Cyril C. Martindale, 'Central Catholic Libraries', *Month*, October 1930, 311, as quoted in Bygott, *With Pen and Tongue*, 219.

More by far than simply a library, Hackett had by then created 'a meeting place for like-minded people, a kind of Catholic salon'.[23] A key scholarly assessment characterises it as 'the pivot on which many of the 1930s Catholic Action activities would turn':

> Material was made available, and opportunities provided, for discussions which both trained and intellectually nourished many of the future leaders of Australian Catholic Action. Here, in the library, Catholics were introduced to overseas writings in philosophy, in theological discussions and social thinking. The library also became a forum for discussion groups and for lecture series organised by Hackett. ... The lectures and the library attracted many of the young Victorian laymen who formed the nucleus of what O'Farrell has described as 'a new Catholic lay movement of dynamic enthusiasm, intellectual and with a deep indeed passionate social commitment'. It was here in the 1930s that the Campion Society was nurtured.[24]

An Auspicious Beginning

When in late 1930 McInerney circularised all known Catholic graduates – some hundreds in number – with a request for their suggestions and assistance in fostering Catholic intellectual activities at the university, Maher was among the seven of them who responded, indicating that he was supportive of stimulating activity among both graduates and undergraduates. McInerney's approach was still on his mind in the course of a chance conversation at the International Tennis at Kooyong on Christmas Day with an old school friend, John Merlo, who had a Master of Arts degree and a diploma in Education, like Maher had been awarded a Wyselaskie Scholarships

23 O'Farrell, *The Catholic Church and Community in Australia*, 317.

24 Bygott, *With Pen and Tongue*, 217–218.

in Economics – albeit also in History – and was teacher at Melbourne High School: 'One chance remark he made … convinced me, "This is the man to begin a Catholic Action Group"'.[25]

Meeting subsequently at Kooyong in Merlo's company with McInerney, Maher outlined to him his idea of a group to study Catholicism in the modern world. It was agreed between them that 'some form of study group' was needed, and that members would discuss books borrowed from Hackett's library.[26] The group met for the first time on 28 January 1931. Of the eight young men present, McInerney and Gerard Heffey were Arts/Law students and Frank Quaine was taking Honours in French language and culture, with a view to further study in Paris. Bill Knowles and Arthur Adams were lawyers and Denys Jackson, like Maher and Merlo, was a secondary school teacher.

No agenda had been prepared – there was 'no clear idea of what it was they were to aim at, no programme of work, no scheme of organization planned'[27] – but the initially tentative proceedings became animated when Jackson took issue over a point with Quaine. By Maher's account:

> He quickly became neither vague, nor formal, nor silent. He and Quaine saved us. We had come together because we felt that we were painfully ignorant of the modern Catholic approach to life, because we had realised we were being poisoned by slow degrees in the pagan atmosphere in which we lived. So we listened humbly and gratefully while Jackson and Quaine

25 Jory, *The Campion Society*, 31–32.

26 Jory, *The Campion Society*, 32.

27 President's Report, Campion Society Quarterly Meeting, 24 January 1934, Heffey/Butler Papers, University of Melbourne Archives.

> gave off fireworks about Latin culture and the neo-classicism of Maritain. We were dazzled and delighted.[28]

It was an auspicious beginning. Heffey wrote: 'I remember attending the first meeting of the Campion with a certain amount of misgivings, and I remember leaving it wondering why no one had ever thought of it before'.[29]

Notable new arrivals included later the same year Kevin Kelly, shortly to establish himself as 'a tower of strength in every way', and 'one of the keenest minds thrown up by the society', and in 1932 'a miniature tornado of ideas and energy', the young B.A. Santamaria.[30] The group's interest was from the outset less by far in numbers than in formation – in the deepening of the understanding by its members of their Faith, and the acquisition of the influence that might make the application of its teachings to their own lives and those of others the more effective. Affirmation of the members' sense of their identity and purpose was evident shortly in their naming of themselves as the Campion Society, in honour of the Jesuit missionary Edmund Campion: 'a University man, a brilliant pamphleteer, an incomparable conversationalist and a gallant martyr'.[31]

The society's objectives, as spelled out in the constitution that it also shortly adopted, read:

> To promote Catholic Lay Action in its intellectual aspect.
>
> To encourage its members to attain a fuller realisation of Catholic Culture.

---

28 F.K.H. Maher, 'Campion Beginnings', *Orders of the Day*, June 1939, Heffey/Butler Papers, University of Melbourne Archives.

29 Gerard C. Heffey, 'Early Days of the Campion', *Orders of the Day*, August 1939, Heffey/Butler Papers, University of Melbourne Archives.

30 Murtagh, 'Australia Comes of Age', 289–290.

31 F.K.H. Maher, 'Prelude to Catholic Action' (Campion Pamphlet No 1), *Australian Catholic Truth Society Record*, 74, 10 September, 1936, 9.

> To encourage the development in harmony of the spiritual and mental lives of members.
>
> To extend the influence of these conceptions so as to assist in the development of a more intense Catholic atmosphere among Australian Catholics.
>
> To place the Catholic viewpoint adequately before non-Catholics when occasion demands it particularly in questions relating to Social order.[32]

Fortnightly meetings of the group focused initially on the Catholic Literary Revival canons, with emphasis on the works such as those of Belloc, Gilbert Chesterton, Ronald Knox, Arnold Lunn, Douglas Woodruff, Christopher Hollis and Christopher Dawson to which Hackett's library provided so comprehensive an access. As recalled by Maher:

> In the new Catholic history being written by Belloc, Dawson, Hollis, Morton and the rest, an entrancingly new view opened up before them of the history of Europe, and the part the Church had played in its culture and achievement. 'Europe is the Faith' became the basic principle of their historical outlook, and this provided a 'patriotism for the Faith' which has increased with the years, and has been the main motive power behind the movement.[33]

Re-organisation and Expansion

With membership increasing from the original eight to thirty-four by the commencement of the 1932 academic year, the original group was subdivided into two, three and ultimately four sub-groups, designated respectively as the Central, Second, Third and University Groups. The Central Group including the founding members of the

32 Jory, *The Campion Society*, 38.

33 Maher, 'Prelude to Catholic Action', 9.

society served as an Executive until their replacement in 1933 by an elected Council. Maher remained president, with a recent newcomer who had been unemployed at the time of his admission, Ken Mitchell, as secretary and Knowles as treasurer.

A re-organisation in 1935 saw the groups re-designated under the names respectively of Thomas More, Thomas Aquinas, Thomas A'Beckett and Pier Giorgio Frassati, while a recently formed Philosophy Group was retained.[34] Regional Campion Groups were established where 'in metropolitan and country areas alike, the Depression era had seen a new solidarity develop among Victoria's Catholic young men, and a new Catholic intellectual consciousness take root among their leaders'.[35] With the introduction of the Chesterton Group in 1936, the society comprised in all five Central Groups, nine affiliated suburban groups and country groups in Wangaratta, Ballarat, Bendigo, Sale and Albury. And further expansion followed in 1937, with a record intake of thirty new members and the addition of country groups at Ararat, Bacchus Marsh, Benalla, Daylesford, Iona and Horsham.

New members were expected to progress through 'a structured three-year course, in which historical topics were alternated with current ideological and social ones'.[36] Groups were limited to no more than sixteen members, and admission of newcomers was subject to the unanimous consent of their existing memberships. Further requirements of members were that they should 'co-operate loyally and cheerfully with the Bishops and members of the clergy' and

---

34 Frassati (1901–1925), a prominent Italian social reformer, anti-fascist and third order Dominican, was inspired by *Rerum Novarum* to adopt as his watchword 'Charity is not enough: we need social reform', and was beatified by Pope John Paul II in 1990.

35 Jory, *The Campion Society*, 48, 51.

36 Jory, *The Campion Society*, 41.

'refrain from all anti-clerical conduct or statements'. And 'neither "the society nor any group thereof" was to "identify as such nor co-operate with any political body"'.[37]

The excitement of it all was infectious. A Joint Newman Society–Campion Society Standing Committee was established to provide lunch hour lectures at the university, lectures at schools commenced and a new Junior Group within the society was established. Individual Campions were invited by Hackett to give 'Catholic Hour' radio talks, with Jackson also shortly acquiring a regular program slot and subsequently a column in *The Advocate*. Visits were paid to the Corpus Christi Regional Seminary with a view to soliciting interest on the part of the seminarians in the society. Approached on behalf of the committee by Kelly, Mannix conferred his 'personal and episcopal approval' on the society and Hackett became its chaplain.

Articles by society members featured on a regular basis in the Catholic Young Men's Society (C.Y.M.S.) journal *Catholic Young Men* from 1934, and five joint C.Y.M.S.–Campion Society Study groups were formed, where 'The well-tried Campion technique of alternating historical with contemporary subjects, sweeping perspectives with closer analysis, was followed throughout'. The society was a high-profile participant in discussions of Catholic Action at the 1934 National Eucharistic Congress in Melbourne. At the concurrent Convention on Catholic Action, Hackett spoke on Catholic Action and Kelly on Cardijn, and Mannix affirmed in his address to its Annual General Meeting:

> His Holiness the Pope himself had been sending a clarion call to the whole world, not directed to the Bishops and priests but to the laity. You are the leaders of the people ... any ideas that

37 Jory, *The Campion Society*, 38.

> you may initiate to make things better than they are at present will receive a cordial welcome, and will be assured of the utmost consideration. And I can assure you that I shall leave nothing undone to give effect to any feasible proposal.[38]

Lunch hour lectures at the university and Hackett's library regularly attracted attendances on average of two hundred predominantly young people, and further spin-offs from the society emerged, such as the Assisian Guild for teachers and for women the Clitherow Society. Links with schools and with the Corpus Christi seminarians were strengthened and the society's first pamphlet, *Prelude to Catholic Action* – effectively a manual of the objects, origins, methods and outcomes of the study group approach – was issued on its behalf in 1936 by the Catholic Truth Society. 'We emphasise', it reads, 'that all this activity is designed simply as a prelude to the real creation of Catholic Action itself':

> The real development can come only when the Hierarchy of Australia decides to organise Catholic Action on a national basis. We shall need an all-embracing scheme eventually – specialist groups for each class of Catholic, young and old, town workers and country workers, employers and employees, University men and women, boys and girls in schools and colleges. It is all working splendidly in France and Holland, Belgium and Spain, Italy and Portugal. It will come here when the Catholic people have awakened to its importance.[39]

Constraints

By Maher's account, there had already by 1935 been 'scarcely a Catholic interested in his religion who has not heard of the Campion

38 As quoted in Jory, *The Campion Society*, 383.

39 Maher, 'Prelude to Catholic Action', 22.

Society'.[40] Two years later it was apparent also that the burden of sustaining so extensive a range of activities was becoming more than a wholly voluntary organisation could readily support, or that the employment on a part-time basis of a prominent society member, W. Gordon Long, to deal with the correspondence could significantly alleviate. Whereas previously Maher had been seeking new projects with which to occupy members, he now had to admit that it was not possible even 'to fulfil all the requests to give lectures'.[41] It was his hope that an official national Catholic Action bureau might – among other things – help to reduce the Society's workload.

Even so, the Campions had little cause for confidence that attitudes on the part either of their fellow Catholics or within the ALP as the party to which traditionally the Church had looked for sympathy and support would necessarily be supportive. As recalled by Heffey, 'On many occasions, other Catholics were surprised at us "bringing religion into everything"':

> I was told by one Campion Society member that when he expressed the intention of joining the Campion Society as a school boy of sixteen, his father, who was a prominent lawyer in the Australian scene, warned him that to dig too deeply into theological matters might have endangered his faith. I can also recall being at a dinner party with several Catholic educated men when a lawyer whose brother was a high ecclesiastic told us we ought to leave it all to the priests – they would sort in due course whatever it was'.[42]

By O'Farrell's account, positive programs for implementing Catholic social principles were widely regarded by Catholic Labor

---

40 Jory, *The Campion Society*, 69.

41 Jory, *The Campion Society*, 73–74.

42 Heffey, *Campion Reflections*, 24.

traditionalists as 'abstruse theology, out of place and gone mad, dangerous fanaticism, the advocacy of impractical formulae alien to the ad hoc temper of Australian politics, and the courting of a sectarian backlash potentially damaging to the Catholic Church, the Labor Party and themselves personally'.[43]

Alienated

Moderate and mainstream opinion within the ALP was alienated increasingly by the perceived antipathy of some Campions towards parliamentary democracy, and support for reactionary and authoritarian regimes. Opinion among the Campions was broadly reflective of the savage critique of Westminster parliamentary democracy that Hilaire Belloc and Cecil Chesterton had set out in their 1912 *The Party System*. 'Parliament', Belloc had written subsequently, was 'irreconcilable with democracy' and public life was stinking 'with the stench of a mortal disease'.

Even the customarily consensus-seeking Maher was no exception. His preference was for an 'organic democracy', whose essential ingredients, consistent with subsidiarity, were 'the preservation or restoration of the "natural associations" and groupings among men' and observance of 'the rule that the tasks of organizations and government are to be left as far as possible to smaller and lesser groupings by the larger and stronger ones'.[44] An accolade to Portugal's dictator, António de Oliveira Salazar, in his *It Can Be Done* in 1942 reads:

> Salazar's delivery of his country from the toils of international finance is one of the greatest economic achievements of the century. It is a reform which sets an example to the world as

43 O'Farrell, *The Catholic Church and Community in Australia*, 396.

44 Henderson, *Mr Santamaria and the Bishops*, 64.

> outstanding as his establishment of a state of Christian social justice ... He has been the saviour of his country, a great Catholic statesman, applying Christian principles to the modern State.[45]

A more informed and objective view may have been that of the resolutely anti-Communist US Secretary of State, Dean Acheson. Salazar was 'a dictator-manager ... maintained by the power of the Army ... to run the country in the interests of the middle class', Acheson wrote.[46]

Extremes

The public face of the Campion Society was less by far the 'neat, suave and restrained' Maher than the 'striking figure, unexpected in dress and somewhat Chestertonian in style' of the abrasively reactionary Denys Jackson.[47] By Brennan's account 'the man most responsible for moulding the current ways of Catholic thought', Jackson wrote on politics and international affairs as 'Sulla' for *The Advocate* from 1933, broadcast as 'Onlooker' for 3AW's 'Catholic Hour' program from 1934, edited Melbourne's second Catholic weekly, *The Tribune* from 1935 and from the mid-1940s was the 'John C. Calhoun' columnist for Santamaria's magazine *Freedom*, which in 1947 changed its name to *News-Weekly*.[48]

What 'passed for democracy', he stated in his 1948 utopian two-part Australian Catholic Truth Society pamphlet, *Australian Dream*, was 'a weary fraud ... where above a vast and inefficient machine of

45 Maher, *It Can Be Done*, 10.

46 Quoted in David F. Schmitz, *Thank God They're on Our Side: The United States and Right-Wing Dictatorships 1921–1965* (Chapel Hill, NC: University of North Carolina Press, 1999) 164.

47 Murtagh, 'Australia Comes of Age', 289.

48 Niall Brennan, *The Politics of Catholics* (Melbourne, Vic: Hill Publishing, 1972) 18.

centralised bureaucracy, a shadow-war was carried out between two political machines, neither of which could be held in a real sense to "represent" the plain man, or to speak for any corporate body of national opinion'.[49] He admired Mussolini, was a disciple of the notoriously violent far-right French monarchist and anti-Semite Charles Maurras, and kept a photograph of Maurras on his desk despite the condemnation by Pope Pius XI in 1926 of Maurras's all-but-openly fascist organisation L'Action Française. He rejected the view that Vichy France was a puppet regime and its leader, Pétain, a puppet ruler, and lauded Pétain as being among those 'who stand for the real national and Christian tradition of the country'.[50]

Nor in any of these respects was Jackson unique among his fellow Campions. Quaine – in Kelly's view 'absolutely steeped in anti-liberal, anti-secularist traditionalist French thought'[51] – also defended *L'Action Française* and Italy's invasion of Abyssinia, and in 1936 praised Maurras as 'probably ... the greatest political philosopher of all time' who had convinced young French militants 'that democracy is a smoke screen for unavowable plutocratic interests pivoted on London'.[52] Finding himself 'so spiritually unattuned to Australia that he went to live in France', Quaine subsequently 'wrote articles for the royalist press, took part in the retreat from Dunkirk and escaped safely on a destroyer'.[53] Observation of the subsequent collaboration of many of his erstwhile heroes with the Nazis and its outcomes, not least for French Jewry, may have left him less naïve. That Jackson and

49 Denys Jackson, 'Australian Dream', *Australian Catholic Truth Society Record*, 393, November 10, 1947, 11–12.

50 Duncan, *Crusade or Conspiracy?*, 36.

51 Duncan, *Crusade or Conspiracy?*, 14.

52 Duncan, *Crusade or Conspiracy?*, 12.

53 Murtagh, 'Australia Comes of Age', 289–290.

Quaine's excesses or idiosyncrasies were compromising of the wider Campion project did not go un-noticed, or fail to concern fellow society members who were of a more moderate or strategic turn of mind.

Kelly cautioned Jackson in 1936 about the danger of Catholicism being identified with views of so extreme a character, and thereby both 'alienating Catholic workers and alarming Protestants'. 'If Catholic workers are led to believe the Church Fascist, all will be lost, humanly speaking', Kelly wrote.[54] His point was well taken, as events in Spain would shortly and in so dramatic a fashion demonstrate. And, as yet all but unsuspected, there was a cuckoo within the Campion nest. For all the apparent impregnability of the ascendancy of Maher and the more senior Campions, they were on borrowed time.

54 Duncan, *Crusade or Conspiracy?*, 13.

Chapter 8

KEVIN KELLY AND THE CAMPION CONSENSUS

Kelly

'A chubby dynamo of physical and mental energy, son of a railway worker, an ardent democrat and radical laborite, whose torrid oratory has been heard from public platform, university rostrum and soapbox',[1] Kevin Kelly figured increasingly as the conscience of the Campion Society and custodian of its consensus: 'The views on the lay apostolate in Australia and of social conditions and of the state of the Church in Australia, reached by the active members of the Campion Society in a period of almost six years' intensive and continuous study'.[2]

His influence in the shaping of the Australian National Secretariat for Catholic Action in its formative years was pervasive, and he was instrumental in particular in bringing about the inception of the Catholic Evidence Guild in Melbourne, the *Catholic Worker* magazine that pre-dated ANSCA, and the Young Christian

1 Murtagh, 'Australia Comes of Age', 289–190.

2 Kevin T. Kelly, 'The Foundation of ANSCA', 3. Copy of unpublished *Memoir*, ND. The memoir is incomplete, and chapters within it are identified by name and pages numbered separately. Kelly's papers, including the original of his *Memoir*, are held by the Kelly family.

Workers movement (Y.C.W.) as the heir ultimately to the Campion values and aspirations.[3] Drawing on European sources, he informed and enriched the outlook and activities of the Campions, the *Worker*, the Y.C.W. and for a time ANSCA with the teachings of Cardijn and Maritain.

'Cardijn sought out young industrial workers for the purpose of studying, penetrating and converting sections of the working class that were no longer Christian', Kelly wrote:

> He gathered but did not isolate his young workers in order to launch a revolutionary attack on contemporary paganism. Paradoxically, he sought to fling good apples into a heap of bad apples so that the bad apples became good. In Cardijn's own words, '... It is useless to propose for the working class mere exterior remedies, from outside or above the working class. It is useless to propose mere interior remedies, whether economic or spiritual. There remains only one means of completely efficacious salvation: the re-making – a re-making, a renewal, at once spiritual and material, temporal and eternal, personal and social, domestic and civic, by the working class apostolate, by the working class laity, by Christ-like Catholic action in and by the working class'.[4]

Consistent with the 'one big thing' of a more widespread ownership of productive property as championed by the encyclicals and the Distributists, a new role was envisaged for the young workers to whose formation the Y.C.W. was dedicated. 'For a long time', Cardijn affirmed, 'the working class has had to be satisfied with demanding material, social and political advances, social security, the eight-hour day, universal suffrage and the rest':

3 Murtagh, 'Australia Comes of Age', 289–290.

4 Kevin T. Kelly, 'Towards the Y.C.W.', in *Memoir* (Unpublished manuscript, Bruce Duncan Papers, ND) 3. Kelly's handwritten amendments to his *Memoir* are in bracketed text.

> Today the time has come when it can and must share in the direction of production and the administration of its own interests. We can no longer imagine a world still moving towards progress and unity without the working class, now spread everywhere and organised, having its true share of responsibility. The working class cannot escape from these responsibilities without handing over the world of today, as well as the unknown possibilities of the future, to anarchy and sterility.[5]

Examining in his 1940 book, *Scholasticism and Politics*, the relation of Catholic Action and political action, Maritain concluded 'If by the teaching it dispenses and the spiritual formation it procures, Catholic action *prepares* Catholic laymen to act as Christians, to participate in struggles of the temporal and to participate in them *as* Christians, to assume social and political tasks to which they consider themselves called, and to assume it *as* Christians, Catholic action, however, restrains itself most carefully from laying the shadow of a finger on this second level'.

> And this is not only because the Church does not want to find itself, at any price, enslaved to temporal things. It is also because ... the competence of an activity belonging to an entirely spiritual order soon finds its limits. There exists a judgement of *Catholicism* about the connections which art and literature have to ethics and to the moral capacities of the average of men; but this judgement does not suffice to tell me what I must think of a book by Joyce or of a poem by Rimbaud, as works of art. There exists a judgement of *Catholicism* about the duty to work on behalf of international peace and of the principles of social justice; but this judgement does not suffice to tell me what I should think of the law of the 40-hour week and of the statute of the League of Nations. *It is my business to judge these problems*

5 As quoted in De La Bedoyere, *The Cardijn Story*, 180.

> *as a Catholic ... but without pretending to speak in the name of Catholicism, nor to draw in my wake Catholics as such.*[6]

Origins

Born the eldest of five surviving children of Irish-Australian parents, at Ballarat on 6 May 1910, and baptised in the local St Alipius Church two days later, Kelly was exposed from an early age to the drama and discourse of the political and industrial labour movements, and the great debates of the day about conscription and the role of government in economic affairs. His childhood memories included attending the 1914, 1915, 1916 and 1917 St Patrick's Day processions with his grandfather Eneas Cull, hearing his father, Ballarat Australian Railways Union branch president John T. Kelly, speak together with Scullin and Mannix at anti-conscription rallies in 1916 and 1917 and being present in the offices of Scullin's outspokenly anti-conscription Ballarat *Evening Echo* immediately following a raid on the paper by Hughes's police.

He was an attentive listener in the family home to news of his unionist father's campaign for a Railways Wages Board and political discussion between his father and grandfather, such as of the prospects and strategies for achieving the quintessentially Distributist 'one big thing' of enabling workers to become owners of their jobs and thereby 'masters of their own destinies':

> While my father favoured the extension of the economic activities of government, my grandfather took the view that it was unnatural for men to be content merely with the status of employees, either in private or government enterprises. Eneas

6 Jacques Maritain, *Scholasticism and Politics* (New York, NY: Doubleday & Co, 1948; this edition 1960) 198–201. Italics added to the last three lines by the author.

> felt that an ideal society should consist of working proprietors, small independent farmers and small independent tradesmen and shopkeepers, protecting themselves by co-operative methods against the encroachments of big business and the State. J.J., on the other hand, took the view that large-scale industries were going to dominate the economy and that in an ideal society the workers in those industries should control them. In the meantime and as an interim measure, he favoured the setting up of government enterprises to compete with large-scale private monopolies.[7]

Further stimulus for Kelly's burgeoning boyhood political consciousness stemmed from the close friendship between the Kelly and Scullin families, who campaigned, socialised and on occasion holidayed together. For the future Prime Minister, he wrote, '... the nationalisation of industry was simply a means to an end, a merely initial phase preceding one in which the management, operation, control and effective ownership of industries would be vested in the workers in those industries under the general supervision of the political officers of the community':

> For Scullin, the 1921 socialisation objective was a long-term prescription for healing the cataclysmic difference between Capital and Labor by giving workers in the great industries a real and direct control over the enterprises and industries in which they worked and for resolving disputes between worker-controlled industries. ... For him it was not nationalisation in the sense that the control of industries was to be vested exclusively in the political officers of the community, for as he said at the time, 'I do not believe the workers will ever make a success of nationalised industry, or of industry controlled by the people collectively, unless they are made responsible themselves. ... Scullin never abandoned the view that wholesale nationalisation,

7 Kelly, 'Bairnsdale', *Memoir.* Kelly's father, John Thomas Kelly, was sometimes called J.J. See Kelly, 'Ballarat', *Memoir*, 1.

> without effective workers' participation and control, was really State Capitalism; in other words, that State Socialism was really State Capitalism.[8]

Befriended and in part mentored by Scullin, Kelly identified with the socially-minded Catholics of his generation whom he saw as 'knowing that Catholic social teaching ruled out completely the transfer of all the means of production, distribution and exchange exclusively to the political officers of the community, groped towards some solution which might give workers in an industry effective control of it without the necessity of first nationalising the industry'.[9]

Consequent, as the family believed, on his Wages Board agitation, Kelly's father was transferred by the Railways management in 1918 from Ballarat to Bairnsdale, where four years later he resigned his position and went into business for himself as a produce merchant and auctioneer. It was during this period that Kelly first acquired what was to prove to be an enduring interest in French language and culture under the influence of the Notre Dame de Sion nun, Mother Athanasius, at the St Mary's Primary School. With the ill health of his father in 1923 from rheumatic fever, the business had to be sold and the family moved to Glen Iris the following year, where they shared a house with Kelly's aunt, and Kelly was enrolled at De La Salle College Malvern.

He qualified for his Intermediate Certificate in 1925 and his Leaving Certificate in 1926 (when concurrently he was co-Dux of the school and co-editor of its magazine, the *Blue and Gold*). In 1927 he studied for Leaving Honours, but took the Leaving Certificate again (and was again Dux), as this was the only means of qualifying

---

8 Kelly, 'Bairnsdale', *Memoir*, 42–3.

9 Kelly, 'Bairnsdale', Memoir, 44.

for the Victorian State Public Service. Precluded from the prospect of full time university study by the need to contribute to the support of his family, in December 1927 he sat the entrance examination to the Victorian State Public Service, coming in second place. In early 1928 he was for a short period a junior teacher at the Toorak Central School, prior to beginning his career in March that year in the Victorian State Public Service. He first worked in the Children's Welfare Branch of the Chief Secretary's Office and later as an assistant to the Public Trustee of Victoria and to the Inspector-General of Penal Establishments; as Secretary to the Wonthaggi State Coal Mine Royal Commission, and as Professional Assistant to the Crown Solicitor of Victoria. In mid-1942 he joined the Royal Australian Navy Volunteer Reserve, serving as a Naval Intelligence Officer until he was demobilised in September 1945. Joining the Campion Society in 1931 as a twenty-one-year-old part-time Melbourne University Arts student majoring in French and English, and already also a Councillor of the Australian Public Servants' Association (Victorian Branch), Labor Party activist and consummate university debater, he recorded of his initial meeting: 'I never enjoyed a night so much'.[10]

Catholic Evidence Guild

Confirmation of his emergence as 'the foremost activist in the Society' and 'a tower of strength in every way' was marked by the creation in November 1933 of the Melbourne Catholic Evidence Guild, as a separate entity, for the provision of Catholic speakers at the popular Yarra Bank Sunday forum.[11] Visiting Sydney the previous August with a letter of introduction to the NSW Master of

10 Jory, *The Campion Society*, 36.

11 Jory, *The Campion Society*, 36, 64.

Catholic Speakers, Peter Gallagher, Kelly had spoken for their Guild from its rostrum in the Domain, and on his return was determined to establish a counterpart body in Melbourne.

Rebuffed in his endeavours to have the Campion Society auspice the new venture, on the grounds that 'actively and as a body, the society cannot, at this stage, engage in work amongst non-Catholics', he and another recent newcomer, Brian Harkin, obtained permission from Mannix for it to be established independently, on an initially provisional basis. Successful from the outset in competing 'with Communist, Evangelical and other pitches for the attention of large crowds of curious or sceptical spectators', the *ad hoc* group, now inclusive also of the future editor of *The Advocate*, Frank Murphy, was instructed shortly by Mannix to prepare a constitution so that its status could be formalised.

Following an inaugural meeting on Wednesday, 8 August 1934, Kelly became Master of the Guild, Murphy its secretary and Harkin the treasurer. Appointed by Mannix as General Clerical Assistants were former members of the Conversion of Australia Movement at Corpus Christi, Fathers James Murtagh, James Cleary and Bernard O'Connor, and as Clerical Secretary the future Bishop of Sandhurst, Bernard Stewart. 'The Guild bore the singular distinction of being the first independent offshoot of Campion enthusiasm', Colin Jory wrote.[12]

The *Catholic Worker*

Concurrent with the creation of the Catholic Evidence Guild, Kelly and Harkin had become aware of the need for 'two new and distinct types of publication':

---

12 Jory, *The Campion Society*, 64–65.

> First, a periodical like the *Jeunesse Ouvrière Chrétienne* of Brussels and Paris, formally designed to promote the religious and intellectual formation of lay people for apostolic work of an ecclesiastical character under the direction of the bishops, and, secondly, periodicals dealing with debatable issues of a temporal and political character, but from the standpoint of a distinctively Christian and Thomistic outlook, 'secular journals of Christian inspiration'.[13]

Impressed by overseas lay publications including *G.K's Weekly* in the UK and in the US *Commonweal* and the *Catholic Worker*, Campion Society members more generally had for some time been canvassing among themselves the prospect of a new paper. Harkin had commenced importing copies of the *Catholic Worker* for distribution by Evidence Guild members from its Yarra Bank rostrum, and through the society's numerous city and suburban study groups. The nineteen year old and hitherto relatively inactive Santamaria had been entrusted with the production of an internal newsletter, *Orders of the Day*, on the society's behalf.[14]

Appearing for the first time on the occasion of the society's Annual Meeting on 13 August 1935 and characterised by Kelly as 'a brilliant broadsheet', *Orders of the Day* 'was written in a forceful and impetuous style, and consisted mainly of snippets from overseas Catholic writers, oddments of news, and exhortations to the Campions to surge on to greater things'. Proclaiming that 'THE CATHOLIC INTERNATIONAL FIGHTS THE WORLD BOURGEOISIE', the inaugural issue of *Orders of the Day* announced that the society had embarked on a three-year plan to obtain three major objectives:

1. To co-ordinate Catholic Action throughout the Commonwealth.

---

13 Kelly, *Memoir*, 'The Catholic Worker', 1.

14 K.T. Kelly, 'Early Campions and the Worker', *The Advocate*, 23 February 1978, 5.

2. To hammer Catholicism into an impenetrable fortress on which heresy will shatter itself.
3. To mould the one and a half million Catholics in Australia into an organic unity ready to assume the Catholic Offensive.[15]

When, frustrated by a seemingly protracted delay in bringing the envisaged larger initiative to fruition, Santamaria at a meeting in late November or early December 1936 announced his intention to commence publication of a local *Catholic Worker* the following February, the *fait accompli* at his hands was accepted, and a provisional committee was appointed to regularise the status of the paper, such that ultimately:

> A Constitution was prepared putting control of the paper into the hands of a Council of twenty men, and below that of a smaller Central Committee. Membership of the Central Committee was a matter of invitation, and the invitations were organised on a relatively informal basis. The Central Committee was the body which met each month to consider the content of the paper and to thrash out the general theme of the articles proposed and to determine what members of the Committee would write the articles. Decisions of the Central Committee were, however, subject to review by the Council.[16]

Meanwhile, Kelly undertook to brief Mannix informally on the proposal in the course of a scheduled December call on the Archbishop in his capacity as Master of the Catholic Evidence Guild.[17] The efficacy of his presentation was evident at a further briefing of Mannix the following month by Santamaria and his fellow Campion, Val Adami: 'Since the paper we proposed to produce carried the

15 Duncan, *Crusade or Conspiracy?*, 17, and Jory, *The Campion Society*, 75.

16 McInerney, *Memoir*, 30.

17 K.T. Kelly, 'Early Campions and the Worker', *The Advocate*, 23 February 1978, 5.

Catholic name, the correct procedure seemed naturally to refer the proposal to Archbishop Mannix for his approval', Santamaria wrote:

> I reminded him that we were inexperienced and that the paper would bear the name 'Catholic', our mistakes might damage the Church. He smiled: 'You will have heard that the man who makes no mistakes, makes nothing'. He extended his hand with an unexpectedly firm grasp. The support which it signified was never withdrawn in any enterprise in which I engaged with him in nearly thirty years.[18]

'The new Communism', the *Catholic Worker* famously declared, in a first issue all but wholly written by Santamaria, 'is only the old Capitalism plus a little missionary fervour. Both are illegitimate off-spring of the same diseased materialism'. Sentiments of so radical a character fell on receptive ears. An overnight spectacular success, and developing rapidly into a national monthly with a circulation of some 50,000 copies, the *Worker* was commended by the Bishops in a joint pastoral following their 1937 Fourth Plenary Council in Sydney. An Apostolic Blessing was conferred on the paper by Pope Pius XI, and a letter of congratulation on its inception was received from Hilaire Belloc.[19]

An anthology of its values, aspirations and policies, edited anonymously by Kelly and John Ginnane in 1944 as *Design for Democrats: The Autobiography of a Free Journal by 25 Men*, carried the dedication 'An Australian Tribute to Hilaire Belloc for his 74th Year', and reportedly sold some 75,000 copies. Its preface read:

> The Australian daily press is not free today. For its readers the Australian daily press is largely a sedative, an irritant or a

18 B.A. Santamaria, *Against the Tide* (Melbourne, Vic: Oxford University Press, 1981) 19.

19 25 Men (ed), *Design for Democrats: The Autobiography of a Free Journal* (Melbourne, Vic: The Advocate Press, 1944) 4.

> diversion; for its proprietors an investment and the most powerful weapon of organised wealth; and for its journalists a means of livelihood in which the right to personal expression no longer exists. In England a generation ago a similar situation prevailed. But Hilaire Belloc and the Chestertons, in 'The Eye Witness', and Alfred Orage in 'The New Age', restored to men of the English tongue the tradition of fighting journalism at the head of which stands the immortal, commanding figure of William Cobbett. In their beginnings, however, these two splendid journals lacked, to some extent a co-ordinating philosophy, and while distinctively national, a strong social and popular basis. To this latter deficiency also must be attributed the difficulties met by the first 'Australia', the vigorous and informed national journal which first saw the light of day in this country during the course of the Great War of 1914–18. Profiting by the inspiration and experience of these three journals, a group of Australian workers and students united in the year 1936 to establish a free newspaper in Australia. For a philosophy they looked to the Catholic Church and for a policy they consulted the needs of the Australian working-class community from which they sprung.[20]

The Distributist character of the *Worker* and its Campion antecedents and their indebtedness to Belloc's writings, including in particular *The Servile State* and *The Restoration of Property*, were affirmed by Kelly's close friend and Evidence Guild associate, Murtagh, in his seminal 1955 *Australia: The Catholic Chapter*. 'In interpreting and applying the principles of *Quadragesimo Anno*, the members, societies and activities fathered by the movement used the Bellocian dialectic in their analysis of the crisis of Christendom, in their criticism of Australian society and in their programmes for social reconstruction', Murtagh wrote.[21]

20 25 Men (ed), *Design for Democrats*, vii.

21 Murtagh, *Australia: The Catholic Chapter*, 174.

A representative 1938 policy statement from the pages of the *Worker*, as incorporated in *Design for Democrats*, read that 'Pope Pius XI calls for the speedy modification of the wage-contract at least by a contract of partnership between owners and wage-earners, by which the latter are made sharers in ownership, management and profits':

> In the light of Australian conditions and following the lead of Chesterton and Belloc, the 'C.W.' advocates an even more radical and revolutionary change in the present economic order. It demands that as many workers as possible be admitted to direct ownership, and that not in the next century but in the present generation. There is no insuperable economic difficulty to prevent the attainment of this policy.[22]

Asserting the paper's Distributist conviction that 'In both cases, the setting up of guilds or vocational groups will enable worker-owners to plan economic activity and to ensure and maintain widespread workers' ownership and the coincidence of political liberty and economic security', the statement nevertheless was sceptical of their capacity to constitute a panacea:

> It is idle to cherish the hope that the mere setting up of a guild in a given industry will overcome the deep-rooted social antagonism arising from wage-slavery and the concentration of property in the hands of a few. To be really effective, the guild must be based on individual or co-operative workers' ownership.[23]

Meanwhile, as McInerney was to recall, the *Worker* had become a prey to internal division: 'Friction developed between the Central Committee and Santamaria arising from the fact that the majority of the Central Committee took the view that Santamaria was not

---

22 25 Men (ed), *Design for Democrats*, 73.

23 25 Men (ed), *Design for Democrats*, 73.

implementing the policy decisions of the Central Committee'.[24] In October 1937 Santamaria was replaced as sole editor by an editorial board comprising, in addition to himself, Kelly and the young railway worker and union activist Frank Keating. Santamaria's attendance at board meetings was sporadic throughout 1939 and by 1940 his severance from the paper was all but complete.

'The breach between members of the "old guard" of the Campion Society in the *Catholic Worker* and Santamaria and members of his "Movement" was partly due to the fact that Santamaria and the "Movement" asserted or allowed it to be asserted that the viewpoint which they presented was the Catholic viewpoint and that there was no other Catholic viewpoint', McInerney wrote:

> The view of the *Catholic Worker* group and of those members of the 'old guard' of the Campion Society who were unable to subscribe to Santamaria's viewpoint, was that Santamaria was presenting a political viewpoint to which he was perfectly entitled, but which was not necessarily the viewpoint of the Catholic Church, and furthermore it was a viewpoint from which Catholics were free to differ.[25]

'I took the view that if they didn't want me, I didn't want to be there … I had plenty to do as it was', Santamaria wrote.[26] The disavowal was disingenuous. Never one to lightly surrender a possible source of advantage, he wrote to Hackett in 1943, suggesting that Mannix 'might sideline the *Catholic Worker*, either by removing the word 'Catholic' from the title, which would limit its church-door sales, or by a takeover, which would make it the official organ of Catholic Action'. Brenda Niall's account reads:

---

24 McInerney, *Memoir*, 30.

25 McInerney, *Memoir*, 34–35

26 Duncan, *Crusade or Conspiracy?*, 21.

> With Kelly and McInerney on war service, Santamaria argued, the paper had fallen into the hands of younger men who, 'though keen and anxious to keep the paper going', had neither the time nor the competence to do the job. A Catholic Action newspaper for workers was needed, but wartime paper restrictions made a new venture impossible. 'I therefore put this thought to you, that you might discuss with his Grace the question of whether this matter is now so important that a decision be reached one way or another'.[27]

Frustrated yet again by the failure of the envisaged takeover of the *Worker* to proceed, Santamaria instead borrowed £700 from his father to establish the four-page, two-penny weekly *Freedom*, which in July 1946 became *News-Weekly*. Niall ascribes the circumstances of its inception to the need to avert a bitter dispute, such as would have been sure to follow 'if Mannix were to sideline the *Catholic Worker* or made a gift of it to Catholic Action' as Santamaria had sought:

> Santamaria was proprietorial about the *Catholic Worker*, which had been his own initiative, and angry at its negative attitude to his policies after he had left it behind. But it would have infuriated the *Worker* group, especially those on war service, to have it downgraded by a title change or appropriated by Catholic Action. Hackett and Mannix found a compromise. The *Catholic Worker* was left alone to pursue its independent line, but through the good offices of Arthur Calwell, then Minister for Information, Santamaria was given the permit necessary to start his paper *Freedom*, which later became *News-Weekly*. The loser in this exchange was Calwell, whom Santamaria did not hesitate to attack in his paper when their policies differed.[28]

So increasingly embittered an estrangement of onetime friends effectively set in train a transformation of the *Worker* into the focus

27 Niall, *The Riddle of Father Hackett*, 238–239.

28 Niall, *The Riddle of Father Hackett*, 259.

and rallying point for the creation of a loyal opposition within the Church, whose members Santamaria sought ceaselessly to stigmatise in populist terms as 'intellectuals' and 'the University Catholics'. A gulf now yawned between Catholics including those associated with the *Worker* who accepted constraints on party political involvement by the Church as so comprehensively spelled out by Maritain, and those associated with Santamaria who as comprehensively rejected and in practice flouted them. It was on the outcome of these differences and such part in their resolution as Mannix might choose to play that great issues for both Church and State would shortly now turn. Not least among them would prove to be whether and if so on what basis a future might be assured for Catholic Action as properly so defined and the Distributism on which the endorsement of the bishops had so unreservedly been conferred.

Chapter 9

PRELUDE TO ANSCA

Kelly warned in *The Advocate* in May 1937 that if Catholic Action in Australia was not soon established on a formal and properly resourced basis, 'the whole movement may be set back for ten years'.[1] Maher called attention publicly the following month to 'the great need for some central secretariat to "direct and inspire" the Catholic Action Movement'.[2] In July, senior members of the Campion Society waited on Mannix with a request that he should 'seek the establishment of a National Secretariat of Catholic Action as a matter of urgency'.[3]

Mannix agreed, and invited the society to prepare a proposal for presentation to the Plenary Council of the Hierarchy of Australasia and New Zealand at its meeting in September. The case for its acceptance by the Council was the more compelling and carried the greater weight for its having coincided with an intensification of well-founded anti-Communist concerns within the Church, following on the assumption of office by aggressively secular governments in the Soviet Union, Mexico and Spain. Catholic papers carried graphic accounts of the anti-religious purges and killings in the Soviet Union in which the clergy was seen to have been all but eliminated. In the 1930s alone, some 100,000 priests, monks and nuns together with

1 Kevin T. Kelly, 'The Crux of Catholic Action', *Advocate*, 20 May 1937.
2 F.K.H. Maher, Speech at Catholic Men's Club, *Advocate*, 24 June 1937.
3 Jory, *The Campion Society*, 89.

great numbers of lay people are now known to have lost their lives, and all told Stalin and his associates may have been responsible for no fewer than thirteen to fifteen million deaths.[4] Catholic reporting of the Spanish Civil War heightened the consternation by ascribing to the Communist Party and the Comintern the responsibility for the killing of some 'thirteen bishops, 4,184 priests, 365 members of other orders and 283 nuns', together with widespread destruction of churches and other church properties, which in reality the Communist authorities had opposed.[5]

Putting the Case for ANSCA

An *ad hoc* Memorandum Committee, consisting of Maher, McInerney, Kelly, Jackson, Mitchell and Long drafted a 15,000-word 'Secretariat of Catholic Action' submission. Major grounds for creation of the Secretariat were identified as the so far insufficiently and ineffectually organised condition of Catholic Action in Australia, and the threat of trade unions both 'coming under the control of Communists' and 'adopting proposals, platforms and policies to which a Catholic may be unable in conscience to pay allegiance'. The thrust of the document was essentially support for both the retention by the Campion Society of its established role and the extension of key aspects of its formation

4 Alexander N. Yakovlev, *A Century of Violence in Soviet Russia* (New Haven, CT: Yale University Press, 2002) 165, and Robert Conquest, *The Great Terror: A Reassessment* (London: Pimlico, 1992) xviii.

5 For statistics of the killings, see Antony Beevor, *The Battle for Spain: The Spanish Civil War 1936–1939* (London: Weidenfeld & Nicolson, 2006) 92. For Communist opposition to them, see José M. Sánchez, *The Spanish Civil War as a Religious Tragedy* (Notre Dame, Indiana: University of Notre Dame Press, 1987) 20, and citing Burnett Bolloten, *The Spanish Revolution: The Left and the Struggle for Power During the Civil War* (Chapel Hill NC: University of North Carolina. Press, 1979), and David Cattell, *Communism and the Spanish Civil War* (Berkley, CA: University of California Press, 1955).

activities under new auspices and by other means.[6] An expanded and better resourced basis was sought to be achieved, commensurate with a formal designation of the Secretariat by the Plenary Council as Catholic Action, and the appointment of an Episcopal Committee to which it would be accountable.

Recognition was accorded at the outset to the envisaged core mission of the Secretariat, as the 'formation of militants and the building up of militant groups ... who are, or who readily become, apostles of Catholic Action', and 'the tremendous reservoir of keenness waiting to be tapped':

> It is the urgent demand of an increasing number for nothing less than Catholic adult education. It is a fact vividly brought home for instance, to members of the Campion Society in recent years. The field is white with the harvest – the labourers are there – if only they know how to reap. While still they are waiting, they must be taught how to reap.[7]

'The attempt to teach them', the document continued, 'has fallen on the shoulders of a few who, subjected to this overwhelming and unnatural strain, are reduced almost to exhaustion':

> This last sentence may seem an exaggeration but it is in fact a correct statement of the position. Something must be done to ease the burden weighing so heavily upon those who captained the movements mentioned. At all costs the groups of militants must be kept going. The information, programmes, reading lists, in short the specialised assistant they require must be provided and dispensed.[8]

---

6 'Campion Memorandum 1: 'Secretariat of Catholic Action' (Typescript, Bruce Duncan Papers, 1937) 4–5.

7 'Campion Memorandum 1', 2.

8 'Campion Memorandum 1', 2.

Priorities were to include the creation of parish, vocational and professional groups, together with the expansion of study groups along Campion lines. Further initiatives for adoption as resources might permit included extensive survey work, publishing and press departments within the Secretariat, and the creation ultimately of a Catholic Workers College was envisaged.

Consistent with the settled values and overall approach of the Society, the Secretariat was to be guided by the Jocist principles and 'See, Judge, Act' inquiry approach of Cardijn and Maritain's seminal differentiation between Catholic Action and 'action by Catholics'. Any vocational group of workers established under the aegis of the Secretariat on a union or trade basis was to be concerned primarily with formation, and would officially organise its members for activity in unions only where religious interests were directly involved: 'All other matters the vocational group should leave to the individual apostolate of its members'.[9] 'The *Jeunesse Ouvrière Chrétienne* is an integral part of official Catholic Action especially in Belgium, France and Canada and is the model which any Australian Youth Organisation should follow'.[10]

Calling together on his return from the Plenary Council representatives of the Society including, along with McInerney, Maher and Santamaria, Ken Mitchell, Kevin Wallace and Val Adami, Mannix advised them that an Episcopal Committee consisting of himself together with Archbishops Norman Gilroy (new Coadjutor Archbishop of Sydney) and Justin Simonds (Hobart) had been appointed to consider the setting up and subsequent activities of the Secretariat. Funding of £1250 had been approved, and advice to

9 'Campion Memorandum 1', 33.

10 'Campion Memorandum 1', 34.

the Committee including the structure, costing and staffing of the Secretariat was sought.

Aware now of resourcing constraints including a staffing limited by the episcopal funding to the positions of secretary, assistant secretary and a single typist, the Campions cautioned in their response against the arousal of unrealistic expectations of the Secretariat. Consistent with its character as 'an institution which will be a source of information and give assistance to every body in Australia carrying on true Catholic Action', priority was to be assigned to three principal functions, namely:

> To assist the development of the study group movement throughout Australia as well as of vocational groups of teachers, doctors, lawyers, chemists, etc. Its aim here is to be the growth of select groups of trained 'militants' who shall provide the leadership of the whole Catholic Action movement as it grows.
>
> To provide up-to-date information on Catholic Action and Catholic Social Problems and to arrange for the dissemination of Catholic principles among Catholics and non-Catholics.
>
> To devote special attention to the formation of groups of Catholic workers.[11]

Tasked principally 'to supply information, direction and inspiration and to show workers in various fields how their abilities may be applied so as to bring the most satisfactory results', the Secretariat 'should not be expected to do much direct organising at present', but 'to utilise the enthusiasm and energy of amateur workers to a very large extent'. Staff should not be expected to arrange functions or demonstrations that were properly the responsibility of the individual organisations

---

11 'Campion Memorandum 2: Catholic Action Bureau' (Typescript 1937, Bruce Duncan Papers) 1–2.

concerned, or 'to attend evening meetings every night of the week – particularly meetings of small groups'.

Responsibility should not be accepted for the work of any individual organisation or body or for coordination between them, other than such as would 'lead to a future general organization of all Catholic Action bodies and their fruitful co-operation'. Subject to the need for each diocese to receive individual attention and for personal contacts to be made and renewed at regular intervals, travelling by the secretary and his assistant should be minimised as 'a waste of time and money when both are precious'. Concentration by the Secretariat should be on 'Youth organizations rather than those of older people'.[12]

Spelling out in more explicit terms a further key constraint specified by the Campions in their initial memorandum, the submission 'pointed out clearly that the Secretariat cannot undertake to direct political action among unionists or control the policy or tactics of Catholic groups of unionists':

> The immediate methods are those of collecting workers together in small groups and giving them a sound general training in Catholic social principles. They are to be 'militants' – trained to work among their fellows. Out of these trained workers will soon arise groups in individual unions. These having special knowledge of the conditions in their own industry will know best what tactics to pursue in their union. *These are the methods recommended by the Holy Father and by Catholic authorities abroad. The Secretariat cannot do more than train militants. It must scrupulously avoid politics and can only indirectly direct group tactics.*[13]

12 Campion Memorandum 2, 2–3.

13 Campion Memorandum 2, 5–6. Italics added.

All action which had been contemplated by individual Catholics where their unions were concerned had, so far, 'been connected only with specifically anti-Communist activities':

> This represents a weakness from two points of view. In the first place it means Catholic unionists themselves are prepared to pay lip service only to the claims for social justice, emphasised by the Pope. This attitude is strange, to say the least, since the economic interests of the Catholic workers themselves are involved in a progressive policy just as much as the interests of the rest of the workers. In the second place, such an attitude is completely mistaken from the point of view of tactics. It is a well-known fact that those union leaders who are Communists are, generally speaking, more determined in fighting for the demands of the men. The latter (who naturally judge by results) are thus inclined to put the Communists into executive positions. So the negative anti-Communist policy defeats its own ends.[14]

Responding to Mannix's request for nominations for appointment to the Secretariat, the submission proposed that Maher be appointed Secretary and Santamaria Assistant Secretary, on salaries respectively of £500 and £250 per annum. Both positions were to be for five years, with twelve months' notice of termination of appointment. 'The persons recommended for the Bureau', the submission read, 'have already made excellent contacts with fellow workers in every capital city':

> They have evolved methods which have proved capable of attracting normal young Catholics of every type. These will have to be adapted to the special needs of groups composed of people of different degrees of education, of different ages and sexes. Out of all this will grow mass movements of Catholic Action

14 Campion Memorandum 2, 8.

> in a natural and organic fashion and along lines best adapted to Australian conditions.[15]

In reality, the nomination of Santamaria for the position of assistant secretary was less assured and the process of arriving at it more fraught than the tenor of the wording might suggest. Kelly and McInerney had been approached initially. According to Kelly, McInerny declined, 'preferring independence in the prosecution of the temporal and ecclesial apostolates'. Kelly also 'declined basically for the same reason as that indicated by McInerney'.[16] By Santamaria's account, 'Kevin Kelly was actually recommended by the senior Campions to Archbishop Mannix as the second man, but his mother was a widow ... so Kelly took the view that his duty was to look after her, and he couldn't risk his job in the public service, and he continued with that'.[17]

'The choice for the second position was then narrowed down to one between Santamaria and Mitchell, at a time when it appeared that Archbishop Mannix's preference for the second position was the 21-year-old Santamaria', Kelly wrote:

> Already recognised as a genius in his speaking, writing and organisational capacities, some of his lay colleagues had certain doubts concerning his ability to appreciate the finer distinctions affecting the frontiers of Church-State relationships and of the distinct but complementary roles of Catholics in their activities as churchmen and citizens. In particular, I entertained

15 Campion Memorandum 2, 13.

16 Kelly, *Memoir*, 'The Foundation of ANSCA', 4.

17 B.A. Santamaria, as interviewed by Robin Hughes for the National Library of Australia Australian Biography Project, 23 April 1997. Tape 2 of 13 tapes transcript, as accessed 21/4/13 at http://www.australianbiography.gov.au/subjects/santamaria/interview2.html. In this interview Santamaria incorrectly states that Kelly's mother 'looked after the railway gates in Hawthorn or Tooronga'. Santamaria has confused Kelly's mother with his aunt, Mary Kate Kelly, who was Station Mistress at Glen Iris.

these reservations, but later recalled my conviction that, as Santamaria was destined to make a significant impact on the Church in Australia and on Australian public opinion, it was better that he should do so as a personality under the strict control in doctrinal matters of the bishops than otherwise. At the time, however, when McInerney and Maher were hesitant about recommending the appointment of Santamaria, Maher inclining to recommend Mitchell and McInerney, I reached the conclusion and informed both Mitchell and Santamaria that Santamaria's nomination would have my support.[18]

Origins

Santamaria was born in 1915, the oldest of six children of Joseph and Maria Santamaria who migrated to Australia from the Aeolian island of Salina in Italy in 1904, and started a grocery shop in Brunswick that by the mid-1930s had become a prosperous licenced grocery. He attended the North Melbourne Christian Brothers College before moving to St Kevin's College in East Melbourne, where Maher was his history teacher. Maher, he wrote, 'was an exceptionally gifted and personally sympathetic teacher whose professional capacities assisted me to obtain the Senior Scholarship':

> His moral influence was even more powerful. It could not but impress a 16-year-old that the religious positions which one would regard as normal coming from the Christian Brothers should be explained and defended with such confidence by a layman with a mind deeply grounded in European History and at home with all the intellectual currents of the day.[19]

Matriculating at the age of 15 and with his scholarship to Melbourne University secured, he repeated his final year at the college

18 Kelly, *Memoir*, 'The Foundation of ANSCA', 4–5.

19 Santamaria, *Against the Tide*, 15.

because he was too young for the university to admit him. Making the most of the hiatus, he debated for the college in inter-school competitions and edited one of its two journals, the *Glendalough Chronicle*. Following an acrimonious exchange with the editor of a rival publication, the *Central Critic*, a teacher, Brother Duffy, cautioned him that he had 'an execrable English style, but unfortunately for you, a good journalistic style. It will get you into trouble'.[20]

Like the more senior Campions of the stature of Maher, Merlo, Heffey and McInerney before him, he achieved outstanding results in the early stages of his five-year Arts-Law course, with the award of a Wyselaskie Scholarship in English Constitutional History and the Harbison Higinbotham Scholarship for his 1934 thesis, 'Italy Changes Shirts: The Origins of Italian Fascism'. Socially, he may have found the university less congenial. By Brenda Niall's account, 'In the small, privileged, class-conscious world of Melbourne University in the 1930s, a working-class Italian Catholic was an outsider on three counts'.[21]

A relevant anecdote by an associate, Peter Ryan, reads 'Writer Chester Wilmot and Santamaria were members of Melbourne University's crack interstate debating team'. Shortly before he died, Santamaria was asked by an author considering writing a biography of Wilmot, if Santamaria could possibly provide any recollections that might be of use. Ryan said he refused and, when asked why, responded:

> 'Chester Wilmot came to Melbourne University gilded by Melbourne Grammar and an establishment background. I was

20 Fitzgerald, *The Pope's Battalions*, 18.

21 Brenda Niall, 'Servant to Whom?', *Australian Book Review*, No 289, March 2007, 12–14.

> an Italian fruiterer's son from Brunswick, and there was not a single day that Chester let me forget it'.[22]

Meanwhile, a promising legal or academic career beckoned, but external events and the fear of Communism determined otherwise: 'Formal studies, however, became increasingly peripheral to the main business of my university years, and the promising results which I had obtained in the first two years of my course shaded downwards to a Law degree at pass standard. ... The future was to be not with, but against, the tide'.[23]

Attitudes

He was introduced to the Campion Society by Maher in 1931. His interests within it gravitated characteristically to action rather than reflection: 'The higher flights of philosophy and history in which men like Maher, Kelly and Denys Jackson were so fully at home were, in those early years, quite beyond me':

> I still recall with a sense of shame that I slept through the first two Campion meetings I attended in 1931, at which Jackson gave two papers on the Byzantine Empire. It took a particular level of philistinism to sleep through two papers delivered by so attractive a speaker ... Although it was later to be written that I was profoundly influenced by the writings of Belloc and Chesterton, in fact whatever influence there was came from the reading of others and listening to their discussion.[24]

The ideological viewpoint to which his exposure to the Campions gave rise was reflected in their newsletter, *Orders of the Day*, in 1935.

22 Peter Ryan, 'Long Shadow Cast by Lay Prince', *Australian*, 20 January 2007.

23 Santamaria, *Against the Tide*, 15–16.

24 Santamaria, *Against the Tide*, 16.

It read: 'Mussolini has declared that the salvation of the world lies in the totalitarian state ... He was wrong. It lies in totalitarian Catholicism. That means integral Catholicism. It means that your whole life and personality must be developed in a Catholic way'.[25] Socialising with him in the course of a visit to Melbourne in 1936 left enduring memories on the part of a group of visiting debaters from Adelaide University. As recalled by the historian Russel Ward in his 1988 autobiography:

> He preached eloquently and incessantly the virtues of Franco's Falange, of the Spanish rebels and of Franco himself, but he was very far from being obsessed with Spanish affairs. To back up these views he passionately expounded a whole theory of authoritarianism. Fascism in Germany, Italy and everywhere else was the best form of government, because the most viable in the modern world, to which modern man could aspire, and all human history went to prove it. Art, science and learning, he argued, had always flourished most under royal, imperial or dictatorial rule; the more authoritarian the better. In this respect the France of Louis XIV, the Sun King, was the *non pareil* of all time, though the absolute and continuing moral authority the Pope ought rightly to wield over all living creatures was even more important.[26]

Spain

Consequent on Kelly's insistence that, as a would-be Catholic Action body, the Campion Society should refrain from direct party political or pressure group activity, its members as such did not involve themselves in the Civil War controversy, but individually some were

25 *Orders of the Day*, No 2, October 1935, as quoted in Duncan, *Crusade or Conspiracy?*, 17.

26 Russel Ward, *A Radical Life: The Autobiography of Russell Ward* (South Melbourne Vic: Macmillan, 1988) 88.

in the forefront of the Nationalist cause. Looking back on his championing of Franco with the advantage of hindsight, and perhaps in the hope of an *ex post facto* vindication, Santamaria wrote in 1983 that 'Those Australian Catholics who believed that Spain was worth a political fight thus did not ... equate the cause of the Spanish Right with absolute Good and that of the Spanish Left with absolute Evil':

> We were not ignorant of the brutal injustices of Spanish society, nor of the apparent affiliation of the higher clergy with the cause of the landed aristocracy, very much in the manner of the *ancien régime* in revolutionary France. Nor were we ignorant of the barbarities committed by the Nationalists against their opponents in many parts of Spain, paralleled, of course, by those committed by the other side, although that provided no justification.[27]

If so, no such nuanced approach or reservations were evident when he and his fellow Campions, Kelly and Stan Ingwersen, argued the affirmative case in a memorable 1937 Melbourne University debate on the proposition 'That the Spanish Government is the ruin of Spain'. Exiting the Public Lecture Theatre to the acclaim of an audience packed overwhelmingly by their supporters, either Santamaria or Ingwersen shouted above the tumult the Nationalist battle cry *Viva Christo Rey!* (Long Live Christ the King!), provoking 'a display of Catholic triumphalism never before witnessed within the confines of the University of Melbourne'.[28]

At a subsequent debate in Ballarat, Ingwersen concluded his final address with the call 'Three cheers for General Franco and the crusaders of Spain'.[29] Reassembling in the street outside a pro-Republic Relief for Spain rally in the Adelaide Town Hall after

27 Santamaria, *Against the Tide*, 34.

28 Fitzgerald, *The Pope's Battalions*, 38.

29 Jory, *The Campion Society*, 84.

their eviction from it by police for their unruly behaviour, he and his followers evoked recollections of persecution and martyrdom with a spirited rendition of the traditional Catholic 'call to arms' hymn 'Faith of Our Fathers'.

Events of the character of the university and Ballarat debates and the Adelaide demonstration were tawdry and short-lived triumphs. The immediate effect of so uncritical and unreserved a support of the Nationalist cause in the eyes of many was to place Santamaria and his associates on the wrong side of history: aligned and identified through Franco with the Nazi and fascist regimes which within so short a space of time were to unleash on the world the horrors of World War II and the Holocaust.

In 1940, Franco and the 'Crusaders' applauded by Ingerswen and his supporters at Ballarat entered into a protocol with Nazi Germany 'committing Spain to join the Axis cause at a date to be decided "by common agreement of the three powers" but after military preparations were complete'. The envisaged alliance would have proceeded had it not been turned down ultimately by Hitler, on the grounds that any gains from it would be exceeded by the costs.[30]

And the wider outcome was to confirm for many the proclivity of the Church for positioning itself in unconscionable company. 'The responsibility of Catholics for the rise of totalitarian, or semi-totalitarian, regimes cannot be denied: Franco's Spain, Mussolini's Italy, Salazar's Portugal, Dolfuss' Austria, Petain's France and the Generals' regime in Argentina are a formidable indictment', Belloc's biographer, Robert Speaight, wrote.[31]

---

30 Paul Preston, 'Franco: A Biography' (London, Fontana Press, 1993) 400.

31 Robert Speaight, 'The Resurrection of France', *Dublin Review*, October 1944, 100–101.

To many, irrespective of denominational affiliations, who shared with the Campions their Christian faith and were as deeply committed to it, the linking of Christ and Christianity with Franco and the Nationalists was morally repugnant, ethically untenable and arguably blasphemous. Highlighting the unfounded attribution by the Spanish bishops, in their internationally circulated 1937 collective letter, of the widespread killing of priests and other religious personnel and burning of churches following the outbreak of the Civil War in 1936 to 'a Communist-directed conspiracy organised by the Comintern', the US historian José M. Sánchez notes that 'The most authoritative studies on the role of the Communist Party reject the notion that it was the motivating force behind the anticlerical fury. … In fact the Communists wanted to end the fury and terror so as to attract moderate Western support for the Republic':[32]

> The bishops had hoped to sway foreign opinion; they instead compromised themselves with a regime that had already begun to commit wartime and reprisal atrocities that no Christian – and especially no cleric – should allow. Thus, the tragedy was compounded; nearly one-eighth of the Spanish clergy were killed by violent anti-clericals; the other seven-eighths found themselves compromised by a violent and barbarous regime. They did not protest their protectors' cruel ways, and the fury came to be compounded by the scandal of silence.[33]

Nor was it self-evident, in the adoption of so partisan a stand as the raising of the Nationalist flag and shouting of its battle cry at

---

32 Sánchez, *The Spanish Civil War as a Religious Tragedy*, 21.

33 Sánchez, *The Spanish Civil War as a Religious Tragedy*, 102. The killings followed on rather than preceded the invasion of mainland Spain by insurrectionist forces under the direction of General Franco – ie. were not the cause of the insurrection as the Catholic press widely reported, but a response to it. See, for example, Hugh Thomas, *The Spanish Civil War* (London: Eyre & Spottiswoode Ltd, 1961, and Antony Beevor, *The Battle for Spain: The Spanish Civil War 1936–1939* (London: Orion Books, 2006).

the university debate signified, that adequate or indeed any account had been taken of the opposition to the insurrection by Catholics otherwise in good standing among the Campions, 'who strongly contested the apocalyptic worldview and the concepts of holy war or crusade'.[34] Had greater attention been paid to passionate critiques of the insurrection such as by Maritain, Luigi Sturzo, François Mauriac and Georges Bernanos, which were freely available in periodicals to which Hackett's library subscribed, the Campions arguably may have forfeited less credibility and spared themselves much grief. The effect was to engender a measure of mutual wariness or antipathy on the part of much of centre-left opinion and moderate Catholic activism towards one another by which ultimately neither was well-served. The ALP Split of the middle 1950s stemmed in part from the suffering of the Spanish people, and was watered with their tears.

Postscript

A significant postscript to the Civil War controversy from a recent biography of Mannix reads: 'Ingwersen's chivalric sense of honour was outraged when, in one debate on Spain, Bob [Santamaria] brilliantly extemporized a crunching response, citing statistics, to a sharp unexpected question'.

> On being congratulated afterwards (where on earth did he come across such happy numbers?), Santamaria admitted cheerfully: 'I made them up'. Ingwersen never spoke to him again. An outraged soul of honour, Stan would refer to Bob after that as 'that Sicilian bandit'. But for Bob there had been no breach of

34 Duncan, *From Ghetto to Crusade: A Study of the Social and Political Thought of Catholic Opinion-Makers in Sydney During the 1930s*, PhD thesis, Department of Government, University of Sydney, 1987, 200.

> integrity; at worst a sporting peccadillo, at best a winning hit for Christ. It was part of a lifelong habit.[35]

As subsequent events so strikingly attest, the Ingwersen experience was in no sense unique or unrepresentative. John Molony recalls of documents from the 1957 Second World Congress of the Lay Apostolate obtained by him at Santamaria's request that 'Bob had them picked up from the airport holding them for a week or so before sending them to me in Ballarat':

> I received and read some of them just after I finished reading an article by Bob in the Melbourne Catholic paper, the *Advocate*, of 14 November, on the conclusions of the Congress. The documents were in Italian, and, as soon as I read Bob's article, I saw that the text had been interpreted, misinterpreted if the truth be known, in order to make it seem that the Congress, and the pope himself, agreed with lay involvement in the political sphere in the way Bob and his Movement engaged in it. ... I have been quoted since as saying in an interview in 1977, 'From that moment I had no further trust in Santamaria and vigorously and publicly opposed his concept of the lay apostolate'.[36]

Frank Mount – otherwise well-disposed and a onetime close associate – writes that the greatest problem he had with Santamaria throughout their association was that 'he was not always a man of his word':

> For example he'd agree on a deal over lunch and perhaps shake your hand on it and a few days, weeks or months later deny that the conversation had ever happened. He didn't always do this, but it occurred often. Others had the same experience, regularly. NCC officials like Norm Lauritz and Gerald Mercer and the

35 James Griffin, *Daniel Mannix: Beyond the Myths* (Mulgrave, Vic: Garratt Publishing, 2012) 311.

36 John Molony, *Beyond Wendouree* (Ballan, Vic: Connor Court Publishing, 2010) 311.

> DLP senators put up with it during the long fight against Communist totalitarianism, but when that faded, the situation changed. All but one of the five DLP senators, while they were senators, broke with Bob over this issue, as did independent Senator Brian Harradine.[37]

Nor was he averse to urging action in similar vein on others. By Fr Duncan's account, Santamaria proposed to the Victorian bishops in 1967 that 'for six years 10 per cent of the expected $1,800,000 from new per capita grants to Catholic schools be allocated instead to build up a capital fund for the NCC':

> Santamaria suggested that the Victorian dioceses hire 'Catholic Adult Education Association Ltd', the incorporated name of the NCC, as consultants at such a commission. The bishops undoubtedly did not agree to this, but it was an astonishing request given the Vatican's clear direction in 1957 to end direct support for the Movement. What would a government or public have made of such a use of public funds?[38]

Reservations

As recalled by McInerney, 'Some of us – including Kelly and myself – had reservations as to how far Santamaria could work with Maher'. Unforeseen or insufficiently appreciated in his or Kelly's calculations was the extent to which emerging trends and future developments would so shortly marginalise their influence and incomparably advantage Santamaria to Maher's detriment. 'The senior members of the Campion Society were settling into married life and the bringing up of children, while at the other end of the scale the younger members

---

37 Frank Mount, *Wrestling with Asia: A Memoir* (Ballan, Vic: Connor Court Publishing, 2012) 347.

38 Duncan, *Crusade or Conspiracy?*, 384.

of the Society were becoming increasingly exposed to the chances of the call-up for service in the military forces', McInerney wrote:

> From September 1939 when at the Campion Spring School at Xavier College we adjourned to hear Menzies' broadcast announcing Australia's entry into the War, we all lived in the shadow of the call up and industrial conscription. Some of the most promising young recruits of the Campion Society were among those who were first called up, others enlisted in the Army or the Air Force or the Navy. By the time Japan entered the War there were few in the Campion Society who were not liable to be called up into the armed forces and even they were liable to have their activities directed by the Director of Manpower ... When the pre-war Campions came back from the services their priorities were in most cases to find employment or to complete their educational or professional qualifications and for those who had married during the War there was the problem of finding a house and raising a family.[39]

Spared in exceptional and controversial circumstances from the exigencies of the call-up and the critical scrutiny by the senior Campions which his activities otherwise might have attracted, Santamaria was able to devote his considerable energies to a shaping of the Secretariat along lines which diverged increasingly and to ultimately disastrous effect from those set out in the Campion memoranda and endorsed by the bishops. A perceptive assessment reads: 'Maher found it impossible, granted his personality, to impose either his view or his will on the young Santamaria'.[40] Nor were expectations of a 'strict control' at the hands of the bishops themselves fulfilled. 'It was not Pius XII who formed the minds of the bishops in the 1940s: it was Mr Santamaria', Kelly wrote.[41]

39 McInerney, *Memoir*, 27–28.

40 Peoples, *Santamaria's Salesman*, 149.

41 Duncan, *Crusade of Conspiracy?*, 388.

Chapter 10

ANSCA: THE MAHER YEARS 1938–1946

Inception and Achievements

Recalled to the episcopal residence, Raheen, on 3 November 1937, in their capacity as representatives of the Campion Society, McInerney, Maher, Kelly and Santamaria 'were first received privately by Archbishop Mannix, who told us of his success in convincing his three colleagues of the utility of the Campion plan, and discussed with us certain difficulties he had experienced with his colleagues':

> Twenty minutes later, his three colleagues entered the room and we were introduced to them. Archbishop Mannix then requested Archbishop Simonds to read to us the Minutes of the meeting of the Episcopal Committee held that afternoon and this he did. In accordance with the specific recommendations of the *ad hoc* group, Maher had been appointed Secretary and Santamaria Assistant Secretary to a National Secretariat of Catholic Action.[1]

The Episcopal Committee on Catholic Action (ECCA) was to be chaired by Mannix with Simonds as its secretary. Meanwhile, not all the concurrent developments were as auspicious. In place of the Belgian/French 'Jocist' model, whereby the emphasis was on lay

1 Kelly, *Memoir*, 'The Foundation of ANSCA', 4.

initiative and the overall movement was subdivided consistent with the natural social groupings of age, sex, locality of parish, trade or profession or other definitive activity or attribute, Gilroy abruptly proposed on behalf of the Sydney diocese an alternative. Consistent with Italian practice, Catholic Action within each parish was to be divided into groups simply of men and women and older and younger members, and subject to the proviso that 'as a general principle all organising Secretaries should be priests'.[2] When, on the basis of a third submission on the proposal prepared by the Campions at Mannix's request, the Episcopal Sub-Committee confirmed its original decision and adherence to the Jocist tenets, Gilroy withdrew Sydney from the national movement to establish a diocesan Catholic Action network of its own.[3]

The Australian National Secretariat for Catholic Action opened for business on 24 January 1938, in premises rented in the Bank of New South Wales building at 368 Collins Street, where Maher had practised briefly as a partner in the firm of Adami & Maher. Maher and Santamaria agreed at the outset on a division of responsibilities whereby Santamaria's primary focus would be on the provision of information to trade union groups and the creation of a National Catholic Rural Movement (NCRM). Maher would have the carriage of all such other projects as the Campion memoranda had specified and the Plenary Council and ECCA had endorsed. For all that the Secretariat's resources were from the start meagre, its achievements in the short to intermediate term incomparably exceeded its limitations.

---

2 Jory, *The Campion Society*, 91.

3 'Campion Society Memorandum 3: Catholic Action Bureau': Memorandum prepared by the Campion Society for the Episcopal Sub-Committee on Catholic Action (Bruce Duncan Papers) 4.

Maher was able to report to ECCA in December 1940 that an initial phase of the key task of preparing 'militants' for the role of 'action by Catholics' had been completed. Discussion groups 'to bring together the people most interested to educate them in the principles of the Movement, and to discover, by practical experiment, the type of specialised movements really needed under our conditions' had been 'crowned with success in producing all the results which had been expected and which were required as a foundation for future development':

> The transition from 'discussion group' to 'national specialised movement' is only now taking place – two and a half years after the development of the Secretariat – but it would have been unwise to have 'forced the pace' by endeavouring to establish the specialised movements earlier. … A large number of groups have been formed throughout Australia, even though developments in some dioceses have been uneven. There are now some hundreds of young Catholics ready to be trained as leaders of specialised movements, and their early interest, aroused in discussion groups, will bear fruit in the near future. … The transition is being accomplished naturally, and, if the main Movements can be placed on a proper foundation before the end of the next year, it seems that they should be ready to make progress then and to render valuable service to the Church and Australia.[4]

Specialised movements which had been identified in the course of the previous two and a half years as being the most necessary, and for which handbooks had been prepared, were to cater respectively for:

4 F.K.H. Maher, *Report of the Australian National Secretariat of Catholic Action to December 31st, 1940* (Melbourne, Vic: Australian National Secretariat for Catholic Action, ND) 5.

Rural Population

Adult Workers

Young Workers

Schools

University Students

Girls 14–25

Married Women.

Meanwhile, translations of Fernand Lelotte's *Fundamental Principles of Catholic Action* and Pierre Bayart's *Specialised Catholic Action* had been prepared and published, together with some 5000 copies of study program guides for discussion groups, and 80,000 copies of pamphlets issued in conjunction with the Catholic Truth Society. Pamphlet titles included *What to Read*, *For Social Justice*, *The Catholic Revival*, *The World Moves On*, *What the Church Has Done for the Worker (Parts 1 & 2)* and *The Manifesto of the NCRM*. Lecture tours featuring distinguished visitors had attracted large audiences throughout various parts of Australia, and numerous 'Catholic Hour' radio talks had been delivered.

A monthly Catholic Action *Bulletin for Leaders* had been launched, and special articles on aspects of Catholic Action had been prepared for diocesan periodicals. In advance of the other proposed specialised movements, the NCRM was already in being, with an 'eminently successful' National Rural Conference behind it, a constitution drawn up, and a distinctive magazine of its own, *Rural Life*, appearing on a regular basis. Fifty Rural Groups had been 'consolidated into a unity' and re-organised on a regional basis, and further groups were being formed.[5] Individuals engaging in

5 Maher, *Report of the Australian National Secretariat of Catholic Action to December 31st, 1940*, 7.

controversies on matters of social justice and apologetics in the secular press and professional journals had been assisted with advice and information, and 'considerable quantities' of the Secretariat's material had been dispatched in response to queries about Catholic Action from overseas: 'England, Ireland, Colombo, India, Fiji, Singapore and many cities in USA'.

The Distributist vision of a new social order had begun to be spelled out in the series of Social Justice Statements that were drafted on ANSCA's behalf for the bishops mainly by Santamaria, from 1940 until 1954. Consistent with the key tenets of the social encyclicals, Distributism and the personalist philosophers, the Social Justice Statements advocated an all but explicitly Distributist widespread ownership of property including workers owning and controlling their workplaces, which were to be grouped through Industry Councils, along lines broadly reminiscent of the medieval guilds which Belloc and the Chesterton brothers so greatly admired and eloquently championed. Introduced in an initial statement by Simonds in 1940, their Distributist agenda was codified and accorded its most explicit expression in the 1943 statement *Pattern for Peace* and the 1945 statement *The Land is Your Business.*

Patterns for Peace set out recommendations for the government of the day, which included:

> The formation of industrial councils as the instrument for the control and regulation of industry.
>
> That industrial policy should be directed to the most widespread possible distribution of the ownership of production (a) by means of co-partnerships of workers in industrial enterprises; and (b) by marshalling the incentive resources of the nation to secure the greatest possible reduction in the size of industrial units consistent with efficiency in production.

> The right of the worker to share in the control of the policy of the industry in which he is engaged shall be made effective by his participation on terms of equality with the employer in the industrial council.
>
> That special measures are called for in the public control of monopolies and the regulation of 'Big business' to curb the power derived from immense financial resources.
>
> That each industrial council will seek to preserve the class of small owners in the industry which it controls.
>
> That family farms, linked together by a network of co-operative institutions, shall be recognised in principle as the basis of our rural civilisation.[6]

The Land is Your Business stated:

> We want co-operatives to develop – and to develop fast. We want buying co-operatives, selling co-operatives, insurance co-operatives, credit co-operatives and co-operatives of half-a-dozen other kinds.

It recommended that:

> Every State should pass legislation on the lines of the NSW Co-operation Act, which recognises and regulates co-operatives of all types, and encourages their development. In addition, all Governments should establish or extend Agricultural Extension Services so that farming communities are constantly being trained in the methods of co-operation. ... The Government can also help by assisting financially all those movements which are engaged in the extension of co-operatives.[7]

---

6 'Pattern for Peace: A Twenty-Point Program for Social Reconstruction', in Michael Hogan, *Justice Now! Social Justice Statements of the Australian Catholic Bishops First Series 1940–1966* (Sydney, NSW: Department of Government and Public Administration, University of Sydney, 2006) 43–44.

7 'Pattern for Peace', in Hogan, *Justice Now!*, 71, 75.

'We are satisfied', Maher's report concluded, 'that the end of three years of official Catholic Action shows a considerable advance in the following respects':

> There is now a fairly clear knowledge in the minds of many priests and lay leaders of what Catholic Action implies in practice and of the methods which, if applied consistently, will bring satisfactory results.
>
> There is a very great amount of latent enthusiasm among the laity in every diocese and every milieu, and tens of thousands could be enrolled fairly quickly if it were possible to set up the organization to direct their energies.
>
> The National Secretariat, which has received generous support from the Bishops, is in close touch with the leading personalities in Catholic Action in nearly every part of Australia and New Zealand.
>
> We feel we have the confidence of the Diocesan Organisers everywhere and we have been assured that they will co-operate with us in any general schemes of development which may be drawn up.
>
> That, with only a few exceptions, all bodies doing work of a Catholic Action nature are thus working to a common plan and we feel that there is sound reason for believing that the confusion and rivalry which has marred Catholic Action in other lands are well on the way to being eliminated in Australia and New Zealand.
>
> Unless the war spoils everything, we are confident that the existing organizations will make steady progress during 1941, particularly in the rural and worker movements.[8]

The hopes for the Secretariat in the subsequent short to medium term were not disappointed. Maher was able to report further in 1945, in a seemingly all but standard response to inquiries raised in

8 Maher, *Report of the Australian National Secretariat of Catholic Action to December 31st, 1940*, 19–20.

correspondence, that 'The Rural Movement, after tremendous difficulties at the beginning, is now flourishing very well and has some 250 groups of men and women, together with nearly five thousand members':

> This, in view of petrol restrictions and transport problems and the whole war situation is very encouraging, and this Movement is now solidly on its feet. Meanwhile, I have been encouraging the growth of the Young Christian Workers for boys in the cities between 14 and 25, the National Catholic Girls' Movement for girls in the cities from 14 to 25 and the Young Catholic Students' Movement for senior students in secondary schools. These are also well established; the Y.C.W. having about 8000 members, the NCGM about 4000. And the YCS about 2500. As each of these Movements grew to some kind of maturity and there were priests and laity with some kind of knowledge of these methods, I withdrew from the active direction and a National Council was set up in each case under one of the Bishops. This National Council is now responsible for the policy of the Movement, and I keep in touch with all the National Councils by sitting in on their meetings. ... All are following the Jocist methods of Enquiry, Gospel Discussion, Contact, Specialisation and Services.[9]

National Catholic Rural Movement

Even so, for all Maher's apparent optimism, underlying divergences of both principle and practice between himself and Santamaria were emerging, which the NCRM in particular exemplified. Far from Santamaria's direction of the NCRM being observant of the ANSCA commitment to formation of the Catholic conscience and 'the Jocist methods of Enquiry, Gospel Discussion, Contact, Specialisation and

9 F.K.H Maher to Rev Father Quinlan, 23 May 1945, B.A. Santamaria Papers, Series 5 Box 3. MS13492.

Services' that the bishops had so explicitly endorsed and Maher's reports so consistently reaffirmed, it was from the outset unambiguously non-consultative, 'top down' and authoritarian. As recalled by T.R. Luscombe, a onetime NCRM Administrative Secretary and, in general, supportive of Santamaria, 'Once again it was a case of Santamaria dominance':

> Looking at it in retrospect, one cannot escape the conclusion that, despite its undoubted achievements in some directions, it was an artificial organization created from the city and run by city intellectuals and theorists ... There was certainly no room for the non-conformist or the individualist. The acid test consisted of the acceptance of policy as defined and imposed from the top. ... The obvious danger in an arrangement of this nature was that such an organization, while ostensibly solely concerned with rural matters, would increasingly be expected to become a mouthpiece for policies, both national and international, decided in a broader context. ... In practice it resulted in the Rural Movement, during the final years of Santamaria's association with it, degenerating into a country cousin of the industrial movement. ... The old spontaneous quality was swamped by a sombre, depressing anti-Communism that very often turned the pages of *Rural Life* into a nagging, mechanical recital of the theme poured out week after week in the deadly serious *News-Weekly*.[10]

By the early 1960s, the NCRM was reduced to little more than a compliant cash cow for the Santamaria Movement, in its ultimate iteration as the National Civic Council. Citing the discovery, in his capacity as an NCRM organiser from 1959 until 1961, of a £5000 NCRM loan to the Catholic Adult Education Association, Kevin Peoples notes that 'Adult Education was a euphemism for describing Bob's NCC':

---

10 Luscombe, *Builders and Crusaders*, 194–195.

> This umbrella account, first established in 1948 with a slightly different title, was a means of enabling monies to flow to different accounts under Bob's control either through loans or simply moving money from one account to another. Bank overdrafts were made available at cheaper rates of interest if some accounts had credit balances. I had no idea that my efforts were at times directly supporting the coffers of the NCC. Monies from the NCRM, a formal Catholic Action body working directly to the bishops, should never have been made accessible to the NCC, a civic body of Catholics actively involved in politics.[11]

Admitting to NCRM members in 1968 that he had made mistakes 'when we developed the idea of independent farming many years ago', Santamaria added 'Your mistake was to listen to me too easily and not to controvert'.[12] That something more in the nature of a comprehensive apology and a modicum of humility may have been called for seemingly did not occur to him. Responding to a friendly reference to his supposed Distributist convictions by the onetime Labor Leader W.G. ('Bill') Hayden in 1996, he wrote 'In fact whatever economic ideas I express are not "Distributist" in the Chestertonian sense of that word'.[13] It was a low-key leave taking from so longstanding an affiliation.

---

11 Peoples, *Santamaria's Salesman*, 53.

12 Duncan, *Crusade or Conspiracy?*, 400.

13 Santamaria, *Santamaria: A Memoir*, 193.

Chapter 11

THE SANTAMARIA HEGEMONY

Santamaria

With indications of a modest economic recovery evident from the mid-1930s and the emergence of new tensions internationally, Mannix's priorities changed. It was to the twenty-one-year-old Santamaria that he looked increasingly for a less constrained response than that of Maher and the more senior Campions to the threat of Communism that now supplanted the deficiencies of Capitalism as his major concern, and the fulfilment of the wider political hopes for which he had so long striven.

Santamaria, he confided to Denys Jackson, 'was the son he never had'.[1] In the fiery young student activist and soon-to-be law graduate, he perhaps sensed something of the flamboyance, theatrics, predisposition to hyperbole and disregard for inconvenient constraints of his younger self, and glimpsed possibilities akin to where classically 'When Cicero spoke, men marvelled. When Caesar spoke men marched'. His sentiments were reciprocated. As recalled by Brenda Niall, 'The most revealing words I ever heard

1 Duncan, *Crusade or Conspiracy?*, 389.

from Santamaria – never one to talk about his own feelings – showed his devotion to Mannix "whom I love more than my own father"'.[2] Santamaria wrote that Mannix and the poet James McAuley 'were really the only close, intimate friends I have ever had'.[3] In Kelly's view, Santamaria acted as 'a kind of prime minister to Mannix'.[4] So close-knit an inner circle was not necessarily receptive to external advice or admonition.

As was to become clear increasingly, nothing about Santamaria's ANSCA appointments in his view obligated him to an observance of the Secretariat's core values and principles, as set out in the Campion memoranda and endorsed by the bishops. 'Even before 1942, the Central Committee of the "C.W." had been looking askance at a number of informal and, as it were, extra-official activities impinging on the temporal plane that appeared to be initiated at least in part by B.A. Santamaria', Kelly wrote:

> In the event, it was later to be disclosed that, on the evening of Friday 14 August 1942, Santamaria, while holding the position of Assistant Secretary of ANSCA and doubtless with the noblest of motives in mind, but with an imperfect appreciation of the doctrinal issues at stake, inaugurated, with himself as its effective head, an organisation which was to involve him and many others in intensive political work at first in Catholic Action groups and other Catholic societies, [then] in trade unions and other organisations, and ultimately in the internal affairs of political parties. This supplementary or extra-official activity of Santamaria, on both the spiritual and temporal planes, was to involve him, in the words of Maritain, in asking 'Catholics to form a single bloc on the level of political action;

2 Niall, *The Riddle of Father Hackett*, 252.

3 Duncan, *Crusade or Conspiracy?*, 389.

4 K.T. Kelly, 'Mannix: The Full Story has Still to Come', *Catholic Weekly*, 12 December 1984.

> and so of annihilating and sterilising, in the long run, their best efforts on the level of Catholic Action'.[5]

'To understand the relationship between Santamaria and his colleagues of the "Movement" on the one hand and what I might call the "Old Guard" of the Campion Society and the *Catholic Worker* on the other it is necessary to say something about the geographical situation of the Secretariat and the *Catholic Worker* respectively', McInerney wrote. When the Secretariat had established itself in the A.P.A. building at 379 Queen Street, its offices were on the second floor of the building and, 'given the closeness of the friendship which existed between senior members of the Campion Society and Frank Maher, and in those days Bob Santamaria', it was natural that senior members of the Campion Society and later the Central Committee of the *Catholic Worker* frequently brought their lunches down to the Secretariat offices and discussed matters of mutual concern:

> When the War ended and those of us who had been absent from Melbourne on war service returned to our peacetime avocations, we renewed the practice of dropping in at 379 Collins Street at lunchtime. By that time the second floor offices of the Secretariat were peopled by a number of men who were not with the Campion vintage but were associated with Bob Santamaria in some way which was never made clear. … With Frank Maher absent on leave in England in virtually the whole of 1946 it was more and more usual for myself and others to resort at lunch to the *Worker* offices rather than to the Secretariat offices. Our tendency to resort at lunch to the *Worker* offices rather than to the Secretariat offices increased as we became aware – at first only vaguely – that there was some secret activity emanating

5 Kelly, *Memoir*, 'The Foundation of ANSCA', 16. Bracketed text is from Kelly's handwritten amendments to the original typescript.

from the Secretariat offices to the existence and nature of which we were not privy.[6]

The Anti-Communist Struggle

Anti-Communist sentiment reached fever pitch throughout Australia in the decade subsequent to World War II. The postwar world was in many respects an unfamiliar and even frightening place. Old certainties were being challenged, old allegiances such as to Britain crumbling, wartime allies were becoming enemies and enemies allies, and familiar maps being re-drawn in new and frequently disturbing or threatening ways. Legitimate struggles by trade unionists to retain improved wages and working conditions and ensure the fulfilment of wartime expectations of full employment and 'a land fit for heroes' were ascribed routinely to subversive rather than industrial motivation.

Hiroshima and Nagasaki raised new spectres of nuclear devastation or annihilation. Mounting all but exponentially with the advent of the Cold War, the Communist takeover of China, the outbreak of hostilities in Korea and the persecution of the Church and its adherents within the Soviet Bloc and China, Catholic fears were intensified by high-profile instances of anti-Catholicism, such as the show trial and protracted imprisonment of Hungary's Cardinal Josef Mindszenty, and the expulsion of foreign missionaries from China and persecution of Chinese Christians.

Nor domestically was there felt to be room for complacency in the light of a largely uncritical wartime sympathy and support for the Soviet Union and by extension Soviet Communism, as reflected in

---

6 McInerney, *Memoir*, 37, 21.

part by the concurrent rise of Communist Party membership and influence in the industrial sphere. Party membership increased from around 4000 in 1940 to a peak in the middle 1940s of some 23,000. In an overall unionised workforce of some 1.3 million, the party at its zenith controlled unions with a membership of 275,000 and in others totalling 480,000 members was significantly influential.[7] Fred Paterson – 'Rhodes scholar, ex-theology student, union activist and radical barrister' – won the state seat of Bowen in Queensland in 1944, as the only openly Communist Party candidate ever to secure election to an Australian parliament.[8]

The 1945 Australian Council of Trade Unions Congress adopted on the motion of Communist delegates resolutions requiring respectively that decisions of future congresses should be binding on the union movement as a whole, and that all members of the interstate executive of the ACTU should in future be elected directly by the Congress rather than in part by its affiliated Trades Hall Councils. That ratification of the affiliates resolution was rejected subsequently by a majority of the THCs, and its intent to further enhance the party's prospects of controlling future Congresses to that extent thereby frustrated, was little consolation for those who saw in its adoption a new high-water mark of party influence within the peak body. A further Congress decision authorized affiliation by the ACTU with the predominantly Communist-influenced World Federation of Trade Unions (WFTU), and the prominent Communist secretary of the Federated Ironworkers Union, E.W. ('Ernie') Thornton, was elected as its first WFTU delegate. Vacancies on the Executive

---

7 Robin Gollan, *Revolutionaries and Reformists: Communism and the Australian Labor Movement 1920–1950* (Sydney: George Allen & Unwin, 1975) 130.

8 Ross Fitzgerald, *Fred Paterson: Australia's Only Communist Party Member of Parliament* (St Lucia, Qld: University of Queensland Press, 1997) xii.

were without exception filled from a party ticket incorporating both Communist and ALP candidates.

In March 1949 the then secretary of the Communist Party, Lance Sharkey, told a Sydney journalist that Australian troops would welcome Soviet troops 'pursuing aggressors' in Australia as workers in Europe had welcomed the Red Army, and was gaoled for three years on grounds of sedition.[9] The national coal strike that crippled Australian industry throughout much of 1949 and arguably resulted directly in the downfall of the Chifley government at the 1949 elections was by the admission of subsequent party secretary, Bernard ('Bernie') Taft, 'a last desperate attempt' by the CPA leadership to precipitate a crisis and supplant the ALP as the workers' party.[10] The prominent Communist Party member, Eric Aarons, acknowledged to its Central Committee in 1956 that 'had we been in power, we too could have executed people we considered to be objectively, even if not subjectively helping our enemies'.[11]

Exaggeration and Exacerbation

Exaggeration and exacerbation of the general disquiet were rife. Writing under the pseudonym of Michael Lamb in a 1942 pamphlet, *Red Glows the Dawn*, that sold some 35,000 copies, the then Deputy Leader of the Victorian Parliamentary Labor Party and future Deputy Premier, Bert Cremean, warned of penetration by Communist Party cadres into strategic industries and the Volunteer Defence Corps, in

9 Alistair Davidson, *The Communist Party of Australia: A Short History* (Stanford, CA: Stanford University Press, 1969) 108–109.

10 Bernie Taft, *Crossing the Party Line: Memoirs of Bernie Taft* (Newnham, Vic: Scribe Publications, 1994) 63.

11 Eric Aarons, *What's Left: Memoirs of an Australian Communist* (Melbourne, Vic: Penguin Books, 1993). As quoted in Duncan, *Crusade or Conspiracy?*, 396.

preparation for 'a violent, bloody, terrible uprising' to eliminate their class enemies:

> Every effort is being made by the Communists and their supporters to infiltrate the VDC because membership means the possession of arms, and because rifles and cartridges are necessary to the future of the movement in this country. In every factory or annex where there is a Red employed you may be certain that there is a campaign in existence for enlistment in the Corps.[12]

Warming to Cremean's theme, the Jesuit priest Harold Lalor electrified predominantly Catholic audiences with his 'five minutes to midnight' predictions of imminent insurrection, for which he claimed to possess not only the plans but the locations of the Communist arsenals and machine-gun ammunition.[13] A perceptive account of the climate and circumstances of the day concludes 'With this sort of propaganda ringing in Catholic ears, it is hardly surprising that there were some bizarre activities in the parishes as the faithful were prepared for the imminent takeover of Australia':

> One Sydney convent, under advice from Movement people, stocked up on civilian clothing so that nuns could disappear into the community when the Communist revolution came. In a Melbourne Catholic school, girls were encouraged to watch out for Communist submarines in Port Phillip Bay, using a telescope from the school roof. Around the countryside, commando courses were organized for guerilla training against the Communists.[14]

---

12 Herbert M. Cremean (as Michael Lamb), *Red Glows the Dawn*, Melbourne: NP, 1942) 36. An alternative account estimates sales at 50,000 copies.

13 Paul Ormonde, *The Movement* (Melbourne, Vic: Thomas Nelson (Australia) Limited, 1972) 17.

14 Paul Ormonde, 'The Movement – Politics by Remote Control', in Paul Ormonde (ed), *Santamaria: The Politics of Fear* (Richmond, Vic: Spectrum Publications Pty Ltd, 2000) 166.

Even at so late a point as the 1958 elections, Lalor argued that an ALP victory would 'soon give way to a full-blooded Red regime, and another nation would have fallen to the Terror'.[15]

Nor were hyperbole and fomentation of hysteria in the wider community less endemic. Calling for the suppression of the Communist Party in 1940, the then Leader of the Country Party, A.G. ('Archie') Cameron, declared that it must be 'torn from Australian soil, root, branch and seed'.[16] Following the Communist takeover of Czechoslovakia in 1948, Victoria's Liberal Premier, T.T. ('Tom') Hollway, likened his state's situation to that of the Czechs, declaring that the 'Communist menace was no less real there than in Czechoslovakia, the latest country to come under the heel of the Soviets'.[17] In 1951, the Prime Minister and Liberal Party Leader, R.G. Menzies, foreshadowed a possible outbreak within three years of a world war between the Western and Soviet blocs. In the event of war, Communists and the Communist Party would act as a fifth column, Menzies said.

Akin to Senator Joseph McCarthy and his Congressional Un-American Affairs Committee counterparts in the US, the anti-Labor parties and conservative media of the day routinely conflated left

---

15 A paper circulated by Santamaria in 1974 to national officers of the National Civic Council (NCC), as the Movement had by then become, reads: 'The organisation's fundamental responsibility is to preserve the constitutional democratic order against the threat of a totalitarian "coup" which, the practical situation indicates, could only come from the Communist parties and the extreme left. Whereas in the past … there was considerable scepticism as to such a possibility, there is now a more widespread acknowledgement that runaway inflation has made it possible, even in the short to medium term'. B.A. Santamaria, 'National Situation' (ND, Lalor Papers), as quoted in Duncan, *Crusade or Conspiracy?*, 347.

16 David Carment, 'Australian Communism and National Security September 1939 – June 1941', *Journal of the Australasian Historical Society*, 6, Part 4, March 1980, 250.

17 *Argus*, 1/3/1948, as quoted in Fitzgerald, *The Pope's Battalions*, 81.

of centre opinion with Communism and vilified the ALP as being 'soft on communism'. Its leader H.V. ('Bert') Evatt was pilloried as being pro-Communist for his role in defeating on civil liberties grounds the Menzies government's 1951 referendum seeking powers, previously disallowed by the High Court, to outlaw the Communist Party and require 'named' Communists to prove their innocence, in contravention of the accepted principle in British law that an accused person is innocent until proven guilty. The Country Party Leader and Deputy Prime Minister, Arthur Fadden, questioned publicly during the 1954 election campaign whether the electorate could afford to make Evatt its 'trustee' and rely on him to give effect to the findings of the Petrov Royal Commission, in the light of 'his association with Communists and communism over the years'.[18]

Origins of the Santamaria 'Movement'

Santamaria was drawn into the organised anti-Communist struggle by Cremean in 1938. Impressed by his Civil War debate address and hard on the heels of recommending him to Mannix as Deputy to Maher at ANSCA, Cremean invited him to the Melbourne Trades Hall for a series of lectures on Communist aims and tactics by a former party member, Dinny Lovegrove, who had fallen out with the party, joined the ALP and along with Calwell and the ALP State Secretary, Pat Kennelly, become a leader of 'a growing anti-Communist faction' within it. Introductions followed to the Secretary of the Melbourne Trades Hall Council, Vic Stout, and the president of the ACTU, Percy Clary, who were under Communist challenge in their respective spheres, and his assistance was sought

18 Murray, *The Split*, 151.

shortly to combat the 'seeming inevitability of the defeat of the non-Communist forces'.[19]

'What Cremean was asking for was a kind of Catholic crusade against Communism, not one that would be based on mass meetings and ringing pronouncements, but one that would base itself on direct organization within the trade union movement', Santamaria wrote.[20] He, Cremean and Calwell supported incipient anti-Communist insurrections such as were emerging at the Newport Railways Workshops, at the instigation respectively of the young trade unionist Campion Frank Keating and the future state Labor MP and minister, Frank Scully.

At a meeting attended in Santamaria's home in August 1941 by Cremean, the future state and later federal ALP MP Stan Keon and a local ALP 'numbers' man, Frank Hannan, the nucleus of a new anti-Communist organisation was formed. Known severally to its members as 'the Freedom Movement', 'the Show' or more commonly throughout its successive iterations as simply 'the Movement', the fledgling body was to be kept secret, reportedly on the insistence of Stout, Clarey and Kennelly, who feared a sectarian backlash if its existence became public knowledge.[21]

At Cremean's suggestion, he and Santamaria called on Mannix in late 1941, 'to discuss the Communist threat and see whether the Archbishop could be persuaded that the challenge to the party which held the allegiance of almost all Catholics should be resisted through

---

19 Santamaria, *Against the Tide*, 31.

20 B.A. Santamaria, *Santamaria: A Memoir* (Melbourne, Vic: Oxford University Press, 1997) 346.

21 Jack Kane, *Exploding the Myths: The Political Memoirs of Jack Kane* (North Ryde, NSW: Angus & Robertson Publishers, 1989) 19–20.

a broader effort than its leaders could organize'. Santamaria's account reads:

> Archbishop Mannix dealt with the situation as Cremean described it. He said that if we advanced a practical plan of action he would be disposed to back us. Somewhat timidly, I mentioned the question of financial support. What did we need? Unprepared, I could do no better than to say that a piece of propaganda we proposed to produce for the railways would cost £25. He did not even refuse. He simply changed the subject. ... Some months later, when, with Cremean, I went to the Archbishop with the practical plan the latter had requested, I told him we needed £3000. He did not demur. When I referred to the bypassing of our original request for £25, he smiled: 'Now I know you are serious'.[22]

Endorsement for the Movement was forthcoming from meetings of unionists from Catholic parishes convened by Santamaria respectively on 14 August 1942 and 4 January 1943. Between the first and second meetings, attendance rose from twenty to three hundred unionists and representation from a dozen parishes to virtually all those in the city area. Organised consciously on lines similar to those of the Communists, Movement cells had by 1943 begun to be established in Victorian unions and workplaces. Pamphlets written in the course of the year by Santamaria under various pseudonyms and distributed through Freedom Movement channels included *Through Violence to Fascism*, *Nine Reasons Why Labor Won't Have Communism* and *The Fight for Red Trade Unions.*

Freedom/News-Weekly

Freedom was edited initially in Santamaria's ANSCA office, but neither the ANSCA connection nor the identities of the publisher

22 Santamaria, *Santamaria: A Memoir*, 64–65.

and contributors were disclosed, and the paper was not to be sold from churches so that 'the Catholic connection will not be too clear'.[23] Questioned about its antecedents and affiliations, Mannix answered disingenuously 'I personally do not know of any connection between *Freedom* and the Catholic Church'.[24]

In the event, *News-Weekly* as the paper became known from 1946 fell short conspicuously of its promise of a 'fighting paper' for 'social reconstruction based on the inspiration of Christianity', justice among all classes and militant defence against fascist and communist extremists.[25] Duncan's account characterises its style and content as having been from the outset 'alarmist in the extreme, inflated and apocalyptic in their forecasts for post-war Australia'.[26] Niall Brennan resigned from the editorial staff on the grounds of its 'deliberate falsification of reports and news'. 'Invective and falsehood may both be normal to many people in the morasses of politics, but they have no place among men posturing as Christians engaged in a Christian crusade', Brennan wrote.[27]

Following 'vituperative' attacks by *News-Weekly* against the ALP and its leaders for their opposition to the proposed dissolution of the Communist Party at the 1951 referendum, the party's Federal Executive banned the paper, and threatened members distributing it with expulsion.[28] Denouncing the ban as 'a hasty and ill-advised act

---

23 Santamaria to Bishop O'Collins, 30 September 1943, as quoted in Duncan, *Crusade or Conspiracy?*, 64.

24 Duncan, *Crusade or Conspiracy?*, 62.

25 Duncan, *Crusade or Conspiracy?*, 64.

26 Duncan, *Crusade or Conspiracy?*, 64, and Fitzgerald, *The Pope's Battalions*, 62.

27 Brennan, *The Politics of Catholics*, 63.

28 Patrick Weller and Beverley Lloyd (eds), *Federal Executive Minutes 1951–55: Minutes of the Meetings of the Federal Executive of the Australian Labor Party* (Melbourne, Vic: Melbourne University Press, 1978) 478.

of repression', Mannix added with a perhaps not wholly unconscious irony 'If the paper has at any time made enemies by being provoked into personalities, I regret this extremely'.[29] Santamaria defended the 'acerbic' tone of *News-Weekly*, on the grounds that 'Not to attack is to condone. It is a genuine dilemma'.[30]

Progress

Santamaria was able by the end of 1945 to report significant progress. Membership of the Movement had increased to some 3000 and local groups had been formed in 72 parishes in Sydney, 52 in Melbourne and 12 in Newcastle.[31] Some 120,000 pamphlets had been sold, circulation of *Freedom* was stabilizing at around 16,000, numbers of smaller unions had been won back from the Communists and some twenty ALP branches in Victoria had been either secured or newly created under anti-Communist control. Even so, much remained to be done, with major unions for the most part still in the hands of the Communists and their sympathizers or supporters, and associates of Calwell and Kennelly only by the narrowest of margins staving off defeat at the ALP's 1945 Victorian State Conference.

His strategy for the Movement was for it to become 'a disciplined national organization which will be modelled completely on the Communist Party and which will work on the same principles'.[32]

---

29 Duncan, *Crusade or Conspiracy?*, 167. On succeeding Mannix in 1963, Simonds banned the sale of *News-Weekly* at Catholic Churches. In 1988, a subsequent Santamaria periodical, *AD2000*, was banned from sale on Church property by Archbishop Frank Little, 'for its attacks on other Catholics and particularly on the education guidelines of the Melbourne Archdiocese'. Duncan, *Crusade or Conspiracy?*, 71.

30 Duncan, *Crusade or Conspiracy?*, 394.

31 Campion, 'A Question of Loyalties', 8.

32 As quoted in Campion, 'A Question of Loyalties', 8.

'The battle', he believed, 'should be essentially one of cadre against cadre, cell against cell, fraction against fraction'.[33] Akin to the Leninist democratic centralism of the Party, the Movement in its several iterations was designedly and by his direction 'democratic and at the same time authoritative':

> It is authoritative to this extent – that in the groups members are not in a position to know precisely what is going on, and therefore must accept the advice of HQ. There is only one body in the position to know precisely what is going on – the national headquarters of the organization. Without fear of contradiction, national HQ is in a better position than any other body in Australia to know what is going on in most places at most times.[34]

It was no part of the duty of prospective leaders of the Movement's local branch structure to query the policy of HQ, since they 'may not be in possession of all the facts'.[35] In the event that a member was unhappy with so uncompromisingly authoritarian a management style, 'he should get out'.[36] Regimentation prevailed over the personal formation which, in his ANSCA capacity, he was obligated to uphold.

Inception of the CSSM

Following insistent requests by Santamaria for endorsement and funding of the Movement as Catholic Action, a meeting of the bishops on 19–20 September 1945 created the Catholic Social Studies

33 Santamaria, *Santamaria: A Memoir*, 66.

34 B.A. Santamaria, 'How the Organisation Works'. As quoted in Gerard Henderson, 'B.A. Santamaria, Santamariaism and the Cult of Personality' in Paul Ormonde (ed), *Fifty Years of the Santamaria Movement* (Eureka Street Papers No 1, Richmond, Vic: Jesuit Publications, 1992) 51.

35 B.A Santamaria, 'State Organisation: Address to a CSSM Meeting', as quoted in Henderson, 'B.A. Santamaria, Santamariaism and the Cult of Personality', 51.

36 Santamaria, 'State Organisation', 51.

Movement (CSSM), as a national agency, independent of ANSCA and tasked to combat Communism through the defeat of Communist office-holders and candidates at trade union elections. At Simonds's insistence explicitly 'not to be regarded as the mandated movement of Catholic Action', the CSSM even so was endowed to its advantage with the defining Catholic Action attributes of episcopal control 'both in policy and finance', through a specially constituted Episcopal Committee of the Catholic Social Studies Movement (ECCSSM) and an annual grant from the collective episcopal purse of £10,000.[37] And, as previously, members were required to take a pledge never to disclose 'the existence or the activities of the Movement'.[38]

The outcome was unambiguous, albeit frequently misrepresented. The CSSM was now by the wish and formal resolution of the bishops vested with their authority, and an inescapable responsibility on their part for its utterances and actions had been incurred. The Movement in its new guise was of its own volition and at Santamaria's explicit request no longer a lay body but an arm of the Church, and subject like any other to episcopal control. Irrespective of whether by the exercise or default of their right of direction to the CSSM, the bishops could not but shape the course of its development and determine its destiny.

Serious as the intentions of the bishops may have been in their imposition of constraints on the Movement, such attempts as may have been made to secure compliance with them were ineffectual, nor would the outcomes necessarily have survived closer moral scrutiny than may have seemed expedient. As recalled in the memoir of a Sydney journalist whose father was a Movement activist, 'After my

37 Simonds to Maher, 2 September 1945, as quoted in Duncan, *Crusade or Conspiracy?*, 83.

38 Santamaria to O'Collins, 1 May 1946, as quoted in Duncan, *Crusade or Conspiracy?*, 103.

father's death I found membership cards in his name for numerous unions that covered occupations in which he had never been active, such as the Painters and Decorators' Union':

> At the union meetings they were supposed to disperse throughout the hall, stay quiet and vote the right way. But Dad never could stay quiet. At one Painters and Decorators' Union meeting a big fellow turned round and demanded: 'Show us yer hands! You've never been a painter in your life.' Tony watched as three big men threw Dad out.[39]

By virtue of the acquisition of so incontestably official a status, the CSSM and 'the bishops, priests and laymen backing it' enjoyed the best of all possible worlds:

> On the one hand they could and did rally support and demand discipline by presenting the Movement as the official – but secret – instrument of the bishops in the industrial and political fields. Opposition to its policies appeared to be opposition to the Church itself. The word was widely whispered, and rarely, if ever, denied within the Church, that it was Catholic Action.[40]

'Critics', by the account of the onetime 'Movement' activist, Fr Edmund Campion, 'were told that their criticism made them disloyal to the church, at odds with "the mind of the hierarchy", almost like traitors in wartime'.[41] 'Indeed one of the characteristics of the "Movement" was that many of its leading clerical supporters and episcopal supporters used phrases such as "The Mind of the Church" or "The Mind of the Bishop" in a quite impermissible context, to clothe the political decisions of the leaders of the "Movement" with

39 Greg Sheridan, *When We Were Young and Foolish: A Memoir of My Misguided Youth With Tony Abbott, Bob Carr, Malcolm Turnbull, Kevin Rudd and Other Reprobates* (Crow's Nest, NSW: Allen & Unwin, 2015) 18–19.

40 Ormonde, *The Movement*, 70.

41 Campion, 'A Question of Loyalties', 10.

an ecclesiastical sanction, while at the same time the views of those Catholics who differed from the political views from time to time espoused by members of the "Movement" were denounced as "pro-Communist" or as "anti-Catholic"', MacInerney wrote.[42]

A succinct summary by the poet and onetime *Catholic Worker* committee member Vincent Buckley of the intended chilling effect reads:

> The Movement could not be mentioned
> *Because it was not known to exist*
> It could not be criticized
> *Because it was known to have the bishops' special favour*
> It could not be actively opposed
> *Because the bishops did not want it mentioned.*

'As one pro-Movement intellectual explained to me, when I objected that I could not follow the wishes of the bishops unless they told me what they were, you learned these things by "calculated hearsay"', Buckley wrote.[43]

Major new opportunities for the CSSM emerged with the creation by the ALP in NSW in 1945 of accredited Industrial Groups to take up the anti-Communist cause within individual unions, and their extension subsequently to other states, including in particular Victoria. Campion characterises their rank and file as 'working people who, by class and tradition, belonged to the industrial and political wings of the Labour Movement':

---

42 McInerney, *Memoir*, 26.

43 Buckley, *Cutting Green Hay*, 111–112.

> They were not, as the Communists alleged, outsiders brought in to split and weaken the institutions of Australian workers. They were workers themselves, formed and energised by the Church to live their faith in their daily lives. They were generous people – generous of themselves, their leisure, their prospects, their money, even their families.[44]

A possibly inflated account by Santamaria in 1949 of CSSM involvement in the Groups reads '90% of their membership is composed of our people. All the impetus in them comes from our members and they would not survive any mass withdrawal of our members'.[45] Welcoming the more broadly based and high profile 'Groupers' as a cover for the covert CSSM, he wrote 'Previously in the battle against Communism in the factory, Movement activists were compelled to act individually':

> Wherever they concentrated in groups it was obvious that the group were Catholic ... Today they have the cover of the Labor Party. They carry on the fight as the executives of these factory 'discussion groups' and none can effectively question their bona fides.[46]

Relegation of Maher

Santamaria became the CSSM's executive officer jointly with his ongoing post as Maher's deputy at ANSCA. In 1946, he replaced Maher, to assume the management concurrently of both bodies. Maher returned from an overseas study of Catholic Action, suggested

44 Campion, 'A Question of Loyalties', 9.

45 B.A. Santamaria, *Report to the National Executive of the Movement*, 1949, as quoted in Fitzgerald, *The Pope's Battalions*, 76–77.

46 B.A. Santamaria, 'Confidential Memorandum to the Hierarchy, 1945' (Second Annual report to the Freedom Movement), Santamaria Papers, as quoted in Fitzgerald, *The Pope's Battalions*, 73.

to him by Santamaria and funded by Mannix, only to find that he had been relegated by ECCA to the position of Research Officer and assigned a room off-site from the ANSCA offices, at Newman College.

The circumstances of his removal admit the interpretation by Gerard Henderson in a 1994 research paper that it was 'a cleverly designed manoeuvre' by Santamaria and Mannix to clear the way for the ongoing politicising of ANSCA which Maher had consistently opposed.[47] Maher's 1947 report on the study tour opened with an eloquent and perhaps defiant affirmation of Jocism and 'the wisdom of the Bishops in establishing Catholic Action in the particular form now existing in Australia':

> Our movements all derive from the 'new model' of the Jocist Movement. In the last ten years that particular method has not only survived the most terrible tests of war and persecution: it has emerged as easily the most effective form of the lay apostolate. There is no sign of any novel or rival form; all the principles of Jocism have been confirmed by time and experience: these principles are constantly giving birth to fresh movements.

'I have no doubt whatsoever that in essentials Catholic Action here is soundly based and that it will be very successful *if the lines laid down by the Bishops here are followed as they should be*', Maher wrote.[48] While relations between the Maher and Santamaria households

---

47 Gerard Henderson, *Frank Maher and Bob Santamaria Circa 1946* (privately circulated research paper, 1994) 1. Copy courtesy of the author. Henderson was able to read both sides of the correspondence, and the letters from Santamaria to Maher are reproduced in Morgan, *Santamaria: Your Most Obedient Servant*, but Maher's letters to Santamaria appear to be missing from the Santamaria Papers as held currently by the State Library.

48 F.K.H. Maher, *Report by F.K. Maher on Visit to England February–October* (Melbourne, Vic: Australian National Secretariat for Catholic Action, 1947). Santamaria Papers, Series 5 Box 1 Part 4. Italics added.

reportedly remained cordial, a 1957 letter from Maher to Heffey attests to an ongoing embitterment.[49] It reads:

> Since my own work was wrecked by the quarrels among our own people, I have retired to the study of matters of no practical importance. Judging by the ferocity of the conflict now going on and the disputes which now seem to create lasting breaks in our ranks, I was wise. There are times when I regret we started The Campion or the 'Worker'.[50]

Commenting subsequently to Brenda Niall that 'Bob saved us', he displayed a magnanimity that was not reciprocated.[51] Interviewed in 2009, his son, Paul Maher, recalled him as having become 'clearly a sad man':

> The family has always assumed this was because of Bob [Santamaria] elbowing Frank out of the Catholic Action organization. ... The family theory was that Frank was doing the job all right, but not in the way that Bob would have liked it done. Bob actively manoeuvred, with Mannix's help, to get Frank out of the position. ... He was probably a compliant man and he accepted the result rather than white-anting Bob.[52]

An alternative view consistent with Niall's reservations may be that Maher and his wife, Molly, saw Mannix rather than Santamaria as having been the instigator of Maher's undoing, but were constrained by their loyalty to the Church to remain silent even within the family circle. For all Maher's disappointment, he was not wholly silenced nor was he backward in the exercise of his capacity to rebuke. Maintaining his advocacy of formation in the Cardijn mould through a

49 For relations between the Maher and Santamaria households, see Brenda Niall, *Mannix* (Melbourne, Vic: Text Publishing, 2015) 296.

50 Maher to Heffey (letter, received 26/1/1957 or 2/2/1957). Heffey-Butler Papers.

51 Niall, *The Riddle of Father Hackett*, 232.

52 Praetz, *The Church in Springtime*. Interview with Paul Maher, 17 April 2009, 14.

stream of Research Officer bulletins and culminating with his 1948 *Studies in Catholic Action: A Practical Approach*, he reaffirmed in the face of Santamaria's new ANSCA orthodoxy that 'The remarkable thing about what is called the 'Jocist technique' is that it is equally effective in every environment'.

> Adapted intelligently, it works with farmers, school children, lawyers, teachers, sailors; for it is after-all a kind of inspired common sense, a method of organization that is eminently suited to 20th Century conditions. Twenty-five years action in every country, in peace and in war, among the learned and the ignorant, the young and the mature, have revealed clearly its extraordinary strength and resilience. It has solved problems of education and co-operation which many thought hopeless to tackle. If one conceives Catholic Action as a missionary enterprise (as it is) here is the grand strategy ready at hand.[53]

The composition of the ECCSSM was nominally Gilroy, Mannix and Bishop James O'Collins of Ballarat, but Gilroy indicated from the outset that he would not be travelling to Melbourne for meetings. With his unexpected nomination of O'Collins as a proxy less close in outlook to himself than to Mannix, the hegemony of Mannix and Santamaria was assured. Reminiscing about the episode in later life, Santamaria recalled the delegation by Gilroy of O'Collins as having been 'not without its humour'.[54] 'As the new head of ANSCA, without the check or accountability Maher had provided, Santamaria was free to utilise ANSCA more fully to buttress and expand the CSSM', Duncan concludes.[55]

---

53 F.K.H. Maher, *Studies in Catholic Action: A Practical Approach* (Melbourne, Vic: The Hawthorn Press, 1948) 8.

54 As quoted in Fitzgerald, *The Pope's Battalions*, 75.

55 Duncan, *Crusade or Conspiracy?*, 91.

Chapter 12

SANTAMARIA AND THE Y.C.W.

As a protracted confrontation with the Young Christian Workers was so shortly to demonstrate, the upshot of Santamaria's elevation was an acute conflict of interest. The constraints on involvement by the Church in party political activity which, wearing his ANSCA hat, he was required to uphold, he now ridiculed, repudiated and subverted in his CSSM capacity.

Impressed by Kevin Kelly, Hackett had encouraged him as early as 1932 to prepare for the French Jesuit publication *Les Dossiers de l'Action Populaire* an article on the history of the ALP, with special reference to its Socialist Objective. Receiving in lieu of payment copies of the journal and other French Catholic publications, Kelly 'became aware, for the first time, of a new organisation of Christian workers, *La Jeunesse Ouvrière Chrétienne* or the J.O.C.':

> I at once began to steep myself in its doctrines and techniques and to spread, especially in Campion circles, a knowledge of its methods, spirit and ideology. ... From my study of the documentation in French during 1934 and 1935 and from a comparison of the way in which the industrial environment was having the same effect on young workers in France and Australia, I became convinced that the specialised techniques of the Y.C.W. could play a decisive role in the adult education of

> young Christian workers in Australia and that I should devote as much of my spare time as possible to an effort to establish the Y.C.W. in Melbourne.[1]

'It was Cardijn's genius to pursue a radically different course of action, selecting only young men who shared the same social interests, who spoke, thought, worked and lived in the same milieu or environment', Kelly wrote:

> For him, the hierarchy and the clergy were powerless of themselves to combat and conquer modern paganism nor was the parochial ministry nor were parochial organisations in any better case, for modern paganism was, as it still is, beyond their reach. They themselves, he said, could not combat and conquer it on its own ground, in its own milieu, in its own institutions, in its own manifestations. For that the organisation and training of the laity for action in the lay milieu was essential.[2]

Cardijn's expectations were explicit and uncompromising. The Y.C.W. was to be 'at once and indissolubly':

> *A school of lay apostolate* in their life, their environment, within the mass of their comrades ... not a theoretical school, or a purely doctrinal school, but a school in which they exercise themselves, and work out and perfect their own training; an essentially active and acting school, with its enquiries and activities imparting a social sense, a social spirit, a social conduct, in a much more gripping way than any lessons and lectures which leave the listeners passive and inactive.
>
> *A service of lay apostolate* in their life, their environment, within the mass of their comrades. ... a concrete, practical, methodical service, which so provides all the help and assistance necessary for their life as young workers, so that the effort which is

1 Kelly, *Memoir*, 'Towards the Y.C.W.', 1.

2 Kelly, *Memoir*, 'Towards the Y.C.W.', 3–4.

> demanded from them may be proportional to their lives and capabilities; service for all the aspects of their lives; intellectual, moral, spiritual, professional, recreational.
>
> *A representative body of lay apostolate* in their life, their environment, within the mass of their comrades ... which, in the name of working youth takes action, makes demands, influences public opinion, and creates the necessary favourable conditions for the integral uplifting of all working youth.[3]

Initially under the impression that the JOC was a French organisation, Kelly learned shortly that it was the French counterpart of the Belgian body of the same name, as founded by Cardijn and with its general secretariat in Brussels, where Cardijn was assisted by 'an altogether remarkable priest', the Abbé Robert Kothen. A 'fascinating correspondence' with Kothen ensued, which was to end only with his premature death in 1953. 'We are greatly delighted', Kothen wrote to Kelly on 22 May 1936, 'that you are taking an interest in our movement. ... From this moment I pray that Australia will soon have a powerful movement of Young Christian Workers'.[4]

Prelude to the Y.C.W.

Appointed formally by the Belgian Y.C.W. in 1939 as its official Australian correspondent, and in receipt of a personal expression of the esteem of its founder in the form of an autographed photograph of Cardijn, Kelly was already well advanced in setting out in conjunction with three young workers Eric Nilan, Tom Hogan and Dave Nelson 'to introduce to Australia the spirit and techniques of the Y.C.W.'. Measures taken included the foundation on an *ad hoc*

3 Josef Cardijn, 'The Y.C.W.', 1938, in Eugene Langdale (ed), *Challenges to Action* (London: New Life Publications, 1955) 91–92.

4 Kelly, *Memoir*, 'Towards the Y.C.W.', 2.

basis in Oakleigh of the nation's first Y.C.W. group, and the creation of an informal 'JOC Propaganda Group' to foster informed support among priests and within other influential Catholic circles, including the Catholic Young Men's Society (C.Y.M.S.) and the Catholic Boys Legion (CBL):

> It was our hope that an Australian Y.C.W. might be brought into being as a movement parallel to the C.Y.M.S. and the Boys' Legion, the Y.C.W. being primarily an organization of militants and the other two organizations constituting as it were mass movements. ... By 1938 there were some 40 branches of the C.Y.M.S. in Melbourne, 23 of which had formed groups of activists belonging to the C.Y.M.S. Legion. In that year some 7–800 boys belonged to the 10 branches of the Catholic Boys' Legion and some 8 or 9 parochial boys' clubs run independently of it.[5]

Early milestones included the publication on 31 July 1939, of the 34-page Australian Catholic Truth Society pamphlet *Young Christian Workers*, that was edited by Kelly and with contributions from Cardijn, Kothen and the South Australian activist Paul McGuire. A further pamphlet, *How to Start the JOC*, was published by ANSCA in March 1940. Concurrently, a young Northcote curate, Fr Frank Lombard, had begun experimenting with the application of the Jocist approach and the inquiry method at the Northcote Catholic Boys Club: 'the first continuous Jocist militants group in Australia'.[6]

In early 1940, Mannix designated Lombard – 'a charismatic man with a great appeal to youth and a stirring public speaker'[7] – as Archdiocesan Chaplain to the CBL. Appointment followed of a

5 Kelly, *Memoir*, 'Towards the Y.C.W.', 4–5.

6 Kehoe, Unpublished Draft History of the Melbourne Y.C.W., 1932–58, Chapter 3, 7.

7 Duncan, *Crusade or Conspiracy?*, 23.

Priests Committee to conduct an intensive study of the Y.C.W. concept, chaired by Lombard and including Frs P. Ford, J.H. Cleary, J.F. Kelly, P. Hansen, A. Morgan, G. Coughlan and T. Murray, and a long-running Committee journal commenced publication, with iterations successively as *The Chaplain*, *The Priest in Catholic Action* and ultimately *The Catholic Action Chaplain*.[8] 'Knowing that I was about to leave Melbourne for armed service they called on me and I handed over to them much of the literature on the Y.C.W. which I had gathered through the preceding five years', Kevin Kelly wrote.[9]

The Melbourne Y.C.W.

The CBL was mandated later in 1940 as Melbourne's official Catholic Action movement for young workers aged from 14 to 18. In 1942 it became formally the Y.C.W., with the motto 'A New Youth to Build a New Australia'. Governance of the new entity was by the Priests Committee in conjunction with a lay Central Council – later the Diocesan Council – to whose Executive the powers of the Committee gradually came to be delegated, thereby enabling it to become 'the real source of policy initiatives'.[10] Organisation was on the basis of local parishes, grouped regionally and with parish priests or curates as their chaplains.

As with the Belgian model, the structure in each instance consisted of a leaders' group and a wider mass membership. Uniformity of

8 Ted Long, *Notes on the Early History of the Y.C.W. and its Works*, 2005, as presented to Archbishop Denis J. Hart at the Cardijn Community Australia Conference, Cardinal Knox Centre, 4 November 2011.

9 Kelly, *Memoir*, 'Towards the Y.C.W.', 4–6.

10 Kehoe, Unpublished Draft History of the Melbourne Y.C.W., 1932–58, Chapter 3, 61.

meeting procedures was secured through the adoption of prescribed agendas. Iterations in their initial form comprised respectively for the Leaders' Group:

Gospel Meditation

Chaplain's Talk

Minutes of the Last Meeting

Report on Work Done

Inquiry (eg. Leisure)

Allocation of Work

and for the General Meeting:

Opening Prayer

Minutes of the Previous Meeting

Short talk by priest or perhaps a member of the leaders' group

General Business (not to exceed 9 o'clock)

Syllabus Items

Closing prayer (10 pm).

Prospective leaders were introduced to Jocism at well-attended training camps in Mornington over the 1940–41 Christmas to New Year period, at Hanging Rock the following Easter and at Mentone in 1942. Some six hundred members appeared publicly in their new capacity for the first time at the Catholic Youth Rally at Xavier College on 26 October 1942, and again the following week in a Eucharistic procession at the Salesian boys' home in Sunbury:

> Imitating the European Jocist movements, the young workers wore special uniforms, and each branch marched behind its own banner. The uniforms were the white shirts and grey trousers of the Belgium Y.C.W.; the banners were emblazoned with the Y.C.W. shield, a red crusaders cross on a white

> background under the letters 'Y.C.W.', on a background of local parish colours.[11]

Subsequent Xavier rallies were organised wholly by Y.C.W., as 'an outstanding event, rivalling the St Patrick's Day March and Sunbury Eucharistic Festival as the major annual demonstrations of the Catholic tribe in the nineteen-forties', and with attendances averaging some 25,000.[12] In 1942 the former CBL football competition became the Y.C.W. Football Association, and, as of 1943, there were 38 Under 18 football teams, 13 Under 16 football teams and 30 Senior and 8 Junior cricket teams, together with athletics, swimming and boxing competitions.[13] Branch football teams played one another on a regional basis for regional premierships. Other services introduced early on – albeit not in all cases universally available – included a savings scheme, 'Learn to Dance' classes and vocational guidance counselling.

Major capital outlays were incurred for projects including the purchase of the 'Maiya Wamba' leadership training centre in Cheltenham in 1943, an accommodation centre in Albert Park for orphanage boys from Geelong and other young workers without families or working away from them in 1945, and in 1949 a hostel in Hawthorn for young British migrants and a permanent holiday camp site at Smith's Beach on Phillip Island. The Y.C.W. administration was housed in rental accommodation behind the St Francis Church at 312 Elizabeth Street and at 99 Queen Street prior to settling in

11 Kehoe, Unpublished Draft History of the Melbourne Y.C.W., 1932–58, Chapter 3, 64, 78.

12 Kehoe, Unpublished Draft History of the Melbourne Y.C.W., 1932–58, Chapter 3, 81.

13 Kehoe, Unpublished Draft History of the Melbourne Y.C.W., 1932–58, Chapter 3, 92–93.

premises of its own at 355 Lonsdale Street. Costs for the property acquisitions together ultimately with significant annual contributions to recurrent expenditure were in large part met by a group of men initially recruited by Lombard to support the Xavier rallies involvement, and reconstituted in a mainly fund-raising capacity as an ongoing Y.C.W. Men's Extension Committee.

From 1943, the Y.C.W. was placed by the bishops on a national footing, with a £477 annual grant and a governance structure comprising a National Conference and a National Council. Simonds and Lombard became respectively the founding Episcopal Chairman of the new entity and its founding Chaplain, and a National Headquarters was established in Melbourne. Following an initial National Conference of some 130 Melbourne-based priests in Abbotsford between 19 and 23 October 1943, Frank McCann – Melbourne Y.C.W. football registration secretary since August 1941, and as of November its State Secretary – became jointly the first National Secretary and full-time national organiser.

Ted Long

As with Manning, Moran or Mannix and *Rerum Novarum*, Maher and the Campions, or Kelly and the inception of ANSCA, the hour and the man found one another, in the person of Ted Long. Long's parents were farmers at Knowlsley, near Bendigo. The third of their eight children, he was born on 1 July 1921, and educated to Merit Certificate level at the Knowsley Primary School, and from 1935 to 1938 as a boarder at St Patrick's College in Ballarat. 'I didn't mind the school work and I loved the sporting activities' he told a Credit Union Historical Co-operative (CUHC) interviewer in 1992:

> At St Patrick's College, Ballarat, the Christian Brothers as a group were a big influence and one brother in particular, Brother O'Malley, was sports master there and a prominent teacher. His temper was pretty hot at times, but he was a lover of sport and he got on very well with the boys.[14]

Recognising that 'there wasn't an opportunity for all of us to stay home on the farm', Long took up a Public Service appointment with the Department of Air in Melbourne in 1939, and enrolled as a part-time Batchelor of Commerce student at Melbourne University. Boarding for several years with Frank McCann's family in their North Melbourne home, the close ties that developed there with Frank, his fellow Y.C.W. activist and future priest brother, Charlie, and his sister, Kathleen, may well have been instrumental in alerting the country boy to the harsh realities of working class life in the inner suburban Melbourne of the day, and sowed the seeds for an enduring commitment to radical reform and a new social order consistent with the Church's social teachings.

Kehoe's summary of a 1979 interview with Frank McCann reads in part:

> Frank McCann was intensely aware that his parents, who lived in O'Shannassey Street, North Melbourne, in what was regarded at the time as a slum area, had to pay rent for housing accommodation all their life because the normal family charges on his father's weekly wage to feed, clothe and educate a growing family had prevented them from saving a deposit to obtain a loan to build a house. Theirs was not an isolated case. In 1938, North Melbourne, along with Collingwood, consistently

---

14 Ted Long. As interviewed by Richard Raxworthy for the Australian Credit Union Historical Society Co-operative, Melbourne, 3 November 1991. Tape 1 Side A of three tapes. Transcript courtesy of the Australian Credit Union Archives, Sydney, 2007, 3.

> registered in indicators of poverty above the national average among other inner suburbs.[15]

Leaving school at thirteen to work as an apprentice motor mechanic, Charlie McCann was recruited to the CBL as the founder president of its North Melbourne Branch in April 1940, and, following his ordination, succeeded Lombard as national Y.C.W. chaplain jointly with Fr Kevin Toomey. As recalled by a close family friend, Fr Cyril Hally, 'I used to visit the McCann family and Kathleen McCann was a leader in the Y.C.W. girls':

> Members of the Y.C.W. would listen to groups of young people deciding where to go out for the evening, for example, and the one who made the decisions in the group was invited to become part of the Y.C.W. I was at the McCann home for a birthday party and Kathleen was late. She was working on the leader of the Children of Mary to talk her into joining the Y.C.W. This was the thirteenth time that Kathleen had gone to visit her and the first time she was home. This was the sort of dedication they showed. They believed deeply. They had a theory and acted on it.[16]

Long was attracted initially to the under-18 football competition of the Kensington Boys Club and later the CBL: 'I was invited to become a leader in the Y.C.W. and became very involved with it':

> The War started in 1939 when I was employed in the Department of Air – an essential service and a reserved occupation – and it required a lot of overtime. Between the overtime and my becoming interested in the Youth Movement, which took up a lot of my other spare time, I discontinued the university course

15 Kehoe, Unpublished Draft History of the Melbourne Y.C.W., 1932–58, Chapter 6, 44.

16 Praetz, *The Church in Springtime*, 52.

> in 1942 after I had a pass in five subjects. I never got back to resuming it.[17]

He served subsequently as Melbourne Y.C.W. President from 1942 until 1944 and again from 1948 until 1950. On Frank McCann's becoming ill with tuberculosis in 1943, Long took over from him in the role of National Secretary in an acting capacity, thereby giving up his Public Service career and abandoning a promising Victorian Football League future after having played some ten games with the North Melbourne Football Club.

In June 1944 a national Y.C.W. monthly, *New Youth*, commenced publication, while the age limit for membership was raised by Simonds from eighteen to twenty-five, with provision for more extended retention of members such as Long, whose services were seen to be indispensable to the wellbeing of either their branches or the wider movement. The provisional National Committee met on a preliminary basis in Melbourne on 10 August 1944, and for the first time formally in the course of a first National Conference of Priests and Leaders in Melbourne between 15 and 21 October.

Concurrently with the conference, the first national training course for leaders was conducted, at 'Maiya Wamba'. Membership peaked in 1947, when the Melbourne Y.C.W. consisted of 66 branches, comprising in all some 3300 registered members, 61 leader groups totalling 305 leaders and 9900 users of Y.C.W. services. In the same year, the Australian Y.C.W. comprised some 7000 members and 180 branches spread over eighteen dioceses.

---

17 Long, Raxworthy Interview, Tape 1 Side A of three tapes, 1.

Headaches and Heartaches

With Kelly assigned for the duration of the war to Naval Intelligence and the Kothen connection severed by the Nazi occupation of Europe, Lombard and his fellow priests struggled with the exigencies of matching the fledgling Y.C.W. to the Belgian model. Nor was the situation in any way assisted by the competing demands on their availability of recurrent absences in their capacity as military chaplains, or the armed forces call-ups that so repeatedly depleted the ranks of the lay leadership.

Appointed by Mannix to the Armed Forces Chaplaincy as a Captain Chaplain, Lombard was absent in the course of the subsequent year for at least two three-monthly tours of duty at the army's Puckapunyal camp in Seymour.[18] Of the eight members of the new 1942 Executive, only Long and McCann completed their terms of office without either enlisting or being conscripted: 'Soon after, Kevin Toomey became the third member of the depleted Executive. During the next eighteen months, this triumvirate effected the final consolidation of the Melbourne Y.C.W.'.[19] The outcome was a hybrid body, combining attributes of the Y.C.W. as envisaged by Cardijn and Kelly with those of a youth movement in the more traditional Catholic mould.

A central cause for concern was class: more white collar than blue collar workers were being attracted to the Y.C.W., and its influence was less effective among blue collar than white collar members. 'There is

18 Kehoe, Unpublished Draft History of the Melbourne Y.C.W., 1932–58, Chapter 5, 12.

19 Kehoe, Unpublished Draft History of the Melbourne Y.C.W., 1932–58, Chapter 7, 7.

something wrong' Simonds told the Fourth National Conference of the Y.C.W. in Adelaide in September 1947:

> One of the reasons why we are not influencing the general mass is that we may be losing sight of the fact that we are a specialised section of Catholic Action. It was the genius of Pius XI that conceived the idea of Catholic Action. Pope Pius XI said that in order to be a success, Catholic Action must be specialised, ie, members of a particular group must be of the class to which they belong.[20]

A relevant observation by Kehoe reads:

> By implication, the leaders were being selected by Chaplains from the devout middle class and skilled apprentices of the labour aristocracy rather than the leaders of gangs of unskilled youths. This had been the public wisdom of Melbourne Chaplains from the beginning. The principle of specialisation meant that one member of a class would be able to communicate with another member of a class in their own social language or dialect. The breakdown in influence in the Melbourne and Australian Y.C.W. was not surprising considering the policy for selection of leaders.[21]

Nor was this all. Headaches and heartaches abounded. Consistent with clerical priorities, the focus at the outset was squarely on winning back to regular attendance at Mass the mostly unskilled young workers or 'roughies' who were seen as severing their connection with the Church at the point of their leaving school and entry to the workforce, rather than on the workplace and working life issues which might more effectively have gained and retained their attention.

---

20 *Catholic Worker*, No 142, November 1947.

21 Kehoe, Unpublished Draft History of the Melbourne Y.C.W., 1932–58, Chapter 5, 8.

CHAPTER 12

Not all members drawn to the Y.C.W. by its football competition and other sporting and recreational activities necessarily were found to be as willing to comply with the *quid pro quo* of attending the general meetings on Friday nights, or sign up for further formation. And formation even where sought was not necessarily of sufficient depth or duration to be fully effective. As Arizmendiarrieta was so shortly to discover and the Mondragón experience now so plainly confirms, formation of the character required for a transformation of the social order such as Long and his associates envisaged was a more exacting and protracted undertaking than they and even Cardijn may have supposed.

An unintended consequence of the financial support of the Men's Extension Committee for property purchases and other capital and even recurrent outlays was a diminution of the acceptance by members of the direct and personal responsibility for the financing and financial management of their organisation, which Cardijn saw as being indispensable to both its institutional wellbeing and the formation process. The upshot ultimately was chronic arrears of unpaid member dues and recurrent financial crises, and an insufficiency of seasoned Jocists at junctures when, as in the course of the co-operatives project, the need for them was acute.

Wages were low and administrative costs tightly circumscribed. Faced with a budgetary crisis in 1950, a special Executive meeting adopted a package of emergency measures which included a reduction of the staff from four to two employees and the acceptance of an offer by Dan Callahan to reduce his pay to a subsistence level of £1 per week, plus board at one of the Y.C.W. hostels: 'Only Ted

Long, who had a young family, continued to receive his previous wage'.[22]

Prompted – or perhaps shamed – by Callahan's magnanimity, Executive members agreed to donate 10/- weekly from their own pockets to supplement his meagre earnings. It was a sound investment. Callahan served on as Treasurer in 1950, Secretary in 1951 and in 1958 President. So low were the wages accepted by Long and McCann at a later stage of their Y.C.W. employment that 'Frank McCann, with the approval of Archbishop Simonds, commenced bookmaking as a sideline, with Ted Long as his penciller'.[23]

Jim Ross – a further Y.C.W. state organiser, State President and National Secretary – recalls how even as late as 1956 establishing branches 'wasn't an easy job':

> I never owned a car and I always had to hitchhike so it meant that I was never certain how long It was going to be or how long it would take to get from one place to another. That was pretty awkward. Sometimes it was quite stimulating, and particularly when you got good responses from people, but often it was just very hard work – waiting for three or four hours on a back road for a lift, for example.[24]

Asked by Kevin Peoples in the course of a visit to Terang where he had spent the previous night, Ross replied 'I often sleep out and last night I slept on the beach at Warrnambool'. 'So after that I thought I should join the Y.C.W. ... I became a leader in the Y.C.W. because Jim

---

22 Kehoe, Unpublished Draft History of the Melbourne Y.C.W., 1932–58, Chapter 4, 25.

23 Kehoe, Unpublished Draft History of the Melbourne Y.C.W., 1932–58, Chapter 6, 69.

24 'Interview with Jim Ross 17 November 2009', in Praetz, *The Church in Spring Time: Remembering Catholic Action 1940–1965*, 101.

Ross didn't have a bed', Peoples' account recalls.[25] A tribute by John Molony to Catholic Action co-workers including Ross and Peoples 'who devoted their lives to fulltime work for the Y.C.W.' reads:

> They received a pittance as a 'salary'; they left home and lived in poor circumstances; they put off entering into close relationships; and relinquished many of the normal ways of 'having a good time' common among the young. In short, being full time workers demanded that they spent practically every moment of the day, and often well into the night, giving of themselves for the good of other young workers. I was then, and I remain today, in awe of them.[26]

Visiting Australia in 1958, Cardijn affirmed to his Australian hosts that 'Your Y.C.W. has developed as I dreamed a Y.C.W. should develop'.[27]

Santamaria's Response

Like the Campions before it, the Y.C.W. was insistent from its inception that its Catholic Action status precluded it from involvement in party politics. Its Episcopal Chairman, Simonds, stated that 'Catholic Action is a purely spiritual apostolate for the salvation of souls and the extension of the Kingdom of Christ, and can never become a political activity'.[28] Santamaria's rejection of the proposition was adamant. His priority was for the specialised movements including the Y.C.W. to be brought to heel and co-operate with the CSSM in its mobilisation against Communism and perhaps as yet undisclosed wider objectives. Irrespective of whether taken up by Santamaria to

25 'Interview with Kevin Peoples 14 April 2010', in Praetz, *The Church in Spring Time*, 83.

26 Molony, *By Wendouree*, 320.

27 Accessed 17/1/2014 at http://www.yourfaithproject.com.au/article.aspx?aeid=29122.

28 Henderson, *Mr Santamaria and the Bishops*, 29.

a high place and shown the principalities of the world or bludgeoned by him with unwarranted anathemas, the Y.C.W. leaders stuck resolutely throughout to the principles with which the Campions and the bishops had at the inception of ANSCA endowed them.

A 1943 recommendation to the bishops by Santamaria in his Freedom Movement capacity, that top priority should be given to the creation of a factory-based Y.C.W. to develop committed leaders, was followed up in early 1944 with a complaint, ostensibly by ANSCA, that 'the National Catholic Girls' Movement (in 12 dioceses with 172 groups), the Y.C.W. (in 13 dioceses) and other Catholic organizations were resisting Santamaria's plans to use them as recruiting and training grounds for the Movement'.[29] Seeking to allay fears on the part of Simonds that Catholic Action was becoming 'too political', and ANSCA was giving 'a wrong direction' to the Y.C.W., Santamaria wrote to him on 28 July, offering assurances that 'its work was solely spiritual' and Catholics were duty bound 'to take the offensive and become the effective leaders of all Australians' to tackle social and economic problems when they were fundamentally moral matters.[30] A further letter from him to Simonds in August 1945 read that it was 'imperative for the CSSM to have the assistance of all Catholic Movements and of their members as long as the crisis lasts':

> I would have preferred that the development of Catholic Action should have been on the lines which appeared normal when the Secretariat was first founded. Now I am asking that the

29 B.A. Santamaria, 1943, 'Report of Anti-Communist Campaign' and 'Report of the Fifth Meeting of the Episcopal Committee on Catholic Action, 17–18 April 1944', as quoted in Duncan, *Crusade or Conspiracy?*, 71.

30 Santamaria to Simonds, 28 June 1944, as quoted in Duncan, *Crusade or Conspiracy?*, 71. A footnote to Duncan's account reads 'Fr Lalor's copy of Santamaria's report found its way into the hands of the security police, who unsuccessfully tried to infiltrate the Movement'. Duncan, *Crusade or Conspiracy?*, FN 88, 418.

> work of the Industrial Movement [ie. CSSM] should be given real priority among all Catholics because I believe ... that an appalling disaster faces the Church in this country, and all [Catholic Action] Movements whose policy is now in question, unless we win this fight immediately, unless the Industrial Movement can be given an effective priority.[31]

Nor was it from Santamaria alone that the pressure to conform was forthcoming. Summoned to 'Raheen' in November 1945, the Y.C.W. Chaplain, Fr Frank Lombard, and Fr Tom Murray, were briefed by Mannix on the seriousness of the Communist problem, and Lombard was able in response to put the Y.C.W.'s case:

> As the meeting progressed, it did not appear as if the Archbishop would make a definite declaration, so Fr Lombard asked what would happen if the Y.C.W. did not carry out the Archbishop's commands. Dr Mannix retorted that he did not command Fr Lombard to do anything but he expected him to interpret the wishes of his bishop. He then left the room. In great trepidation, Fr Lombard then stuck by his decision. But the Archbishop did not order the Y.C.W. to co-operate with the CSSM on Mr Santamaria's terms. He continued to appear at Y.C.W. functions and support its work. In 1948 he described the Y.C.W. as having 'one of the most powerful methods of combating Communism'.[32]

Rebuffed consistently by Simonds and Lombard, Santamaria warned Mannix two years later that 'At the moment there is a real danger that members of the youth movements may be told that if they belong to the Industrial Movement they cannot simultaneously be members of leaders groups in Catholic Action':

31 Santamaria to Simonds, August 1950, as quoted in Henderson, *Mr Santamaria and the Bishops*, 30.

32 Interview with Fr Tom Murray, 2 November 1978, in D.M. Kehoe, Unpublished Draft History of the Melbourne Y.C.W., 1932–58, Chapter 7, 69. NB: Pages are numbered separately for the respective chapters.

> This seems to be wrong in principle, while in practice it would mean that the very people who should be trained in action for future leadership of industrial life will be disqualified from fulfilling that task because of their very loyalty to Catholic Action. There is a real danger that as those who are now active in the Industrial Movement advance in years, the people who should carry on will not be there to do so.[33]

Returning to his theme on a note of heightened concern in 1952, he wrote again to Mannix that consequent on the Y.C.W.'s stand 'The problem is simply that the life-blood of the Secretariat and the Social Studies Movement is being drained off, and that in a relatively short time – whatever the bishops may wish – it will be unable to recruit members in sufficient numbers or of sufficient ability to do its work':

> For many years now, as a result of the deliberate and avowed policies of those who control the Y.C.W., all the leaders of this organization have been taught that there is something reprehensible about the activities of the Social Studies Movement. … Today, it is clear that it has involved the Church in an absolute disaster. We are winning union elections in all States. A relatively large number of full-time union positions have had to be filled. We are now facing a situation that we no longer have the men to fill them. As a result, the Church is now deprived of positions of industrial and political importance … It is worrying, to the point of distraction, to find that we are able to win the positions, and then see the fruits of victory dissipated in this fashion.

Subversion of the CSSM likewise was claimed to have spread to the Catholic secondary schools and the universities, in whose regard the letter alerted Mannix to the existence of 'a definite plan of action,

33 Santamaria to Mannix, 28 May 1947, in Morgan, *Santamaria: Your Most Obedient Servant*, 24.

in which the chaplains of the Universities of Melbourne, Sydney and Brisbane, and a number of close supporters, are involved, to destroy the influence of the Secretariat, the Social Studies Movement and the Campion Society in these universities':

> If the secondary schools and universities are finally closed to us, and to this is added the long-standing boycott by the Y.C.W., I would submit to Your Grace that we have no future. Quite apart from the numbers involved, the loss of intellectual quality will be irreplaceable. … I may sum up by saying that my colleagues have never been afraid of the Communist Party. But they are more than afraid of this organised internal dissention which can destroy all of our work and which can never be tracked down and answered.[34]

And no more was Santamaria willing to concede any merit to the Y.C.W.'s 'See, Judge, Act' technique of changing essentially hostile environments through the transformation of individual consciences – of enabling its members to apply moral standards within their workplaces and working lives:

> The emphasis which has been placed on the Inquiry method would seem to imply that the great problems of the different human environments are not already known, or that, even if they are known to officials at Headquarters, they have not penetrated the consciousness of ordinary leaders of the Movements. I believe such a proposition to be untrue. … I believe that the problems to be faced by each Movement are clear – almost transparently so – and that it is a complete waste of time – almost a criminal waste of time in the revolutionary situation with which the Church is faced – to be examining problems

34 Santamaria to Mannix, 11 December 1952, in Morgan, *Santamaria: Your Most Obedient Servant*, 76–79.

> from all angles and to be substituting individual acts of charity for the large-scale action which the times demand.[35]

Following Maher's resignation as ANSCA Research Officer in 1951, a memorandum from the Y.C.W. to Simonds in his capacity as secretary of ECCA recommended the replacement of the Research Officer position by one of Assistant Director, to which Long as the most outstanding Y.C.W. activist of his generation would then be appointed, but the new designation was not adopted nor was the vacancy filled. The implicit slight was indicative of the heavy cost incurred by the Y.C.W. for the upholding of its principles. In the face of the fraught circumstances of the day and embittered divisions within both lay and clerical circles, it was unsurprising that so strong and sustained a stand against the CSSM by the Y.C.W. should result in a reluctance or failure on the part of pro-CSSM priests or bishops to pass on information about Y.C.W.'s activities through their pulpits or assist it in encouraging the younger members of their respective congregations to become or remain Y.C.W. members.

Confrontation

The Y.C.W. Priests Committee in its turn directed attention in a mid-1952 memorandum to the contrast between annual payments by the bishops respectively of £250 to individual Catholic Action specialised movements including the Y.C.W. and £7000 to the CSSM. And it was argued further by the Committee that the discrepancy was the greater still by reason of Santamaria's salary, secretarial and rental

35 B.A. Santamaria, 'Personal Statement, March 1949', in Patrick A. Morgan, *B.A. Santamaria: Running the Show: Selected Documents 1939–1996* (Melbourne, Vic: The Meigunyah Press in Association with the State Library of Victoria, 2008) 47.

expenses as Director of ANSCA representing effectively a further subsidy to the CSSM consequent on the allocation of the greater part of his time to CSSM rather than ANSCA work. The CSSM was claimed also to have taken over the office space previously occupied by the specialised movements, and thus: 'This financial advantage given the Movement has made organization of their work more widespread, with the result that many people have gained the idea, either that it almost supersedes the need for Catholic Action, or that it is Catholic Action'.[36]

Meeting in Melbourne on 21 October 1953, the ANSCA, Y.C.W., National Catholic Girls Movement (NCGM) and Young Catholic Students (YCS) diocesan chaplains of the day drafted and disseminated a declaration that:

> Considerable confusion exists in the public mind and in the minds of many Priests as to the real distinction between official Catholic Action and the [Catholic] Social Studies Movement. This association is detrimental to the progress of Catholic Action and is brought about by the following factors:
>
> The official Chaplain to ANSCA and to the CSSM being the same person,
>
> The headquarters of both organizations being located in the same building, and
>
> The Administrative Officer of ANSCA and the CSSM being the same person.

The bishops were requested by the meeting 'to define the duties of the ANSCA chaplain as being connected with ANSCA and its associate Catholic Action bodies only and in no way with the

36 Kehoe, Unpublished Draft History of the Melbourne Y.C.W., 1932–58, Chapter 7, 75.

CSSM, to consider locating the offices of the CSSM and ANSCA in different premises, and to see that the same person did not hold the directorships of both ANSCA and the CSSM.[37]

Consideration of the declaration by the bishops at the ECCA meeting on 17 November failed to achieve a consensus, with Simonds and Adelaide's Archbishop Beovich supporting the separation of the two organisations, and O'Collins in opposition to it. A ruling by Mannix as Chairman against the proposal provoked strong dissent from Simonds, who then 'stalked out of the meeting', thus leaving the members deeply divided: 'with Mannix, O'Collins and Henschke supporting the Movement; and Simonds, Beovich, Toohey and presumably Duhig, opposed (Tweedy was absent)'.[38]

Such, however, was not to be the last word. Following further consideration by the bishops at their annual conference on 28 and 29 April 1954, Mannix's ruling was overturned, and Catholic Action declared to be a separate organisation from the CSSM *de jure et de facto*. Advised by Santamaria that if required to choose between ANSCA and the CSSM his choice would be to retain the latter, an ECCA meeting on 23 September accepted further recommendations from him to the effect that ANSCA should be abolished and its staff – 'himself, an assistant chaplain, an accountant and two secretaries' – reassigned together with the lion's share of its resources to the CSSM:

> The Catholic Action movements were to be under their own episcopal chairmen, who would be responsible directly to the whole episcopal conference. Apart from £400 which went to each of the YCS, the NCGM and the Y.C.W., and £250 to the

37 Kehoe, Unpublished Draft History of the Melbourne Y.C.W., 1932–58, Chapter 7, 78.

38 Duncan, *Crusade or Conspiracy?*, 200.

> Rural Movement (a total of £1450 which was to be collected by Bishop Brennan) the balance of the existing £5000 quota for Catholic Action was allotted to the Movement, and collected annually from the bishops by Bishop O'Collins. There was no ruling on who would prepare the social justice statements, but Santamaria continued to do this, and remained secretary.[39]

The CSSM moved to new premises in Gertrude Street, Fitzroy, in March 1954, and in April the ANSCA offices were closed. 'However, the deeper issues had not been faced', Duncan concludes:

> The Movement was still under episcopal patronage and receiving even more direct Church funding than before. The problem of its political scope had not been resolved, nor the question of accountability. The Rural Movement was officially Catholic Action, and hence supposed to stay out of the political arena, yet it remained linked with the CSSM under Santamaria's direction.[40]

39 Duncan, *Crusade or Conspiracy?*, 221.

40 Duncan, *Crusade or Conspiracy?*, 221.

Chapter 13

MISSION CREEP AND POLITICAL DEBACLE

'The Position in the Political Field'

That the broader ideological mandate with which Santamaria saw the Catholic Social Studies Movement as having been conferred exceeded by far the anti-Communist intentions and expectation of the bishops was apparent in a series of three seminal addresses, commencing with 'The Position in the Political Field' in January 1950 and culminating in 1953 with 'The Movement of Ideas in Australia' and 'Religious Apostolate and Political Action':

> As time passed, the Movement went into unions that could hardly be called Communist-run. The Groupers, as they and their ilk were called, were targeting Labor men whom they found unacceptable. ... Unintended or not, the Movement was becoming a faction within the Labor Party, the emergency fire brigade was settling down to party politics. It was a faction like every other faction, with this difference – it spoke with the authority of the Church.[1]

Expanding exponentially the definition of the enemy to encompass groups other than the Communists as originally targeted, Santamaria's 'The Position in the Political Field' address reads:

1 Campion, 'A Question of Loyalties', 14.

> The primary task in relation to Labor is not that we should fight to maintain the status quo – for the status quo cannot be maintained – but that in the inevitable struggle with the forces of the Left Wing we should emerge victorious and that the victors should emerge with the name and with the organization of the Australian Labor Party attached to them. ... The conflict can only be won if at the effective level in the Labor organization – that is to say, among Federal and State Labor members and among delegates to Federal and State Labor conferences – our viewpoint is represented by individuals with a Christian outlook.

Categorising the CSSM and its following as the 'New Christians', the address identified as their adversaries a broad spectrum of 'Old Christians', Social-Democrats, Democratic Socialists and 'Labourist' trade unionists. 'Old Christians', as traditional Catholics within the party including former senior ministers in the recently defeated Chifley government were styled, had undergone their intellectual development 'at a time when the energies of religious bodies were concentrated on other and more immediate questions than those of social policy':

> As a result, the 'Old Christians' did not receive that Christian intellectual formation on social matters which would have given them one integrated Christian viewpoint on all social matters. They became 'split' personalities. Their religious formation went on under the direct aegis of religious organizations. Their social formation was achieved under the aegis of men who were influenced by the Socialist theories of the last century. Not that they became logical and convinced Socialists. In social matters, their outlook was a rather muddled mixture of Christianity and Socialism, with Socialist ideas predominating. ... They are extremely critical of religious influence within the Labor Party, even though they themselves profess religious loyalty. ...

> Seemingly, they have neither philosophy nor objective, and are concerned only with returning to office as soon as possible.

Attacking Chifley and his ministers via the proxy of their closest advisors, the address characterised the battle within the party as 'best described as a struggle between the new and vigorous school of Fabian Socialists on the one hand, and on the other the equally new and equally vigorous influence which might be described as that of the "New Christians"'. Had the government survived, 'the real victors would have been the new Left Wing bureaucracy, the emergence of which was possibly the most important permanent effect of the Chifley administration':

> Dr Coombs as Governor of the Commonwealth Bank, Dr Burton as head of the Department of External Affairs, the ex-professor Crisp as Director of the Department of Post-war Reconstruction, Dr Lloyd Ross until recently one of the senior officials of that Department – all of them represented one school of thought on socio-political matters. Their appointment to the top positions in the Federal Public Service signified not only the rise to the leadership of that club of some men of outstanding ability, but the conversion of the Public Service into an instrumentality of men whose intellectual heritage descended from the London School of Economics. There was nothing to show that as the older Departmental heads retired their place in all the Departments, whose work had social content, would not have been taken by men drawn from outside the ranks of the Public Service and representing the same intellectual trend.

'One in mind with the men who have so recently been promoted to the top positions in the Public Service' were 'the young economists who have written and will continue to write the pamphlets and brochures of the Australian Fabian Society':

> They are Socialists by conviction, and direct or indirect products of the London School of Economics by training. They are cold, confident, ruthless, intellectually strong and able to appeal to the native Socialist group which has been present as one of the composite factors of the Australian Labor Party since the days of its foundation. This new ideological group within the Labor Party possesses, therefore, three points of strength:
>
> It is possessed of an intellectually strong and philosophically coherent social outlook.
>
> It represented a very strong political interest within the Labor Party by speaking for the interests of the new bureaucracy.
>
> It can appeal to one part of the historical tradition of the Labor Party – to that Socialist element which has been present within Australian Labor since the days of its foundation.

'Outside the Fabians altogether' but allied with them were 'the extreme industrialists whose primary loyalty is to the union movement although they are not Communists':

> This force is altogether opposed to any Government legislation whatsoever in relation to the trade unions, and, in fact, opposed all the trade union legislation of the Chifley Government from the amendments to the Arbitration Act concerning union elections to the 'freezing' legislation on the occasion of the coal strike.

Overall, the 'New Christians', on the other hand, suffered from 'a very grave weakness':

> Whereas the Fabians know where they are going, the 'new Christians' as yet do not. With relatively few exceptions, they do not realise that Labor's only real alternative to the adoption of a completely Socialist policy is the adoption of a policy based upon the small unit – the small political unit, the small State, the small town, the small industrial unit, the small farm bound

> together in co-operative association. They do not realise that the socialisation objective, even with the 1921 interpretation, is a temporary compromise rather than a final policy. As a compromise, it is no doubt necessary for a period in which the 'new Christians' are not possessed of the political strength with which to assert themselves. If ever they do obtain this strength, however, it will be a cardinal error which will lead to their defeat if they do not press forward from the temporary compromise to the final conversion of the Labor objective into one which is in harmony with Christian social teaching.[2]

'The Movement of Ideas'

Highlighting the clash at recent Sydney Trades and Labour Council elections between a Catholic, J.D. Keenahan, who was not a Grouper, and a Grouper, Jim Shortell, who was not a Catholic, Santamaria's 'The Movement of Ideas' address characterised the CSSM and its Grouper allies as having arraigned against them in the ALP and the trade union movement a new and formidable force. Akin allegedly to the Bevanite wing of the UK Labour Party and to Tito's Yugoslavia, it was argued to be reflective of 'a doctrine of political agnosticism, that in the political struggle today there is no absolute truth, that it is to be not that Moscow is better than Rome, but neither Rome nor Moscow'.

> That policy today represents the majority view of the Federal Executive and the Federal Conference of the ALP. It represents the majority view of the interstate executive of the ACTU and the majority of the delegates to the ACTU Congress and if you could count the heads in the Federal Parliamentary Caucus, it would represent the majority view there today ... It brings about

2 B.A. Santamaria, 'The Position in the Political Field', 1950, in Morgan, *B.A. Santamaria: Running the Show*, 165–173.

> this degree of disbelief in any absolute, and in the end what it does is it destroys your will to act.

Others including former supporters or sympathisers such as Lloyd Ross were singled out as spreading the view that 'the forces which knew and were strong enough to defeat Communism in the trade union movement are finished, they've got no positive policy, they don't know where they are going, and it is necessary now to embark on the next stage to take over from these people'. How was this development to be dealt with?: 'The fact that this force does exist, its doctrines and the reputation of its doctrines must be worked out clearly and intellectually':

> We have got to win the argument of ideas. It can be answered alright, but unless you describe it and dispose it and answer it, you won't know what you are fighting. And the people whom you are trying to influence will deny the existence of the very enemy against whom you are coming today … We mustn't call it a third force, as I have called it for the purpose of convenience, because a third force between Communism and anti-Communism is tremendously attractive to the people who have not got any stomach for the fighting … It must be given a name so that like any disease it can be isolated and labelled, diagnosed and dealt with.

The repudiation of Chifley was no longer implicit, as previously in his 'The Position in the Political Field' address, but overt: 'The order of infallibility given to these arguments by the Chifley legend' had to be destroyed: 'People might not follow Dr Evatt or Mr Calwell. But the Chifley legend is held to be strong enough to make orthodox any policy that they put forward, and to condemn any policy that we put forward':

> Within the Labour Movement we must fight to destroy their use of the Chifley legend. You are always against a disadvantage today when they can say Chifley said this in foreign policy, Chifley said that on bank nationalisation. ... you can destroy the Chifley legend by appealing to the now forgotten Curtin legend, and the meaning of Mr Curtin's actions in the field of foreign relationships was to call on America instead of Great Britain ... There is a big task of research to be done in Chifley's own speeches, to show that the doctrines of Chifley in the last year of his life, were not the doctrines that he held in the previous five or six years.

So far in the battle against Communism it had been the Catholic workers, tradesmen, members of unions, who had 'borne the whole brunt of the struggle':

> The educated Catholics, the people with secondary and university education have come into the fight hardly at all, and because they are not in the fight their actions and their statements today, in argument, in Catholic papers, are very often irresponsible and dangerous. They have got to be brought into the struggle and won to the struggle. Then you not only side-track that line of argument but you bring into the fight all of the intellectual resources of which the Church in Australia is capable.[3]

'Religious Apostolate and Political Action'

Santamaria's 'Religious Apostolate and Political Action' address in 1953 – published by Cardinal Gracias in the official organ of his Bombay diocese, the *Bombay Examiner*, in June 1955 – asserted the legitimacy of the CSSM as a means of securing through 'Catholic organizations linked to the Hierarchy' the adoption of Catholic policies and programs':

---

3 B.A. Santamaria, 'The Movement of Ideas: Address to the 1953 National Conference of the Catholic Social Studies Movement' (typescript courtesy of the State Library of Queensland).

> That an official Catholic organization, ie an organization of Catholics designed for political action and 'united to the Hierarchy' may legitimately undertake political action is made clear by the statement of the Holy Father to Catholic Action as delivered on May 3 1951: 'Catholic citizens as such can well unite themselves in an association for political activity' ... This statement contradicts a view which is often expressed that it is legitimate to select and train Catholics, but that it is not legitimate to keep them organised in one body once trained. This view is opposed to common sense.

Pressure group activity and Catholics acting as individuals were rejected in favour of an 'Action by Way of Permeation' approach on the part of an organisation 'united with the Hierarchy' in three steps, namely:

> The conscious training of individuals in political and industrial life;
>
> The development and maintenance of machinery to keep together in association individuals possessing the same ideals so that their views will make an effective impact and be of consequence.
>
> Continuous guidance by an authorised body entrusted with this work by a competent authority to ensure that these individuals are guided in all their actions by the moral law and principles of Christianity.

Moreover, 'When a Catholic organization is charged with the responsibility for political action, it is failing to discharge that responsibility if it makes no effort to remove from the conduct of public organizations "unworthy or incapable men"':

> Individuals involved in graft or similar forms of dishonesty;
>
> Individuals whose only purpose in public life is their own aggrandisement;

> Individuals who are ready to urge false and dangerous policies as a means of keeping themselves or their party in office, or to preserve their own supremacy within the party;
>
> Individuals who refuse to fight organised atheism or who, in fact, objectively side with it or its supporters;
>
> Individuals who oppose the broad policies laid down, for instance in the Social Encyclicals.[4]

Characterisation by Santamaria of the 'Religious Apostolate and Political Action' address as a hypothetical or tentative proposal was contradicted in the covering letter that accompanied a copy of it sent by him in June 1953 to an employee of the League of St Thomas Moore, John Dynon. The letter reads that the address 'represents the fixed direction of our work, and as we are completely under way with this operation, it is not something that can be changed'.[5]

The address was 'adopted enthusiastically by the Movement's March 1953 Conference' and 'a shortened version was presented on 2 December, with no qualifications about it being "tentative", as the conclusions of discussion by the Movement's national executive'. 'Astonishingly, despite the increasing conflict over the Movement, it was circulated around Australia, presumably as the basis for Movement action', Duncan wrote.[6] Having heard the address read to him by Kevin Kelly in the US in 1958, Maritain responded 'Why, that's the purest theocracy'.[7]

4 B.A. Santamaria, *Religious Apostolate and Political Action*, paper delivered to the Movement Summer School, January 1953, 1–10.

5 Santamaria to Dynon, 1 June 1953, Simonds Papers, Correspondence Box, Melbourne Archdiocese Archives.

6 Duncan, *Crusade or Conspiracy?*, 194, 204.

7 Kelly to McInerney, 26 January 1958, as quoted in Duncan, *Crusade or Conspiracy?*, 385.

New Opportunities

Movement voices and viewpoints dominated Victoria's Catholic media. Santamaria and his close associates such as Jackson accounted for much of the political and international affairs coverage in the columns of *The Advocate* and on the long-running 'Catholic Hour' radio program, and dissident opinion struggled for expression, with even letters to the editor repeatedly refused publication. Santamaria was the public face of Catholic television's 'Sunday Magazine' program until informed by Simonds following Mannix's death in 1963 that his services were no longer required.

Accepting the offer by Australia's most reactionary media proprietor, Sir Frank Packer, of the comparable segment on Channel Nine that became 'Point of View', Santamaria likened Simonds's decision to 'an attack on the policy and memory of the dead Archbishop'.[8] Simonds was more circumspect: 'Nobody was more pleased than I was when I learnt that Mr Santamaria now has a TV programme of his own'.[9] In reality, Santamaria had little cause for complaint. The new program provided him for the first time with a voice in NSW, and was for twenty years 'a weekly Australian institution'.[10]

Hubris

Defeated by the Industrial Groups and the CSSM in the major unions which it had for so protracted a period controlled, all but universally discredited in the eyes of the public and with its membership depleted to all but vanishing point, the Communist Party was by the middle 1950s in no position either to arrest or reverse

8 Santamaria, *Against the Tide*, 255.

9 'Archbishop Explains Ousting of Santamaria', *West Australian*, 23 November 1963.

10 Fitzgerald, *The Pope's Battalions*, 192.

its losses. Unions lost to the party either wholly or in part included the Federated Ironworkers' Association, the Victorian Branch of the Australian Railways Union, the NSW Branch of the Clerks' Union, the Amalgamated Engineering Union and one or more of the state branches of the Boilermakers' Union, Waterside Workers' Federation, Builders Labourers' Union, Electrical Trades Union, Painters' Union and Amalgamated Postal Workers Union.[11] 'By the beginning of 1953, Communist power was to all intents and purposes broken', Santamaria wrote.[12]

Meanwhile, the replacement of Communist union officials by CSSM operatives or supporters was indirectly but inexorably altering the balance of power within the ALP's union-dominated ruling bodies. By 1954, their control of its all-powerful Federal Executive was all but complete. Nor were Santamaria and his associates slow to recognise the historic opening that now beckoned. The vulnerability of the ALP to external takeover via its union affiliates of which he had warned the bishops in 1942 was now to his advantage, and the party seemingly ripe for the taking.

Reminiscent of Shakespeare's 'confident and o'er lusty French' on the eve of Agincourt, the CSSM conference in May 1952 resolved 'to secure control of the Federal Executive and Conference by men with a satisfactory policy by July 1952'. A letter from Santamaria to Mannix on 11 December 1952 reads:

> The Social Studies Movement should within a period of five or six years be able to completely transform the leadership of the Labor Movement, and to introduce into Federal and State spheres large numbers of members who possess a clear

11 P.L. Reynolds, *The Democratic Labor Party* (Milton, Qld: Jacaranda Press, 1974) 7.

12 Santamaria, *Against the Tide*, 115.

> realisation of what Australia demands. Without going into details, they should be able to implement a Christian social programme in both the State and Federal spheres, and above all, to achieve co-ordination of the states in so doing. This is the first time that such a work has become possible in Australia, and, as far as I can see, in the Anglo-Saxon world since the advent of Protestantism.[13]

In the view of some, the aspirations and activities of Santamaria and the CSSM as regards the ALP fell short of a wholesale takeover of the party, but evidence brought to light by Patrick Morgan in his 2007 *B.A. Santamaria: Your Most Obedient Servant: Selected Letters 1938–1996* indicates otherwise. Morgan's cross-referencing of the substance of the 'smoking gun' letter to Mannix with others of broadly concurrent date corroborates the commonsense conclusion that, in addressing himself privately to the friend and mentor whom he had revered throughout his adult life, Santamaria 'wrote what he meant and meant what he wrote'.

It was not to be. The CSSM's grab for power was by now exceeding its grasp. Santamaria's analysis underestimated the extent of the antipathy towards the CSSM and its Industrial Group allies that was developing consequent on their perceived exceeding of their mandate – on their having been put to use for purposes other than those envisaged in their original brief. Mission creep of so extensive a character could not but engender a comparable resistance, evocative of Shakespeare's defiant Henry V: 'Bid them achieve me and then sell my bones. The man that once did sell the lion's skin while the beast yet lived was killed with hunting him'. Erstwhile founders or friends of the Groups such as Lloyd Ross and the future senators Jim

13 Santamaria to Mannix, 11 December 1952, in Morgan, *B.A. Santamaria: Your Most Obedient Servant*, 73.

Ormonde and Tony Mulvihill in NSW and in Victoria Vic Stout, Pat Kennelly and Dinny Lovegrove increasingly turned against them. Arguing as early as 1953 for the right of unionists to compete in elections even against Grouper candidates, Ormonde warned: 'The Groups are over-reaching themselves and endangering the Labor machine':

> Having defeated Communists they are now in the position of deciding who are the militants. That is the situation which Mr Chifley warned against.[14]

And memories lingered of the young Santamaria's sympathy for Mussolini and stridently partisan championing of Franco in the Spanish Civil War – sentiments that recall the characterisation of Belloc by the early Chesterton biographer Dudley Barker. Barker wrote: 'In all this, Chesterton was pushed by Belloc, who was soon to be detecting Masonic plots against the noble Italian [Mussolini], and who, during the Civil War in Spain, could acclaim Franco as the saviour of us all'.[15]

Was the Santamaria who had so vehemently denounced the atrocities of one side in the Civil War while turning a blind eye to those of the other necessarily to be trusted with so great a power as control of the ALP seemed likely to confer on him? It was by no means sectarians alone who detected a whiff of authoritarianism about Santamaria's Catholicism. Nor did Australian attachments to notions of 'a fair go' and the fitness of things necessarily sit easily with the prospect of so sweeping and decisive an influence being exercised over a major political party by a man who had adamantly refused to

---

14 James P. Ormonde, 'Will Industrial Groups Split the Labour Machine?', *Voice*, February 1953.

15 Dudley Barker, *G.K. Chesterton: A Biography* (London: Constable & Co, 1973) 275.

belong to it. 'Few things were more alien to me than membership of a political party', Santamaria wrote with perhaps inadvertent irony:

> I disliked the necessary compromises of politics, and was only too aware, from many examples before me, of the consequences of political ambitions once aroused. I did not believe that I was likely to be any better than anyone else in politics.[16]

Former assertions and associations were now a millstone around his neck, of which proverbially, like Brer Fox with the Tar Baby in Joe Chandler Harris's *Tales of Uncle Remus*, he was unable readily to rid himself. Simonds stated at a lunch following the installation of Eris O'Brien as Archbishop of Canberra and Goulburn in 1954:

> I am sure that he (Eris O'Brien) will set his face against any attempt to involve the Church in underground political intrigue. Anything of that nature is completely foreign to his character, and he is too well vested in history to imagine that the Church's divine apostolate gains any permanent fruit when any of her misguided children seek to capture power in her name.[17]

Nemesis

Hubris having emerged, nemesis followed. On 5 October 1954, a press release by the Labor Leader, Evatt, attacked 'a small group of Labor members', whom it accused of being 'disloyal to the Labor Movement and to the Labor leadership' and so 'deflecting the Labor Movement from the pursuit of established Labor objectives and ideals'. The statement continued 'It seems certain that the activities of this small group are largely directed from outside the Labor

16 Santamaria, *Santamaria: A Memoir*, 72.

17 Henderson, *Mr Santamaria and the Bishops*, 38.

Movement. The Melbourne *News-Weekly* appears to act as their journal'.[18] The target of the charges was identified shortly as the 'Santamaria-Keon-McManus group'.

Initial denials by Santamaria of the existence of the Movement and the involvement of the bishops were unpersuasive. He was reduced shortly to the fallback of misrepresenting Evatt's allegations as having been to the effect that the CSSM had been conceived in order to assume control of the ALP, rather than that, as in reality had occurred, its subsequent success had been exploited opportunistically in order to achieve a takeover that at the outset had been unforeseen. Evatt was thereby to be made to appear to be opposing anti-Communism and exploiting sectarian sentiment, rather than legitimately protecting the independence of the party against a mainly external influence.

Had the 1952 CSSM conference decision, Santamaria's December 1952 letter to Mannix and the 1953 'Religious Apostolate and Political Action' address become public concurrently with Evatt's statement or in its immediate aftermath, their likely effect can be gauged by the reactions on the part of his onetime close associates and admirers, Gerard Henderson and Frank Knopfelmacher, to the publication for the first time in 1983 of extracts from the letter in Henderson's seminal *Mr Santamaria and the Bishops*. Evatt's stand would have been vindicated, the charges of sectarianism levelled against him would have been shown conclusively to be unfounded, and the Split may well have been alleviated or averted.

In Henderson's view, the letter unmasked Santamaria as having pursued the 'unrealistic' objective of creating 'a Catholic social order

---

18 Alan Dalziel, *Evatt: The Enigma* (Melbourne, Vic: Lansdowne Press, 1987), as quoted in Murray, *The Split*, 179–180.

... within an Anglo-Saxon democratic society ... in a secretive and conspiratorial manner' ... through operating techniques 'which involved the infiltration of organizations by minorities in a way that was somewhat reminiscent of the organisational techniques of Lenin'.[19]

Knopfelmacher, a high-profile Melbourne University academic and outspokenly anti-Communist public intellectual, was less restrained. His review of Henderson's book for ABC Radio 2 in 1982 reads:

> After reading Henderson, it is no longer possible to sustain the thesis that Evatt was a Communist sympathiser, as I had hitherto sincerely believed. ... The wealth of astounding revelations ... reveal that before and throughout the Split, the principal aim of the Movement was not Australia's security but her conversion to, or political manipulation into, a fundamentalist brand of Catholicism ... Henderson's story convincingly supports the following conclusion: *A fundamentalist Catholic outfit, supported by part of the Hierarchy, set up a secret organisational weapon for the purpose of penetrating and dominating the traditional domiciles of Australian Irish Catholicism – the unions and the ALP – and through them, Australia.*[20]

Others concur. Fr Campion sees the 1940s and 1950s as having witnessed 'a serious and vigorous attempt by Catholics to take over the political life of the nation, in order to legislate, in their turn, their version of the good life'.[21] Bruce Duncan concludes that 'Santamaria aimed to determine public policy and to replace the Labor leadership with Movement associates and sympathisers':

19 Henderson, *Mr Santamaria and the Bishops*, 173–174.

20 Frank Knopfelmacher, 'Review of *Mr Santamaria and the Bishops*' (ABC Radio 1982, transcript by courtesy of the ABC). Italics in the original.

21 Edmund Campion, 'People and Politics: The Australian Catholic Tradition', in *Australian Politics: Catholic Perspectives* (Sydney, Uniya Jesuit Social Justice Centre, Discussion Paper No 6), 5.

> At what stage could such a degree of influence properly be termed 'control'? Had the Communists been in a position of such influence, the Movement would undoubtedly have considered it amounted effectively to 'control' of the ALP.[22]

Out-manoeuvering Santamaria and the CSSM in a series of frequently brutal clashes culminating with a Special Conference of the Party in Hobart on 14 March 1955, the Evatt forces were able to set in train the dissolution of the Industrial Groups and secure control of the key Victorian and NSW State Executives. The party then split, with the creation of the breakaway ALP (Anti-Communist) Party by the so-called 'Coleman-Barry' group of dissident Victorian MPs expelled for crossing the floor in the state and federal parliaments.

Re-badged as the Democratic Labor Party (DLP), and with a foothold and following ultimately in every state and territory, the breakaway group was able through the disciplined direction of the preferences of its mainly Catholic voters to deny the ALP office federally until 1972 and until 1982 in Victoria. It was not until the double dissolution of the federal parliament in 1974 that the DLP finally lost its frequently pivotal Senate presence, and as late as 2012 a rump remnant of it had regained single seat representation respectively in the Senate and the Victorian Legislative Council.

Persecution

Meanwhile, dissident Catholic voices were at times sought to be silenced or stifled by denunciations from pulpits throughout the diocese that remained unchecked and unrebuked.

---

22 Duncan, *Crusade or Conspiracy?*, 407.

Calwell in particular was singled out for vilification, as the polarisation between pro- and anti-Movement elements within the Church intensified. 'It was an abiding scandal that a man like Arthur Calwell who to the best of my belief was, so far as circumstances permitted, a daily communicant throughout his life had been exposed to such criticism in his own [St Brendan's] parish church as to cause him to cease attending that church', McInerney wrote.[23] Calwell's account reads 'When I left St Brendan's, I attended thereafter when in Melbourne the Church of St Francis Assisi in Elizabeth Street':

> I re-named it the 'Church of the Catholic political refugee' because at St Francis's church I heard the gospel preached pure and undefiled. There were no sideswipes at people who were in a position where they could not hit back.[24]

Admiring of then Premier of Victoria, Labor's John Cain Snr, but despising the breakaways' leader Bill Barry – 'a key figure in the John Wren machine, who was named in a corruption scandal in the 1940s' – the Legislative Council leader of the day, Jack Galbally, told an interviewer in 1979 that 'One night in April 1955, Archbishop Mannix sent a Monsignor to his home, directing him to join the Coleman-Barry group':

> Galbally refused, telling the Monsignor: 'Would you ask the Archbishop: is he aware that the leader of his party, Barry, is a crook?' The next night, the Monsignor returned and told him: 'The Archbishop feels that if that is your view, then you should retire from politics'.

23 McInerney, *Memoir*, 43–44.

24 Arthur A. Calwell, *Be Just and Fear Not* (Melbourne, Vic: Rigby in Association with Lloyd O'Neill, 1978), 143.

'Galbally ignored the directive and stayed in the ALP', the interviewer's account continues, 'but for years afterwards he, like Calwell, was snubbed by Melbourne's Catholic hierarchy. Of the five Catholics in the Cain ministry, he was the only one to stay in the party'.[25]

Addressing priests at a conference subsequent to the Split and the inception of the DLP, Mannix stated that they could invite whoever they pleased to their public functions, but added 'I will not appear with any of those who have been false to their principles'.[26] 'It followed naturally and inevitably that every Catholic politician, Federal or State, who refused to join the DLP was excluded from Church functions', Calwell wrote.[27]

Following disclosure of the activities of the CSSM by the *Catholic Worker* in its April 1955 issue, Mannix effectively banned the sale of the paper on Church property. A circular sent to all parish priests in the diocese over the signature of his Vicar-General, Msgr Fox, on 30 March 1955 reads:

> Reverend and Dear Father
>
> The issue of April 1955 of the *Catholic Worker* has been sent to the distributors this week against the advice of the chaplain who also acts as censor of this newspaper.
>
> I myself am forbidding its sale at the Cathedral and at the churches in the Cathedral parish from next Sunday onwards. The parish priests, of course, are not bound to follow my example, but the Archbishop has asked me to let you know the above facts, and that he does not approve of certain matters appearing in this issue.[28]

---

25 Tim Colebatch, *Dick Hamer: The liberal Liberal* (Melbourne, Vic: Scribe, 2014), 152.

26 Calwell, *Be Just and Fear Not*, 141–142.

27 Calwell, *Be Just and Fear Not*, 142.

28 Ormonde, *The Movement*, 87.

In the immediate aftermath of an all but complete compliance with the ban, circulation of the *Catholic Worker* fell from 35,000 to 15,000 copies, declined subsequently to no more than 5000 copies, and was obliged ultimately to cease publication in 1976. Asked by a *Catholic Worker* committee member at a meeting in 1960 whether he would lift the ban, Mannix replied 'I have never banned anything'.[29] Fox's allegations were in significant respects unfounded. McInerney's analysis reads:

> It is to be observed that the *Catholic Worker* had no chaplain and although as a matter of practice the Reverend John Pierce had for a number of years acted as the paper's advisor on faith or morals, he did not hold the role of censor of this newspaper, and indeed, as readers of Mr Santamaria's biography, *Against the Tide*, will recall, the Archbishop, when first approached in 1936 about the question of the publication of the *Catholic Worker*, declined to appoint any censor. It is also to be observed that in the 1955 article there was nothing contrary to faith or morals. The issue was one of the political line taken by Mr Santamaria and by Archbishop Mannix and other Bishops.[30]

Alerted privately by McInerney to a particularly egregious attack by one of Santamaria's subordinates on the Catholicity of members of the Central Committee of the *Catholic Worker* and asked 'to take steps to ensure that the untrue aspersion was not repeated and that the subordinate concerned should not make that sort of attack in the future', Santamaria declined to accede to his request 'substantially on the grounds that those who gave aid and comfort to Communists

---

29 McInerney, *Memoir*, 39. On succeeding Mannix in 1963, Simonds banned the sale of *News-Weekly* at Catholic churches. In 1988, a subsequent Santamaria publication, *AD2000*, was banned from sale on Church property by Archbishop Frank Little, 'for its attacks on other Catholics and particularly on the education guidelines of the Melbourne Archdiocese'. Duncan, *Crusade or Conspiracy?*, 71.

30 McInerney, *Memoir*, 39.

could not complain if they were attacked by Catholics'. 'I was disappointed by Santamaria's reply', McInterney's account of the incident concludes, 'as I was and am of the view that members of the "Movement" were not exempt from the obligations of justice and charity towards all, including those men of the *Catholic Worker* who considered that members of the "Movement" were mistaken in their methods and practices in what were, in reality, political activities'.[31]

A relevant anecdote by Beovich's biographer reads 'On 21 December 1953 Matthew Beovich sat at a dinner table in Sydney with Archbishop Romolo Carboni, the new apostolic delegate to Australia':

> In his diary later that night, Beovich recounted that he (Beovich) had praised the work of 'the Movement', the secretive anti-communist organisation led by B.A. Santamaria, and told Carboni that Mr Santamaria was 'the best Catholic layman in Australia'. At some later date, after Carboni had become an enthusiastic supporter of Santamaria, Beovich went back to his diary entry and wrote in the margin alongside it: 'Mea Culpa'.[32]

In 1962, he banned Santamaria from speaking 'at any Catholic function in Adelaide'.[33]

Opening the 7th Annual Catholic Press Conference in 1961, Simonds deplored that Catholics had become bitterly divided and the Church was 'split from top to bottom over issues that are political

31 McInerney, *Memoir*, 44.

32 Josephine Laffin, *Matthew Beovich: A Biography* (Kent Town, South Australia: Wakefield Press, 2008) 167.

33 Edmund Campion, 'A Question of Loyalties', in Paul Ormonde (ed), *50 Years of the Santamaria Movement* (Eureka Street Papers No 1, Richmond, Vic: Jesuit Publications, 1992) 21.

rather than doctrinal'. The Church, he affirmed, 'should put herself far above the sordid strife of party political jobbery'.[34] Addressing the diocesan clergy for the first time following Mannix's death and his accession to the See in 1963, he reported that he had in his hands 'seventeen letters of protest from Catholic lay people who named priests as having offended by using their pulpits for political purposes'. 'I intend to forget these incidents', he warned, 'but if it happens again, I will deal with it severely'.[35]

Rome's Ruling

Ostensibly united at the outset in the show of support for the CSSM to which their 1955 Easter Pastoral Letter gave expression, the bishops in reality were already divided among themselves. Gilroy's auxiliary, Bishop James Carroll, affirmed in a letter to his Brisbane counterpart, Archbishop Patrick O'Donnell, in April 1955 that the Movement aimed 'to control ALP Executives and Conferences ... by force of numbers of its own representatives, and control of these representatives by their obedience to the authority of the Organisation, that is, ultimately by religious authority' and that the ALP naturally resented such outside control. A new approach would not dictate 'in the name of the Church what should be economic, industrial or international policy'.[36] Appalled by the turn of events in Victoria and concerned fundamentally that Santamaria and his associates were 'usurping the bishops' authority and dictating partisan political activity in the name

34 Calwell, *Be Just and Fear Nothing*, 175, and as quoted in Anon, *Archbishop Daniel Mannix 1864–1963* (Melbourne: Catholic Education Office, 1999).

35 Calwell, *Be Just and Fear Nothing*, 144.

36 Carroll to O'Donnell, 'Future Programme', April 1955 (Brisbane Archdiocesan Archive). As quoted in Duncan, *Crusade or Conspiracy?*, 255.

of the Church', Gilroy and Carroll, moved swiftly to separate the NSW Movement from its national counterpart.[37]

With support for the CSSM on the part of the other dioceses declining subsequently to the point where it was confined largely – albeit far from exclusively – to Victoria, the outstanding issues were referred finally for resolution by Rome in 1956. In 1957 the Vatican and Pope Pius XII in their turn ruled against Santamaria and Mannix, and to the effect that the Catholic Social Movement (CSM), as the CSSM in a further iteration had by then become, should set aside all direct action in the political field and be re-constituted to form 'the social and moral conscience of Catholics, with special attention to the battle against Communism'. Meeting in Melbourne from 16 to 19 December 1957, the CSM dissolved itself, and was re-birthed as the nominally independent National Civic Council (NCC). Rarely can defeat have been snatched so comprehensively from the jaws of victory.

Luscombe wrote in his *Builders and Crusaders* that Santamaria 'doubtless sorrowed at the political destruction of many men, Federal and State Members of Parliament, who tied their allegiance to Movement-supported policies':

> The 1954 split in the Labor Party cut short the political careers of a group of men who could have retained office if they had been prepared to sacrifice principle to expediency. Santamaria was too honest and sincere not to suffer with them.[38]

But was Santamaria frank with them about his intentions, as spelt out to Mannix? And had they been fully taken into his confidence, would all or any of them have persisted in their political apostasy?

---

37 Duncan, *Crusade or Conspiracy?*, 69.

38 Luscombe, *Builders and Crusaders*, 192.

Luscombe also wrote that 'one unfortunate result of the Split' was that 'The figure of Santamaria is firmly fixed in the minds of numerous Australians as a sinister political manipulator, a Machiavellian character who would have imposed his own Fascist-like dictatorship in Australia if his plans had not been foiled.'[39]

But was he too less than fully informed about Santamaria's intentions? Had the 'smoking gun' letter to Mannix been public knowledge when he wrote, might not he have arrived at a less sweepingly exculpatory a conclusion?

Departures

By Kelly's account, if Santamaria himself did not envisage this dénouement, 'practically all his old colleagues in the Campion Society and in the *Catholic Worker* organization came to do so':

> And as when they became aware of his sincerely motivated activities on the temporal or political plane, they would, faithful to the teachings of the Popes and the exposition of those teachings by Maritain, have nothing to do with those activities. There thus developed in Victoria a breach in the ranks of Catholics which was to have disastrous consequences, personal, social, political, ideological, national and religious.[40]

With the end of the war in sight, Kelly was thinking about new employment opportunities with an international affairs dimension. In March 1945, while in New Guinea with Naval Intelligence, he applied for temporary Research Officer positions in the Department of External Affairs (DEA), and was successful. On being demobilised, he left Melbourne for Canberra and a distinguished career in DEA,

39 Luscombe, *Builders and Crusaders*, 193.
40 Kelly, 'The Foundation of ANSCA', 16.

culminating with postings as Ambassador to Argentina from 1964–1966 and to Portugal from 1970–1974.[41] Retiring from DEA in 1975, he completed the ANU's Legal Workshop course in 1976 and was admitted to practice as a Barrister and Solicitor in the Supreme Courts of the ACT and Victoria in 1977.[42]

Out of sympathy increasingly with the post–Vatican Council Church, Santamaria was reported in 1990 as believing 'Insofar as they [the Australian bishops] think at all about the Movement or the NCC, they've come to regard it as their enemy':

> Only a few bishops would talk to him today, he says, despite the fact he has 'followed a line of policy that was followed unanimously by Catholic bishops for fifteen years without a dissentient vote'. Asked about his work, he says, 'I don't think it matters much. … Basically I haven't achieved anything I set out to achieve'.[43]

'Santamaria had compromised the Church with his politics, destroying "the whole magnificent aspiration" of Catholic Action', the prominent Sydney layman and onetime associate editor of the *Catholic Weekly* and editor of Brisbane's *Catholic Leader*, Brian Doyle, wrote.[44] Even so, the ideal survived the setback that had been inflicted upon it. The aspirations in reality outlived the structures that were to have given effect to them. The Distributist torch had passed into new hands.

---

41 Taking leave of absence from the Office of the Crown Solicitor of Victoria, Kelly commenced work in DEA on 14 October 1945. He resigned from the Victorian State Public Service on 24 June 1946 on being made a permanent officer of DEA.

42 Kelly had graduated LLB from the University of Melbourne on 14 December 1940.

43 John Lyons, 'Against the Tide', *Good Weekend*, 17 March 1990.

44 Duncan, *Crusade or Conspiracy?*, 388.

Chapter 14

THE Y.C.W. CO-OPERATORS

With the waning of the Campion presence and influence, and the abolition of ANSCA, it was the Young Christian Workers that took over the carriage of the Distributist 'one big idea' of a widespread ownership of productive property and ran with it. Kevin Peoples's memoir captures the essence and tenor of the Y.C.W. experience. It reads:

> The Y.C.W. lifted up my head and made me look at the stars. Anything was possible. I realised at the time that not all my peers took so seriously the theological basis of the Y.C.W. For some young workers the emphasis was more on worker and justice issues. I wanted both. I needed the integration and for me the Y.C.W. provided a winning formula that had the potential to change my life. And it did.[1]

Y.C.W. members and alumni, including Ted Long, Frank McCann, Bob Maybury and Leon Magree, set out to give practical effect to the papal encyclicals by co-operativist means, culminating with the rapid growth of credit unions and credit unionism as from the 1950s, and a bold bid to bring together co-operatives of all kinds within a single movement. 'The drastic and unsocial effects of the aftermath of the

1 Peoples, *Santamaria's Salesman*, 35.

Industrial Revolution increased the propertyless people of the world', Long wrote in characteristically Distributist terms, reminiscent of Belloc and the Chesterton brothers:

> People can build a middle course upholding the rights of the individual and serving the common good. ... Co-operators do not believe only in economic co-operation. They want a balance of private ownership, socialised ownership where justified, private enterprise where justified, private enterprise and co-operative enterprise.[2]

Opening a Y.C.W. co-operatives conference in 1952, the organisation's Episcopal Chairman, Archbishop Justin Simonds, affirmed in similar terms: 'There is a need for a policy that will overcome the evils of unrestricted capitalism (which makes workers little better than slaves) and brutal socialism which destroys the dignity of the individual'.[3] The motto of the Y.C.W. co-operatives became 'Not for us but for all'. David Kehoe's draft 'History of the Melbourne Y.C.W. 1932–1959' characterises them as 'the largest and most lasting material attempt by Melbourne Catholic Actionists to re-Christianise Australian society'.[4]

An intimation of things to come was Long's role in the establishing of a savings scheme as a Y.C.W. service: 'This was run voluntarily in parish groups and money was collected from the young workers each week and banked in a savings account, the idea being that this was teaching them the habit of saving', Long said:

> In 1942, I think it was, Mr Chifley, then Federal Treasurer, advised us we were breaking the law because the scheme couldn't

2 Ted Long, 'Helping Each Other Through Co-operatives', *The Australian Catholic Truth Society Record*, No 1375, 10 January 1962, 22–23.

3 *New Youth*, 11 November 1953, p 6, as quoted in Kehoe, *Towards the Y.C.W.*, Chapter 6, 64.

4 Kehoe, *Towards the Y.C.W.*, Chapter 6, 33.

> be conducted under the Banking Act. So we had to wind that up. This caused the Committee to look at getting something legal which would help encourage savings. Our enquiries took us to look at NSW legislation and we learned of terminating co-operative societies.[5]

The timing of the savings inquiry was serendipitous, as the post-war housing shortage would shortly reveal. Inspiration and guidance as to the wider application of co-operatives and co-operativism stemmed from an increasing awareness on the part of Long and his associates of Rochdale consumer co-operation and Canada's Antigonish Movement co-operatives. Reflections by Murtagh on a visit to Antigonish while studying in the US in the early 1940s were serialised in *The Advocate* in 1944, and incorporated in his exceptionally detailed Catholic Truth Society pamphlet, *The Story of Antigonish: The Extension Movement for Adult Education and Economic Co-operation of St Francis Xavier's University of Nova Scotia.*

Murtagh's account fired the imaginations of Long and his associates with its stirring narrative of apostolic initiative and community empowerment. It reads:

> During the years 1930 to 1938, Dr Coady travelled the length and breadth of the Maritimes, expounding his vision. He visited countless little fishing villages along the coast, he sought out the miners and steelworkers of the north, he talked to the little people of the inland farms. Most of the time it was in winter, when mines were idle and there was little work on land and sea. He travelled by car, by cart, by sledge, over bad roads, in snow and rain and mud. Sometimes, meetings were large, often there was a handful of people to listen to him. But gradually his vision and his homespun eloquence began to fire minds. The Extension Department built up a staff of trained writers, leaders

5 Long, Raxworthy Interview, Tape 1 Side A of three tapes, 2.

> and organisers ... And the people of the Maritimes began to take their first steps towards the mastery of their own destiny. A modern Moses was leading them slowly out of the wilderness.[6]

Not one to settle for half measures or modest in his ambitions, 'Our objective is democracy' Coady wrote:

> Our objective is to demonstrate that this can be done in Eastern Canada, a territory with a population of a little over a million people. When we set loose the proper forces in this area the people in the rest of Canada will be on the way too. Then we federate with them for a national movement which will have repercussions in the political field. We need to control only a small percentage of business to do this. I would say the control of 15% to 25% of the evident feasible economic processes would give them the power to wield the other instruments that control society via political action, socialisation, labour union activity, and proper control of private business.[7]

Articles by a newcomer from England, Steve Neate, in *The Advocate* between December 1948 and 1949 expanded on Murtagh's material with additional information on the principles and practice of Rochdale co-operation, and further encouragement and example were forthcoming from the Australian Antigonish Movement which Fr John Gallagher formed in Lidcombe in NSW following discussions with Coady in Antigonish in 1952.

Gallagher, by Long's account, 'came into our office in Melbourne in the early 1950s and made himself known to us', and Long in his turn visited Sydney in May 1954, to talk further with Gallagher and observe at first hand the Association's experiment with 'the

---

6 James Murtagh, 'The Story of Antigonish', *The Australian Catholic Truth Society Record*, No 315, July 20 1944, 19–20.

7 As quoted in Dan MacInnes, 'Masters of Our Destiny: The Ideal and the Reality'. Notes for an address to the 2nd Topshee Conference, Antigonish, 21 June 1985, 3.

Antigonish method of the organic establishment of co-operatives from the grass-roots by local credit unions'. He admired Gallagher's ideas and regretted their failure to gain greater traction in NSW, but differed from him in that 'We whilst appreciating the need for philosophy and education, felt that there had to be more widespread progress to try and involve greater numbers of people'.[8]

But were the numbers and degree of formation among the Y.C.W. co-operators sufficient to hold so ambitious an undertaking on its intended course? And had their understanding of the Antigonish experience kept abreast of its development? A more rigorous scrutiny may have resulted in a less optimistic assessment. Returning via Antigonish from the Y.C.W.'s 1957 International Pilgrimage to Rome, its joint chaplain Kevin Toomey was the last of its members to speak directly to Coady, who died in 1959. So vaulting a vision from so many impeccably credentialed sources could not but inspire emulation, albeit at the risk of disillusionment and strategic miscalculation if its claims were insufficiently scrutinised and tested or its lessons misunderstood.

Housing Co-operatives

Instrumental along with other interested parties in securing the adoption of the Victorian Co-operative Housing Act on 18 December 1944, the Y.C.W. was among the first of them to avail itself of the Act's provisions. A contemporary's summary reads:

> A co-operative housing Society relied on the Victorian government guarantee which we were able to take to a lending institution, either a bank or an insurance company, and then borrow a lump sum, in those days perhaps half a million dollars,

8 Long, Raxworthy Interview, Tape 1 Side B of two tapes, and Kehoe, Unpublished Draft History of the Melbourne Y.C.W., 1932–58, Chapter 6, 64.

> or the equivalent thereof, and that was lent individually to a number of people for housing. But the single loan was paid back as individuals paid back the Society, so it was a co-operative in the sense that we borrowed as one and the surpluses that we might make by way of interest and so forth were in fact rebated to members as we went along.[9]

Notice of intention to establish the Y.C.W. (Number 1) Co-operative Housing Society was given at a public meeting of some 150 prospective members on 19 October 1945, the society's registration was completed on 10 March 1946 and it opened for business as of that date with Kel O'Mullane as Senior Administrative Secretary and offices at the Y.C.W. headquarters in Elizabeth Street. Neville Finn became Junior Secretary as of the following year and Leo Moore – a former President of the Surrey Hills Y.C.W. – and Ted Long were appointed to clerical positions, respectively in 1949 and 1950.

An informal advisory committee comprised of the chairmen of the societies was re-constituted in 1949, as a consolidated board of which all directors were as-of-right members, together with the Y.C.W. in an observer capacity. With the resignation of O'Mullane and Finn in 1951, Bob Maybury – a former president of the Y.C.W. Deepdene Branch and East Region, and currently a Diocesan Executive member and Number 7 Co-operative Housing Society director – became the Senior Secretary of the Security Housing Co-operative, as the Y.C.W. Housing Co-operatives Group had been renamed, and the position of Junior Secretary was gained by Vic Burns.

All told, 26 terminating societies were formed, and some 2800 houses funded, but underlying issues of corporate governance and

9 Robert Maybury. As interviewed by Richard Raxworthy for the Australian Credit Union Historical Society Co-operative, Melbourne, 28 February 1992, Tape 1 Side A, transcript courtesy of the Australian Credit Union Archives 2007, 2.

worker enfranchisement and empowerment arising from the resignations remained unresolved to the project's long-term detriment. Was the conduct of the housing co-operatives, as by law independent bodies, to be determined by the Y.C.W. or independent of it, by their respective boards and managements in conformity with normal business practice? And if by the Y.C.W. whether and to what degree should the outcome be reflective of the organisation's commitment to economic and industrial democracy? Difficulties in securing quorums for the annual general meetings of the societies suggest that the implications and obligations of the co-operativist message had yet to be effectively communicated or understood.

With finance for further terminating societies unavailable from the banks between 1953 and 1956, and thereafter intermittent and uncertain, a Y.C.W. permanent building society – the Security Permanent Building Society – was established in 1958, where young workers were encouraged to accumulate savings, which in turn could be used as security against a society loan for a house or land purchase:

> The Permanent Building Society could not supply home finance as quickly as a terminating housing society but offered greater long-term security in obtaining home finance in general as well as encouraging saving. Eventually, Y.C.W. sponsored terminating societies ceased forming in the 1960s and all investment in home finance by Y.C.W. clients was made in the Security Permanent Building Society.[10]

Reflective of an increasing awareness of the need for greater co-operation between co-operatives, the Y.C.W. affiliated with the wider terminating and permanent housing society peak bodies, and was

10 Kehoe, Unpublished Draft History of the Melbourne Y.C.W., 1932–58, Chapter 6, 63.

active at their meetings and conferences. Maybury served terms as a state and national president of the Union of Permanent Building Societies and the Union's international vice-president, and in the course of overseas travel on behalf of a number of co-operative bodies in 1964 attended a school for building societies in London and visited credit unions and other co-operatives in Ireland, Canada, the United States and Fiji. 'A highlight of a visit to Canada by any person interested in co-operatives is a visit to the University of St Francis Xavier at Antigonish, Nova Scotia', Maybury wrote:

> It was from this university and the small town surrounding it that the ideal of co-operatives as a means of adult education and community development as well as an economic force was spread throughout Canada and later to many parts of the world.[11]

The Y.C.W. Trading Society

With the housing societies successfully bedded down, the attention of Long and his associates turned to further challenges and co-operatives of other kinds: 'We found that long term lending through the housing co-operatives enabled people to buy a house, but then they often were short of funds to buy furniture for their house at reasonable prices', Long said.[12]

The Y.C.W. Co-operative Trading Society Pty Ltd was registered in 1948 under the *Industrial and Provident Societies Act (1928)*, opened for business the following year 'in a back room of the Melbourne Y.C.W. headquarters', and finally in 1960 acquired premises of its own

11 Robert Maybury, 'Antigonish', *The Co-operator*, 5, No 3, August–October 1964, 4.

12 Long, Raxworthy Interview, Tape 1 Side A of 2 tapes, 3.

at Lombard House in A'Beckett Street.[13] Emphasising his support for co-operatives and co-operativism in remarks at the opening of the Lombard House showrooms, Simonds affirmed that 'It would be difficult to name a more valuable social service than that of setting up young families in their own homes by their own co-operative efforts':

> Co-operative effort is also sound social theory in harmony with the teachings of the Holy See. It enables young people to steer a course between the monopolists who exploit their needs and the type of socialism which depresses their personal initiative.[14]

Even so, for all Simonds's enthusiasm an initially slow take-up of memberships of the new entity calls into question whether support for the co-operatives as a Y.C.W. venture within a Church increasingly polarised between pro- and anti-Santamaria and CSSM elements was necessarily unanimous, or its advocacy from parish pulpits universal. As has been seen, bad-mouthing of the Y.C.W. and belittling of its inquiry method by Santamaria and the CSSM in the late 1940s and early 1950s was a source of significant reputational damage to the organisation in influential Church circles, damaging morale and diverting attention and resources from the more productive uses to which they might more profitably have been put.

McCann became the society's secretary-manager and Long chaired an inaugural Board of Directors comprising, along with Neate, Messrs H.C. Broderick, C.E. Clements, W.F. Davey, F.W. Landy and E. Piper. As of 1951, Davey, a prominent Melbourne glass merchant who had offered to assist the Y.C.W. after reading about its

13 Kehoe, Unpublished Draft History of the Melbourne Y.C.W., 1932–58, Chapter 6, 69.

14 'Opening Gives Co-op Impetus', *The Co-operator*, 1, No 1, August–October 1960, 1.

ideals in a copy of *New Youth* purchased from a street seller, took over as Chairman from Long, who in turn became successively the co-operative's Secretary and Education Officer and, on McCann's retiring in 1978, its Chief Executive Officer.

Initially trading in furniture, blinds, floor coverings, bedding, electrical goods, and bicycles, the co-operative shortly branched out to offer baths and other prime cost building requisites, and subsequently school desks and uniforms. As of 1962 some 12,000 desks – 'attractive stove enamelled, stackable metal framework, high-grade woodwork, packaged to ensure safe delivery, compact units enabling more desks to be used per room, yet providing comfort for students' – had been sold, 'in 400 locations throughout five states of the Commonwealth'.[15] By Maybury's account:

> It was one of the great success stories of co-operatives generally in that there had only been one or two suppliers of school desks in the whole of Australia and when the Y.C.W. came in it, although it had only a very small fraction of the market, it was able to produce desks at a considerably lower rate than was available elsewhere. In fact the price of desks through the whole of Australia fell as a result of that activity, because it was the first time competition had entered into that particular field.[16]

The Y.C.W. Co-operative Trading Society Chairman, Davey, reported on its entry into the school uniforms market in July 1966 that as demand was growing there had not been sufficient space in Lombard House to accommodate the service, and property in Elizabeth Street had had to be leased: 'We invite members, parents' organizations and teachers to inspect the showroom at their convenience', Davey wrote.[17]

---

15 'Desk Enterprise – A Co-operative Success Story', *The Co-operator*, Vol 3, No 2, May–July 1962, 6.

16 Maybury, Raxworthy Interview, Tape 1 Side A, 3.

17 'New Showroom Opened', *The Co-operator*, 7, No 5, August 1966, 3.

The Co-operative Education Committee

Buoyed in spirit by the launch of the trading society, Long and his associates moved to ensure the maintenance of the attendant momentum, through the auspicing by the society of a co-operatives education conference at the St John's parish hall in East Melbourne on 12 July 1952. Arising from the conference proceedings, an informal Co-operatives Education Committee (CEC) was formed, together with five working parties comprising in all some 30 members from its own and the housing societies' ranks, and tasked to study and report back on co-operatives in the spheres severally of finance, consumption, production, marketing and service.

Early outcomes of the working party's deliberations included the mainly Y.C.W.-inspired enactment by John Cain Snr's Labor government in 1953 of an *Act to Provide for the Formation, Registration, and Management of Co-operative Societies and for Other Purposes* such as had existed in NSW since 1923, with provision for the formation of co-operatives respectively for producers, trading, community settlement, community advancement, credit and investment, together with associations of societies and unions of associations. Co-operative Housing Societies Registrar Ted Ebbels was appointed to the new position of Registrar of Co-operative Societies, a Co-operatives Advisory Council was established and the trading society migrated from the *Industrial and Provident Societies Act (1928)* to re-register under the new legislation as simply the Y.C.W. Co-operative Society.

Incorporated as a new division of the trading society in 1953, a previously independent home building group – 'the first experiment by the Melbourne Y.C.W. co-operatives in worker management and profit sharing among employees as well as shareholders'[18] – was disbanded two years later, ostensibly on its being seen as 'not a financial success'.[19] The situation may have been less simple. By Kehoe's account, 'Davies [the manager], following the published charter of the Building Division which incorporated the Distributist ideals of Catholic social theory on worker management and profit-sharing, decided to distribute one-third of the first year profits among the workers':

> Hearing of this decision, Fr Lombard countermanded it. … Nevertheless, the bonus was paid to the workers. For twelve months they had been expecting to receive it if a profit was accrued. Their on-site education in Catholic social theory taught them to expect it. In fear of appearing inconsistent the Y.C.W. Co-operative Society relented. It paid the bonus only on the condition that it would not be paid again. … Frustrated idealism proved to be a deep source of division and passion.[20]

The upshot was effectively a watershed in the affairs of the Co-operators, with a characteristically Australian pragmatism on the part of Lombard effectively blurring Davies's deeply felt Distributist ideals and convictions. No further worker ownership projects were undertaken and consideration of alternative measures such as hybrid worker/member co-operatives seemingly did not occur.[21]

---

18 Kehoe, Unpublished Draft History of the Melbourne Y.C.W., 1932–58, Chapter 6, 84. 'Y.C.W. dominated' in as much as the board of management of the group prior to its incorporation in the trading society consisted of Ted Long as chairman, together with Fr Lombard, Bob Maybury, Bill Davies, Don McDonald and Don Carr.

19 'The Story of the Y.C.W. Co-operatives', *Development Review*, April–June 1961, 7.

20 Kehoe, Unpublished Draft History of the Melbourne Y.C.W., 1932–58, Chapter 6, 86.

21 For an in part Catholic inspired but more broadly based home building co-operative, see Ruth Scollay, *Lalor: The Peter Lalor Home Building Co-operative 1946–2012* (Sydney, NSW: University of New South Wales Press, 2012).

Meanwhile, a profitable household fire and theft insurance division of the society was created in 1954, a separate Waverley and District Co-operative Ltd was registered in June 1961 as a provider of uniforms for schools in the Syndal, Glen Waverley and Mount Waverley parishes and in 1963 Maybury's Security Permanent Building Society formed a Home Land Co-operative division to acquire, subdivide, service and make available at cost land for prospective home builders.

With the funding by the trading society in 1960 of a new journal, *The Co-operator*, members and well-wishers of the Y.C.W. co-operatives were enabled for the first time to exchange news and views with one another on a regular basis. The journal's initial editorial reads:

> *The Co-operator*, in this its first issue, asks its readers to face the question – can we improve the economic conditions of our country? Can we provide a distribution of property and wealth more in keeping with the rights of individuals? With the rights of families? Can we bring about a democratic ownership and control of the supply of goods and services we need? ... The true co-operative with active and interested members will find the right answers, because co-operators think not of their own gain, but of the benefit for all. Thus our motto: 'Not for us, but for all'.[22]

Co-operatives Management Committee

Efforts by Long and his associates to bring about closer coordination between the housing and trading co-operatives in the face of their increasingly disparate activities and demands were unceasing and indefatigable. Sharing of accounting services between the housing

22 'We Ask You', *The Co-operator*, 1, No 1, August–October 1960, 2.

societies and the trading society was introduced as from 1952, and in 1954 agreement was reached between them on the creation of a Co-operatives Management Committee (CMC) to superintend the employment, salaries and staff of the respective bodies and adjudicate on such disputes as might arise over the work priorities of the accounting section.

The committee comprised two housing society and two trading society representatives together with non-voting representatives of the Y.C.W. and its chaplains and Long in the capacity of the new entity's General Secretary and Education Officer. Long's responsibilities were (1) education, (2) supervision and coordination of all activities of the Y.C.W. co-operative movement including the housing co-operatives, with over-riding authority over its departmental managers, and (3) expansion and development of the existing and new co-operative ventures.

Consistent with the encyclicals and Antigonish Movement principles and practice, education of both directors and members of co-operatives was assumed increasingly by both the CEC and the CMC to be the key to the sustainability of the co-operatives project. A dual approach was favoured, with members to be educated 'on the spirit of co-operation, what it could do for them and their neighbours and also how to effectively and responsibly handle their money and financial commitments'.[23]

Directors in their turn were to receive instruction additionally on the philosophy, background and relationship to Christian social teachings of co-operation, together with the technical information

23 Susan Pepper, *Giving Credit to the People: A History of the Credit Co-operative Movement In Victoria* (Windsor, Vic: The Victorian Credit Co-operative Association Limited, 1985) 45.

required to run a successful credit co-operative. Annual education conferences under the auspices initially of the trading society were introduced, with Fr Leahy from Rockhampton in Queensland speaking on worker ownership through co-operatives as an alternative to the contemporary joint stock company in 1953, Maybury on 'Financing the Family' in 1954, and in 1955 Long and Maybury heralding new departures and priorities on the part of the movement with their joint presentation on 'How to form a Credit Union'. And it was to credit unions and credit unionism that the attention of the Y.C.W. co-operators increasingly now turned.

Y.C.W. Credit Unions

Established in anticipation of the impending legislation at a meeting on 23 March 1952, a new Y.C.W. Central Co-operative Credit Society (Y.C.W.CCCS) with a bond encompassing members of both the Y.C.W. and its housing and trading societies was so vigorous in its promotion of credit unions and credit unionism as to prompt the Registrar, Ted Ebbels, to declare on the occasion of the proclamation of the Act 'I will make a point of registering your credit union as number one'.[24] Susan Pepper's 1985 *Giving Credit to the People: A History of the Credit Co-operative Movement in Victoria* credits the movement's inception with having 'represented the beginnings of a new era for credit co-operatives in Victoria that went well beyond the significance and importance of the society itself and the facilities it offered its members'.[25] 'It was obvious that the basic co-operative which was best promoted was the credit union and that was the thing

24 Maybury, Raxworthy Interview, Tape 1 Side A, 5.

25 Pepper, *Giving Credit to the People*, 22.

that we could make people aware of co-operatives generally through', Maybury said.[26]

Co-operatives and co-operative movement historian Gary Lewis notes in his 1996 *People Before Profit: The Credit Union Movement in Australia* that credit union development in Victoria 'remained sluggish until around 1960':

> In June of that year, still only 39 credit unions had registered in Victoria and not all these were functioning. Barely 4000 people were members, although perhaps a few more were associated with unregistered societies. Six years later, 144 credit unions were registered in Victoria with 20,756 members. This compared with 250 credit unions in New South Wales with 111,479 members. Growth rates in Victoria, however, were impressive. Membership had increased by 38 per cent since 1960, assets by 50 per cent, loans by 35 per cent and deposits by 38 per cent. Approximately 75 per cent of the Victorian credit unions were parish or community based.[27]

As with the Antigonish Movement, the preferred means for securing the inception of new credit unions was home discussions. 'Numerous home discussions between say 1956 and 1962 were conducted by staff and members of the Y.C.W. Co-operative in their spare time', Long said:

> In metropolitan suburbs it was relatively easy, but it required considerable organization because sometimes we had to service up to four separate meetings in one parish on the one night. I also organised home discussions in parishes such as Bendigo, Echuca, Swan Hill, Mildura, Kerang, Geelong, Bacchus Marsh, Warragul and others. When we went to home discussions in those places we returned to Melbourne very late the same

26 Maybury, Raxworthy Interview, Tape 1 Side A, 5.

27 Gary Lewis, *People Before Profit: The Credit Union Movement in Australia* (Adelaide, SA: Wakefield Press, 1996) 123.

> night. After about three months we would get a credit society formed.[28]

As recalled by the then housing societies worker, Leon Magree, 'The whole idea would be thrashed out in the living room':

> For example, I would have held one in my own home in Bulleen and I would have invited neighbours and other people from the parish into my home. There might have been perhaps 12 people present and some of them in turn would conduct similar cottage meetings in the home. So by doing this over a number of weeks in a parish you would eventually cover 40 or 50 people and if you thought you had enough interest in the formation of a credit society then you would convene a formal meeting that would be required. ... In one week we formed five new credit unions which was unusual but they all came to a culmination at the one time.[29]

The popular appeal and competitive advantage of credit unions and credit unionism stemmed significantly from their character as a means of averting exploitation at the hands of the usurious hire purchase rackets of the day. Home buyers could qualify – albeit at the cost of frequently protracted queuing – for bank loans re-payable over 30 years at a fixed interest rate of three and a half per cent. However, when furnishings, floor coverings, a car or consumer durables such as a refrigerator or washing machine were required, they would be referred to a hire purchase company – frequently a subsidiary of the bank which was already their home loan provider – at interest rates which were grossly and punitively disproportionate.

Characteristically, Catholic families gathered round card tables in their church foyers after Mass, to pool such savings as they had, and in turn queue to borrow at interest rates which were affordable for

28 Long, Raxworthy Interview, Tape 2 Side A of three tapes, 1.

29 Magree, Raxworthy Interview, Tape 2 Side A of three tapes, 4.

them. An account of the Box Hill Credit Union in its early stages by a founder Director and subsequent senior credit movement activist, Tom Stubbs, reads:

> We only used to operate on a Sunday morning. We had a room in the hall outside the church and we had a tin box which people used to put their pass-books in with their money in an envelope, leave it on their way into Mass. The Directors, who were the volunteers for that particular Sunday, took the books and did the necessary work involved on them. They were ready for the people when they came out from Mass.[30]

A little later, neighbouring households of other faiths or none metaphorically looked over the fences of the churches, saw what a good thing the parishioners had going for them, and sought and secured admission, thereby setting in train the conversion of the parish credit unions into community credit unions. Later again, trade unions and some employers recognised that workplaces were as much communities as were parishes or suburbs, and industrial credit unions were established. And over time, individual credit unions linked up with one another, through associations and auxiliary bodies.

The Association of Catholic Co-operative Credit Societies

Chairing a meeting of representatives of the Y.C.W.CCS together with the East Thornbury, St Gabriel's and St Peter's credit co-operatives at 312 Elizabeth Street, Melbourne, on 29 October 1957 to consider the creation of a credit co-operatives association, Long urged them 'to co-operate for their common good, to pool resources

30 Tom Stubbs. As interviewed by Richard Raxworthy for the Australian Credit Union Historical Society Co-operative, Melbourne, 27 February 1992, Tape 1 Side A of 2 tapes. Transcript courtesy of the Australian Credit Union Archives 2007, 2.

and information, improve administration, combine in lobbying for legislative improvements, develop new credit co-operatives, co-ordinate policy and methods, and generally advance the co-operative cause in the service of fellow citizens'.[31] A motion by the Y.C.W.CCS and the St Peter's credit society for the formation of the Association of Catholic Co-operative Credit Societies (ACCCS) was accepted and rules adopted.

The Y.C.W.CCS Chairman, Jim Ryan, was appointed Acting ACCS Chairman, together with Long as Secretary and Maybury as Treasurer, and the Association was registered on 11 December 1957 with a board comprising one director from each member society. Meeting for the first time in their new capacity, the directors confirmed Ryan's appointment and agreed in principle on a per society member subscription, which subsequently was set at one shilling (10 cents) per member or, as Ryan dubbed it, 'a bob a nob'.[32] On Ryan's resignation due to ill health in 1961, his position was taken over by Leo Stewart.

Unable initially to afford paid staff, the ACCCS operated from 1957 to 1965 on an honorary basis. Taking over from Maybury as Treasurer in 1960, Magree voluntarily devoted much of his time outside business hours to developmental work on behalf of the Association, and in 1965 became its manager and first full-time employee:

> We did quickly appoint a secretary, a secretary-typist you might say, and just the two of us ran the Association. We were fortunate that we were able to share offices, or rent offices, from the overall Y.C.W. group of housing co-operatives, so if both of us were not in the office any one day we could be sure the phone was

31 Lewis, *People Before Profit*, 126.

32 Pepper, *Giving Credit to the People*, 42–43.

> answered and orders taken for stationery, whatever particular service inquiry was received.[33]

Support services as introduced progressively by the ACCCS included central banking with the Association in 1957, insurance respectively for the cancellation of outstanding loan balances on the death of borrowers in 1959 and fidelity cover for society officers in 1963, lobbying such as of governments over taxation and stamp duty on loan agreements from the late 1950s, and from 1961 a handbook for society secretaries was regularly updated:

> Compiled by Arthur Carter, a Director of St Leonard's Credit Co-operative Society, Glen Waverley, it was designed as a reference manual on procedures. Over 100 pages in length, it interpreted the requirements of the law for credit societies, detailed accounting practices, the role and responsibilities of directors, how to hold a meeting as well as a history of the movement. The handbook was greatly appreciated within the parish co-operatives, because it was the first manual for their use.[34]

Standardised credit union stationery was made available on request to affiliated societies, together with 'discussion papers exploring possible future developments including a stabilisation fund and loan committees, and technical papers considering best practice'.[35] As from 1958, conduct of the movement's annual education conferences was taken over from the trading society and the CEM, with the ACCCS seeking 'to broaden the understanding of credit unions and consider such matters as interest rates, insurance, taxation, administration, the role of credit unions in the co-operative movement and the

33 Magree, Raxworthy Interview, Tape 1 Side B of three tapes, 1.

34 Pepper, *Giving Credit to the People*, 36.

35 Lewis, *People Before Profit*, 127.

philosophical tenets of co-operation'.[36] By 1966, ACCCS-affiliated societies comprising some 10,000 members and 5000 non-member depositors had made loans totalling $8 million, and the Association's assets totalled $115,380.[37]

The Co-operative Development Society

Concerned in 1961 that the then current co-operative education measures were insufficiently extensive or inclusive, Long in his capacity as secretary jointly of the CMC and the ACCCS recommended to the ACCCS Board the creation of a new body, tasked to assume responsibility for the education function in all its aspects and comprising 'individuals to be drawn from the experienced staff of the various Y.C.W. co-operative societies, their chaplains like Fr Toomey and Fr Lombard and a few experienced individuals from the various Y.C.W. co-operative societies, including one from each credit society'.[38]

Formed at a meeting of ten Y.C.W. co-operators on 24 January 1961 and registered on 2 February with a board comprised of Brian Waldron (Chairman) and Ted Long (Secretary), together with Directors Bob Maybury, Frank McCann, Chris Stocks and Jim Ryan, the Co-operative Development Society (CDS) was endorsed formally by the ACCCS at its May 1962 annual general meeting as the sole educational unit for the Y.C.W. co-operative movement.

The inspiration and motivation for the new venture was again explicitly Antigonish. 'We believed what the Antigonish Movement of Nova Scotia, through the St Francis Xavier University there, was

---

36 Lewis, *People Before Profit*, 127.

37 Pepper, *Giving Credit to the People*, 35.

38 Pepper, *Giving Credit to the People*, 44.

propagating, that co-operatives are a means to an end whereby you can gain greater personal freedom and that is something that is most essential for Christian living' Long said:

> We viewed co-operatives as a means of making a contribution to the reform of society. We didn't say the community or the society or the economy has got to go all co-operative. But we were saying that the world or community has socialism, it has capitalism and bits of each mixed up at times, and there is a need for a third order and co-operatives could be that third order. If there was a proper mix of capitalism, socialism and this form of private enterprise which is co-operative, you would finish up, probably with a better society.[39]

A summary of the responsibilities taken over by the CDS from the Association or otherwise assumed reads:

> Publication of the quarterly *Co-operator*,
>
> Publication of the quarterly *Development Bulletin*,
>
> Building up of a Co-operative Library at Lombard House,
>
> Preparation of suitable publicity brochures for various types of co-operatives,
>
> Provision of speakers for various Annual meetings and other meetings,
>
> Consideration of main principles for Christian co-operatives,
>
> Organising Retreats for Co-operators.[40]

As of July–September 1961, the quarterly CDS *Development Bulletin* was introduced as a more specialised companion paper for the *Co-operator*, 'to develop an educational programme for those on

39 Long, Raxworthy Interview, Tape 1 Side B of two tapes, 5.

40 'The Co-operative Development Society Progresses', *Development Bulletin*, 1, No 2, July–September 1961, 2.

whose efforts the future of our Co-operative Movement depends – namely our Directors, employees and honorary officials':

> The bulletin is directed towards developing 'whole' co-operators – not only 'one-type' co-operators. For instance, we want to help our co-operators understand there is no such thing as a true co-operator who believes only in a Co-operative Credit Society and will take no interest in the further development of co-operative trading or insurance.[41]

Long's CDS and Catholic Truth Society pamphlet *Helping Each Other Through Co-operatives* had to be re-printed, as had also John Giddens's subsequent *Invest in the Future of Your Credit Union*, and circulation of the *Co-operator* reportedly peaked at 17,750.[42] Conducted at Lombard House over six successive Tuesdays from 24 September to 29 October 1963, an initial CDS 'School on Co-operatives' featured addresses by eleven speakers, on themes including 'Why are co-operatives necessary?', 'Why should Christian men and women form and develop co-operatives?', 'Have co-operatives a bigger job to do than that of economic benefit?' and 'What is the future of the Y.C.W. co-operatives?'.[43] Regional schools at centres including Mitcham, Glen Waverley, Bentleigh, Oak Park, Bendigo and Geelong followed in October 1964, a further three-night school at Lombard House in 1965, and in 1966 and 1969 residential weekend schools respectively at Melbourne University's Newman College and International House.

Reviewing as from 1964 'What should be the future policy of what had become known as the Y.C.W. Co-operative Movement?',

---

41 'Why the Development Bulletin?', *Development Bulletin*, 1, No 1, April–June 1961, 2.

42 Lewis, *People Before Profit*, 127.

43 'Means to a Higher End', *The Co-operator*, 4, No 3, November–December 1963, January 1964, 1.

the CDS decided at its Annual Meeting in 1965 that it should 'work for the development of a general co-operative movement in Victoria open to all who are prepared to accept co-operative principles including education':

> By March 1966 all affiliated groups and sponsoring bodies had endorsed the Development Society's 1965 decision. ... The Development Society is now working for the formation of a Co-operative Trading Association and then a Co-operative Union. The Society regards itself as trying to fulfil some of the functions of a Union until such is formed, and will cease to exist in favour of the Union once the latter is formed. The Development Society in its history and in its present effort is trying to provide a means to fulfil one of the principles recently defined by the International Co-operative Alliance: 'That there should be active co-operation between co-operatives'.[44]

Following the success of lobbying by the CDS in securing a representative for the co-operative movement on the Victorian Co-operative Societies Advisory Council in 1969, Long was appointed to the position and remained a member until 1989.

The Victorian Credit Co-operatives Association

Concurrently with the Development Society's committing itself to the creation respectively of activity-specific co-operative associations and an overall co-operative union or federation, moves were afoot to convert the ACCCS from an exclusively Catholic body to one to which all credit unions could belong. Responding to notice of the convening by the La Trobe Valley Credit Co-operative of a meeting to consider the formation of a state association, a special meeting of

44 'History of the Co-operative Development Society', *The Co-operator*, 8, No 7&8, October–December 1967, 6.

ACCCS Board on 31 August 1965 'welcomed the attempt by La Trobe Valley to form a state association for the many societies not affiliated with a central body'.[45]

At a meeting in the Nurses Memorial Centre at 431 St Kilda Road, Melbourne, on 4 November, representatives of ACCCS and thirty-four credit co-operatives heard Maybury argue forcefully: 'We will have to open our doors. We will have to become the Victorian Association'. So altruistic and affirmative an outlook was not universally shared. As recalled by the future Manager of the Administrative and Clerical Officers Association Credit Union, Ralph Lewis, 'A guy got up … and in the broadest of Irish accents said "Why should we help these other people?"'.[46] A ten-member sub-committee was established to review the rules of the NSW League and the Victorian Co-operation Act and model rules and bring forward to a further meeting a formal recommendation on 'the desirability or otherwise of an Association in Victoria'.[47] Rejecting the option of separate bodies, the sub-committee's recommendation was for the retention of the ACCCS with a new name and amended rules.

Agreement was reached on the ACCCS Board 'to recommend to societies that they endorse the decision to work towards the formation of a State association, open to all credit societies that are prepared to accept co-operative principles, including education'.[48] A meeting of forty people from twenty-five ACCCS affiliates on 10 December 1965 endorsed the board's decision, and Simonds's approval for the

45 Pepper, *Giving Credit to the People*, 68.

46 Ralph Lewis, as interviewed by Richard Raxworthy for the Australian Credit Union Historical Society Co-operative, Melbourne, ND. Tape 1 Side A of two tapes. Transcript courtesy of the Australian Credit Union Archives 2007, 4.

47 Pepper, *Giving Credit to the People*, 69.

48 Pepper, *Giving Credit to the People*, 70.

change of name was obtained on the basis 'that the co-operatives are a legal mechanism concerned with economic problems, and as such, not directly subject to the authority of the Church'.[49] Following on the adoption by the ninth Annual Meeting of the ACCCS on 16 September 1966 of a special resolution changing the name and rules of the association, 'the Victorian Credit Co-operative Association (VCCA) became a reality'.[50] It was an epiphany of sorts for the Y.C.W. Co-operators – the Cortes moment when, like the great conquistador and his men, they 'looked at one another with a wild surmise, silent upon a peak in Darien'.

Achievements

The outcome of the efforts of the Y.C.W. Co-operators in the short to medium term exceeded their expectations. Evocative of Victor Hugo's great adage 'Nothing is so powerful as an idea whose time has come', the credit unions and credit unionism in which they had so comprehensively invested their hopes seemingly swept all before them. Key performance indicators increased exponentially. In an astonishing growth spurt between 1983 and 1995, credit union membership nationally rose from 1.9 to 3.4 million and assets under management from $3 billion to $14 billion.

The inception of national ancillary bodies, such as a Credit Union Foundation of Australia for the fostering of credit unionism in developing countries and the Credit Unions Historical Society Co-operative for the archiving of the movement's memories and records and study of its development, attested to a strong sense on the part of the movement of its corporate identity, and an acceptance by credit

49 Pepper, *Giving Credit to the People*, 70.

50 Pepper, *Giving Credit to the People*, 71.

unions of social and community obligations aside and apart from those of conventional financial services providers.

Weekend residential schools held annually at the Warburton Chalet guest house renewed and reinforced solidarity among key movement activists, and functioned as a forum for the exchange of information and ideas about future directions and opportunities. Following the loss of the guest house in a fire in 1973, and the failure of subsequent efforts to replace it with a Jubilee Lake co-operative conference centre at Daylesford, regional chapters together with institutes respectively of directors and managers emerged as alternative sources of education and training. So highly valued had been the Warburton schools and their Y.C.W.-style formation function, that the VCCA went close to bankrupting itself over the Daylesford project.[51]

Meanwhile, households were enabled to access consumer loans at interest rates that were affordable for them or assisted in their household budgeting and the resolution of financial crises. The ravages of pay-day lending were curtailed, and usurious hire purchase industry practices significantly mitigated. Credit unions collectively came to comprise in all but narrowly regulatory or legislative terms a people's bank, servicing predominantly low and modest income memberships.

Setbacks and Disappointments

For all these initial successes, the upshot ultimately was far from being as the Y.C.W. Co-operators had envisaged it. Antigonish was losing its inspirational quality, as the co-operatives there were shown increasingly to have fallen short of the hopes which had been invested in them, and already at the point when Murtagh's pamphlet

---

51 Lewis, *People Before Profit*, 139–146.

first drew attention to them to have entered upon a marked decline. As so eloquently demonstrated by Professor Dan MacInnes of the Department of Sociology at Antigonish's University of St Francis Xavier in a 1985 conference paper, the movement had become in the intervening decades 'the most dangerous of all Celtic mythic creatures – a live ghost':

> As a live ghost, the movement appears to have life, co-op stores exist, and to all intents and purposes it is possible to point out the externalities of life. This appearance of life is more confusing for visitors since frequently people closely associated with the movement pretend that things have turned out pretty well as had been planned. Hardly anyone curses the darkness. Instead, commonly people speak of how the movement made things better pointing at today's flickering torches, Bergengren, Eastern Dairyfoods, and UMF.[52] Few users ask how these co-operative businesses are different from those run according to the profit motive; few are aware that these concerns ought to be part of an integrated economic strategy.[53]

Deprived by the deaths of Simonds and Lombard respectively in November and December 1967 of its principal clerical supporters and protectors and distracted by the ongoing turmoil within and around the Church following the CSSM debacle, the botched ALP takeover bid and the inception of the NCC and the DLP, the wider Y.C.W. was in no position to augment the efforts of the Co-operators and no successor generation within their ranks was fostered or forthcoming. Too few in number by far and hampered all too frequently by an interrupted or otherwise insufficient or ineffectual formation process,

---

52 Bergengren was at the time the major regional credit union and Eastern Dairyfoods and the United Maritime Fishermen (UMF) producer co-operatives. The UMF was placed in receivership in 1988.

53 MacInnes, *Masters of Our Destiny: The Ideal and the Reality*, 5.

those in both the central and local spheres found themselves overwhelmed by the administrative and organisational demands of the explosive growth of the credit unionism whose inception their efforts had so triumphantly engendered, and impotent increasingly to arrest its drift from the wider objectives which had been their expectation of it. Managers recruited of necessity from elsewhere in the financial services sector including hire purchase companies were not necessarily aware or appreciative of co-operative and mutualist values and principles, and in some instances rejected or resisted them. Opportunities to implement employee ownership measures consistent with the encyclicals as in the case of the school desks project and the home building project were overlooked or insufficiently explored.

The altruistic and ecumenical sentiments that motivated the conversion of the ACCCS into the secular VCCA and the subsequent shelving of the distinctively Catholic Co-operative Development Society proved ultimately to be self-defeating. Education was found to be a necessary input for co-operative and mutualist development, but an insufficient antidote or panacea for a marked diminution of member involvement and creeping bureaucratisation. The intended wider role of the credit unions in instigating and facilitating the development of an effective peak body for the co-operatives sector and perhaps also for mutuals more generally did not eventuate. Rather than a means of transitioning to a more just and equitable social order consistent with the encyclicals as was the Y.C.W.'s stated intention, credit unionism became increasingly in hands other than those of Catholics an end in itself.

Starved in their turn of attention and resources by the demands of the burgeoning credit unions initiative, the Y.C.W. co-operatives and the fledgling trading societies association faltered and fell short of their objectives. The Y.C.W. Trading Society was deregistered on 10 October 2000 as was on 5 July 2011 the Waverley and District Co-operative. The Security Permanent Building Society merged with the IOOF Friendly Society, which in turn was acquired ultimately by a proprietary limited company, the Bendigo Bank. As of 2013, the Y.C.W. Central Co-operative Credit Society and the Co-operative Development Society retained their registrations, but in realty were moribund and non-compliant with their statutory obligation to provide the Registrar with annual reports.

New Challenges

Meanwhile, the focus of intervening generations of mainstream Y.C.W. leaders had shifted to new challenges, both domestically and in the international sphere. Writers such as Ivan Illich and Brazil's Archbishop Dom Hélder Camara were read, praxis and liberation theology were taken to heart and solidarity was affirmed with fellow Y.C.W. members in other countries such as Brazil, Argentina and Chile, where in the course of the so-called 'dirty wars' young workers were being tortured and killed for their pursuit of basic rights:

> The common ground was to seek a liberation from unjust economic, political or social conditions in the under-developed region where an elite class exploited resources and labour largely for its own benefit – and that of the rich world with which they traded. It was to be expressed in what Gutiérrez, in the movement's seminal work, *A Theology of Liberation* (1971), called the 'preferential option for the poor' – the radical idea that in the Bible God takes sides and gives preference to the impoverished, the marginalised and the oppressed.[54]

54 Paul Vallely, *Pope Francis: Untying the Knots* (London: Bloomsbury, 2013) 42.

Closer to home, the emphasis was on taking the movement into the workplaces where young people were employed. Rather than leaders being asked to work full time for the Y.C.W. in supporting parish groups, they were encouraged to take jobs in the factories where the movement's message could most effectively be spread. Unions were valued and membership of them promoted. Leaders perceived themselves as being part of an international worker movement, with whose engagement and activities those in the local milieu were consistent. Even so, linkages with the worker ownership ideals and aspirations of Cardijn, their YCM Co-operator forebears and the Campions were not recognised or if recognised not pursued.

The issue effectively remained unfinished business on the Y.C.W. agenda, with rich potential for revival at a later date. 'We are not achieving the objects that we who started the Y.C.W. co-operatives had hoped. That doesn't mean they can't do so in the future, but it will be harder', Long said.[55] Unbeknown to him, the way ahead was already manifest, in the small steel-working town in a hitherto obscure valley in the Basque region of Spain to whose experience and example worldwide attention would increasingly now turn.

55 Long, Raxworthy Interview, Tape 1 Side B of two tapes, 5.

Chapter 15

ARIZMENDIARRIETA AND MONDRAGÓN

Working predominantly through the local Catholic Action and Y.C.W. groups, Fr José María Arizmendiarrieta imparted new depth and duration to the formation process over an extended period from 1941 to 1956, in preparation for the inception of the great worker co-operatives complex at Mondragón in the Basque region of Spain.

Born the son of a smallholder farmer in Markina in 1915, he was educated from the age of 13 at the Seminary of the Diocese of Vitoria, by 'a brilliant generation of intellectual priests committed to the social question and what Catholics called the "redemption of the worker's world"':

> Two teachers influenced Arizmendiarrieta profoundly. The first was Jose Miguel de Barandiaran, whose modern perspective included new disciplines such as sociology and anthropology, along with a virtuous notion of life and work that was saturated with peasant religiosity ... The other outstanding figure was Juan Thalamas, a priest trained at the Saint Sulpice Seminary in Paris one of the most important intellectual centres of Catholicism.[1]

1 Fernando Molina and Antonio Miguez, 'The Origins of Mondragón: Catholic Co-operativism and Social Movement in a Basque Valley (1941–59)', *Social History*, 33, No 3, August 2008, 287.

Introduced by Thalamas to the personalist thought of Maritain and Mounier as featured in *Espirit*, his reading closer to home included the official newspaper of the Basque Nationalist Party, *Euzkadi*, the social questions journal *Gizarte Auzia* as edited by the Basque priest Juan Bautista Eguzkitza and the pamphlets of the Basque Group for Social Action. He joined the Spiritualty Movement – a body which called priests to 'a life of personal sacrifice for the social redemption of the Christian community' – and acquired a further mentor in Rufino Aldabalde, a Guipizcoan priest who had worked to improve the housing of impoverished communities of Spanish agricultural workers in the south of France, and, following the Civil War, became the Spiritual Director of the Vitoria Seminary.

Meanwhile, Arizmendiarrieta's studies were interrupted by the hostilities. Following service in the Republican cause as a writer and editor on the trade union paper *Eguna*, he became a prisoner of war in 1936, and narrowly escaped execution by Franco's victorious Nationalist forces. The museum of the Otalora Institute in Mondragón includes among its exhibits the executioner's list on which the names of prisoners including Arizmendiarrieta were to be crossed off as they were taken out to their deaths. Arizmendiarrieta's name was passed over:

> There was one crucial question. How had he been supporting himself? After a moment's hesitation, he said he had been a soldier in the Basque army. That answer saved his life. A man who had worked with him on the newspaper identified himself as a journalist and was executed.[2]

2 William Whyte and Kathleen Whyte, *Making Mondragón: The Growth and Dynamics of the Worker Cooperative Complex* (Ithaca, N.Y.: ILR Press, 1991), 28.

In all, sixteen Basque priests – among them Arizmendiarrieta's immediate predecessor in Mondragón, Fr Joaquin Arin – were shot, and hundreds more imprisoned in concentration camps, deported or driven into exile.

The exiles included the Basque archbishop Mateo Mujica. Responding to Arin's murder, Mujica told Cardinal Goma that 'It would have been better if Franco and his soldiers had kissed Father Arin's feet instead of shooting him'.[3] His successor, Francisco Lauzurica y Torralba, may have differed. 'I am one more general under the orders from the Generalissimo to smash nationalism', Lauzurica declared.[4] From Rome, Mujica was able to intervene with the Catholic hierarchy to stop the excommunication of priests who had been supportive of the Basque nationalists and discourage further executions.

Free at last from his incarceration, Arizmendiarrieta resumed his studies at the Vitoria Seminary in 1938, and with Aldabalde's encouragement launched in 1940 a new periodical, *Surge*, for the Spirituality Movement. As his ordination approached in 1941, he applied to Lauzurica for permission to study sociology at the University of Louvrain, but was rebuffed, and instead sent to Mondragón as an assistant to its more senior local clergy. 'By denying Arizmendiarrieta's petition', the authors of an early Cornell University study of the cooperatives, William and Kathleen Whyte, conclude, 'the monsignor deprived the Basque country of a sociologist with academic credentials and opened the way to a development of applied sociology whose extraordinary achievements would outweigh any set of credentials'.[5]

3 Roy Morrison, *We Build the Road as We Travel*(Philadelphia, Pa.: New Society Publishers, 1991), 43.

4 Whyte and Whyte, *Making Mondragón*, 248.

5 Whyte and Whyte, *Making Mondragón*, 28.

His assigned task of 're-Catholicising' the community in conformity with the social encyclicals was formidable. As he was to recall in later life:

> We lost the Civil War, and we became an occupied region. In the post-war period the people of Mondragón suffered severely in the repression. I had known some people of Mondragón, but when I came after the war they had all either died, or were in gaol, or in exile.[6]

The predicament of survivors was not in any sense enviable. Spain was in the grip of what many remember as its 'Hunger Years', a period characterised by extensive unemployment, under-employment and privation:

> Working people were desperately poor and oppressed by unemployment, run-down and overcrowded housing, and an outbreak of tuberculosis. People spoke a spirit of hopelessness. They saw themselves as a conquered people, living under a regime that offered neither political freedom nor economic opportunity.[7]

Within Mondragón, a postwar population of some 9000 found itself internally divided:

> Roughly equivalent numbers of inhabitants had been on either side of the conflict: as socialist or Basque nationalist supporters of the Basque Republic or as traditionalist rebels. Thirty-seven of its inhabitants had been killed by firing squads when the city fell into the hands of the rebel troops of General Franco. The Civil War had been fought between the inhabitants of Mondragón and had filled its narrow streets with hatred and grudges. The harsh post-war years and the effects of the Second World War led to increased rationing, hunger, misery, sickness and crowding, while at the local level those who had 'lost the

6 Whyte and Whyte, *Making Mondragón*, 242.

7 Whyte and Whyte, *Making Mondragón*, 26.

> war' were politically, socially and culturally excluded from every sphere of life.[8]

Two-thirds of the town's workers were employed by a local iron and steel combine, the Union Cerrajera of Mondragón, and its subsidaries. Advancement through admission to the company's School of Apprentices was restricted to relatives of current employees and no more than twelve other applicants, who upon completion of their courses were ranked as industrial masters and became eligible for middle management positions in the related enterprises. Working initially in close co-operation with the *Union Cerrajera*, Arizmendiarrieta set out 'to promote apostleship for the working world':

> After their classes at the School of Apprentices or work in the factories and shops, hundreds of young people would come to hear him speak on sociological and theological topics at the Catholic Action centre of Mondragón or at the School for Apprentices. Little by little he formed a core group of those who consistently participated in the social activities he promoted at the centre: plays, fund-raising for children and indigents, sporting activities, etc. ... They gradually took on leadership and management tasks, according to their age and ability. Arizmendiarrieta began to teach them classic values from Catholic social doctrine, which they applied in their local milieu: enthusiasm for work, austerity in the social sphere, dedication and self-sacrifice for community ideals, faith in social initiatives, self examination and personal integrity in collective tasks.[9]

A letter he addressed to the Chairman of the *Union Cerrajera* in 1942 reads: 'Our general objective for the next school year is to

---

8 Molina and Miguez, 'The Origins of Mondragón', 289.

9 Molina and Miguez, 'The Origins of Mondragón', 290.

mobilise the youth of our town. While training and maintaining a nucleus of the best of them, we are going to act upon the masses'.

Reflecting on the process in later life, he characterised it as one of 'theoretical and practical mobilization, conscience-raising and preparation, for the purpose of self-government and self-management by which young people … organized raffles, lotteries and other public events that funded their endeavours and gave them – particularly those who were most active – an opportunity to receive the highest level of practical training'.

As recalled by a onetime protégé and co- founder of the co-operatives, José María Ormaechea:

> The Study Circles in *Acción Católica* and in JOC (Young Christian Workers Movement) continued at progressively higher levels … under the aegis of the Diocesan Secretariat in Vitoria, Father Arizmendi organized specialist courses on sociology to which he invited economics professors … His ecclesiastical training led him towards being a practical apostle. He not only tried to give guidelines on what should be the model for the ideal enterprise, but he put that social enterprise to which he aspired into practice.

'In calculations we were making in 1956, we counted more than 2000 circles of study that he conducted. Some for religious and humanistic orientation; others for social orientation', Ormaechea wrote.[10]

The report of the Cornell University study reads:

> Thus from 1941 on, Arizmendi conducted at least one study session every 2.7 days, not counting holidays and vacations, in

10 José María Ormaechea, *The Mondragón Co-operative Experience* (Mondragón: The Mondragón Corporacion Cooperativa, 1991) 20. 'Arizmendi' as customarily abbreviated from 'Arizmendiarrieta'.

> addition to teaching his regular schedule. As one of his former students told us, 'He taught classes in religion and sociology – and really his religion classes were mainly sociology'. Sessions with those who had been his first students focused particularly on discussions of conflicts between labour and capital, reform of private enterprise management and the participation of workers in ownership. … In his sermons and writings, he stressed that work should not be seen as a punishment but as a means of self-realization. There should be dignity in any work. He stressed the need for co-operation and collective solidarity. He combined a social vision with an emphasis on education for technical knowledge and skills.[11]

Following the rejection by the Union Cerrajera of a request by him for admissions to its apprenticeship school to be enlarged, he proposed the creation of a technical school independent of the company. A parents' association was formed to publicise the project and raise the necessary funds. The campaign culminated with the placing of boxes on street corners to receive pledges of cash or other contributions. Those responding were offered membership of the association, with the right to vote for its office-holders and determine its policies.

In the event, pledges from 600 well-wishers – roughly 15 per cent of Mondragón's adult population at the time – were received, and the Escuela Politécnica Profesional opened in October 1943 with twenty students. Adding a new level as soon as the students had completed the previous one, the school is seen by the Cornell researchers as having 'provided the base for the creation and development of the co-operatives that would build the Mondragón complex'.[12]

Enrolments increased steadily, with the addition of new levels of instruction – first *oficialla*, then *maestria* and ultimately *peritaje*

11 Whyte and Whyte, *Making Mondragón*, 29.

12 Whyte and Whyte, *Making Mondragón*, 31.

industrial – as the preceding ones were completed. In 1948 the parents' association was formalised as Hezibide Elkartea, or the League for Education and Culture. The new entity was notable in particular for a structure that foreshadowed the future shape of the Mondragón co-operatives as it was then evolving in Arizmendiarrieta's mind.

Enabled at Arizmendiarrieta's initiative to proceed on the completion of the education available to them in Mondragón to study *in absentia* with the University of Zaragoza, eleven of the twenty young men enrolled by the Escuela Politécnica Profesional at its inception secured degrees in technical engineering from the university. In the early 1950s, five of them – Ormaechea, Luis Usatorre, Jesus Larrañaga, Alfonso Gorroñogoitia, and Javier Ortubay – told Arizmendiarrieta that 'they were determined to start a new company organized along the lines they had been discussing'.[13]

What eventuated in 1956, as a handful of workers in a disused factory using hand tools and sheet metal to make oil-fired heating and cooking stoves, is now a massive complex of some 260 manufacturing, retail, financial, agricultural, civil engineering and support co-operatives and associated entities, with jobs for 83,800 workers, and annual sales in excess of $US20 billion. The Basque region's largest industrial conglomerate and the fifth largest in Spain, the Mondragón co-operatives now own or joint venture some 114 local and overseas subsidiaries, and are committed to their conversion to employee ownership on a case-by-case basis, consistent with local laws, customs and other cultural and economic considerations.

As equal co-owners of their workplaces, members enjoy job security together with individual capital holdings, equal sharing of

13 Whyte and Whyte, *Making Mondragón*, 31.

profits on a proportionate basis and an equal 'one member, one vote' say in their governance. Remuneration within the co-operatives is egalitarian, with the highest rates payable other than in exceptional circumstances being no greater than six and a half times the lowest. Members share at one remove in ownership of a unique system of secondary support co-operatives, from which the primary or frontline co-operatives draw resources including financial services, social insurance, education and training, and research and development. Hybrid primary co-operatives within the group include its worker/consumer Eroski retail co-operative and worker/farmer agricultural co-operatives. Multi-stakeholder structuring plays a key role in endowing the co-operatives both individually and collectively with their impressive cohesiveness and resilience.

Reflective of the high priority attached by the primary co-operatives to the competitive advantage of cutting edge research and development is the augmenting of the original Ikerlan research and development support co-operative with thirteen sister bodies, specialising in the needs of particular aspects of manufacturing activity and product development. Annual outlays for research and development total some $75 million, and in 2010 21.4 per cent of sales comprised new products and services which had not existed five years earlier.

Faced as have been the co-operatives repeatedly throughout their existence by adverse trading circumstances, they have been able to avail themselves of significant flexibilities. For example, non-members employed on a temporary basis can be put off until conditions improve. Members can agree to forfeit or postpone entitlements such as one or more of their fourteen per annum pay packets or the payment of interest on their individual capital accounts, or in extreme circumstances authorise individual capital account draw-downs. And in the event of failures such as of the group's Fagor domestic appliances co-operative in 2013, displaced workers will either be re-located to other co-operatives which are expanding, enabled to take early retirement or have access for up to two years of generous income maintenance entitlements. As of approaching two years later, some 1500 of the 1800 members whose jobs were lost had been re-allocated to other co-operatives and those not reassigned were on 80 per cent of salary together with health and related benefits.

Confronted in the aftermath of the Global Financial Crisis with circumstances where unemployment was in excess nationally of 25 per cent, and among young people at around 45 per cent, Mondragón was instrumental in helping hold jobless levels in the Basque region initially to under half the national average. 'Our commitment is not to capital but to the creation of sustainable jobs', Mondragón CEO Txema Gisasola states:

> This is not magic. We are in this market, competing in the capitalist world, and the only difference is how we do things and why we do things. We have to be competitive, we have to be efficient, we have to have quality in our products and give satisfaction to our clients, and we have to be profitable. In that sense we are no different from anyone else. The difference is how we organize ourselves. Some will ask if [the co-operative structure] is a disadvantage, but it is the complete opposite. The company's workers are the owners of the project, so who is better than them to fight for its interests? They come to work because it is their project.[14]

---

14 Miles Johnson, 'Drivers of Change: Workers United', *Financial Times*, 21 March 2013.

Mondragón in America

Green shoots of Distributist initiative are emerging from previously less hospitable soils. Announcing a formal partnership between his 850,000 member union and Mondragón in 2009, the United Steelworkers (USW) president Leo Gerard put its essence in the proverbial nutshell:

> Too often we have seen Wall Street hollow out companies by draining their cash and assets and hollow out communities by shedding jobs and shutting plants. We need a new business model that invests in workers and invests in communities. We see Mondragón's co-operative model with 'one worker, one vote' ownership as a means to re-empower workers and make business accountable to Main Street instead of Wall Street.[15]

Mondragón Internacional president Josu Ugarte noted:[16]

> What we are announcing today represents a historic first, combining the world's largest industrial worker co-operative with one of the world's most progressive and forward-looking unions to work together so that our combined know-how and complementary visions can transform manufacturing practices in America.

A 2012 report by the USW in conjunction with Mondragón and the Ohio Employee Ownership Centre (OEOC) differentiates between union and traditional worker co-operatives on the basis of the capacity of workers in a union co-operative to appoint a management team, from within their own ranks or from outside the co-operative, to bargain collectively on issues including wage rates, health

15 Amy Dean, 'Why Unions are Going into the Co-op Business', *Yes! Magazine*, 5 March 2013.

16 Erbin Crowell, 'Mondragón and the United Steelworkers: New Opportunity for the Co-op and Labor Movements?', *Cooperative Grocer*, January–February 2010.

care and other benefit packages and a process for grievances and arbitration of workplace disputes. Mondragón's co-operative bank agreed in September 2013 to partner with the Washington based National Co-operative Bank in the creation of co-operative stakeholder businesses throughout the United States.[17]

Designedly modest, and consistent with both subsidiarity and Schumacher's great 'Small is beautiful' dictum, inspiration in the implementation of the USW/Mondragón collaboration has stemmed at the outset from examples such as of Cleveland's Evergreen Co-operatives, with thirty worker-owners currently cleaning an annual four million tons of local hospital laundry, and planning underway for the creation of a solar installers' co-operative and a greenhouse co-operative that grows high-end salad vegetables and herbs for the hospitals, universities and restaurants.

The objective ultimately is to make 'Mondragón' a household word, and the adoption of its model an objective whose legitimacy is universally accepted, and to whose adoption communities and industries universally will aspire.

Australia

Likewise in Australia developments potentially conducive to the adoption of Gerard's Distributist in all but name 'new business model that invests in workers and invests in communities' are evident. Significant gains to date have included the organising by the Australian Secretariat for the 2012 United Nations Year of Co-operatives of a comprehensive year-long program of promotional and consciousness-raising events culminating with the featuring of

17 PRN Newswire, 4 September 2013, accessed at http://finance.yahoo.com/news/laboral-kutxa- mondragon-bank-national-175900469.html.

a Mondragón representative, Mikel Lezamiz, at a major conference at Port Macquarie; the enactment by state and federal parliaments in 2012–13 of uniform and highly supportive national co-operatives legislation; and the inception in 2013 of the Business Council of Co-operatives and Mutuals as a body tasked to furnish the wider sector with 'opportunities for sharing knowledge, skills and best practice, through wider communication, industry talks, international speakers, case studies and advocacy'. Despite the demutualisation tsunami that has overtaken all but a handful of Australia's former friendly societies, permanent building societies and mutual assurance societies, the nation's top 100 co-operatives and financial mutuals retain an annual turnover of some $17 billion and the assets of the financial mutuals alone total some $83 billion.

Chapter 16

CONCLUSION

An Upwards Trajectory

What the foregoing has documented is successive stages in an uneven upwards trajectory of social teachings, consciousness-raising and lay activism, extending over the greater part of a century and cut short needlessly in Australia in a political debacle of epic proportions, the reverberations of which still linger. Encouraged by the advocacy and support of Cardinal Manning and his continental allies, Leo XIII establishes in *Rerum Novarum* guiding social principles for the Church that are reflective of the dignity of the human person and human labour, and responsive to calls such as for the relief of poverty, more widespread ownership of property, protection of worker rights, including the right to trade union representation, and the resolution of industrial disputes through agreed frameworks for conciliation and arbitration.

The English translation of the encyclical prepared at Leo's request by Manning and Archbishop Walsh, and Manning's commentary in the *Dublin Review*, add weight to Leo's implicit endorsement of the right to strike, and distinguish between England's predominantly mutualist Socialism and the more statist continental Socialism that the encyclical had condemned. Affronted by the too frequent and widespread indifference of many among his more prominent co-religionists to working-class privation, Manning does not hesitate to make common cause with allies frequently of other faiths, such as Gladstone, the Salvation Army's General Booth, leading trade unionists of the stamp of Ben Tillett and John Burns, and adherents of the burgeoning co-operative and mutualist movements. The Secretary of the Royal Commission on the Housing of the Working Classes, to which he was appointed in 1884, remarks that 'If there had been some half dozen Mannings England would have run some risk of being converted to Christianity'.[1]

Patrick Moran is assigned by his uncle, Cardinal Cullen, to assist Manning in securing the adoption by the First Vatican Council of papal infallibility in 1869. Deeply admiring of so notable a colleague, inspired by his concern for the wellbeing of workers and their families, and following in his footsteps, Moran is guided throughout his Australian episcopate by comparable labourist and mutualist sentiments and sympathies. Determined to be 'an Australian among Australians', he champions the encyclical, supports strikes and affirms in an early press interview that 'The present labour organizations are really only the old Catholic guilds formed to secure to the workman just payment for his skill and labour'.

The gravamen of his great 1891 Masonic Hall address and its commitment to mutualist and co-operative enterprises is echoed by the 1905 Second Plenary Council of the Hierarchy of Australia in a Joint Pastoral Letter. Like Manning an instinctive networker, Moran cultivates connections in influential quarters including the nascent Labor Party, and enters into such informal alliances as he believes are

1 John F. Fitzsimons, *Manning: Anglican and Catholic* (London: Catholic Book Club, 1951), 138.

supportive of workers' wellbeing and the public interest. His approach is institutionalised in an overall pattern of clerical counselling and negotiation to which subsequent NSW episcopates broadly adhere. He endorses overtures by Archbishop Carr for consideration by the Irish hierarchy of Archbishop Mannix as his coadjutor in Melbourne.

More insular by background than Manning or Moran and by nature introspective and distrustful of other denominations, Mannix largely eschews networking and the cultivation of external alliances such as they have practised, and personifies instead historian Patrick O'Farrell's 'confrontation, challenge, conflict'. Positioning himself in the hiatus following Moran's death in 1911 as the champion of the antipodean Church and *Rerum Novarum*'s social agenda, he looks increasingly to lay activism such as initially the Catholic Federation exemplifies for the furtherance of the encyclical's objectives, along with the struggle for State Aid for Catholic schools and his more distinctively Irish preoccupations. Accorded heroic status in the eyes of Catholics throughout Australia, he is scornful of papal constraints on involvement by the Church in party politics, adopts a high-profile role in major political controversies such as over the conscription issue, and, before the crushing defeats of Patrick Cleary's Democratic Party at the 1920 and 1922 New South Wales elections, seemingly entertains hopes for the creation of an overtly confessional party or 'Christianised' Labor Party.

The expansion of access to higher educational opportunities for young Catholics for which he is in part responsible gives rise to a cadre of talented graduates whose passionate commitment to the deepening of their faith and the exploration of its wider implications and prospects for hands-on application he welcomes and endorses. Prompted in part by Fr William Hackett SJ and the inception in 1931 of his Catholic Central Library, Frank Maher, Murray McInerney and John Merlo convene a discussion group, which shortly is formalised as the Campion Society and tasked to deepen the Catholic identities and understandings of its members. The example of the English Distributists is embraced as the basis for a distinctively Australian understanding of the principles of economic democracy, worker ownership and subsidiarity as set out by Pius XI in *Quadragesimo Anno*. Sub-groups and courses are created as the need for them arises, and study guides, reading lists and discussion materials are developed. A speakers panel is established and publications including a pamphlet series and in 1935 a Campion Society newsletter, *Orders of the Day*, are introduced.

As an early newcomer to the society and already a Labor Party and trade union activist, Kevin Kelly infuses and galvanises its thinking with the teachings of Joseph Cardijn and Jacques Maritain to which his European interests and Y.C.W. connections have introduced him. New ventures spun off from the society include the Catholic Evidence Guild, the Assisian Guild for teachers, the Clitherow Society for women and in 1936 an independent monthly, the *Catholic Worker*. So great is the interest to which the activities of the society give rise that the demands on it outstrip by far the ability of its members to respond to them in their capacity as volunteers.

Alerted by Maher and Kelly to the impending crisis in the Campion Society's affairs and the need for a National Secretariat of Catholic Action to be established as a matter of urgency, Mannix invites the Society to prepare a proposal for presentation by him to the 1937 Plenary Council of the Hierarchy of Australasia and New Zealand. Drawing on submissions shaped predominantly by Kelly's input and influence, he obtains endorsement by the bishops of the creation and funding of the Australian National Secretariat for Catholic Action (ANSCA). The new entity's mission is agreed to be formation of militants to combat Communism and secure through 'action of Catholics' the implementation of the Church's social teachings, and there is to be no involvement by it in party-political activity. Maher becomes its Director and Santamaria the Deputy Director.

Adhering initially to its agreed mandate for the formation of Catholic militants to combat Communism and ensure through lay activism the implementation of the teachings of the encyclicals, ANSCA achieves significant success, which Santamaria in part compromises by his use of its facilities for the covert anti-Communist network, the 'Freedom Movement' or 'Show', which he heads concurrently from 1941. Undermined progressively by Santamaria and exhausted emotionally and physically by the disproportionate demands on the chronically under-resourced Secretariat, Maher accepts the offer extended to him by Mannix at Santamaria's instigation in 1945 of a twelve-month European study tour, only to discover on his return that he has been replaced as director by Santamaria, relegated to the newly created position of Research Officer, and out-posted from the Secretariat offices to a room grudgingly made available to him by the university's Newman College.

Santamaria completes an effective co-locating of the activities of the Freedom Movement within the Secretariat – by McInerney's account 'some secret activity emanating from the Secretariat offices to the existence and nature of which we were not privy'.[2] The creation by the ALP in 1945 of its Industrial Groups as an effective anti-Communist mechanism is welcomed by him as affording a cover for the Movement: 'Wherever they concentrated in groups it

2 McInerney, *Memoir*, 37, 21.

was obvious that the groups were Catholic ... Today they have the cover of the Labor Party ... They carry on the fight as the executives of these factory "discussion groups" and none can effectively question their bona fides'.[3]

Top-down management and a militarised organisational model increasingly supplant the Secretariat's former formation focus: 'Members are not in a position to know precisely what is going on, and therefore must accept the advice of HQ. There is only one body in the position to know precisely what is going on – the national headquarters of the organization'.[4] Nurturing of lay initiatives pursuant to the implementation of the encyclicals, such as the creation of mutuals and co-operatives including nascent National Catholic Rural Movement (NCRM) credit unions and the Maryknoll and Whitlands rural settlement projects, is all but wholly forgone, and dissidents such as the *Catholic Worker* group are harassed and vilified.

Challenged by Archbishop Simonds as to the new ANSCA dispensation's legitimacy as Catholic Action, the bishops formalise the Movement as the covert anti-Communist Catholic Social Studies Movement, with Santamaria as director of both it and ANSCA. The inflammatory and frequently defamatory rhetoric of *News-Weekly* and supportive MPs including Stan Keon and Jack Mullens alarms and alienates moderate opinion, as exemplified by the impeccably anti-Communist credentialed Heinz Arndt and Lloyd Ross. As Arndt writes in a letter to which Santamaria does not respond, 'I am prepared to believe that the moderation that you display in your letter is not purely for my benefit, and that the Keons and McCarthys disgust you as much as they do me. Why then do you not sometimes

3 Fitzgerald, *The Pope's Battalions*, 73.

4 Ormonde, *50 Years of the Santamaria Movement*, 8.

speak up against them … I would be happy to know that you condemn them as strongly as do I'.[5]

Confident by 1953 that Communist power has been 'to all intents and purposes broken', and aware increasingly that the replacement of Communist union officials by CSSM operatives and supporters is indirectly but inexorably altering in his favour the balance of power within the ALP's union-dominated ruling bodies, Santamaria turns his attention to securing control of the party.[6] Polarisation between non-Catholic and predominantly Catholic elements within the party is incited around issues including opposition to the Menzies government's Communist Party dissolution legislation and Evatt's appearances respectively in the High Court for the Waterside Workers' Federation challenge to the legislation and before the Petrov Royal Commission. New threats and enemies singled out for strategic targeting and denunciation include 'Old Catholics' such as Calwell and Kennelly, 'the young economists who have written and will continue to write the pamphlets and brochures of the Australian Fabian Society' and the 'extreme industrialists whose primary loyalty is to the trade union movement'.

The 'Chifley legend' is condemned in his 'The Movement of Ideas' address and his 'Religious Apostolate and Political Action' address asserts the legitimacy of the CSSM as a means of securing through 'Catholic organizations linked to the Hierarchy' the adoption of Catholic policies and programs. The May 1952 CSSM conference resolves to 'secure control of the Federal Executive and Conference by men with a satisfactory policy by July 1952', and the intended takeover of the party is spelled out in December 1952, in Santamaria's

5 Arndt, 'The Catholic Social Movement', 191.

6 Santamaria, *Against the Tide*, 115.

'smoking gun' letter to Mannix. Required by the bishops to choose between his ANSCA and CSSM positions, his choice is to retain the CSSM. ANSCA is wound up on his recommendation, and its funding is re-directed predominantly to the CSSM.

Pre-empted and out-manoeuvred politically by Evatt and his associates in the aftermath of Labor's 1954 election defeat, repudiated by the NSW hierarchy and required ultimately by the Vatican to end its party-political involvement, the CSSM dissolves itself and is re-birthed as the National Civic Council. CSSM members and sympathiser MPs expelled from the ALP for voting against it in the Victorian and federal parliaments form the Labor Party (Anti-Communist) which in turn is re-badged nationally as the Democratic Labor Party (DLP). Insistent initially that Catholics are duty bound to support the DLP, Mannix shortly prior to his death in 1963 executes an about-face, stating that they are free to support any party other than the Communist Party. Direction by the DLP of its preferences against the ALP at successive elections denies the party office federally until 1972, and until 1982 in Victoria.

Shell-shocked and gun-shy in the face of their internal dissentions and the overall turmoil, the bishops are concerned primarily to return the Church to some semblance of normality. The heir effectively to the mutualist, co-operativist and Distributist agenda and aspirations of the now moribund Campion Society and the defunct ANSCA, the Y.C.W. creates housing and consumer co-operatives and engenders the inception of the credit union movement, but is unable in the face of the movement's explosive expansion to hold it to the spirit and values of the encyclicals or achieve its intended integration within a wider sectoral body representative of co-operatives of all kinds and perhaps also of mutuals more generally. No successors to Long and his fellow

Y.C.W. co-operators emerge, and Mondragón's triumphant vindication of their convictions and aspirations is all but wholly unnoticed and unremarked. The encyclicals and their teachings are relegated to a relative obscurity from which they have yet to re-emerge.

Counter-factual Scenario: What Might Have Been

That none of this need have occurred – that more fruitful, productive and enduring outcomes might have been achieved and setbacks and disappointments averted – is suggested if a counter-factual scenario is constructed for the all but thirty-year period from the inception of ANSCA in 1938 to the secularising in 1966 of the Association of Catholic Co-operative Credit Societies. In this wholly fictitious account, let us imagine the war does not intervene. Let it be imagined also that the senior Campions including Kelly and McInerney are available to support Maher in restraining Santamaria from his more egregious departures from ANSCA's episcopal mandate for the formation of militants and abstention from party-political involvement.

Maher carries on as Director, and Santamaria is required to resign on becoming Director of the newly created CSSM. More attentive exercise by the bishops of the supervision of the CSSM ensures that the constraints of its anti-Communist mandate are observed, and groups other than Communists and including fellow Catholics are not ostracised or vilified. Control of the ALP is not sought and the party split is not precipitated.

The attempted bringing to heel of the specialist Catholic Action agencies is not undertaken and the abolition of ANSCA and diversion of its resources to the CSSM does not occur. Contact between the Y.C.W. and its European counterpart is not interrupted, and Kelly's ongoing input ensures that its adherence to the teachings of Cardijn and Maritain is maintained and the number and quality of the militants trained by it is such that the requirements of the credit unions movement and wider aspirations of the Co-operative Development Society can be met in full. Better resourced for research and evaluation, the Y.C.W. co-operators are alerted at an earlier stage to the decline of the Antigonish Movement and the vulnerability of its model to the generation–degeneration cycle, and exploration of distinctively Distributist worker ownership options such as through its short-lived home building co-operative is more vigorously pursued.

Distributism is not erased from political agendas as wholly as if for practical purposes it had never arisen, the fruitful cross-fertilisation between Distributist, Democratic Socialist and Social-Democratic elements within the ALP as demonstrated by Arndt and Ross is not forfeited, and the Church does not resile from advocacy of the encyclicals and the wider Distributist agenda which the Social Justice Statements have so comprehensively articulated. Pure fantasy, perhaps, but there is some pertinence in such 'counter-factual' speculation. The fact that none of these things happened is indicative that failure was not the proverbial orphan, but had many fathers. Kelly's death in 1994 and the death of Santamaria four years later rule off the ledger and mark the end of an era.

What Might Yet Come to Be

Extrapolation of this speculative approach to a near future time-frame identifies a way forward. Under the new pontificate of Francis, awareness of the Church's moral critique of Capitalism is re-kindled, and the Church rediscovers its rich heritage of concern for the rights and wellbeing of workers, support for nationalisation where necessary to break up monopolies, opposition to the concentration of wealth in the hands of the few and participation by workers in the ownership and control of their workplaces.

Incontrovertibly a product of the Church's social teachings and Y.C.W. formation in the Cardijn mould – 'an example of the application of ideas flowing from the "Fountain of Christian social thought"'[7] – Mondragón is afforded the acclaim that its achievements so plainly justify. Seizing the day, the Australian hierarchy initiates a renewed and distinctively Distributist lay apostolate such as that of the Y.C.W. co-operators, in concert with the resurgent wider co-operative, mutualist and employee ownership movements and sympathetic elements within bodies including think tanks, trade unions and community groups.

Consistent with the insights and example of Cardijn and Arizmendiarrieta, current and future priests are exposed in the course of seminary and in-service training to a more extensive coverage of *Rerum Novarum* and *Quadragessimo Anno* and their significance in the context of the Mondragón experience and connection. The absolute primacy and indispensability of formation and its implementation in the extended form pioneered by Arizmendiarrieta at Mondragón – of Evolved Formation in the service of Evolved Distributism – is acknowledged, its lessons are absorbed and applied and new methodologies and opportunities for its improvement and application are sought. Mondragón is brought to attention from pulpits on a regular basis.

A Jocist-style 'See, Judge, Act' public inquiry is conducted, with the objectives severally of interrogating and highlighting the Mondragón experience and determining whether and if so by what

7 Bernard Manzo, 'Was Chesterton Right?', *Tablet*, 1 August 2009.

means adaptations of the Mondragón model might yet become going concerns, not least in decentralist locations such as Rockhampton, Wollongong or Geelong. Explicit papal endorsement for the project consistent with the social teachings advocacy of Pope Francis is sought, and economic context is derived from authoritative investigations and insights into rising inequality such as those of the French scholar Thomas Piketty in his seminal and widely read *Capitalism in the Twenty-First Century.*[8]

The need for worker co-operatives to assume a broader profile is acknowledged. Given significant progress in the US via means including the Mondragón/United Steelworkers pact, why not also in Australia? A distinctive worker ownership entity within the wider co-operative and mutualist movement is seen to be required, such as will facilitate workers in the sharing of the ownership and management of their workplaces. Education, formation, leadership of a high order, a strong philosophical grounding and an abundance of practical know-how are seen to be essential in order for the transition to be effective.

Links are forged with advocacy groups including the longstanding Australia and New Zealand Employee Ownership Association and the emergent Business Council of Co-operatives and Mutuals. Support is sought for further improvement of the current uniform co-operatives legislation along the lines of its far more advanced counterparts such as in Spain, Italy and France, and for re-instatement of the capacity for proactive engagement with the sector such as previously was provided by Registries of Co-operatives in Victoria and New South Wales.

---

8 Thomas Piketty, *Capital in the Twenty-First Century* (Boston, Mass: Harvard University Press, 2014).

Innovative reports such as that of Victoria's Ministerial Advisory Committee on Co-operation on *The Co-operative Way: Victoria's Third Sector* in 1986 are revisited and the relevance and likely effectiveness of their recommendations are reassessed.[9] The currently moribund Co-operative Development Society is re-activated and properly re-sourced as a mark of continuity with past measures, and forerunner for a Centre for the Study of Co-operative, Mutualist and Distributist Enterprises within a suitably supportive university. The inception of an International Mondragon Studies Association is instigated.

Manning's Children

Prospects so pregnant with promise are Manning's legacy to us. Were he to have witnessed the course of relevant events in the century subsequent to his death, his assessment may well have been mixed. Welcome to him in particular would have been the postwar settlement in advanced industrial societies whereby the worth of each person was respected, as was also the right to secure employment and the aspiration to ownership such as of a home, a business or on a shared basis a workplace. No less would he have been appalled by the settlement's subsequent breakdown and regression. As so presciently summarised by the UK scholar and former MP David Marquand, 'Capitalism is off the leash':

> Not surprisingly it is behaving much as it did before its tamers put it on the leash during the extraordinary burst of institutional creativity which followed the Second World War. ... One of the central themes of the golden age was 'embourgeoisement': the spread to the working class of the job security, career ladders and lifestyles which had formerly been the prerogatives of the

9 Accessed 30/6/2013 at http://education.victoria.coop/index.php/resources/maccreport1986.

> middle class. … Now the engines have gone into reverse. … The decasualisation of labour, which a generation of trade union leaders saw as its life's work has given way to re-casualisation – and in what used to be the middle class as well as the working class. Down-sizing, delayering, outsourcing and re-engineering haunt the suburbs as well as the inner cities, mocking the commitments and hollowing out the institutions which once were the lodestones of the salariat.[10]

Nor necessarily will worse not follow from an increasing dispossession and effective disenfranchising of the many. The spectre of Orwell's 'If you want a vision of the future, imagine a boot stamping on a human face – forever' endures. As does also that of the Morlocks of H.G. Wells's *The Time Machine*, returning nightly from habitats beneath the earth to feed on the effete Eloi whose ancestors – reminiscent of UK Prime Minister Baldwin's 'hard-faced men' in the 1930s – consigned them to their subterranean exile. Political democracy in the absence of economic democracy is a fragile construct that may not indefinitely avert arbitrary abrogation.

Even so, at a time when both the advocates of the statutory corporation school of State Socialism and their 'greed is good' counterparts in the corporate sphere have simultaneously and comprehensively discredited themselves, the way is open for Distributism to assume the larger role – locally, regionally, nationally and on a global basis – to which its merits so plainly entitle it. As a contemporary adage affirms: 'The future is not set. There is no fate but what we make of it ourselves'.[11]

---

10 David Marquand, *The New Reckoning: Capitalism, States and Citizens* (Cambridge: Polity Press, 1997) 3–5.

11 James Cameron, *Terminator 2: Judgement Day* (Movie, 1991).

BIBLIOGRAPHY

Papal Documents

Leo XIII, *Rerum Novarum*, Encyclical Letter (1891).
Pius XI, *Quadragesimo Anno*, Encyclical Letter (1931).
John XXIII, *Mater et Magistra*, Encyclical Letter (1961).
John Paul II, *Centesimus Annus*, Encyclical Letter (1991).
Francis, *Evangelii Gaudium*, Apostolic Exhortation (2013).
Francis, *Laudato Si*, Encyclical Letter (2015).

Interviews

Praetz, Helen (ed). *The Church in Springtime: Remembering Catholic Action 1940–1965*. Oral Archive of recordings and transcripts deposited in the Melbourne College of Divinity Repository. April, 2011:
Paul Maher
Max Charlesworth
Jack Keating
Marilyn Puglesi
Tom Hayes
Cyril Hally
Jim Griffin
David McKenna
John Molony
Kevin Peoples
Jim Ross.
Raxworthy, Richard. Transcripts of interview conducted on behalf of the Credit Union Historical Society (Sydney: Australian Credit Union Archives):
Leon Magree (03/11/1991 & 12/02/1992)
David Dinning (10/02/1992)
Ken Ploog (10/02/1992)
Wally Winter (10/02/1992)
Keith Glover (11/02/1992)
Ian Larsson (11/02/1992)
Alan Dash (11/02/1992)
Richard Crosbie (11/02/1992)
Gavin Cook (11/02/1992)
Les Harcourt (11/02/1992)
Rob Davey (12/02/1992)
Philip Elliot (13/02/1992)

Philip Doughty (14/02/1992)
Arthur Carter (14/02/1992)
Warren Edwards (14/02/1992)
John Galvin (24/02/1992)
Ted Long (25/02/1992)
Donald Matlock (25/02/1992)
Marlene Jackson (25/02/1992)
Brendan Griffin (26/02/1992)
Peter Weston (26/02/1992)
Peter Hodgkinson (27/02/1992)
Ray Bowyer (27/02/1992)
Tom Stubbs (27/02/1992)
Bob Maybury (28/02/1992)
Tim Dyce (28/02/1992)
Bob Moffatt (28/02/1992)
Don Harris (23/03/1992)
Roger Bell (25/03/1992)
Ralph Lewis (ND).

Santamaria, B.A., interviewed by Robin Hughes for the National Library of Australia Australian Biography Project, as accessed 23 April 1997 at http://www.australianbiography.gov.au/subjects/santamaria/interview1.html.

Books

Alexander, Anne. *The Antigonish Movement: Moses Coady and Adult Education Today*. Toronto, ON: Thompson Educational Publishing Inc, 1997.

Andrews, Eric M. *The Anzac Illusion*. Melbourne, Vic: Cambridge University Press, 1994.

Anon. *Australians and the Spanish Civil War*. Melbourne, Vic: Red Pen Publications, 1986.

Anon. *Archbishop Daniel Mannix 1864–1963*. Melbourne, Vic: Catholic Education Office, 1999.

Arizmendiarrieta, José María. *Pensamientos*. Mondragón: Otalora, ND.

Azurmendi, Joxe. *El Hombre Cooperativo: Pensamiento de Arizmendiarrieta*. Mondragón: Otalora, ND.

Arnold, Mary Ellicott. *The Story of Tompkinsville*. New York, NY: The Co-operative League, 1940.

——— *Father Jimmy of Nova Scotia*. Chicago, IL: The Co-operative League of the USA, ND.

Barker, Dudley. *G.K. Chesterton: A Biography*. London: Constable & Co, 1973.

Barnett, Corelli. *The Collapse of British Power*. London: Eyre Methuen, 1972.

Beevor, Antony. *The Battle for Spain: The Spanish Civil War 1936–1939*. London: Weidenfeld & Nicolson, 2006.

Belloc, Hilaire. *Essays in Liberalism*. London: Cassell & Co, 1897.

——— *Danton: A Study*. London: James Nisbett & Co, 1899.

——— *Paris*. London: James Arnold, 1900.
——— *Robespierre*. London: James Nisbett & Co, 1901.
——— *The Path to Rome*. London: George Allen & Unwin, 1902.
——— *Esto Perpetua*. London: Duckworth & Co, 1906.
——— *The French Revolution*. London: Williams & Norgate, 1911.
——— *The Servile State*. London: Constable & Co, 1912.
——— *Europe and the Faith*. London: Constable & Co, 1912.
——— *The Jews*. London: Constable & Co, 1922.
——— *Economics for Helen*. Bristol: Arrowsmith, 1924.
——— *The Cruise of the 'Nona'*. London: Constable and Company Limited, 1925.
——— *Napoleon*. London, Cassell & Co, 1932.
——— *An Essay on the Restoration of Property*. London: The Distributist League, 1936.
——— *The Crisis in Our Civilisation*. London: Cassell & Co, 1937.
——— *The Place of Chesterton in English Letters*. New York: Steed and Ward, 1940.
Belloc, Hilaire, and Chesterton, Cecil. *The Party System*. London: Stephen Swift, 1911.
Belloc Lowndes, Marie. *'I Too Have Lived in Arcadia': A Record of Love and Childhood.* London: Macmillan & Co, 1943.
Bentley, Eric C. *Those Days*. London: Constable & Co, 1940.
Berlin, Isaiah. *The Hedgehog and the Fox: An Essay on Tolstoy's View of History*. London: Weidenfeld & Nicolson, 1953.
Beveridge, William. *Power and Influence*. London: Hodder & Stoughton, 1953.
Birchall, Johnston. *The International Co-operative Movement*. Manchester: Manchester University Press, 1997.
Birchall, Johnston (ed). *The New Mutualism in Public Policy*. London: Routledge, 2001.
Black, Antony. *Guilds & Civil Society in European Political Thought from the Twelfth Century to the Present*. London: Methuen & Co Ltd, 1984.
Blasi, Joseph R. *Employee Ownership: Revolution or Ripoff*. New York, NY: Harper Business, 1988.
Blatchford, Robert. *Merrie England*. London: Clarion Newspaper Co, 1895.
——— *My Eighty Years*. London: Cassell & Co, 1931.
Boland, Thomas P. *James Duhig*. St Lucia, Qld: University of Queensland Press, 1986.
——— *Thomas Carr: Archbishop of Melbourne*. St Lucia, Qld: University of Queensland Press, 1997.
Boyle, George. *Father Tompkins of Nova Scotia*. New York, NY: P.J. Kennedy & Sons, 1953.
Brady, Edwin J. *Dr Mannix: Archbishop of Melbourne*. Melbourne, Vic: The Library of National Biography, 1934.
Brennan, Niall. *A Hoax Called Jones*. London: Sheed and Ward, 1962.
——— *Dr Mannix*. Melbourne, Vic: Rigby, 1964.
——— *The Politics of Catholics*. Melbourne, Vic: Hill Publishing, 1972.
Britain, Ian. *Fabianism and Culture: A Study in British Socialism and the Arts c. 1884–1918*. Melbourne, Vic: Cambridge University Press, 1982.

Bryan, Cyril. *Archbishop Mannix: Champion of Australian Democracy.* Melbourne, Vic: NP, 1918.

Bryant, Chris. *Possible Dreams: A Personal History of the British Christian Socialists.* London: Hodder & Stoughton, 1996.

Buckley, Ken, and Wheelwright, Ted. *No Paradise for Workers: Capitalism and the Common People in Australia, 1788–1914.* Melbourne, Vic: Oxford University Press, 1988.

Buckley, Vincent. *Cutting Green Hay: Friendships. Movements and Cultural Conflicts in Australia's Great Decades.* Ringwood, Vic: Penguin Books, 1983.

Buhlman, William. *With Eyes to See: Church and World in the Third Millennium.* London: Oxford University Press, 1990.

Bygott, Ursula L. *With Pen and Tongue: The Jesuits in Australia 1865–1939.* Carlton, Vic: Melbourne University Press, 1980.

Calwell, Arthur A. *Labor's Role in Modern Society.* Melbourne, Vic: Lansdowne Press, 1963.

——— *Be Just and Fear Not.* Melbourne, Vic: Rigby in Association with Lloyd O'Neill, 1978.

Canovan, Margaret. *G.K. Chesterton: Radical Populist.* New York, NY: Harcourt Brace Jovanovich, 1977.

Cardijn, Msgr Joseph. *The Young Worker Faces Life: Addresses of Monsignor Joseph Cardijn.* Melbourne, Vic: Y.C.W., 1960.

Carlson, Allan C. *The New Agrarian Mind: The Movement Toward Decentralist Thought in Twentieth-Century America.* New Brunswick: Transaction Publishers, 2000.

——— *Third Ways: How Bulgarian Greens, Swedish Housewives and Beer-Swilling Englishmen Created Family-Centred Economies – And Why They Disappeared.* Wilmington, DE: ISI Books, 2007.

Carson, Kevin A. *Studies in Mutualist Political Economy.* Kevin Carson, 2007.

Champion, Henry Hyde. *The Great Dock Strike in London, August 1889.* London: Swan, Sonnenschein & Co, 1887.

Charlesworth, Max. *Church, State and Conscience.* St Lucia, Qld: University of Queensland Press, 1973.

Cheney, George. *Values at Work: Employee Participation Meets Market Pressure at Mondragón.* Ithaca, NY: Cornell University Press, 1999.

Chesterton, A.K. *The New Unhappy Lords.* London: The Candour Publishing Co, 1965.

Chesterton, Cecil. *G.K. Chesterton: A Criticism.* London: Alston Rivers Ltd, 1908. This edition Seattle, WA: Inkling Books, 2007.

Chesterton, Mrs C. *The Chestertons.* London: Chapman & Hall, 1941.

Chesterton, Gilbert Keith. *Heretics.* London: John Lane, 1905.

——— *Orthodoxy.* London: John Lane, The Bodley Head, 1908.

——— *What's Wrong With the World.* London: Cassell and Company Limited, 1910.

——— *Utopia of Usurers.* New York, NY: Boni & Liveright, 1917. This edition Norfolk, VA: IHS Press, 2002.

——— *The Outline of Sanity*. London: Methuen & Company, 1926.
——— *Autobiography*. London: Hutchinson & Co, 1937.
Chesterton, Gilbert Keith, Shaw, George Bernard, and Belloc, Hilaire. *Do We Agree?* London: Cecil Palmer, 1928.
Clarke, Arthur C., *2001: A Space Odyssey*. New York: New American Library, 1968.
Coady, Moses. *Masters of Their Own Destiny: The Story of the Antigonish Movement of Adult Education through Economic Cooperation*. New York: Harper & Brothers Publishers, 1939. This edition Antigonish NS, Formac Publishing Company Limited, 1980.
Cole, Margaret. *The Story of Fabian Socialism*. London: Heinemann, 1961.
Colebatch, Tim. Dick Hamer: The liberal Liberal. Melbourne: Scribe, 2014.
Colloms, Brenda. *Victorian Visionaries*. London: Constable, 1982.
Conlan, D.J. (ed), *G.K. Chesterton: A Half Century of Views*. Oxford: Oxford University Press, 1987.
Conquest, Robert. *The Great Terror: A Reassessment*. London: Pimlico, 1992.
Cooksey, Robert. (ed). *The Great Depression in Australia*. Canberra, ACT: Australian Society for the Study of Labour History, 1970.
Corbett, E.A. *We Have With Us Tonight*. Toronto, ON: The Ryerson Press, 1957.
Coren, Michael. *Gilbert: The Man Who Was G.K. Chesterton*. New York, NY: Paragon House, 1990.
Corrin, Jay P. *G.K. Chesterton and Hilaire Belloc: The Battle against Modernity*. Athens, OH: Ohio University Press, 1981.
——— *Catholic Intellectuals and the Challenge of Democracy*. Notre Dame, IN: University of Notre Dame Press, 2002.
——— *Catholic Progressives in England After Vatican II*. University of Notre Dame Press, Notre Dame, IN, 2013.
Coutino, Boavida. *Community Development through Adult Education and Cooperatives*. Rome: Institute of Pastoral Sociology, 1966.
Cremean, Herbert M. (as Michael Lamb). *Red Glows the Dawn*. Melbourne, Vic: NP, 1942.
Crisp, L.F. *The Australian Federal Labour Party 1901–1951*. Melbourne, Vic: Longmans Green & Co, 1955.
Cunneen, Christopher. *William John McKell: Boilermaker, Premier, Governor-General*. Sydney, NSW: University of New South Wales Press, 2000.
Dale, Alzina Stone. *The Outline of Sanity: A Life of G.K. Chesterton*. Grand Rapids, MI: William B. Eerdmans Publishing Company, 1982.
Dangerfield, George. *The Strange Death of Liberal England*. London: MacGibbon & Kee Ltd, 1935. This edition 1966.
Davis, Ed, and Lansbury, Russell. *Democracy and Control in the Workplace*. Melbourne: Longman Cheshire, 1986.
Davidson, Alistair. *The Communist Party of Australia: A Short History*. Stanford, CA: Stanford University Press, 1969.
De la Bedoyere, Michael. *The Cardijn Story*. Milwaukee, WI: The Bruce Publishing Company, 1959.

Delaney, Ida. *By Their Own Hands: A Fieldworker's Account of the Antigonish Movement*. Hansport, BC: Lancelot Press, 1985.
Denniss, Richard, and Baker, David. *Who Knew Australians Were So Co-operative? The Size and Scope of Mutually Owned Co-ops in Australia*. Australia Institute Paper 10. Canberra, ACT: The Australia Institute 2012.
De Soderini, Eduardo. *The Pontificate of Leo XIII*. London: Burns, Oates and Washbourne, 1934.
Develtere, Patrick. *Co-operative Development: Towards a Social Movement Perspective*. Saskatoon, SK: University of Saskatchewan Centre for Co-operative Studies, 1992.
Distributist Perspectives Volume I, *Essays on the Economics of Justice and Charity*. Norfolk, VA: HIS Press, 2004.
Distributist Perspectives Volume II, *Essays on the Economics of Justice and Charity*. Norfolk, VA: IHS Press, 2008.
Doyle, I. *The Antigonish Idea and Social Welfare*. Antigonish, NS: St Francis Xavier University Press, 1964.
Duncan, Bruce F. *The Church's Social Teachings: From Rerum Novarum to 1931*. North Blackburn, Vic: Collins Dove, 1992.
——— *Crusade or Conspiracy? Catholics and the Anti-Communist Struggle in Australia*. Sydney, NSW: University of NSW Press, 2001.
——— *Social Justice: Fuller Life in a Fairer World*. Mulgrave, Vic: Garratt Publishing Pty Ltd, 2012.
Ebsworth, Walter A. *Archbishop Mannix*. Armidale, Vic: The Graphic Workshop, 1977.
Evatt, Herbert. V. *Australian Labour Leader: The Story of W.A. Holman and the Labour Movement*. Sydney, NSW: Angus and Robertson, 1945.
Fagerberg, David W. *The Size of Chesterton's Catholicism*. Notre Dame, IN: University of Notre Dame Press, 1998.
Fanfani, Amintore. *Catholicism, Protestantism and Capitalism*. Norfolk, VA: IHS Press, 2003.
Ffinch, Michael. *G.K. Chesterton: A Biography*. San Francisco, CA: Harper & Row, 1986.
Fievez, Marguerite and Meert, Jacques. *Cardijn*. Preston, Lancs: T. Snape & Co, ND.
Finnane, Mark. *J.V. Barry: A Life*. Sydney, NSW: University of New South Wales Press, 2007.
Fitzgerald, Ross. *'Red Ted': The Life of E.G. Theodore*. St Lucia, Qld: University of Queensland Press, 1994.
——— *Fred Paterson: Australia's Only Communist Party Member of Parliament*. St Lucia, Qld: University of Queensland Press, 1997.
——— *The Pope's Battalions: Santamaria, Catholicism and the Labor Split*. St Lucia, Qld: University of Queensland Press, 2003.
Fitzpatrick, Brian, *The Australian People 1878–1945*. Carlton, Vic: Melbourne University Press, 1946.
Ford, Patrick. *Cardinal Moran and the ALP: A Study in the Encounter between*

Moran and Socialism, 1890–1907: Its Effects upon the Australian Labor Party: The Foundation of Catholic Social Thought and Action in Modern Australia. Carlton, Vic: Melbourne University Press, 1966.

Fremantle, Anne. *This Little Band of Prophets*. London: George Allen & Unwin, 1960.

——— *The Social Teachings of the Church*. New York, NY: The New American Library, 1963.

Freudenberg, Graham. *A Certain Grandeur: Gough Whitlam in Politics.* South Melbourne, Vic: Macmillan, 1977.

Fitzsimons, John F. *Manning: Anglican and Catholic*. London: Catholic Book Club, 1951.

Fitzsimons, John, and McGuire, Paul (eds). *Restoring All Things*. London: Sheed and Ward, 1939.

Gargan, Edward T. (ed). *Leo XIII and the Modern World.* New York, NY: Sheed and Ward, 1961.

Gates, Jeff. *The Ownership Solution: Towards a Shared Capitalism for the 21st Century*. Reading, MA: Addison-Wesley, 1998.

Gilchrist, Michael. *Daniel Mannix: Priest and Patriot.* Melbourne, Vic: Dove Communications, 1982.

——— *Wit and Wisdom: Daniel Mannix.* North Melbourne, Vic: Freedom Publishing, 2004.

Gollan, Robin. *Revolutionaries and Reformists: Communism and the Australian Labor Movement 1920–1950.* Sydney, NSW: George Allen & Unwin, 1975.

Gould, Nathan. *Town and Bush.* London: George Routledge, 1896.

Grant, James, and Serle, Geoffrey. *The Melbourne Scene 1803–1956.* Carlton, Vic: Melbourne University Press, 1957.

Gray, Robert. *Cardinal Manning: A Biography.* New York, NY: St Martin's Press, 1985.

Green, David, and Cromwell, Lawrence. *Mutual Aid or Welfare State: Australia's Friendly Societies.* Sydney, NSW: George Allen & Unwin, 1984.

Greenwood, D.F., and González, J.L.G. *Industrial Democracy as Process: Participatory Action Research in the Fagor Co-operative Group of Mondragon*. Assen/Maastricht: Van Gorcum, 1992.

Griffin, James. *Daniel Mannix: Beyond the Myths.* Mulgrave Vic: Garratt Publishing, 2012.

Gregory R.G. and Butlin N.G. (eds). *Recovery from the Depression: Australia and the World Economy in the 1930s*. Melbourne: Cambridge University Press, 1988.

Grierson, Edward. *The Imperial Dream: British Commonwealth and Empire 1775–1969.* London: Collins, 1972.

Hardy, Dennis. *Utopian England: Community Experiments 1900–1945*. London: E & F.N. Spon, 2000.

Hattersley, Roy. *The Edwardians*. London: Little, Brown, 2004.

Haynes, E.S.P. *The Lawyer: A Conversation Piece*. London: Eyre & Spottiswoode, 1951.

Head, Brian, and Walter, James. *Intellectual Movements in Australian Society.* Melbourne, Vic: Oxford University Press, 1988.
Heenan, John C. *Cardinal Hinsley*. London: Burns, Oates and Eastbourne, 1944.
Henderson, Anne. *Enid Lyons: Leading Lady to a Nation.* North Melbourne Vic: Pluto Press, 2008.
Henderson, Gerard. *Mr Santamaria and the Bishops.* Sydney, NSW: Hale and Iremonger, 1982.
——— *Santamaria: A Most Unusual Man*. Carlton, Vic: The Miegunyah Press, 2015.
Henderson, Leslie M. *The Goldstein Story*. Melbourne, Vic: Stockland Press, 1973.
Himmelfarb Gertrude. *Poverty and Compassion: The Moral Imagination of the Late Victorians*. New York, NY: Alfred A. Knopf, 1991.
Hogan, Michael. *Australian Catholics: The Social Justice Tradition.* Blackburn, Vic: Collins Dove/HarperCollins Publishers (Aus) Pty Ltd, 1993.
——— *Justice Now! Social Justice Statements of the Australian Catholic Bishops First Series 1940–1966.* Sydney, NSW: Department of Government and Public Administration, University of Sydney, 2006.
——— Hogan, Michael (ed). *Australian Politics: Catholic Perspectives.* Sydney, NSW: Uniya Jesuit Social Justice Centre, Discussion Paper No 6.
Hollis, Christopher. *The Seven Ages: Their Exits and Entrances.* London: Heinemann, 1974.
Holmes, J Derek. *The Papacy in the Modern World.* London: Burns & Oates, 1981.
Holt, Stephen. *A Veritable Dynamo: Lloyd Ross and Australian Labour 1901–1987.* St Lucia, Qld: University of Queensland Press, 1996.
Husslein, Joseph. *Social Wellsprings: Fourteen Epochal Documents by Pope Leo XIII.* MI: The Bruce Publishing Company, 1949.
Hyndman, H.M. *The Record of an Adventurous Life*. London: Macmillan & Co, 1911.
——— *Further Reminiscences*. London: Macmillan & Co, 1912.
Hynes, Samuel. *The Edwardian Turn of Mind.* Princeton, NJ: University Press, 1968. This edition London: Pimlico, 1991.
——— *The Auden Generation: Literature and Politics in England in the 1930s*. New York, NY: The Viking Press, 1977.
Jebb, E. & R. *Testimony to Hilaire Belloc*. London: Methuen & Co, 1956.
Jones, Peter d'A. *The Christian Socialist Revival 1877–1914: Religion, Class and Social Conscience in Late-Victorian England.* Princeton, NJ: Princeton University Press, 1968.
Jory, Colin H. *The Campion Society and Catholic Social Militancy in Australia 1929–1939.* Sydney, NSW: Harpham, 1986.
Jupp, James. *Immigration.* South Melbourne, Vic: Sydney University Press in Association with Oxford University Press, 1991.
Kane, Jack. *Exploding the Myths: The Political Memoirs of Jack Kane*. North Ryde NSW: Angus & Robertson Publishers, 1989.
Kasmir, Sharryn. *The Myth of Mondragon: Co-operatives, Politics and Working Class Life in a Basque Town*. New York, NY: State University of New York Press, 1996.

Kiernan, Colm. *Calwell: A Personal and Political Biography.* Melbourne, Vic: Thomas Nelson (Australia) Limited, 1978.

——— *Daniel Mannix and Ireland.* Morwell, Vic: Alella Books, 1984.

Laffin, Josephine. *Matthew Beovich: A Biography.* Kent Town, SA: Wakefield Press, 2008.

Laidlaw, Alexander F. *The Campus and the Community: The Global Impact of the Antigonish Movement.* Montreal, Q: Harvest House Limited, 1961.

Laidlaw, Alexander F. (ed). *The Man from Margaree: Writings and Speeches of M.M. Coady.* Toronto, ON: McClelland and Stewart Limited, 1971.

Langdale, Eugene (ed). *Challenges to Action.* London: New Life Publications, 1955.

Lanz, Tobias J. (ed). *Beyond Capitalism and Socialism: A New Statement of an Old Idea.* Norfolk, VI: IHS Press, 2008.

Lawrence, Dennis. *The Third Way: The Promise of Industrial Democracy.* London: Routledge, 1988.

Lelotte, Fr P. *Fundamental Principles of Catholic Action.* Melbourne, Vic: Australian National Secretariat for Catholic Action, ND.

Leslie, Shane. *Henry Edward Manning: His Life and Labours.* New York, NY: P.J. Kennedy and Sons, 1921.

Lewis, Gary. *A Middle Way: Rochdale Co-operation in New South Wales 1859–1986.* Sydney, NSW: Australian Association of Co-operatives, 1992.

——— *People Before Profit: The Credit Union Movement in Australia.* Adelaide, SA: Wakefield Press, 1996.

——— *The Democracy Principle: Farmer Co-operatives in Twentieth Century Australia.* Sydney, NSW: Co-operative Federation of New South Wales, 2006.

Lowndes, Susan (ed). *Diaries and Letters of Marie Belloc Lowndes 1911–1947.* London: Chatto & Windus, 1971.

Lotz, Jim, and Webb, Michael R. *Father Jimmy: Life and Times of Jimmy Tompkins.* Wreck Cove, Cape Breton, NS: Breton Books, 1997.

Luscombe. T.R. *Builders and Crusaders: Prominent Catholics in Australian History.* Melbourne, Vic: Lansdowne Press, 1967.

MacDonald, J.D.N. *Memoirs of an Unorthodox Clergyman.* Truro, NS: Co-operative Resources, 1986.

Mackenzie, Norman and Jeanne. *The First Fabians.* London: Weidenfeld & Nicolson, 1977.

Mackenzie, Norman and Jeanne (ed). *The Diaries of Beatrice Webb* (3 Volumes). London, Virago, 1965–1982.

MacLeod, Greg. *From Mondragón to America: Experiments in Community Economic Development.* Sydney, NS: University College of Cape Breton Press, 1997.

McCarthy, John. *Hilaire Belloc: Edwardian Radical.* Indianapolis, IN: Liberty Press, 1978.

McClelland, Vincent A. *Cardinal Manning: His Public Life and Influence 1865–1892.* London: Oxford University Press, 1962.

McBriar, Alan M. *Fabian Socialism and English Politics.* London: Cambridge University Press, 1962.

McEntee, Gillen P. *The Social Catholic Movement in Great Britain*. New York, NY: The Macmillan Company, 1927.

McKenna, Mark. *The Captive Republic*. Melbourne, Vic: Cambridge University Press, 1996.

McLaren, John. *Journey Without Arrival: The Life and Writing of Vincent Buckley*. Melbourne, Vic: Australian Scholarly Publishing, 2009.

McManners, John. *Church and State in France. 1870–1914*. New York, NY: Harper and Row, 1972.

McQuillan J. and Others. *Flee to the Fields: The Founding Papers of the Catholic Land Movement*. London: Heath Cranton, 1934. This edition Norfolk VA, IHS Press, 2003.

Maher, F.K.H. *An Introduction to Social Principles*. Carnegie Vic: Catholic Social Guild and Renown Press, ND.

——— *Studies in Catholic Action: A Practical Approach*. Melbourne, Vic: The Hawthorn Press, 1948.

Mandle, W.F. (ed). *Ireland and Irish-Australia: Studies in Cultural and Political History*. London and Sydney, NSW: Croom Helm, 1986.

Mann, Tom. *Tom Mann's Memoirs*. Melbourne, Vic: Labour Publishing Company, 1923.

Manning, Henry E. *What One Work of Mercy Can I Do This Lent? A Letter to a Friend*. London: NP, 1847.

——— *Miscellanies* (3 Volumes). London: Burns and Oates, 1888.

Maritain, Jacques. *Scholasticism and Politics*. New York, NY: Doubleday & Co, 1948. This edition 1960.

Marquand, David. *The Unprincipled Society: New Demands and Old Politics*. London: Jonathan Cape, 1988.

——— *The New Reckoning: Capitalism, States and Citizens*. Cambridge: Polity Press, 1997.

Masterman, C.F.G. *The Condition of England*. London: Methuen & Co, 1909. Re-set 1960.

Mathews, Race. *Australia's First Fabians: Middle-Class Radicals, Labour Activists and the Early Labour Movement*. Melbourne, Vic: Cambridge University Press, 1993.

——— *Jobs of Our Own: Building a Stakeholder Society*. Sydney, NSW: Pluto Press, 1999.

Mazioux, Abbe. *How to Form Leaders*. Melbourne, Vic: National Secretariat of Catholic Action, ND.

Médaille, John. *The Vocation of Business: Social Justice in the Marketplace*. New York, NY: Continuum, 2007.

Messner, Johannes. *Dolfuss: An Austrian Patriot*. Norfolk, VA: IHS Press, 2004.

Ministerial Advisory Committee on Co-operation. *The Co-operative Way: Victoria's Third Sector*. Melbourne, Vic: Ministry of Housing, 1986.

Molony, John. *The Worker Question: A New Historical Perspective on Rerum Novarum*. Melbourne, Vic: Collins Dove, 1991.

——— *Luther's Pine: An Autobiography*. Canberra, ACT: Pandanus Books, 2004.

——— *Beyond Wendouree*. Ballan: Vic: Connor Court Publishing, 2010.
Morgan, Patrick A. *B.A. Santamaria: Your Most Obedient Servant: Selected Letters 1938–1996.* Melbourne, Vic: The Meigunyah Press in Association with the State Library of Victoria, 2007.
——— *B.A. Santamaria: Running the Show: Selected Documents 1939–1996.* Melbourne, Vic: The Meigunyah Press in Association with the State Library of Victoria, 2008.
——— *Melbourne Before Mannix: Catholics in Public Life 1880–1920.* Ballan, Vic: Connor Court Publishing, 2012.
Morrison, Roy. *We Build the Road as We Travel.* Philadelphia, Pa: New Society Publishers, 1991.
Morrissey, Thomas J. *William J Walsh, Archbishop of Dublin 1841–1921: No Uncertain Voice.* Dublin: Four Courts Press, 2000.
Mounier, Emmanual. *A Personalist Manifesto*. London: Longmans, Green & Co, 1938. This edition 1952.
Mount, Frank. *Wrestling with Asia: A Memoir.* Ballan, Vic: Connorcourt, 2012.
Murphy, Frank. *Daniel Mannix: Archbishop of Melbourne 1917–1963.* Melbourne, Vic: The Polding Press, 1972.
Murray, Robert. *The Split: Australian Labor in the Fifties.* Melbourne, Vic: Cheshire, 1970.
Murtagh, James G. *Australia: The Catholic Chapter*. Melbourne, Vic: Angus & Robertson, 1959.
Nairn, Bede. *Civilising Capitalism: The Labor Movement in New South Wales 1870–1900.* Canberra, ACT: Australian National University Press, 1973.
Nairn, Bede and Serle, Geoffrey (eds). *Australian Dictionary of Biography* Volume 10: 1891–1939. Carlton, Vic: Melbourne University Press, 1986.
Newman, J. *Co-responsibility in Industry: Social Justice in Labour Management Relations*. Dublin: M.H. Gill & Son Ltd, 1955.
Newsome, David. *The Parting of Friends: The Wilberforces and Henry Manning*. Grand Rapids, MI: William B Eerdmans Publishing Company, 1993.
Niall, Brenda. *The Riddle of Father Hackett: A Life in Ireland and Australia.* Canberra, ACT: National Library of Australia, 2009.
——— *Mannix*. Melbourne, Vic: Text Publishing, 2015.
Oakeshott, Robert. *Jobs and Fairness: The Logic and Experience of Employee Ownership*. Wilby, Norwich: Michael Russell, 2000.
O'Connor, J. *Father Brown on Chesterton*. London: Frederick Muller, 1937.
O'Farrell, Patrick. *The Catholic Church and Community in Australia: A History*. Melbourne, Vic: Thomas Nelson (Australia) Limited, 1977.
Ormaechea, J.M. *The Mondragón Co-operative Experience*. Mondragón: The Mondragón Co-operative Corporation, 1993.
Ormonde, Paul. *The Movement.* Melbourne, Vic: Thomas Nelson (Australia) Limited, 1972.
Ormonde, Paul (ed). *50 Years of the Santamaria Movement.* Richmond, Vic: Jesuit Publications, 1992.
——— *Santamaria: The Politics of Fear.* Richmond, Vic: Spectrum Publications Pty Ltd, 2000.

Pearce, Joseph. *Wisdom and Innocence: A Life of G.K. Chesterton.* San Francisco, CA: Ignatius Press, 1996.

——— *Old Thunder: A Life of Hilaire Belloc.* London: HarperCollins Publishers, 2003.

——— *Literary Giants: Literary Catholics.* San Francisco, CA: Ignatius Press, 2005.

Pearsall, Ronald. *Edwardian Life and Leisure.* Melbourne, Vic: Wren Publishing Pty Ltd, 1973.

Pease, E.R. *The History of the Fabian Society.* New York, NY: International Publishers, 1926.

Peoples, Kevin. *Santamaria's Salesman: Working for the National Catholic Rural Movement 1959–1961.* Mulgrave, Vic: John Garratt Publishing, 2012.

Pepper Susan. *Giving Credit to the People: A History of the Credit Co-operative Movement In Victoria.* Windsor, Vic: The Victorian Credit Co-operative Association Limited, 1985.

Pierson, Stanley. *British Socialists: The Journey from Fantasy to Politics.* Cambridge, MA: Harvard University Press, 1979.

Potts, David. *The Myth of the Great Depression.* Melbourne: Scribe Publications, 2009.

Preston, Paul. *Franco.* London: HarperCollins Publishers, 1993.

——— *Comrades! Portraits from the Spanish Civil War.* London: HarperCollins Publishers, 1999.

——— *We Saw Spain Die: Foreign Correspondents in the Spanish Civil War.* New York: Skyhorse Publishing Inc, 2009.

Pugh, Patricia. *Educate, Agitate. Organise: 100 Years of Fabian Socialism.* London: Methuen, 1984.

Purcell, E.S. *Life of Cardinal Manning, Archbishop of Westminster* (2 Volumes). London: MacMillan and Co, 1896.

Pybus, Cassandra. *The Devil and James McAuley.* St Lucia, Qld: University of Queensland Press, 1999.

Ransome, Arthur. *The Autobiography of Arthur Ransome.* London: Jonathan Cape, 176.

Reckitt, Maurice. *Faith and Society: A Study of the Structure, Outlook and Opportunity of the Christian Social Movement in Great Britain.* London: Longmans, Green & Co, 1932.

——— *As It Happened.* London: J.M. Dent & Sons, 1941.

Reckitt, Maurice (ed). *For Christ and the People: Studies of Four Socialist Priests and Prophets of the Church of England.* London: Society for the Propagation of Christian Knowledge, 1968.

Reynolds, P.L. *The Democratic Labor Party.* Milton, Qld: Jacaranda Press, 1974.

Rivett, Rohan. *Australian Citizen: Herbert Brookes 1867–1963.* Carlton Vic: Melbourne University Press, 1965.

Robertson, John R. 'Scullin, James Henry (1876–1953)' in Serle, Geoffrey (ed) *Australian Dictionary of Biography,* 1891–1939, Vol II. Melbourne, Vic: Melbourne University Press, 1988.

Rochford, Fr Vincent. *The Young Christian Workers.* Melbourne, Vic: Y.C.W. Headquarters, ND.

Rowntree, Seebohm. *Poverty: A Study of Town Life.* London: Macmillan & Co, 1901.

Sánchez, José M. *The Spanish Civil War as a Religious Tragedy.* Notre Dame, IN: University of Notre Dame Press, 1987.
Santamaria, B.A. *The Earth – Our Mother.* Melbourne, Vic: Araluen Publishing Co, 1945.
——— *The Price of Freedom: The Movement after Ten Years.* Melbourne, Vic: The Campion Press, 1964.
——— *Against the Tide.* Melbourne: Oxford University Press, 1981.
——— *Daniel Mannix: The Quality of Leadership.* Carlton, Vic: Melbourne University Press, 1984.
——— *Daniel Mannix: A Biography.* Carlton, Vic: Melbourne University Press, 1984.
——— *Santamaria: A Memoir.* Melbourne, Vic: Oxford University Press, 1997.
——— *The Movement 1941–60.* Melbourne, Vic: The Hawthorn Press, ND.
Sassoon, Donald. *One Hundred Years of Socialism.* New York. NY: The New Press, 1996.
Schmitz, David F. *Thank God They're on Our Side: The United States and Right-Wing Dictatorships 1921–1965.* Chapel Hill NC: University of North Carolina Press, 1999.
Schumacher, Barbara. *E.F. Schumacher: His Life and Thought.* New York, NY: Harper and Row, 1984.
Schumacher, E.F. *Small is Beautiful.* London: Anthony Blond, 1973.
Scollay, Ruth. *Lalor: The Lalor Home Building Co-operative 1946–2012*, Sydney: University of New South Wales Press, 2012.
Sewell, Brocard. *My Dear Time's Waste.* Aylesford: St Dominic's Press, 1966.
——— *G.K.'s Weekly: An Appraisal.* Aylesford: The Aylesford Press, 1990.
Shaw, George Bernard (ed). *Fabian Essays in Socialism.* London: The Fabian Society, 1889.
Sheridan, Greg. *When We Were Young and Foolish: A Memoir of My Misguided Youth With Tony Abbott, Bob Carr, Malcolm Turnbull, Kevin Rudd and Other Reprobates.* Crow's Nest, NSW: Allen & Unwin, 2015.
Shinnick, David (ed). *1997 – Turning Point: Celebrating the Centenary of 'Rerum Novarum' and the Future of Catholic Social Teaching.* Adelaide SA: Archdiocese of Adelaide, 1992.
Speaight, Robert. *The Life of Hilaire Belloc.* London: Hollis & Carter, 1957.
——— *Recollection of a Divided Life.* London: Collins & Harvill Press, 1970.
——— *Georges Bernanos: A Study of the Man and the Writer.* London: Collins & Harvill Press, 1973.
Speaight, Robert (ed). *Letters from Hilaire Belloc.* London: Hollis & Carter, 1958.
Swinnerton, Frank. *The Georgian Literary Scene 1910–1935: A Panorama.* London: Hutchinson & Co, 1935.
Taft, Bernie. *Crossing the Party Line: Memoirs of Bernie Taft.* Newnham Vic: Scribe Publications, 1994.
Taylor, A.J.P. *English History 1914–1945.* Oxford: Oxford University Press, 1965. This edition Readers Union, 1967.

Thomas, Henk, and Logan, Chris. *Mondragon: An Economic Analysis.* London: George Allen & Unwin, 1982.
Thomas, Hugh. *The Spanish Civil War.* London: Eyre & Spottiswoode Ltd, 1961.
Thompson, E.P. *The Making of the English Working Class.* London: Victor Gollancz, 1965.
Thornley, Jenny. *Worker's Co-operatives: Jobs and Dreams.* London: Heinemann Educational Books Ltd, 1981.
Tillett Ben, *Memories and Reflections.* London: John Long, Ltd, 1931.
Titterton, W.R. *G.K. Chesterton: A Portrait.* London: Alexander Ousley, 1936.
Trevor, Meriol. *Newman: Light in Winter.* London: Macmillan, 1962.
Truman, Tom. *Catholic Action and Politics.* Melbourne, Vic: Georgian House, 1959.
25 Men (ed). *Design for Democrats: The Autobiography of a Free Journal.* Melbourne, Vic: The Advocate Press, 1944.
Vanek, Jaroslav. *Self-Management: Economic Liberation of Man.* Harmondsworth, Middlesex: Penguin Education, 1975.
Vansittart, Robert. *The Mist Procession: The Autobiography of Lord Vansittart.* London: Hutchinson, 1958.
Van Thal, Herbert, and Nickerson, Jane Soames. *Belloc: A Biographical Anthology.* London: George Allen & Unwin, 1970.
Vaughan, Roger B. *Pastorals and Speeches on Education.* Sydney, NSW: Edward F. Flanagan, 1879.
Ward, Maisie. *Gilbert Keith Chesterton.* London: Sheed and Ward, 1944.
——— *Return to Chesterton.* London: Sheed and Ward, 1952.
Ward, Russell. *A Radical Life: The Autobiography of Russell Ward.* South Melbourne Vic: Macmillan, 1988.
Watkins, W.P. *The International Co-operative Alliance 1895–1970.* London: International Co-operative Alliance, 1970.
Webb, Sidney & Beatrice. *A Constitution for the Socialist Commonwealth of Great Britain.* London: Longman, 1920.
Weigel, George, and Royal, Robert (eds). *Building the Free Society: Democracy, Capitalism and Catholic Social Teaching.* Grand Rapids, MI: William B. Eerdmans Publishing Company, 1993.
Weller, Patrick, and Lloyd, Beverley (eds). *Federal Executive Minutes 1951–55: Minutes of the Meetings of the Federal Executive of the Australian Labor Party.* Melbourne, Vic: Melbourne University Press, 1978.
Welsh, Fr J.J. *Socialism, Individualism and Catholicism.* London: Sands Co, 1910.
Welton, Michael R. (ed). *The Origins and Development of the Antigonish Movement.* Toronto, ON: Oise Press, 1987.
——— *Little Mosie from Margaree: A Biography of Moses Michael Coady.* Toronto, ON: Thompson Educational Publishing Inc, 2001.
Wilson, Andrew N. *Hilaire Belloc.* London: Hamish Hamilton, 1984.
——— *God's Funeral.* London: John Murray, 1999.
——— *The Victorians.* London: Hutchinson, 2002.
——— *After the Victorians: The World Our Parents Knew.* London: Hutchinson, 2005.

Whyte, William, and Kathleen Whyte, *Making Mondragón: The Growth and Dynamics of the Worker Cooperative Complex*. Ithaca, N.Y.: ILR Press, 1991.
Yakovlev, Alexander N. *A Century of Violence in Soviet Russia*. New Haven, CT: Yale University Press, 2002.

Articles

Anon. 'Capitalism and Religion', *Australian Catholic Truth Society Record* 18 (15 July 1934).
Anon. 'For Social Justice', *Australian Catholic Truth Society Record* 53 (10 February 1938).
Anon. 'What to Read: Book Lists for Discussion Groups', *Australian Catholic Truth Society Record* 136 (30 May 1938).
Anon. 'The Foundations of Catholic Sociology', *Australian Catholic Truth Society Record* 365 (ND).
Arndt, Heinz. 'The Church and Socialism', *Australian Observer* 2 (October 1948) as appended to Arndt to Santamaria, 6 August 1956. B.A. Santamaria Papers Series 5 Box 3. MS13492.
——— 'The Catholic Social Movement', *Australian Journal of Politics and History* 1&2 (1955–1957): 181–195.
Boland, Thomas P. 'The Growth of Australian Catholic Historiography', *Journal of the Australian Catholic Historical Society* (January 2006). Accessed at htpp://www.accessmylibrary.com/coms2/summary_0286-33678441_ITM, 21/6/2013.
Brendain G. 'Impressions and Memories of Monsignor Mannix', *Austral Light* XIII No 9 (1912): 707–719.
Buxton, Sydney. 'Cardinal Manning – A Reminiscence', *Fortnightly Review* 65 No 59 (1896): 591–592.
Cahill, Anthony E. 'Catholicism and Socialism – The 1905 Controversy in Australia', *Journal of Religious History* No 1 (1960): 89–101.
——— 'Cardinal Moran's Politics', *Journal of Religious History* No 15 (1989): 525–531.
Calderwood, Glenn. 'A Question of Loyalty: Archbishop Daniel Mannix, the Australian Government and the Papacy, 1914–18', in *Australasian Studies* 17 No 2 (2002): 55–94.
Campion, Edmund. 'Were Irish & Catholic Synonymous?', *Tinteán* (March 2008): 18–19.
Coleman, Peter. 'Missionary Legacy of a Fiery Pamphleteer', *Sydney Morning Herald* (26/2/1998).
Collins, Paul. 'Abbott and Santamaria's Undemocratic Catholicism', *Eureka Street* (August, 2010). Accessed at http://www.eureka street.com./article.aspx?aeid=2283.
Costar, Brian, and Strangio, Paul. 'Santamaria: A True Believer?', *History Australia* 1 No 2 (2004).
Dalton, Leo. 'Red Menace in Australia: A Companion to the Encyclical "Atheistic Communism Australia"', *Catholic Truth Society Record* 104 (10 July 1937).

Dynon, James. 'The Social Doctrine of Leo XIII and Australia', *Twentieth Century* 6 No 2 (Spring 1951): 13–20.
Flanagan, Martin. 'An Unshakeable Belief in His Own Truths', *Age* (26 February 1998).
Giddens, John. 'Invest in the Future of Your Credit Society', *Australian Catholic Truth Society Record* 1418 (20 October, 1963).
Gilley, Sheridan. 'Manning and Chesterton', *The Chesterton Review* XVIII No 4 (November 1992): 491.
Griffin, James. 'Cardinal Moran and the ALP', *Twentieth Century* XXI No 1 (Spring 1966).
——— 'Revisionism of Reality: Daniel Mannix in ADB 10', *Tirra Lirra* 6 No 1 (1995): 18–23.
——— 'The Santamaria Legacy', *Eureka Street* (April 1998): 26–30.
Henderson, Gerard. 'Labor Split Warrior Dies at 82', *Sydney Morning Herald*, 26 February 1998.
Jackson, Denys. 'Australian Dream: A Journey to Merrion Part 1', *Australian Catholic Truth Society Record* 393 (10 November 1947).
——— 'Australian Dream: A Journey to Merrion Part 2', *Australian Catholic Truth Society Record* 401 (20 February 1948).
Johnston, Fr Thomas SJ. 'Abyssinia and Christianity', *Australian Catholic Truth Society Record* 130 (30 March 1938).
Kelly, Kevin T. 'James Henry Scullin', *Canberra Historical Journal* (September 1975): 104–106.
Keogh, Dermot. 'Mannix, De Valera and Irish Nationalism Part 2', *Australasian Catholic Record* (July 1988): 349.
Leys, M.D.R. 'An Introduction to Political Economy', Oxford, Catholic Social Guild, 1934.
Long, Ted. 'Helping Each Other Through Co-operatives', *Australian Catholic Truth Society Record* 1375 (10 January 1962).
Lord, Daniel A. 'God and the Depression', *Australian Catholic Truth Society Record* No 14 (30 April 1933).
Lewins, Frank. 'Continuity and Change in a Religious Organisation: Some Aspects of the Australian Catholic Church', *Journal for the Scientific Study of Religion* 16 No 4 (1977): 371–382.
Lyons, John. 'Against the Tide', *Age/Good Weekend*, 17 March 1990.
Madden, Edward. 'It Can Be Done', *Australian Catholic Truth Society Record* 264 (20 July 1942).
Maher, F.K.H. 'Prelude to Catholic Action: Campion Pamphlet No 1', *Australian Catholic Truth Society Record* (10 September 1936).
——— 'For Social Justice', *Australian Catholic Truth Society Record* 732 (10 February 1938).
——— 'The World Moves On', *Australian Catholic Truth Society Record* 786 (30 January 1937).
——— 'The Catholic Revival', *Australian Catholic Truth Society Record* 786 (30 July 1938).

Mahon J.M. 'Cardinal Moran's Candidature', *Manna* 6 (1963): 63–71.
Manning, Henry E. 'A Pope on Capital and Labour: The Significance of the Encyclical *Rerum Novarum*', *Dublin Review* (July 1891).
McClelland, Vincent A. 'Manning's Work for Social Justice', *The Chesterton Review* XVIII No 4 (November 1992): 532.
McClelland, Jim. 'End of a 40-year Chill', *Sydney Morning Herald* (26 February 1998).
Molina, Fernando and Miguez, Antonio. 'The Origins of Mondragon: Catholic Co-operativism and Social Movement in a Basque Valley (1941–59)', *Social History* 33 No 3 (August, 2008).
Morgan, Patrick. 'The Austral Light Group', *Australian Journal of Irish Studies* 1 (2001): 90–98.
——— 'New Light on Bob Santamaria', *News Weekly*, No 2750 (3 March, 2007). Accessed at http://www.newsweekly.com.au/article.php?id=3052.
Murray, Robert. 'Relentless Crusader of the Right'. *Australian* (26 February 1998).
Murtagh, James G. 'Australia Comes of Age: A Sketch-portrait of a Continent Commonwealth', *Commonweal* (9 January 1942): 286–290.
——— 'The Story of Antigonish', *The Australian Catholic Truth Society Record* 315 (20 July 1944).
——— 'The Sociology of Industry', *Twentieth Century* 3 No 2 (1948): 55–58.
——— 'Workers' Control', *Twentieth Century* 5 No 4 (1951): 5–16.
——— 'The Servile State – Forty Years After', *Twentieth Century* 8 No 1 (1953) 89–44.
Niall, Brenda. 'Servant to Whom', *Australian Book Review* No 289 (March 2007) 12–14.
O'Brien Eris. 'Cardinal Moran's Part in Public Affairs', Part I, *Royal Australian Historical Society Journal and Proceedings* XXVIII No 2 (1942): 29.
Odriozola, U.L., Monasterio, J.M.L. and Berriobalgoitia, I.A. 'Mondragon before the Crisis', *Projectics* 2 (2009): 31–53.
Ormonde, Paul. 'Our Grey Eminence', *Sydney Morning Herald*, 3 February 2007.
Pell, Cardinal George. 'B.A. Santamaria, Strategist and Prophet', *News Weekly* 2787 (30 August, 2008). Accessed at http://www.newsweekly.com.au/article.php?id=3327.
——— 'Archbishop Pell's Tribute to B.A. Santamaria', *AD 2000* 11, No 3 (April 1998). Accessed at http//www.ad2000.com.au/articles/1998/apr1998p10_560.html.
Quinn, Dermot. 'The Historical Foundations of Modern Distributism', *The Chesterton Review* 21 No 4 (November 1985): 464.
——— 'Manning, Chesterton and Social Catholicism', *The Chesterton Review* XVIII No 4 (November 1992): 502.
Richardson, Charles. 'Fusion: The Party System We Had to Have?' *Policy* 25 No 1 (2009): 13–19.
Robbins, Harold. 'A Land Movement', *GK's Weekly* (3 August 1933): 349.
——— 'The Last of the Realists: G.K. Chesterton and his Work', Part III, *The Cross and the Plough* 15 No 3 (Michaelmas 1948): 16.

Ross, Lloyd. 'Socialism and Distributivism', *Twentieth Century* 1 No 4 (June 1947): 32–47.
——— 'Labour, Catholicism and Democratic Socialism', *Twentieth Century* 1 No 6 (December 1947): 3, No 2 74–89.
——— 'Labor and Production', *Twentieth Century* 4 No 1 (September 1949): 58–68.
——— 'Australian Labour Now: Defeat or Opportunity', *Twentieth Century* 10 No 1 (Spring 1955): 7–16.
Taft, Bernie. 'Crossing the Great Divide to Build Friendship With a Foe', *Age*, 26 February 1998.
Santamaria, B.A. 'The Pattern of Valley Development', *Twentieth Century* 5 No 2 (1950).
Shapiro, Edward S. 'Decentralist Intellectuals and the New Deal', *The Journal of American History* 58 No 4 (March 1972).
Sheehan, Archbishop. 'Socialism and Labour', *The Australian Catholic Truth Society Record* 5 (15 December 1930).
Speaight, Robert. 'The Resurrection of France', *Dublin Review* (October 1944): 100–101.
Warhurst, John. 'Abbott, Santamaria and Catholic Liberals', *Eureka Street* (March, 2010). Accessed at http//eurekastreet.com.au/article.aspx?aeid=20247.
Woodhouse, Fay. 'Catholic Action and Anti-Communism: The Spanish Civil War Debate at the University of Melbourne, March 1937', *Journal of Australian Studies* 26 No 73 (2002).
Young Christian Workers Movement. 'Including Enquiries on "Savings", "Teenage Behaviour" and "Trade Unions"', *Campaign Bulletin for Leaders* (Melbourne: October–December 1957).

Theses and Private or Unpublished Papers

Ayers, Tony. 'The National Catholic Rural Movement 1939–1955', BA (Hons) Thesis, University of Melbourne, 1986.
'Campion Memorandum 1: Secretariat of Catholic Action' (Ms, 1937, Bruce Duncan Papers).
'Campion Memorandum 2: Catholic Action Bureau' (Ms 1937, Bruce Duncan Papers).
'Campion Society Memorandum 3: Catholic Action Bureau' (Ms 1937, Bruce Duncan Papers).
Close, Cecily. 'The Organisation of the Catholic Laity in Victoria 1911–1930', MA Thesis, University of Melbourne, 1972.
Downing, Ian G. 'The Radicalisation of Archbishop Mannix in Australia: A Consideration of Daniel Mannix's Radical Behaviour in Australia 1913–1934 and Its Connection with His Irish Antecedents', MA Thesis, Monash University, 1999.
Duncan, Bruce F. 'From Ghetto to Crusade: A Study of the Social and Political Thought of Catholic Opinion-Makers in Sydney during the 1930s', PhD Thesis, University of Sydney, 1987.

Dutton, Robyn Anne. 'Italian Catholics and the Social Question', PhD Thesis, Australian National University, 1990.
Heffey, Gerard. 'Campion Reflections' (Ms, 1990, Bruce Duncan Papers).
Heffey, Gerard, and Butler, Tom. Papers. University of Melbourne Archives.
Henderson, Gerard. 'Frank Maher and Bob Santamaria Circa 1946' (privately circulated research paper, 1994).
Kehoe, David M. 'The Origins of the Australian Secretariat of Catholic Action: The Response of Catholic Lay Intellectuals to a Crisis in Western Civilisation, 1931–38', BA Honours Thesis, Melbourne University, 1976.
——— 'Draft History of the Melbourne Y.C.W. 1932–58' (Melbourne: Y.C.W. Holdings).
Kelly, Kevin T. 'Memoir' (Ms, ND, Bruce Duncan Papers).
Knopfelmacher, Frank. 'Review of *Mr Santamaria and the Bishops*' (ABC Radio 1982). Transcript by courtesy of the ABC.
Long, Ted. 'Notes on the Early History of the Y.C.W. and its Works 2005', as presented to Archbishop Denis J. Hart at the Cardijn Community Australia Conference, Cardinal Knox Centre, 4 November 2011.
MacInnes, Dan. 'Masters of Our Destiny: The Ideal and the Reality'. Notes for an address to the 2nd Topshee Conference, Antigonish, 21 June 1985.
McInerney, Murray. 'The Campion Society and the Catholic Action Secretariat' (unpublished Ms, 1987, Bruce Duncan Papers).
Molony, John. Notes for his presentation to the 'Meeting the Show' panel discussion, State Library of Victoria, 26 August 2008.
Murtagh, James G. Papers. Diocesan Archives, Melbourne.
Newland, William J. 'Mannix Depression: Challenging the biographies' "Mannix Legend" with an examination of Archbishop Daniel Mannix during the Great Depression period', BA (Honours) Thesis, University of Melbourne 2005.
Noone, Val. 'A New Youth for a New Australia: Young Christian Workers Around 1960'. Paper for the Australian Association for the Study of Religions, Australian Catholic University, Aquinas Campus, Ballarat, 6–9 July 1995.
Praetz, Helen. 'The Church in Spring Time: Remembering Catholic Action 1940–1965'. Oral History Archive deposited in the Melbourne College of Divinity Research Repository, 2011.
Santamaria, B.A. Papers. State Library of Victoria.

Online and Other Electronic Publications

Corcoran, Hazel, and Wilson, David, 'The Worker Co-operative Movement in Italy, Mondragon and France, 2010'. Canadian Worker Co-operative Federation Research Paper. Accessed 8 July 2013 at http://canadianworker.coop/files/CWCF_Research_Paper_International 16-6-2010_fnl[1].pdf.
Wise, Bernard R., *The Making of the Australian Commonwealth* (1913). This edition a digital text sponsored by the New South Wales Centenary of Federation Committee, University of Sydney Library, 144. Accessed 17 July 2011 at http://adc.library.usyd.edu.au/data-2/fed0038.pdf.

Pamphlets and Ephemera

Anon. *Catholic Action at Work.* Sydney: Australian Communist Party, 1942.
Anon. *Pattern of Deceit: The N.C.C. and the Labor Movement.* Melbourne: Committee to Defend the ALP, 1980.
Anon. *Leaders' Preliminary Training Programme.* Melbourne: Y.C.W. National Headquarters, ND.
Belloc, Hilaire. *The Church and Socialism.* London: Catholic Truth Society, ND.
Cardijn, Cardinal Joseph. *The Workman and His Family.* Ballarat Vic: Cripac Press, 1967.
——— *The Hour of the Working Class.* Melbourne: Y.C.W. National Headquarters, ND.
——— *Cardijn Speaks on Person, Family and Education.* (ND)
Catholic Bishops of Australia. *International Social Justice: An Episcopal Statement on the World Population Problem.* Surrey Hills NSW: The Catholic Press, 1960.
Cohalan, Bishop D. *Capital, Capitalism and Communism.* Dublin: Catholic Truth Society of Ireland, 1937.
Chesterton, A.K. *Beware the Money Power: A Warning to the British Nations.* South Croydon, Surry: Candour Publishing Company, 1954.
Keane, Fr W. SJ. *A Great Evil and its Remedy: Three Lectures on Social Justice.* Brisbane, Qld: *The Catholic Leader*, ND.
Keating, Fr Joseph SJ. *The Things That Are Caesar's.* London: Catholic Truth Society, 1924.
Ryan, Fr John A., and McGowan, Fr R.A. *The Labour Problem: What It Is – How to Solve It.* New York: Social Action Department National Catholic Welfare Conference and The Paulist Press, 1921.
Santamaria B.A. *The Pattern of Christian Society.* Kew Vic: Institute of Social Order, 1956.
——— *The Mission of the Layman: An Analysis of the Thought of Pius XII on the Mission of the Layman in the Modern World.* Melbourne: Australian Catholic Publications, 1957.
Shepherd, A.W. *Catholic Action and Australian Labor.* Sydney: Morgan Publications, 1955.
Somerville, Henry. *Why the Church has Condemned Socialism.* Oxford: Catholic Social Guild, ND.
Voorhis, Jerry. *A New Look at the Principles and Practices of Cooperatives.* Chicago: The Cooperative League of the USA, 1956.
Watt, Fr Lewis SJ. *Leo XIII and the Social Movement: The Background to Rerum Novarum.* London: Catholic Truth Society; and Oxford: Catholic Social Guild, 1941.
——— *Communism and Religion.* London: Catholic Truth Society Studies in Comparative Religion R38, ND.
——— *Elements of Economics.* London: Catholic Social Guild, ND.
Young Christian Workers Movement Australia. *Leaders' Preliminary Training Programme.* Melbourne: Y.C.W. Movement National Headquarters, ND.

Newspapers and Magazines

Advertiser (Adelaide)
Age (Melbourne)
Argus (Melbourne)
Catholic Weekly (Sydney)
Catholic Worker (Melbourne)
Co-operator (Melbourne)
Cork Examiner (Ireland)
Daily Telegraph (Sydney)
Development Bulletin (Melbourne)
Freedom
Freeman's Journal (Sydney)
Herald (Melbourne)
G.K.'s Weekly (London)
Good Weekend (Melbourne)
News-Weekly
New Witness (London)
Sun News-Pictorial (Melbourne)
Sydney Morning Herald (Sydney)
Tablet (London)
West Australian (Perth)
Yes! Magazine (US)

INDEX

CPSIA information can be obtained
at www.ICGtesting.com
Printed in the USA
LVOW10*2018060318
568854LV00011B/312/P

9 780268 103415